Praise for *Loving Sylvia Plath*

"[Emily] Van Duyne's lived experiences create an identification with Plath that, far from undermining Van Duyne's credibility . . . convinces the reader of her ability to recognize in Plath what she, too, once suffered. Her work reveals the scholarly power of identification, or experience as a lens—what she calls the 'communion of women who know what [Plath] went through.'" —Lynne Feeley, *Nation*

"[Van Duyne] carefully, almost tenderly, combines research with experience." —Bethanne Patrick, *Los Angeles Times*

"In *Loving Sylvia Plath*, Emily Van Duyne sets out to radically reimagine the last years of Plath's life and recontextualize her legacy by undoing her silencing and exploring the brilliance of her work. This book is perfect for lovers of poetry and literary history alike."
—Michael Welch, *Chicago Review of Books*

"Van Duyne rejects any notion that Plath was a bad mother or merely a morbid poet. She maintains Plath ought to be remembered as a complicated woman, a formidable writer—one who outshined Hughes—and almost certainly a victim of domestic abuse."
—Krysta Fauria, *Associated Press*

"Impassioned. . . . [E]ffective in [its] takedown of the literary establishment that closed ranks around Hughes to protect him against feminist pushback from the 1970s on. . . . [C]ompelling and well argued." —Wendy Smith, *Boston Globe*

"Emily Van Duyne takes a deeper look at Plath and does away with the trappings of her sad-girl persona—perpetuated, in many ways, by Plath's husband, the writer Ted Hughes—to focus on her accomplishments and the enduring power of her work. This book is part

celebration and part repossession, looking at the writer on her own terms instead of through the lens for her that others have created."
—Adam Rathe, *Town & Country*

"Bold and original. . . . Ms. Van Duyne, a superb reader of both Plath's writing and her biography, identifies key moments in a marriage that was violent from the beginning. . . . Only a critic as steeped in the literature of Sylvia Plath could have produced such an innovative book."
—Carl Rollyson, *New York Sun*

"Van Duyne is a provocative and intriguing writer who understands both the visible and invisible forces that come to play upon women who refuse to cower into silence. She will leave many a female reader thinking about how they present themselves to the world and perhaps encourage them to think how they might do otherwise."
—Elaine Margolin, *Book and Film Globe*

"[*Loving Sylvia Plath*] examines the many myths surrounding the poet before taking them apart, wiping off the grime, and reconstructing a new vision of Plath for the future."
—Emily Temple, *Literary Hub*

"This disquieting debut from Van Duyne . . . examines how Ted Hughes's physical and psychological abuse of his wife, Sylvia Plath, shaped her life, work, and legacy. . . . An incriminating account exposing the depths of Hughes's cruelty, [*Loving Sylvia Plath*] is sure to reignite debate in literary circles."
—*Publishers Weekly*

"A fresh melding of scholarly investigation and personal reflection."
—*Kirkus Reviews*

"A deeply researched analysis of how the popular myth of Plath's life, one that subordinates her poetry to her depression and her suicide, was constructed by Hughes and maintained by critics from the time of her death in 1963 to the present." —*BookPage*

"Brilliant, lyrical, and moving, *Loving Sylvia Plath* is a riveting story of misogynistic abuse, gaslighting, and the way our culture protects treasured male heroes at the cost of female victims. A must-read for any feminist, any lover of literature, and anyone who simply values a gripping story." —Kate Manne, author of *Unshrinking*

"*Loving Sylvia Plath* is indeed a reclamation, and one that not only centers but in many ways resurrects Plath's own voice to speak her own truth."
—Gail Crowther, author of *Three-Martini Afternoons at the Ritz*

"Emily Van Duyne reveals Plath as she was: the best of her, the worst of her, the parts she hid in plain sight, the parts she made harder to find. I inhaled *Loving Sylvia Plath: A Reclamation* like (what else?) air."
—Jessica DeFino, *Guardian* columnist and beauty reporter

Loving Sylvia Plath

A RECLAMATION

Emily Van Duyne

W. W. NORTON & COMPANY
Independent Publishers Since 1923

This book is dedicated with gratitude
to Peter E. Murphy, Patricia Goldstein,
Dzvinia Orlowsky, and Maria Koundoura,
in whose classrooms I learned to
love, and reclaim, Sylvia Plath.

In memory of Beth Vesel (1957–2024).

Copyright © 2024 by Emily Van Duyne

All rights reserved
Printed in the United States of America
First published as a Norton paperback 2025

For information about permission to reproduce selections from this book, write to
Permissions, W. W. Norton & Company, Inc., 500 Fifth Avenue, New York, NY 10110

For information about special discounts for bulk purchases, please contact
W. W. Norton Special Sales at specialsales@wwnorton.com or 800-233-4830

Manufacturing by Lakeside Book Company
Book design by Beth Steidle
Production manager: Lauren Abbate

ISBN 978-1-324-11036-1 PBK.

W. W. Norton & Company, Inc., 500 Fifth Avenue, New York, N.Y. 10110
www.wwnorton.com

W. W. Norton & Company Ltd., 15 Carlisle Street, London W1D 3BS

10 9 8 7 6 5 4 3 2 1

> A man can tell a thousand lies
> I've learned my lesson well
>
> —Madonna, "Live to Tell"

> This is not a biography.
>
> —Jacqueline Rose, *The Haunting of Sylvia Plath*

CONTENTS

Introduction: *Gaslight* — 1

Love, My Season: *A Brief History of Sylvia Plath* — 23

Loving Assia Wevill — 59

Nota Bene: *The Dead Girls* — 92

The Haunting of Ted Hughes — 110

How Reliable a Witness? — 128

Harriet the Spy — 155

The House of the Ruler — 182

In the Boneyard — 226

Afterword: *The Heart in the Fire* — 231

Acknowledgments — 231
Notes — 237
Selected Bibliography — 283
Index — 289

Loving
Sylvia Plath

Introduction

Gaslight

—⋘⋙—

If you are dead, no one can criticize
you, or, if they do, it doesn't hurt.

—Sylvia Plath, from her journals, April 23, 1959

IN OCTOBER 2016, HARRIET ROSENSTEIN, A WOMAN WHO spent 1969 to 1978 researching a biography of Sylvia Plath that she never published, contacted Plath's daughter, Frieda Hughes, to alert her that Rosenstein still possessed a number of invaluable documents by and about her mother. In emails between the two women, transcripts of which are now held by Emory University's Stuart A. Rose Manuscript, Archives, and Rare Book Library, they discuss Rosenstein's possession of Sylvia Plath's psychiatric records and letters to her therapist, Ruth Barnhouse Beuscher, none of which had ever been seen by the public. The emails begin with warmth and collegiality. Rosenstein—who had long ago abandoned literary life to become a licensed social worker and therapist—talks about meeting Frieda in 1969, when she visited England to begin her research on Sylvia Plath. Frieda was nine years old then, Rosenstein a graduate student in English literature at Brandeis University. In turn, Frieda sends Rosenstein a copy of *Alternative Values* (2015), her recently published book of poetry and paintings, and expresses gratitude for Rosenstein's long, silent safekeeping of such personal elements of her mother's otherwise historically public legacy.

The emails take a turn in March 2017. That month, Frieda Hughes wrote to Rosenstein that she has been contacted by the British newspaper the *Guardian* for comment on a cache of unpublished letters by her mother that had been put up for sale on behalf of Rosenstein by an antiquarian bookseller named Ken Lopez, in Western Massachusetts, for almost one million dollars. The following month, on April 11, 2017, the *Guardian* broke the story of Plath's letters to her therapist with the headline "Unseen Sylvia Plath Letters Claim Domestic Abuse by Ted Hughes," and a literary scandal was born. The article was followed by similar ones in major newspapers in the United Kingdom and elsewhere, reporting that Plath's allegations of intimate partner violence were "shocking." "Shock" can be caused by moral outrage, surprise, or both, but it was clear from the tone of these articles that we were meant to read Sylvia Plath's revelations of abuse as a surprise, as if her accusations of Ted Hughes's violence were not only anomalous but brand-new. But no Plath scholar I knew was surprised by her allegations of intimate partner violence against Hughes.

Sylvia Plath (1932–1963), an American, met Ted Hughes (1930–1998), born in West Yorkshire, at a party in February 1956 while she was studying in England, at Cambridge University. She married him that June, and they remained so for six and a half years. In July of 1962, Hughes disclosed an affair with a woman named Assia Wevill; he left the marriage that October. In Hughes's absence, Plath wrote the poetry that would eventually change the face of British and American letters. In December 1962, she moved to London, where, two months later on February 11, 1963, she killed herself. Despite being estranged and actively seeking a divorce from Hughes as a result of his infidelity, the couple was still married when she died without a will, ensuring that, as her next of kin, Ted Hughes inherited everything Plath ever wrote. Two years after Plath's death, Hughes published Plath's book *Ariel* in England (it appeared one year later in the United States). It became a runaway bestseller. Later, Hughes would write that prior to the book's release, Plath's British and American publishers "felt the full collection might provoke some outraged backlash," a criticism Hughes took seriously: "Was the whole book simply unacceptable, did it overdo itself?" His response to this critique was to remove the poems he would later call "more personally aggressive." These were poems about a violent marriage and a disrupted love affair, the ones Plath composed in the fall of 1962, when she was left alone in their country house in Devon for the first time since the couple had married. Beginning in 1971, they would be published in various editions over the next forty years.

In the course of that time, Paul Alexander's 1991 biography of Plath, *Rough Magic*, had appeared with serious allegations about Hughes's violence during the couple's honeymoon. Plath's *Unabridged Journals* were published in 2000, with their frank reports of the couple's brutal fights and sexual encounters. As I wrote for the online magazine *Literary Hub* in July of 2017, it was only possible to be shocked by Plath's accusations of abuse if you had ignored or disbelieved her—or, importantly, people writing about her—for the last fifty-one years. This was an old story—not a new one. Moreover, the same year that Frieda Hughes and Harriet Rosenstein wrote back and forth about Sylvia Plath's purloined letters, Chanel Miller, known then as "Emily Doe," the victim in the high-profile Stanford rape case, delivered a searing victim impact statement in a California courtroom that swiftly went viral, changing the landscape for survivors of sexual assault. Plath's "new" allegations against Hughes came shortly after the first Women's March, when half a million people in Washington, DC, and approximately five million across the nation protested the election of Donald Trump, a man repeatedly accused of rape and intimate partner violence. That fall, the #MeToo movement exploded as journalists such as Megan Twohey and Jodi Kantor initiated the disgrace and indictment of Harvey Weinstein for the sexual harassment and assault of actors Rose McGowan, Ashley Judd, and Gwyneth Paltrow, among others. Paltrow had played Sylvia Plath in the biopic *Sylvia*, a movie that, fourteen years prior to #MeToo, depicted scenes of intimate partner violence between Plath and Hughes. It was not simply that this was an old story—it was also one that I suspect was being resurfaced at a politically advantageous time. Plath's voice joined a rising chorus of women who began to refuse, in the words of Chanel Miller, to be "gaslit so often, [they are] expected to tolerate it."

The word *gaslighting*, a complex form of psychological abuse in which a person is deliberately led to doubt their own sanity, comes from the play (and later film) *Gaslight*, in which a violent, conniving husband manipulates his wife into believing she is going mad. He does this in part by turning up the attic gaslights to search for stolen jewels he knows are stashed there, so that the gaslights in the downstairs parlor, where his wife is, flicker. When she complains about the flickering lights, he denies that it's happening. In this way, she literally doubts her own eyes. Gaslighting became a hot topic after the 2016 US presidential election, when the Trump administration's pattern of telling the American public to doubt fact-based news reports brought the term into broad use in the United States. So it was that at the height of Donald Trump's wholesale gaslighting of the nation, I watched as the literary world was gaslit into believing that we had never known that Ted Hughes had abused Sylvia Plath.

But there was more to my sense, that Trumpian spring, that something was wrong with the reporting on Plath's letters about her husband's abuse. I was then thirty-seven years old, in my third year on the tenure track at an American university, and writing a scholarly book about Sylvia Plath, whose work I came to love as a teenager. I had previously researched Plath's journals as an undergraduate and written a long critical thesis on her poetry when I was an MFA candidate. None of this work centered on Plath as a survivor of intimate partner violence, but looking back on it, it was imbued with the kind of emotions that Chanel Miller once said "carry a lot of information." In examining the experiences of sexual assault and intimate partner violence survivors, emotions are largely ignored in a world where, via Miller, "anything that is not a hard fact is discounted." My extensive reading of work both by and about Plath left me with the consistent feeling that major life events had been deliberately left out of her story. This sense of loss moved well past things we know for sure are gone—namely, the journals Plath kept in the last two years of her life: in two different published essays, Hughes admitted to destroying one diary and losing the other. Instead, I felt distinctly that Plath's late poetry was that of a survivor of intimate partner violence trying to feel her way into freedom. It also seemed to me that feminist writers on Plath had read as much, said as much, and *proved* it inasmuch as one can prove such a thing—somewhere along the way. But the proof had been lost in the muck of cover-ups and "he said, she said," as well as the gendered power dynamics that governed so much of the history of Plath publishing.

Why had I always felt that when it came to Sylvia Plath, I was being lied to? When had this feeling begun, since it seemed like it had always been there? Who were the earliest people who had named Hughes's abuse of Plath, and where had they gone, or been relegated to? In 2017, I had the sense that if I began to look for them, I might be able to find them. Which is to say, if I began to examine the emotions I had felt for so long, they might give up some of the information they carried.

This felt risky, given the way women's emotional investment in Sylvia Plath has historically been denigrated. As Janet Badia wrote in *Sylvia Plath and the Mythology of Women Readers* (2011), it is impossible to untangle the history of Sylvia Plath's reception from the ways her readers—usually assumed to be young women—are believed to "[represent] an obstacle to a serious consideration of [Plath's] work," to be "uncritical consumers prone to poor judgment and psychological problems." Outing yourself as a voracious and loving reader of Sylvia Plath means joining a long discourse that sees you as a frivolous and unstable consumer of serious poetry, poetry you will never understand if you read it through the lens of Plath's biography. When Plath became famous in the mid-1960s, the biographical mode of reading was anathema in high literary culture, which was then still dominated by New Criticism. Originated by mid-twentieth-century American and British critics like John Crowe Ransom and I. A. Richards, New Criticism held that a poem was a singular, self-contained thing, and to bring historical or biographical details into it was to destroy the aesthetic experience of reading. This way of reading was, and is, employed like a weapon against readers of Sylvia Plath, many of whom saw in her poetry not only Plath's life story, but their own.

Plath's early fame also coincided with the emergence of the movement for women's liberation, which took as its slogan "the personal is political." *Ariel*, a book that savagely critiqued the institutions of marriage and motherhood, was understandably embraced by second-wave feminists, who believed Plath had turned the personal details of her life into overtly political art. In the mid-1960s, Plath was identified as one of the leading voices of the confessional school of poetry, in which poets like Robert Lowell and Anne Sexton, both of whom Plath knew and cited as influences, mined the stuff of their personal lives for poetry. Plath's association with confessionalism, then at the height of its popularity, understandably compelled her first readers to wonder how much of her life experience went into her poetry. But this wonder was as much a political act as it was an act of mere, or morbid, curiosity, as it would come to be understood by critics who believed that women loved Plath, and wanted to know more about her, only because she had killed herself. Feminists of the second wave began organizing around the act of women speaking about the domestic conditions of their life to prevent, and criminalize, among other things, intimate partner violence and marital rape.

Questions about intimate partner violence and marital rape began to play a significant role in second-wave literature about Sylvia Plath and Ted Hughes when the activist and poet Robin Morgan included Plath's poem "The Jailer," which Hughes had excised from *Ariel*, in her 1970 anthology *Sisterhood Is Powerful*. "The Jailer," a poem about a sadistic husband and an abused wife, includes the line "I have been drugged and raped," prompting readers who self-identified as feminists to ponder just how literally Plath might have been speaking. This became a famous question when, in her debut 1972 collection *Monster*, Morgan included a poem called "Arraignment," in which she claimed that Ted Hughes had raped and murdered Sylvia Plath. Pressed by Random House to pull the poem because of libel threats, Morgan stood by her claims and offered up Plathian texts as evidence for them, and the claims themselves as evidence necessitating changes in the American legal system. As Honor Moore wrote in 2009, when the movement for women's liberation seized on poetry as a tool for political organizing, "We began to read differently as well. In this new context, Sylvia Plath was no longer an isolated victim, but the avatar of a new female literary consciousness."

Despite the serious role Plath's life and work played in 1970s feminist art and reform, backlash against both feminism and Plath's fame continued to denigrate her women readers, who, as recently as 2020, were still being accused of forming a cult around Plath. It remained fashionable to disdain anyone who maintained a fascination with Plath's life story, especially those who believed there was a biographical connection to *Ariel*. Speaking to the *New Yorker* reporter Janet Malcolm in 1992, Plath scholar and critic Jacqueline Rose scoffed at the biographical readings of poems in Ronald Hayman's 1992 biography of Plath. In *Sylvia Plath and the Mythology of Women Readers*, Janet Badia cites the scholar Tracy Brain, who, in her 2001 book *The Other Sylvia Plath*, called reading Sylvia Plath's work biographically "being cheated" by a "fascination with the personal," which "interferes with any serious attentiveness to the writing." In 2017, asked by a friend why "young women" embraced her mother's work, Frieda Hughes replied, "Because she was dead."

It was my strong sense when I began this book in 2017 that if Plath's readership had been cheated of anything, it wasn't our serious attention to her poetry, but of crucial details of the last few years of her life, which offered her poetry vital context. Having these details would have lent credence to my own belief, which I knew others held, that Plath had survived, and tried to leave, a violent, controlling marriage to Ted Hughes. The emergence of Sylvia Plath's letters outlining this violence to her therapist was confirmation that Plath not only felt this—she had told others about it. These kinds of small speech acts, cracks in a facade of perfection, can be the first steps a victim of physical or psychological abuse takes when they make a bid for escape. If these letters existed, I thought, then there was more to this story, and I wanted to find it out.

By "this story," I did not simply mean the end of Sylvia Plath's marriage to Ted Hughes. As a longtime reader of Plath's work with an avid interest in her life, I was fascinated by how we came to know that life in the years after Plath's suicide. During this time, Plath was mythologized as a woman born to die, her suicide an inevitability that was hastened by writing her *Ariel* poetry. Writing about the mythology of Sylvia Plath and her women readers, Janet Badia cites Roland Barthes's definition of myth, which "takes the original sign which had been self-sufficient, impoverishes it of meaning, and turns it into a repository of new meaning. Even as it accomplishes this transformation, however, it also appears devoid of the history which has produced it." Throughout the 1960s and '70s, as Plath's mythology was built, the actual conditions of her life were deliberately obscured. Just as Plath's mythology "[appeared] devoid" of her history, those who had helped to construct that mythology—chiefly Ted Hughes but also the powerful critic Al Alvarez, whom the writer and Ted Hughes biographer Elaine Feinstein called a "kingmaker"—disappeared from the very myth they built. In their place, the feminist writers and activists of the same period, who sought to add Plath's voice to the growing number of women who refused silence and victimhood in favor of speech and empowered advocacy, were held responsible for turning Sylvia Plath into a victim, a martyr, and the "priestess" of their "cult."

AT THE HEART OF SYLVIA PLATH'S mythology is a powerful logical fallacy: a causal relationship between the writing of *Ariel* and Plath's suicide, one that moved fluidly back and forth, with the suicide sometimes credited as a cause of the poems, or the poems the cause of the suicide. The tendency to filter Plath's life and work through her death is by now de rigueur. When her second volume of *Letters* debuted in 2018, the Oxford scholar Jonathan Bate wrote, "The tragedy of Plath's death at the age of 30 is so overwhelming . . . that almost everyone reads the life backwards." Six days after Plath's death, Al Alvarez, whom Plath and Hughes had met and befriended in London in 1960, published "A Poet's Epitaph" in the *Observer*, the London paper where he was the longtime poetry editor. The brief notice included a 1961 photograph of Plath holding Frieda in the kitchen, four of her poems—"Edge," "The Fearful," "Kindness," and "Contusion"—and the observation that she had written the poetry during the last year of her life "almost as though possessed." Alvarez called Plath a genius, "the most gifted woman poet of our time," and said that "the loss to literature is inestimable": the kingmaker signaling to the literati that Plath was now among the great writers of the age. But Alvarez also said she had been "probing" a "narrow, violent" poetics that eventually overwhelmed her.

Alvarez's short obituary had so much influence that by June of 1966, when *Ariel* was published in the United States, *Time* magazine ran an unsigned review claiming that "within a week of her death, intellectual London was hunched over copies of a strange and terrible poem she had written during her last sick slide toward suicide," an evident reference to "A Poet's Epitaph." Taking its cues from the same, the reviewer claimed that "Sylvia hurled herself into a heroic but foolhardy attempt to probe her deepest problems with the point of a pen." That same month, *Newsweek* called Plath "a scapegoat who earned illumination only through the light cast by her own immolation," *Ariel* "a symphony of death and dissolution." In "Dying Is an Art," the critic George Steiner wrote that Plath "could not return from [writing *Ariel*]." Peter Davison, reviewing *Ariel* for the *Atlantic Monthly*, wrote, "At the moment of writing, Sylvia Plath's life was eagerly consuming all its careful preparations. The candle is burnt out, and we have nothing left but the flame." In his foreword to the American edition of *Ariel*, Robert Lowell wrote that the poems "were playing Russian Roulette with six cartridges in the cylinder, a game of 'chicken,' the wheels of both cars locked and unable to swerve."

Not to be outdone, in a 1966 postscript to his 1963 eulogy for Sylvia Plath, Al Alvarez wrote that Plath's poetry "was a murderous art." "The achievement of her final style is to make poetry and death inseparable. The one could not exist without the other," he said, comparing Plath to John Keats, whose "Great Odes" had been written at the same rapid pace as *Ariel*. Prior to writing the Odes, Keats had nursed his brother Tom through his illness and death from tuberculosis, an event Alvarez named as the "cause" of Keats's poetry about death; Keats's death was the "effect" of the poetry—"I think much the same thing happened with Sylvia Plath." Keats had caught a deadly strain of tuberculosis nursing his brother in 1818; he became ill with the disease soon after, and it killed him in February 1821—an inevitability, since there was no effective treatment for tuberculosis at the time. Plath's death by suicide was in every sense avoidable, but writing about it in the context of John Keats's strengthened a false corollary between the two.

In the same essay, Alvarez wrote that Plath's last poems "read posthumously," an oft-repeated quote in popular work about Plath, such as her biography on the Poetry Foundation's website. In this, too, Alvarez was under the influence of Keats, borrowing language from his last letter to his friend Charles Brown, on November 30, 1820, in which he wrote that he "[had] an habitual feeling of my real life having past, and that I am leading a posthumous existence." The feeling of being already dead, as Keats described it, came from the experience of suffering lung hemorrhages. Rather than a "posthumous existence," Plath's last surviving letters describe the intense challenges of life: trying to write for a living while she cared, alone, for her two young children, and navigating the challenge of Hughes's weekly visits. Plath's last recorded letter, written to Ruth Beuscher, describes how badly she wants to get help and survive: "No one can save me but myself, but I need help." The letter ends not in despair, but pragmatism: she must settle the crying babies by taking them to tea.

By writing—falsely—that Keats's interest in death and dying as a subject for poetry was also the cause of his death, Alvarez simultaneously placed Sylvia Plath in great poetic company and treacherous moral waters. To die by suicide because of a grave depression or illness was one thing. To kill yourself because of poetry was something else. Like Alvarez, Robert Lowell made the case that Plath's poetry was undoubtedly great, but that this accomplishment had also killed her: "her art's immortality is life's disintegration." The proliferation of responses to *Ariel* abound with the sentiment that in order to achieve her last poems, Sylvia Plath had sacrificed her life at the altar of her art, abandoning her domestic and maternal obligations, making her an artistic success but a moral failure. Her suicide was therefore also a punishment for this, one which, in the end, discredited her work.

"Are these final poems entirely legitimate?" asked George Steiner. Reviewing Plath's *Collected Poems* in the *New York Times* in 1981, critic Denis Donoghue wrote, "The intensity of Plath's poems is beyond dispute, but not the justice of their complaint." But what was the poems' complaint? According to the logic of these reviews, suicidality was the single focus of Plath's *Ariel* poems; her devotion to the writing of them "destroyed her marriage, then they destroyed her." Rather than address the possibility that Plath was writing an open critique of marriage, intimate partner violence, and the constraints of motherhood, particularly single motherhood, on an artist, Sylvia Plath was punished: posthumously stripped of her identity and relegated to a death-obsessed underworld, one where she produced "the work of a poet possessed by a demon if not by herself."

My understanding of this relegation as a punitive act was born from my own experience as a survivor of intimate partner violence with a man who is now the long-estranged father to my older son. We met as contestants in a poetry contest. I won the contest, but temporarily lost control of my life, and the narrative of my life, as he told anyone who would listen a version of myself unrecognizable to me or to anyone who knew me. In 2016, as Plath's letters to her therapist were about to emerge, I began to write about this experience, tracing the ways poetry brought us together and violence tore us apart, how he seemed to want to punish me for the original sin of having beaten him in the poetry contest, which was also, of course, the origin of our relationship. In exploring the intersection of punishment and gendered violence, a concurrent theme of Sylvia Plath and Ted Hughes began to emerge. By then, several years had passed since I left my ex. The dust had settled. I was a single, working, writing mother, and Plath's story, one I thought I already knew well, began to present itself with a new clarity. Far from the clichéd notion that as a fan of Sylvia Plath, I believed myself to be "like" her simply because I was a poet and had loved a poet, I was instead intrigued by the role retribution had played in the construction of Sylvia Plath's legacy.

This question was thrown into sharp relief by Kate Manne's book *Down Girl: The Logic of Misogyny* (2017), in which Manne offers a new definition of misogyny, a word commonly understood to mean hating women simply because they are women. This original definition—what Manne calls "the naive conception" of misogyny—sees it as a psychological phenomenon, a deep-rooted hatred of women that dehumanizes them, a hatred we possess as a simple result of living in the world. Manne points out that the naive conception of misogyny is interchangeable with sexism in colloquial English, theorizing instead that sexism is a taxonomic, hierarchical system that places a particular kind of person at its top—namely, cis-gendered, white, heterosexual, able-bodied men, who Manne tells us are "subject to fewer social, moral and legal constraints on their actions"—with the rest of us stacked and ranked accordingly below. Misogyny is moralistic, a tool of social control and punishment that reaches out, reliably, to knock us back into place when we act outside of our roles in this sexist hierarchy.

Manne's theory of misogyny as the punishment arm of sexism sheds considerable light on the tenor of Plath's continued reception, one that emerged from a need to discipline and contain a woman writer who had fled the control of her husband, lovers, and teachers and, in doing so, surpassed them. Plath's domestic position as the estranged wife of Ted Hughes, in concert with her place in the literary world at the time of her suicide as a well-published but not yet famous writer, lent itself to this. There were many reviews of women's writing published concurrently with those of *Ariel*, but none, say, of Denise Levertov's poetry, calling her "a literary dragon who in the last months of her life breathed a burning river of bale across the literary landscape." It's similarly impossible to imagine a 1966 review of Adrienne Rich's poems as "blood and brain that . . . seems to . . . splatter the reader." Rich's initial reception, though, is instructive here. When she published *A Change of World* in 1951, W. H. Auden wrote in his introduction that Rich's poems "speak quietly but do not mumble, respect their elders but are not cowed by them, and do not tell fibs." No one in *Ariel* spoke quietly. "Daddy," the book's most immediately (and continuously) famous poem, culminates in the murder of the female speaker's "bastard" father and vampiric husband, after she takes her phone off the hook so she can ignore anyone calling to reproach her or interrupt her work.

Plath's "elders" were some of the most recognizable names in contemporary literature at the time. Auden had been her teacher at Smith College, and Theodore Roethke's fingerprints were so visible in her first book, *The Colossus*, that her American editor at Knopf, Judith Jones, asked her to remove some poems from the collection because she felt they might almost be read as plagiarized, but *Ariel* showed no such influence. As for "telling fibs," Plath's appropriation of a Holocaust victim's identity in "Daddy" and "Lady Lazarus" was widely condemned by critics like George Steiner as "a subtle larceny." Worse, possibly, than all of these infractions was *Ariel*'s popularity, the fact that it remained on the bestseller lists.

Kate Manne contends that misogyny acts against women when *they* act outside of what she calls "history's bad gendered bargains," namely, that women "[are] positioned as human *givers* . . . to the dominant men who look to them for . . . moral support, admiration, attention." This positioning not only takes "moral goods and resources" from women; if she is not there to provide them, she is understood as negligent, having abandoned her moral duties. Manne goes on:

> [M]isogyny . . . directed at female public figures—reflects a . . . deprivation mindset regarding women being giving . . . and attentive, as opposed to power-hungry, uncaring, and domineering. . . . [I]t involves a jealous hoarding of certain positions of presumptive collective moral approval and admiration for the men who have been its historical beneficiaries. Women who compete for these roles will tend to be perceived as morally suspect . . . insufficiently caring and attentive . . . to those in her orbit deemed vulnerable; illicitly trying to gain power that she is not entitled to; and morally untrustworthy.

The extreme responses to Sylvia Plath's sudden rise to fame and her suicide (which took place in the home she shared with her two small children) fit Manne's description of "forms of misogyny . . . directed at female public figures" with near-mathematical precision, given the popular, literary, and financial success of Plath's work. Our perception of Plath as, per Manne, "illicitly trying to gain power that she is not entitled to" is heightened by the fact that she was married to a famous male poet, which results in our seeing her as not just generally going after fame and power, but specifically trying to *take away* the fame and power already secured by her husband. At the time of Plath's death, Ted Hughes was probably the most famous poet in England. Early responses to Plath's work portray her as a cipher, with Hughes the sole authority who might help us crack the code: "Whatever it was I missed then of the true bent, or actually the breach, of Sylvia Plath, what I *did* make out is interestingly ratified by Mr. Hughes's notes."

That Plath was not around to tell us what she was up to in writing *Ariel* is also, unsurprisingly, a recurring theme of these reviews, underscoring our perception of Plath as, via Manne, "insufficiently caring and attentive with respect to those in her orbit deemed vulnerable." Hughes is forced to explain Plath to us because she is seen as having selfishly deserted the people she most owed her "moral goods and resources": her husband and children. She is, to use Manne's words, "morally suspect" and in need of correction.

Reevaluating the construction of Plath's mythology through Manne's formulation of misogyny makes new sense of the continuum of responses to Sylvia Plath's life and work, in which Ted Hughes is frequently presented as a stabilizing factor in Plath's life, and her artistic process that which destroyed her. *Time*'s review of *Ariel* characterizes Plath's poetry and ability with language as violent, weapon-like, and out of control, an obvious nod to their powerful effect on readers. It also tells us that Plath tried to gain control of her life by marrying "Poet Hughes," but the marriage broke up, at which point Plath put on "a shirt of nettles," entered "an inferno" beyond depression, and died "in an Auschwitz all her own." The tastelessness of these lines aside, they make clear that the poetry Sylvia Plath "flung with flat force" into the world had consequences—in this case, her suffering and death, which here rhetorically mimics some of the most horrific scenes in modern history. In this version of writing *Ariel*, Plath dons a penitent shirt like those worn by monks to atone for their sins and dies in Auschwitz, one of the most infamous historical sites of punishment and execution.

This last, it could be argued, was simply a nod to Plath's own use of concentration camp imagery in her poetry. But it's notable that the writer chose Auschwitz, which was associated with the worst horrors of the Holocaust, as the place that ultimately killed Plath. Given its notoriety, our retroactive understanding of those who died there was that they did so both publicly and famously—much like our retroactive understanding, and reconstruction, of the death of Sylvia Plath.

Manne's theory that misogyny operates according to a "deprivation mindset" has the coinciding point that the woman in question "*is* morally in the wrong, as measured by . . . moral standards that . . . protect historically privileged and powerful men from moral downfall . . . [from] the ignominy of shame and the corrosive effects of guilt, [and] the social and legal costs of moral condemnation." By shifting the subject of *Ariel* from a critique of marriage and motherhood to a poetic death wish, critics also ensured that Ted Hughes was excused of any responsibility for either Plath's suicide or the end of their marriage. In the *New Republic*, venerated poet Stephen Spender wrote that *Ariel* was "entirely interior, mental . . . symbols of hysterical vision," the first example of an enduring understanding of Plath's work as the provenance of a deranged imagination, rather than inspired by actual life experiences.

One friend of the Hugheses went so far as to say that Plath deliberately drove Hughes out of the house in an attempt to manufacture the conditions for her work: "That she was creating the situation in which she could write *Ariel*, I'm absolutely convinced of. She needed to be that amount destructive about herself and everything that mattered to her in order to get to the raw material of *Ariel*." There was no possibility, then, that "the raw material of *Ariel*" might have anything to do with Hughes's behavior in the marriage or that the end of the marriage might have reflected the same.

THE "WRONG MORAL STANDARDS" that portrayed Sylvia Plath as throwing her marriage and her life away for the sake of her art also protected Ted Hughes from Manne's "social and legal costs of moral condemnation," casting the events of their lives, and Plath's death, into shadow. In the six years after Sylvia killed herself, Hughes conducted an on-again, off-again affair with Assia Wevill, who gave birth to their child, Shura, in 1965. In 1969, Wevill gassed herself and Shura in the kitchen of their London flat, little-known events that one prominent writer would later characterize as protected by the willful silence of Hughes's friends. Nearly forty years passed before Assia Wevill's story was made public in a 2006 biography, which introduced the likelihood that Ted Hughes's behavior toward his lover and daughter had been alternately neglectful and cruel and certainly contributed to Assia's decision to kill herself and her daughter. Absent the conditions of Wevill's life and death, Plath's suicide and the murmurings about her abusive marriage looked anomalous, rather than part of a larger pattern of Ted Hughes's behavior.

Instead, claims of abuse were shifted onto the women writing about Sylvia Plath, who in the ensuing decades have been characterized as "rabid," a horde, a mob, "the baying pack of feminists who hounded [Hughes] throughout his life." As Plath's mythology crystalized, so, too, did the idea that the feminists who envisioned her as the artistic symbol of their struggle for social, political, and economic equality did so chiefly by terrorizing Ted Hughes. Stories of massive crowds of feminists protesting his readings became legend and were printed and reprinted in the press and in biographies of both Plath and Hughes. But attempts to find contemporary reports of these protests or a single person who attended one have led, per Janet Badia, to "repeated ... dead ends." As she painstakingly reported in *Sylvia Plath and the Mythology of Women Readers*, the only accounts of these so-called protests in print came, without fail, twenty years or more after they were said to have occurred. One of the most prominent came from Jill Barber, Hughes's former lover, whose "credibility as a witness is greatly diminished by other claims she makes ... including her assertion that Hughes had revealed himself as the actual author of *The Bell Jar*."

In short, "The history of feminist attacks on Hughes appears to be largely a history of omissions, elisions, and hearsay, usually repeated by biographers and memoirists without documentation or verifiable details." Yet the mere impression of Hughes as a victim of a rabid horde of feminists allowed for his protection from the kind of moral condemnation Manne speaks of, and further aided in his use of the legal system to silence those trying to write about his abuse of Sylvia Plath.

In 1982, the Australian feminist scholar Dale Spender wrote that feminism was "neither original nor radical; women's ideas about the relationship of women and men are either co-opted or lost by men and have to be recreated every 50 years or so." When Sylvia Plath's letters to her therapist reemerged in 2017, forty-five years had passed since Robin Morgan published "Arraignment." It had been forty-seven years since "The Jailer" was published in *Sisterhood Is Powerful*, about forty-six since Harriet Rosenstein acquired Plath's letters to Ruth Beuscher. And though Rosenstein ultimately hid those letters from the public, Ruth Beuscher did speak to other biographers, trying to reconstruct what she could of the letters from memory. Absent the letters, these claims frequently could not be vetted for publication. Or, if they were printed, they were criticized as flimsy or libelous. For about five years in the 1970s, the story of Sylvia Plath's marriage to Ted Hughes, in her own words, was out. Then it disappeared. But the feeling of it remained, and with it, a buried mine of information. "I wonder," a fellow scholar said to me one night, "how much those early feminists really knew about Plath and Hughes." I wondered, too. I felt in my heart, the place language lived before it found its way out: they knew a lot. I wanted to learn what they knew, and say it.

In "Poetry Is Not a Luxury," Audre Lorde, the Black feminist poet and essayist, and Plath's contemporary, wrote:

> The quality of light by which we scrutinize our lives has direct bearing upon the product which we live. . . . This is poetry as

illumination, for it is through poetry that we give name to those ideas which are—until the poem—nameless and formless, about to be birthed, but already felt. That distillation of experience from which true poetry springs births thought as dream births concept, as feeling births idea, as knowledge births (precedes) understanding.

In Lorde's words about the poem as something "nameless and formless—about to be birthed, but already felt," I read an echo of Sylvia Plath's creativity as she herself described it throughout her life, in her journals. Her *Ariel* poems, so revered in literature, lived inside of her for years as feelings and images before she could put them on the page. "Here are stories: the beautiful popular girl who can't get married. . . . O yes, and the born-writer who can't write," she wrote in her journal on March 29, 1959. "I have a vision of the poems. . . . . When will they come?"

Writing to me about Plath's composition of *Ariel*, her biographer Linda Wagner-Martin said:

> In that collection she destroyed the prowess of all those instructive men—the "daddys" she had learned from, the teachers, the powerful editors of journals who could so easily reject her work. . . . The casual lovers, the casual workers, the men who wanted only a little, a little success, a little money, a little house, a little love. A few affairs rather than one blazing and monumental love.

Before she understood how to turn that prowess and that poverty into poetry, Plath knew it was there. That gendered power imbalance was the stuff of her life. Her knowledge, as Lorde wrote, preceded her understanding; her eventual ability to synthesize both with wild feeling allowed for the creation of what Wagner-Martin, in the same letter, calls "her febrile collection of living, anguishing and angry poems."

The quality of light Plath used to scrutinize her life was sometimes a fever, sometimes a blaze, sometimes a candle's single flame. But it was always a fire, with fire's ability to destroy and, in that destruction, renew and create. Her willingness to sit, silent, in that light—sometimes for years—until the right words came in the right order is a testament to the ways her life embodied Lorde's philosophy that poetry was no luxury, but instead, as Plath said in an October 1962 interview, as essential as bread or water, something she could not survive without. This is why her poetry survives, even as she did not. What is the quality of light by which we scrutinize Sylvia Plath's life, work, and legend?

Plath's readership is associated with fanaticism, but this has never been equated with love. Plath's readers are instead called cult members and cannibals, shadows of the monster we have supposedly made of the woman we read. In 1976, Stanford professor Sandra M. Gilbert framed her admiration for Plath in terms of addiction and compulsion. In "'A Fine, White Flying Myth': Confessions of a Plath Addict," Gilbert apologized for writing about her interest in Plath through the lens of "personal material which might otherwise seem irrelevant," despite the fact that Gilbert was writing about experiences in her life that directly mirrored Plath's own.

The kind of intense affinity many readers felt for Plath, often born from self-identification, was—*is*—discouraged in literary studies, where a cool critical distance is advised. But there is an irony there that begs to be interrogated, since so much foundational critical work on Plath was completed by her husband, male colleagues, and lovers. Stephen Spender knew the Hugheses. He had them over for dinner in the spring of 1960 and later gave Plath tickets to the obscenity trial for *Lady Chatterley's Lover* for her twenty-eighth birthday. Robert Lowell was Plath's teacher and Hughes's friend. Plath wrote in her diary about visiting Lowell and his then-wife, the writer Elizabeth Hardwick, at their home and about the dinner she planned to serve them in her closet-like Boston apartment in the winter of 1959: "lemon meringue pie." Peter Davison was one of her college boyfriends; she broke up with him in the summer of 1955, when she left to pursue a Fulbright Fellowship at Cambridge University. Most of these people never disclosed these relationships in their work on Plath. None, to my knowledge, acknowledged the possibility that, far from a necessary critical distance, the personal animus they bore toward Plath showed up as critical animosity, one they projected onto her readers, women branded as incapable of seeing Plath for who, or what, she was, blinded, instead, by a myth they were said to have created.

Despite her legions of fans, love and the compassionate inquiry that often accompanies it are largely absent from the early writing on Sylvia Plath. Looking back at the early literature about Plath, there is almost nothing in it of grief for this mother of two who was barely thirty when she died. Instead, Plath becomes an object for disdain and almost abject curiosity, and those who profess their love for her work are seen as martyring her, rather than acting out of love for her poetry and her life story. When Heather Clark's biography *Red Comet: The Short Life and Blazing Art of Sylvia Plath* debuted in 2020, it quickly dubbed the definitive book on Plath. But in her 2022 keynote speech at the Sylvia Plath Literary Festival, Clark said that she wrote the book because she couldn't understand why there was as yet no major biography of Plath, a literary genius on a par with Virginia Woolf. While I am grateful for Clark's scholarship on Plath, the answer to her question was not a mystery—it lay with the many ways Ted Hughes and his colleagues kept Plath's life and work in shadow. Clark, who came to Plath studies through her expertise in Ted Hughes, left considerable material about the couple's violent marriage out of her book, possibly because much of it came to light when Harriet Rosenstein sold her archive to Emory University in 2020, the year *Red Comet* was published.

But we cannot understand the blaze of Sylvia Plath's life and art without dragging this material into the light. The reemergence in 2017 of Sylvia Plath as the voice of a survivor of intimate partner violence at the onset of the #MeToo movement, and the subsequent backlash against that movement, points to Plath's continued relevance in a culture that still discounts the stories women tell about their lives. What follows is my best effort to shed as much light as possible on events that have not simply been forgotten or left in the dark, but relegated to the attic, or the ash can, or the metaphorical darkness of fear and shame, and to reignite Plath's fire in the parlor where her fans squint to read by flickering gaslight; above them, the man searches the attic for the jewels he hid too well.

Love, My Season

A Brief History of Sylvia Plath

> How can Lady Lazarus live in a shiny
> pageboy haircut, with polite little pearls
> stuck on her ears? How can we bend both
> into the arc of one life and give it grace?
>
> —Elizabeth Winder, from *Pain, Parties, Work:
> Sylvia Plath in New York, Summer 1953*

A FORWARD READING OF SYLVIA PLATH'S LIFE REQUIRES US TO document an actual history that feels counterintuitive. At Robinson Memorial Hospital, on October 27, 1932, Sylvia Plath was born healthy and thriving to Aurelia Schober Plath and Otto Plath. There were no portents; there were no signs. There was a baby girl, three weeks early, but almost nine pounds, nonetheless. Her parents adored her.

Born in Germany in 1885, Otto Plath emigrated to the United States at the age of fifteen, living with his paternal grandparents in Wisconsin. In 1910, after graduating from Northwestern College with an honors bachelor of arts in classical languages, he took a mas-

Sylvia Plath eating chocolate chip cookies on the beach, summer 1955. (Photograph by Gordon Lameyer, used with permission of the Lilly Library, Indiana University.)

ter of arts in German at the University of Washington. He eventually earned his doctor of science in entomology from Harvard. Aurelia's parents, Frank Schober and Aurelia Greenwood, were Austrian immigrants. Frank arrived in the United States in 1902, Aurelia, 1904. They married in July 1905, and their eldest daughter, Aurelia Frances, was born the following year. She grew up speaking German, writing in the introduction to her 1975 edition of her daughter Sylvia's letters that "our name Schober, with its German sound, resulted in my being ostracized by the neighborhood 'gang,' called 'spy-face,' and at one time being pushed off the bus and dumped on the ground, while the bus driver, keeping his eyes straight on the road, drove off." Aurelia wondered if stories like these, which she shared with her daughter, were responsible for Sylvia's "interest in minority groups."

In 1929, Aurelia met Otto at Boston University, where he taught both biology and German language courses. She was there "to earn a Master of Arts degree in English and German" and enrolled in her future husband's "Middle High German" course. They married in

January 1932. Sylvia was born ten months later. Her father "told his colleagues, 'I hope for one more thing in life—a son, two and a half years from now.'" Their son, Warren Plath, came "only two hours off schedule," an event Plath's biographer Linda Wagner-Martin curiously described as "somewhat chilling." Wagner-Martin's comments, like Aurelia's that her husband was "the man who gets what he wants when he wants it," indicate that Otto Plath was at minimum a taskmaster, at worst, controlling. This quality appears to have subdued Aurelia, who wrote that transitioning into a marriage with her, a woman who grew up surrounded by love and a "free flow of communication" with her parents and siblings, "led to an air of 'rightful' dominance on [Otto's] part."

Despite this, Sylvia Plath's childhood was "if not idyllic, [then] close." Sylvia was precocious and enthusiastic; before she turned three, she read the corner STOP sign as "pots." The Plaths lived in the Jamaica Plain section of Boston, but after Warren's birth in 1934, Sylvia was often sent to her maternal grandparents' home in Winthrop, on the coast, as Warren was prone to respiratory illness and required intensive care. In the fall of 1936, the Plaths bought a home there. By this time, Otto had begun to suffer from the diabetes that would eventually kill him, and Aurelia depended on her parents for childcare. Despite his formidable intelligence, Otto would not see a doctor and wrongly self-diagnosed his disease as cancer. Having witnessed a friend die from lung cancer, he refused to endure what he viewed as the barbaric treatments of the day. Ironically, the diabetes he actually suffered from was treatable, but by 1936, when the family relocated to Winthrop, Otto was becoming an invalid.

Sylvia was already writing. Her mother described an extraordinary moment in Sylvia's childhood when, having brought her two young children out to see the rising new moon, Sylvia spontaneously said, "The moon is a lock of witches hair / tawny and golden and red. / And the night winds pause and stare / at that strand from a witch's head." Plath's early years on the coast of Massachusetts influenced her mature work, in which the ocean careens symbolically between maternal love and wild destruction. In the short essay "Ocean 1212-W," written at the end of her life, the ocean is the center of her childhood world. When she hears the sound of breathing, she can't be sure if it is her mother's breath or the ocean. "My childhood landscape was not land but the end of the land—the cold, salt running hills of the Atlantic." In the essay, a hurricane hits her small shore town and leaves destruction in its wake, "overthrown trees and telephone poles, shoddy summer cottages bobbing out by the lighthouse . . . a dead shark filled what had been the geranium bed, but my grandmother had her broom out, it would soon be right." Women, here, are as elemental as breath and water, able to right disasters with domestic tools. The essay closes with the death of Plath's father: "My father died, we moved inland . . . those first nine years of my life sealed themselves off like a ship in a bottle—beautiful, inaccessible, obsolete, a fine, white flying myth."

The actual timeline was slower. The hurricane hit Winthrop in September 1938, when Sylvia was about to turn six. Otto Plath became gravely ill in the summer of 1940. A minor injury to his toe developed gangrene, and his leg had to be amputated at the hip, an operation that took place in October 1940. He was kept immobile, the standard practice, then, which probably killed him. He died of a pulmonary embolism on November 5, 1940.

His daughter was devastated. Although he was emotionally distant and strict, she adored him and was his special favorite in the household. "She loved his praise," Aurelia said. When he became gravely ill, the nurse who was helping to care for him "cut down a uniform and put it on her and [Sylvia] was her assistant." When Aurelia told Sylvia her father was dead, she said, "I'll never speak to God again." The image of a God who she can't, or won't, speak to, in "his vacuous black," as she wrote in her November 1962 poem "Years," stayed with Plath for the rest of her life. In "Lyonnesse," written in October 1962, a "big God" closes one eye and forgets the people of Lyonnesse, who drown, a reference to the legendary lost Cornish town, but a possible nod to her own overwhelming grief at her father's death, when she lived by the sea. She was not allowed to attend the funeral, a loss that left her, and many subsequent biographers, to posit that this had left her grief unresolved. In 1959, at the age of twenty-six, Plath wrote of a visit to her father's gravestone, that the sight of it caused her to wonder if he had ever really existed. She repurposed this scene for her 1963 novel *The Bell Jar*. When Plath's heroine Esther Greenwood visits her father's grave for the first time, she describes how missing his funeral left her guilty and confused. Finding the stone, Esther says, "I laid my face to the smooth face of the marble and howled my loss into the cold salt rain."

For a brief time after Otto's death, the Plath family remained in Winthrop. Aurelia Plath went back to work, eventually taking a full-time position at her alma mater, Boston University, teaching medical secretarial skills, a course she designed. In 1942, Aurelia moved her family inland to the tony Boston suburb of Wellesley, a step up from working-class Winthrop. Her parents came along. Aurelia was conscious of the fact that she was a widow with little security and two bright children, for whom she and her husband had shared great ambition, which did not die with him. Otto Plath, however, died without life insurance and left Aurelia almost nothing. Wellesley had a first-rate public school system and was the home of Wellesley College, a Seven Sisters school that offered full scholarships to young women who lived in town. The Plath-Schober family moved into a white, three-bedroom house on 26 Elmwood Road; Mrs. Plath and Sylvia had to share a bedroom. This, combined with the loss of her father, began a suffocating closeness between mother and daughter that Plath later wrote about in her journals and letters and in her fiction and poetry. Her October 1962 poem "Medusa," about a mother-daughter relationship, ends, "Off, off, eely tentacle! // There is nothing between us."

Sylvia began school at Wellesley's Marshall Perrin Elementary School and then attended Alice L. Phillips Junior High through the ninth grade. She was, by all accounts, a happy preteen and young teenager, who loved to read, write, and draw. Aurelia loved taking her children into Boston to the theater throughout this time—Sylvia wrote that her mother taking her and her younger brother "Warrie" into Boston to see Shakespeare's *The Tempest* at the Colonial Theater was "too perfect for words." This play would become a crucial part of Plath's poetic influence and lexicon, helping to birth later poems like "Full Fathom Five" and "Ariel." Plath had also begun to use poetry, at least in part, as a way to deal with adverse experiences. Heather Clark describes Plath's thirteenth Christmas, during which her friends were all away for break. The loneliness of the time seems to have upset Plath, and she became ill, "[vomiting and fainting], hitting her head on a table as she fell." She stayed in bed for three days and "channeled her unease into Gothic iambs," like "The night wind moans and plays a game / Of rattling every window frame." Years later, studying at Cambridge University, Plath would have a similar response to emotional isolation.

Sylvia was encouraged by her English teachers, who assured her she was an ideal candidate for a college scholarship, which simultaneously pleased her and increased the pressure on her to achieve at the highest possible level, something that would stay with Plath for the rest of her life. When she graduated junior high in June 1947, she won the Wellesley Award for academic excellence. The school awarded her with a copy of *Understanding Poetry*, by Cleanth Brooks and Robert Penn Warren, two landmark American literary critics who, coincidentally, would later help vault Plath to literary acclaim. She entered Wellesley High School as a tenth grader in the fall of 1947, where she maintained her long string of straight As. This occasionally troubled her, especially when she competed with boys. In her introduction to *Letters Home*, Aurelia described how, in high school, her daughter had to stop dating boys with literary ambitions—they were too jealous of Sylvia's impressive string of publications, which she had begun to rack up in high school, "inject[ing] a sour note in the relationship." This problem of artistic rivalry would eventually haunt her marriage to Ted Hughes.

Plath's most significant influence at Wellesley High School was Wilbury Crockett, her beloved English teacher, who offered advanced students a special three-year, college-level literature course. There, Plath read a range of British and American authors, from Virginia Woolf to Edgar Allan Poe, as well as classical Greek literature and philosophy, Shakespeare, Donne, and other European writers like Goethe and Flaubert. Plath corresponded with Crockett for many years, sending him a signed copy of her first book of poetry, *The Colossus*, to let him know that the poems "took root" in his classrooms. While Crockett's student, she twice won the *Atlantic* student writing contest. And she began to develop a critical stance on American Cold War politics, evident in her 1950 poem "Bitter Strawberries," which she wrote after her summer picking fruit at Lookout Farm. In the poem, a young listener overhears the "adults" in charge wishing America would "bomb [Russia] off the map." The sweetness of the strawberries dies in the speaker's mouth as the anti-Communist rhetoric she hears grows increasingly bitter.

Then, as throughout her adult life, Plath saw poetry as a way to flex her political and artistic muscles, while fiction, especially short fiction, was typically something she produced with the commercial market in mind. Acutely aware of her family's precarious financial state, writing was not simply a creative joy, it was a job: a way to make her more attractive to future educational and professional endeavors, and earn money. Throughout high school, Plath wrote and submitted commercial short fiction to *Seventeen* magazine. She received so many rejections, she wrote about it beneath her yearbook graduation photo: "Future writer . . . Those rejection slips from *Seventeen*." That changed in 1950, the year she graduated high school, when *Seventeen* accepted her story "And Summer Will Not Come Again." This was Plath's first national publication, and it inspired a fan letter from a young man in Chicago named Eddie Cohen, studying English literature at Roosevelt College. The two corresponded for several years, an epistolary relationship that Plath would characteristically try to publish under the name "Dialogue of the Damned."

In Plath's second letter to Cohen, dated August 11, 1950, she describes herself in charming, wry detail—she is "tall" and can eat what she wants without gaining weight (steak, potatoes, and apple pie for that morning's breakfast), and so tan that women on the beach ask for the name of her tanning oil. Although once, Plath writes, she was reading *Brave New World* while her friends were dancing at formals, she now dates so frequently that she's "forgotten what it was like not to have some guy in the kitchen eating mother's cookies and discussing the World Series with my brother." Much like her later letters to Ruth Beuscher, Plath's letters to Cohen reveal her sophistication, wit, and emotional and stylistic range. Writing of her friend Ilo Pill, an Estonian artist she picked strawberries with at Lookout Farm, Plath picks up his accent and cadence, sketching the scene in a few short lines like the novelist she would become: "Out in the strawberry field . . . he suddenly burst out You like Frank Sinatra, ja? He is so sendimendal, so romancic, so moonlight night." But when she tries to do the same for a Black coworker, she descends into racist tropes. These early writings about her time at Lookout Farm foreshadow her later poetic masterpiece, "Ariel," with its stark pastoral imagery and use of a racist slur.

Plath was awarded the town scholarship to Wellesley College, but she was able to turn it down once her "meticulous application" to Smith College led to a full scholarship. She wrote in her journal that with the reality of acceptance to Smith, she knew her life would change forever. In the lead-up to this, Plath expressed frustration about her social life in Wellesley. She was coming of age at the height of Eisenhower's postwar, Cold War political culture, with its emphasis on consumerism, patriotism, and conformity to the raced, classed, and gendered norms of the day. Sex outside of marriage for a young woman of Plath's social class and standing was considered out of the question, a double standard she felt keenly and actively questioned in her diaries. Plath's contemporary Anne Stevenson summed up the attitude of the times in her 1989 biography *Bitter Fame: A Life of Sylvia Plath*: "Middle-class Americans in the 1950s subscribed to an amazing code of sexual frustration. Everything was permissible to girls in the way of intimacy except the one thing such intimacies were intended to bring about."

Plath also questioned the role sexual violence played in this two-faced world. Harriet Rosenstein's papers include notes from her 1971 interviews with Plath's childhood friend William Sterling and with Wilbury Crockett, where both men discuss the time at Plath's high school when "four or five football players had raped a student who was thought to be promiscuous." "WHY SHOULD SUCH A THING HAVE GONE ON?" Plath wanted to know. Rosenstein writes that this "greatly perturbed" Sylvia, as though this was an odd response to a violent crime. Discussing it with Crockett, she mentions Plath's "extreme response" to the "group rape." Rosenstein records that Crockett says this was a result of Plath's being "very disquieted about her sex." Even by 1971, at the height of the second-wave feminist movement, it does not seem to have occurred to any of these three people that Plath may have been "disquieted" about the opposite sex, or disquieted on behalf of her own, in the wake of such an event. The notes are a grim reminder of the misogyny Plath—or any woman—faced in the 1950s.

These sexual mores followed Plath when she entered Smith College in September 1950 as a scholarship student. Plath was under tremendous pressure to maintain her excellent grades; similar pressure existed to maintain a social life that included weekend blind dates, which often involved traveling to Yale and Princeton. Plath's journals from her first year include a vivid description of sexual assault by an army vet named Bill. Plath's writing about this assault is electric with the tension of interpersonal violence, how we know when something that carries the sheen of convention has gone horribly wrong. When Bill asks Plath where she is from and she answers honestly, he replies, angrily, "Don't give me a hard time," intentionally bewildering her. Before long, he wrestles Plath to the ground. She manages to get away, but he tries again to force a sexual encounter while, Plath writes, she says, "No no no no no no," and eventually escapes.

PLATH'S JOURNAL ENTRIES FROM HER first two years at Smith reflect her struggle to find a balance between rigorous academics and social expectations. Without the support of the college, her mother could not afford to send her to Smith; even with that support, it was a financial strain. Plath worked a string of campus jobs and wrote steadily for money throughout her time at Smith. Her journal entries from the fall of 1950 reveal the strain this placed on her social life, with Plath recording snide comments from upper classwomen who mocked her for staying in to study on weekends. Plath later turned this problem into a comedic centerpiece of *The Bell Jar*. When Esther meets up with her boyfriend Buddy Willard for the first time, she tells him she has two forthcoming dates with "Peter the Hermit and Walter the Penniless." Buddy stares back, not getting the joke—"They're from Dartmouth," she deadpans.

Buddy Willard was closely based on Plath's first college boyfriend, Dick Norton, the oldest son of a family who lived near the Plaths in Wellesley; Dick's mother and Aurelia were best friends. Dick was at Yale during Plath's first year at Smith. They began dating and for a time were a fairly serious couple, although Plath felt that Norton could be conformist and patronizing, qualities she spurned in *The Bell Jar*. In a memorably hilarious scene, Buddy Willard "offers" to show Esther his naked self after she admits she has never seen a naked man before. Esther is unimpressed—"The only thing I could think of was turkey neck and turkey gizzards and I felt very depressed."

Norton quickly began to exhibit the competitive envy of Plath's writing that Aurelia wrote about in her introduction to *Letters Home*. When he was diagnosed with tuberculosis in 1952 and sent to a sanitarium to recover, he wrote poetry and short stories he sent to Plath, along with his analysis of *her* poetry. By that time, Plath had won the *Mademoiselle* short fiction contest for "Sunday at the Mintons," a story about an overbearing brother that was based, tellingly, on her relationship with Dick Norton. As a result, she received a letter from Knopf editor in chief Harold Strauss, who told her he would like to see a novel from her someday. In Plath's reply to Strauss, she tells him, "I deeply appreciate the confidence you have expressed in my writing, and I hope within the next few years to justify your encouragement." Norton's condescending "analysis" of her work must have hit a nerve, given the elite literary circles she was already moving in.

By her junior year at Smith, Plath had slipped into a serious depression as a result of the constant academic and social demands she faced, as well as a sense that her identity was being constructed for her by a world she often found troubling and unbalanced. Although her junior year at Smith was as marked by academic and artistic success as her prior two, and she was dating a new, brilliant Yale student named Myron Lotz, whose temperament suited her much better than Dick Norton's had, her journal entries reveal a psychological crisis. In a November 3, 1952, journal entry, Plath describes being close to wanting to commit suicide and asks herself difficult questions: "I can begin to see the compulsion for admitting original sin, for adoring Hitler, for taking opium. . . . Whom can I talk to? Get advice from? No one."

She was buoyed in the spring of her junior year by the news that she had won one of the guest editor positions on *Mademoiselle*'s annual "College Issue." Now out of print, in 1953 *Mademoiselle* was considered the "it" magazine of intellectual young women, publishing erudite short fiction and poetry in between its glossy fashion pages. From 1939 to 1980, it ran a contest for female college students to come and work in its offices for a month, editing that fall's College Issue, an opportunity many now famous writers—Joan Didion, Mona Simpson, Ann Beattie, and Meg Wolitzer—took advantage of when they were unknown. Plath was named managing editor and spent June of 1953 wined and dined all over Manhattan. She was overwhelmed by the month in New York, generally, but also went through some terrible experiences, including a severe case of ptomaine poisoning from bad crabmeat in a test kitchen she visited as part of her work. Elizabeth Winder, in her book *Pain, Parties, Work: Sylvia Plath in New York, Summer 1953*, writes that Plath and guest editor Janet Wagner went with blind dates to a party for the US Open at the West Side Tennis Club in Forest Hills, Queens. Plath's date was a delegate to the UN she called "Jose the Cruel Peruvian" the following month in her diary. "Both men were predators," Winder writes. Plath was the recipient of verbal attacks, but Wagner's date "launched an assault in broad daylight." Wagner responded by elbowing him hard in the mouth: "[his] teeth came crumbling out of his mouth in bloody shards." Although the women eventually left laughing, Wagner reported to Winder that it was a frightening evening: "How were we going to escape these men?"

Plath, physically exhausted and emotionally bewildered, returned home to Wellesley, Massachusetts, for the summer, but not before writing to Wilbury Crockett that she was in "disgrace" and had let everyone down, words that make little sense, given the professional successes she had achieved. In addition to writing considerable copy for the issue of *Mademoiselle* she had been hired to edit, her poem "Mad Girl's Love Song" was also published in its pages. But the brutal glamour of New York City and the feeling of anonymity she experienced there exacerbated Plath's underlying depression of the previous year and brought her to a crisis point. Home in Wellesley, Plath began suffering from prolonged insomnia and claimed she could no longer read or write. Aurelia took her to the family doctor, who recommended a local psychiatrist, a well-intentioned act that had the disastrous consequence of outpatient shock treatments (electroconvulsive therapy, or ECT) for which Plath was given no muscle relaxants or sedatives, an experience she immortalized in *The Bell Jar* as being electrocuted. Heather Clark writes of how ECT was often used to subdue "troubled" or "difficult" women in the mid-twentieth century, revealing that Valley Head Hospital, where Plath was treated, was also the place a young John F. Kennedy sent his wife Jacqueline for shock treatments "after a particularly brutal fight about his infidelity." After her first outpatient shock treatment in *The Bell Jar*, Esther Greenwood wonders what "terrible thing" she has done to be punished in this way.

On August 24, 1953, while her family was out seeing a film of Queen Elizabeth II's coronation, Plath wrote a note that she had gone out for a walk, hid in a basement crawl space, and took a large overdose of sleeping pills. When her family returned, Aurelia knew immediately that something was wrong but couldn't find Sylvia, who was deliberately well hidden, with the serious intention to die. A three-day search ensued, with over two hundred articles published in local and national papers about the "missing Smith beauty." Plath was found when her younger brother Warren heard her groaning and rushed to the basement. She survived because she had taken so many pills that she vomited them up. She was rushed to the local hospital, then transferred to the psychiatric ward at Massachusetts General. Eventually, the writer Olive Higgins Prouty, the benefactor of Plath's scholarship to Smith College who remained both her and Aurelia's lifelong friend, paid for her to be treated at the private psychiatric hospital McLean.

At McLean, Plath struggled to get well and was given insulin treatments, talk and occupational therapy, and eventually another series of ECT, this time administered properly, which seems to have pulled her suddenly out of her suicidality. There she met Ruth Barnhouse Beuscher, then a young resident in psychiatry. The two bonded immediately and formed a lifelong therapeutic relationship; Plath based the character of Doctor Nolan in *The Bell Jar* on Beuscher, who, in combination with ECT, helped her to recover in swift and remarkable fashion. Plath was released from the hospital in January and returned to Smith for the spring term.

The following year, her last at Smith, she applied for a Fulbright Scholarship to study English literature at Oxbridge. It was a tremendous leap of faith. As a result of her hospitalization, she required a character reference from Ruth Beuscher, as well as her academic references, to secure the fellowship. She was granted entrance to Newnham College, the women's college at Cambridge, her tuition and travel funded by the Fulbright Foundation. In the preceding year, despite recovering from a suicidal breakdown, Plath had resumed her excellent grades, won the Glascock Poetry Contest, judged by the venerated American poet Marianne Moore, and published poems in *Harper's*, the *Atlantic Monthly*, and the *Nation*. Plath graduated Smith summa cum laude on June 6, 1955. That September, she sailed for England.

In her first year at Cambridge, Plath lived in her "attic room" at Whitstead, the dormitory for international students at Newnham, and studied Tragedy, Practical Composition & Criticism, and French. She found her dormitory "quaint" but, like much of England, cold and damp, always a trigger for her depression, and she struggled to stay warm. She joined the Amateur Dramatic Club. And she wrote for *Varsity*, the student newspaper, which ran a front-page piece of Plath's that included her modeling a bathing suit—she sent the clipping to her mother with the line, "with love, from Betty Grable." When Plath left for England, she was in love with a young man named Richard Sassoon, whom she had begun dating at Smith in April 1954. They remained in love throughout Plath's first term at Cambridge. Sassoon was studying at the Sorbonne, and Plath went to see him in Paris over Christmas and the 1955–56 New Year. The couple stayed in Paris for several days before taking the train south to Nice, then "traveling by motor scooter to Vence," where Plath had a mystical experience in the Matisse Chapel, a small church Matisse designed and decorated in the 1940s. But some unknown difficulty came between Plath and Sassoon on this trip, and in a letter she received when she returned to Cambridge in January, he asked her not to contact him. Plath was devastated, writing to him in her journal that she could never free herself of his grip on her. Then, the following month, she met a poet and recent Cambridge graduate named Ted Hughes.

BORN AUGUST 17, 1930, IN Mytholmroyd, West Yorkshire, to William Henry Hughes and Edith Farrar, Edward James Hughes was the youngest of three children. His older brother, Gerald, was outdoorsy and worked as a gamekeeper, while his older sister, Olwyn, was as precociously talented at literature as her famous younger brother. Ted Hughes showed an early predilection for poetry writing and literary study and won what was termed "an exhibition" at Pembroke College, Cambridge: "better than a mere place, but below a scholarship," his biographer Jonathan Bate writes. At Pembroke, he studied literature until, famously, he fell asleep writing a required critical essay and dreamed that a creature with the body of a man and the head of a fox came to his window and told him he had to stop writing literary criticism—*You are destroying us*, the dream fox apparently said. Hughes took it as a powerful sign and switched his studies to anthropology. The dream also inspired one of his most famous poems, "The Thought-Fox," which appeared in his first book, *The Hawk in the Rain*.

Hughes was tall and good-looking and had a reputation as a lady-killer, to use the parlance of the day. Plath wrote to her friend Marcia Brown in December 1956 that if she tried to "boss" Hughes, "he'd bash my head in." For his part, when he was at Cambridge, Hughes wrote to his parents that he was dating a nurse he "[kicked] around, and everything goes as I please." The couple's first meeting is frequently characterized as Plath chasing after Hughes, a nobody fangirling after a star. Writing for the *Guardian* in 2017, Danuta Kean said, "Hughes was already an established poet and [Plath] had gone to a party on 25 February of that year with the express desire to meet him." The event in question was a launch party for a new, student-printed literary magazine she admired. Plath did go, but she was hoping to meet not just Hughes, but his friends Lucas Myers and Daniel Huws, also poets, whose work she had also read in the journal. Called *St. Botolph's Review*, Hughes and his friends named it for the falling-down rectory and chicken coop where some of the contributing editors, Hughes included, were staying at the time. It never made it past issue one. None of these three young men were anything close to established. In 1956, Hughes had never published any poetry outside of student magazines like Cambridge's *Chequer*, where he published under a pseudonym.

In a morning journal entry where she anticipates meeting the *St. Botolph's* poets at the coming party, Plath wrote in admiration of Lucas Myers' poetry, but she said nothing of Hughes or his work. At the time, Plath was the established poet. In 1956, at the age of twenty-three, she had already published work in many high-end paying outlets. She continued to write poetry at Cambridge, publishing two poems in *Chequer*. But Plath's ambition was seen as suspect in Cambridge, "too clever, too sophisticated," and her poetry was openly mocked in a published review by Daniel Huws. She attended the *St. Botolph's* party, then, as much to confront Huws as to meet the other poets ("Is this the better or worse half?" she asked Huws when they met that night). And while much has been made of Plath going to the *St. Botolph's* party dressed all in black like a femme fatale to capture Hughes, Hughes was at least as invested in meeting Plath, who, as a brilliant and beautiful American, was a celebrity on campus: "This was not the first time Ted had seen Sylvia. . . . There were some women at Cambridge who were 'very glamorous,' 'public figures . . . a bit like film stars.' . . . Ted . . . thought [she] looked Swedish." Later, he would think the same of Susan Alliston, the poet he was in bed with on the morning Sylvia Plath killed herself.

Hughes was at the *St. Botolph's* party with his current girlfriend, a young student named Shirley, but he danced with Plath when she approached him. Plath quoted his own poem at him and they went into a private room and closed the door. As she wrote the next morning in her journals, they kissed, and then Hughes ripped her earrings and headband from her head. In return, she bit him on the face. Plath was chiefly attracted to Hughes's writing and his "hugeness," as she termed it; Hughes was equally intrigued by the tall American girl whose legs, as he later wrote, "simply went on up." He also knew Plath was a poet, having read her work in *Chequer*, and defended Huws's review to Plath—Dan never would have written it, he said, about an ugly girl. The future couple played a game of tag over the following weeks, with Hughes drunkenly throwing clods of mud at the wrong dorm window while Plath slept. Eventually, they came together in London in March 1956, the night before Plath went to Paris to try and revive her relationship with Richard Sassoon. They slept together for the first time in Plath's London hotel, a night Plath described as a "sleepless holocaust."

In Paris, Plath found Sassoon had left the country for spring break, probably to be with his new girlfriend. She left Paris after a week to travel through Germany and Italy with a former college boyfriend, Gordon Lameyer. Hughes had sent Plath a postcard with a love poem that began, "Ridiculous to call it love," which reached her in Paris at the American Express office. She returned to him in London in mid-April and they began a passionate, public affair, making love in the open air of Cambridge's Grantchester Meadows.

Four months later, on June 16, 1956, with Aurelia Plath the only guest in attendance, they married at St. George the Martyr Church in London's Bloomsbury Square. They honeymooned in Paris, then Spain, for most of the summer of 1956. By the time they landed in Spain, tensions in the new, spontaneous marriage had begun to show. One of Plath's close friends later claimed Plath had told her that Hughes had strangled her on a Spanish hillside. Plath's journal entries of the time describe a bitter fight between the two of them. Nonetheless, Plath wrote joyful letters about their marriage to her mother: "I think he is the handsomest, most brilliant, creative, dear man in the world. My whole thought is for him, to make a comfortable place for him." They returned to England in August, traveling to West Yorkshire, where Plath met Hughes's parents for the first time.

They spent the following year in Cambridge in a small apartment at 55 Eltisley Avenue, near Newnham, where Plath studied on the second year of her Fulbright and Hughes taught at a boys' school. They both wrote copious amounts of poetry, with Plath publishing six new poems in *Poetry* magazine in their first year of their marriage. Plath took on the additional job of promoting Hughes's poetry; she believed he was a genius. In a 1956 letter to her onetime college boyfriend, Peter Davison, by then an editor at the *Atlantic*, she wrote that she had discovered Hughes and was acting as his agent (by the end of the letter, she confesses to having also married him). She typed and ordered Hughes's poems into a manuscript, targeting contests she knew he could win. They hadn't been married a year when his book *The Hawk in the Rain* won a poetry contest sponsored by the Poetry Center of New York City's 92nd Street Y. For the whole of their marriage, Plath played the dual role of secretary and agent for her husband, typing and submitting his work, negotiating his contracts, and managing his finances.

Upon Plath's graduation from Cambridge, she was offered a one-year contract to teach at Smith. She taught the 1957–58 academic year in their English department, while she and Hughes lived in Northampton and struggled to adjust to faculty life. Gail Crowther writes in her dual biography of Plath and Anne Sexton of how challenging Plath found teaching. She was anxious as the returning darling of the English department, where she was now working side by side with the men and women who had been her revered teachers barely two years prior. Plath resented the time that teaching, with its intensive preparatory and grading demands, took away from writing. She was admired by the department as a teacher, regardless, and her colleagues resented her decision not to return the following year so that she could devote herself to writing.

A journal entry from January 1958, describing an encounter with her former professor Alfred Fisher, illustrates the difficulty her colleagues had in grasping her decision. Fisher lectures her about being disloyal to the institution while Plath stares up at his never-to-be-published, seven-volume novel, homebound and perched over his office desk, which, she writes, "must be so ghastly." "What do you need to write?" George Gibian, another former teacher, asked her. The answer was obvious to Plath, and it bewildered her when she tried to articulate it to her colleagues, who inevitably failed to understand. Plath's position as a woman on faculty was also unique. Most of the faculty were men, with wives at home to care for the household, while Plath had the bulk of the domestic duties as well. Clarissa Roche, Plath's good friend, whose husband, Paul, was teaching alongside Plath in the English department, later told reporter Janet Malcolm that she graded all of her husband's assignments to free him to write. By contrast, Plath took on additional grading for other, more established faculty members to bring home extra money.

In the spring of 1958, Hughes took a part-time teaching position at the University of Massachusetts at Amherst, up the road from Smith. This caused tension in the marriage when, on the last day of Plath's spring term in late May 1958, Hughes was absent from the spot they had planned to meet to celebrate. She saw him shortly after, walking with a young woman who was his student. The couple engaged in a violent fight, which Plath described in her journals on June 11. In the same entry, she described their passionate makeup, affirming a love that is "so much the angels might well envy it." The Northampton fight is just one example of a violent breakup/makeup cycle the couple engaged in, almost as soon as they met and which would continue until Plath's death. Plath soothed herself in her diaries that she and Hughes were "intact," now that they had gotten the fight out of their systems. She believed the move away from academia, to a full-time writing life in nearby Boston, which they had planned for the following year, would help their marriage.

The Hugheses spent 1958–59 in Boston in a tiny apartment at 9 Willow Street, in the Beacon Hill neighborhood. Hughes won a Guggenheim, which they depended on for income, while Plath took on occasional part-time jobs, working as a secretary for a professor of Sanskrit at Harvard and transcribing psychiatric records, mining the latter for material that eventually became her short story "Johnny Panic and the Bible of Dreams." She devoted a great deal of her time to writing, publishing poems in *The New Yorker* for the first time—"Mussel Hunter at Rock Harbor" and "Point Shirley," which dealt with the seaside landscape of her childhood. Hughes was by then at work on his second book of poetry, *Lupercal*; *The Hawk in the Rain* had debuted in both England and America to excellent reviews in 1957, and the Hugheses moved in elite Boston literary circles that year as a result. They befriended Robert Lowell and Elizabeth Hardwick and also the poet W. S. Merwin, then married to his British second wife, Dido, who, like Clarissa Roche, later told biographers about her former friend, Sylvia Plath. Plath dined with Adrienne Rich, who she liked very much and also envied, as Rich was by then already an established poet and Plath had yet to publish her first book.

Plath also began seeing her McLean psychiatrist, Ruth Barnhouse Beuscher, regularly and attending Robert Lowell's poetry workshop at Boston University, where she became friends with Anne Sexton and Sexton's lover, George Starbuck. As Sexton wrote memorably in her short piece about her friendship with Plath, "The Barfly Ought to Sing," the three of them would leave the workshop in Sexton's station wagon and park illegally in a loading zone. Why not, Sexton reasoned? They were only going "to get loaded." They drank martinis at the Ritz-Carlton and dined on the bar's free potato chips while having intense conversations about their shared history. Sexton had tried to kill herself multiple times, and would eventually die by suicide in 1974. They grew apart when the Hugheses left Boston in the summer of 1959, but remained in touch.

Plath and Hughes decided to return to England, where, they had been told by the Merwins, it was possible to make a living writing and doing freelance writing and recording for the BBC. Before embarking back across the ocean, they took off on a cross-country road trip throughout America and parts of southern Canada; Plath was newly pregnant with their first child, Frieda. Returning to the East Coast at the end of August, they prepared to spend two months in residence at the renowned artist colony Yaddo, in Saratoga Springs, New York, where Plath wrote many of the poems that would end up in her first book. The couple returned to Wellesley for Thanksgiving, after which they sailed back to England, where Plath would live until her death. Arriving in London in January of 1960, the Hugheses found a tiny flat at 3 Chalcot Square, the spot that now bears one of England's "blue heritage plaques" proclaiming that the poet Sylvia Plath lived there from 1960 to 1961. They rapidly made the house ready for a new baby. The Merwins had also moved to London, and Dido helped set the Hugheses up with her doctor, John Horder, whom Plath continued to see for the rest of her life. On February 11, 1960, a very pregnant Plath signed a contract with William Heinemann, Ltd., the London publishing company that brought out her first book of poetry, *The Colossus*, later that year. It was published two years later in America by Knopf.

Frieda Rebecca Hughes was born at home in the early morning of April 1, 1960, with the help of a midwife. Plath wrote to her friend, the poet Lynne Lawner, "Frieda is my answer to the H-Bomb." The flat, however, was minuscule, and neither Plath nor Hughes had room or much time to write in the first summer after Frieda's birth. By February 1961, Plath was pregnant again, due on August 17, Hughes's birthday. When, one evening, Hughes returned late from a BBC appointment, Plath, suspecting infidelity, tore up some of his papers in a rage. Hughes struck her. Two days later, Plath miscarried. The marriage, always volatile, was never the same. Plath was ill from the miscarriage and generally unwell, and she entered London's St. Pancras Hospital later that same month to have an appendectomy in the hopes her health would improve. Her copious notes from the hospital resulted in strong new poems. These included the famous "Tulips," a work that speaks to the ambivalence she felt for her domestic life. Motherhood, however, was becoming one of her great subjects. The spring of 1961 saw the writing of "Morning Song," about Frieda's birth, with its famous opening line: "Love set you going like a fat gold watch." Later, she would place it as the opening poem of *Ariel*, one of her few editorial decisions for the collection that Ted Hughes honored.

Plath was also writing *The Bell Jar* that spring, up the street in the Merwins' flat, which they had offered as a writing space for Hughes while they vacationed in their French farmhouse in Lacan. That summer Aurelia visited, taking Frieda for several weeks so that the Hugheses could visit the Merwins in Lacan. The visit was, by the sole account we have of it, a disaster. Dido Merwin's 1989 memoir of Plath, called "Vessel of Wrath," centered on the Hugheses' visit to France, and Dido wrote that Plath ate "a fons *foie gras* like it was Aunt Dot's meatloaf." Plath, Dido claimed, ate for lunch what she planned to serve for dinner, and sulked perpetually. The memoir highlights the kind of class differences Plath encountered throughout her time living abroad. Dido was the daughter of the British aristocracy; her other guest that week was Margot Pitt-Rivers, the former duchess of Lerma, a glamorous survivor of the Spanish Civil War. "Aunt Dot's meatloaf" was an easy hit at Plath's middle-class American roots, a barrier to her ever fitting into the world of European sophistication, a world Hughes—British, male, and already crowned a great poet—entered with ease.

By summer 1961, Plath was pregnant again. Returning to England, she and Hughes knew that their tiny flat in London could not possibly sustain a family of four. They purchased their "dream house," Court Green, a crumbling seventeenth-century manor in the small village of North Tawton, Devon, in the southwest of England. The house, in classically English fashion, even had a straw thatch. Since they had signed a five-year lease on their Chalcot Square flat, they let it to a young couple, David and Assia Wevill. David was a Canadian poet; Assia, his wife, was German-Jewish, a famously beautiful advertising copywriter who had fled Hitler's Germany with her family as a child. She was raised in Tel Aviv before emigrating to England. Plath and Hughes were fascinated with the couple, to whom they extended an open invitation to visit Court Green.

The Hugheses worked hard to fix up their new home, becoming friendly with the locals, including Elizabeth and David Compton, to whom Plath later dedicated *The Bell Jar*. They had their first, and last, Christmas together at Court Green in 1961. Hughes had built Frieda, who was a few months shy of two, a cradle for her baby dolls, which Plath painted with flowers and hearts. On January 17, 1962, she gave birth to Nicholas, "my first son . . . with a cross, black frown and oddly low, angry brow, looking up at me." Plath adored her son, but the introduction of a second child to the marriage increased the growing distance between the couple. By the spring of 1962, having come through a cold winter in a drafty, very old house, Plath was writing poems that signaled that distance, such as "Elm," a poem in which an ancient elm tree narrates a terrible vision that reveals itself over time, until the elm can no longer be silent: "A wind of such violence / Will tolerate no bystanding: I must shriek." Finished just weeks before the couple's marriage imploded, "Elm" reads like a harbinger of both its coming end and Plath's *Ariel* poems, which embody witness-bearing in the face of wrongdoing and threat.

In May 1962, the Wevills visited Court Green. On the second day of the visit, Plath walked in on Hughes and Assia Wevill kissing in the kitchen and ordered the couple back to London. By midsummer, Hughes began to come and go between Court Green and London, and Plath realized he had fallen in love with Assia and was conducting an affair. Distraught, she began writing to Ruth Beuscher for advice about how to survive a catastrophic breakup. On July 9, 1962, during a visit from Aurelia, Assia Wevill telephoned Court Green asking for Ted and disguising her voice; Plath knew who it was, and after Hughes finished the phone call, she tore the telephone out of the wall. The couple spent hours in a terrible fight, while Aurelia kept the children occupied, eventually discovering her daughter and son-in-law exhausted, in bed. Embarrassed by the scene, Aurelia left Court Green and went to stay with Plath's midwife, Winnifred Davies. When she left Sylvia at the train station that summer to return to America, it was the last time she saw her daughter.

In September 1962, Plath and Hughes attempted to reconcile and traveled together to Ireland, staying briefly with the poet Richard Murphy in his cottage in the tiny village of Cleggan, on the west coast. They visited Yeats's Thoor Ballylee, which Plath declared the most peaceful place she had ever been. But the peace was short-lived. While at Murphy's, Hughes left early one morning, telling Plath he was going to the painter Barrie Cooke's, but going, instead, to Spain with Assia Wevill. Plath traveled back to England alone. Hughes sent a telegram to Court Green from a London address as a ruse. He returned to Court Green briefly in October to gather his things before leaving permanently. The marriage was over and with it, Plath thought briefly, her life. But she was wrong.

"HOW CAN I EVER GET FREE?" Plath posed this essential question to Ruth Beuscher as Ted Hughes packed his bags to leave Court Green on October 9, 1962. Full of the details of the marriage's end—"[Ted] . . . seems to want to kill me"—Plath swings between despair and the practical realities of dissolving a marriage that included a house, a car, shared bank accounts, and two children. "He has 'agreed' to pay £1000 maintenance. This is scrape pay." Plath wanted to bank on her own writing, but her income from it was still relatively small; the couple had largely depended on Hughes's earnings from his writing, facilitated in part by Plath's work as his functional secretary and agent.

Complex questions of liberation are at the heart of Plath's 1962 letters to Beuscher, a desire for personal freedom that was also a structural question. Her relationship to Hughes was "regressive"; she had tried to turn him into her father, which she now saw as sick, and she wanted to escape. But in 1962, economics and logistics were designed to keep her in place as a mother and wife. The Hugheses' marriage was unusual for its time—it's unusual today—for its creative freedom and shared childcare. Hughes took the children in the morning so Plath could write, Plath the afternoon so Hughes could, which allowed for both of them to earn a risky, difficult living. With Hughes gone and Plath living alone with the children, this was next to impossible.

She began rising at 4 a.m. to write until the babies woke at 8. It worked until it didn't—most of *Ariel* was written this way—but it also took a physical and emotional toll. In the summer and fall of 1962, she began running mysterious high fevers. A new nanny would make her life livable, she wrote to Beuscher, indicating that she knew this was an unsustainable career plan. But a good nanny required a dependable income, and freelance writing was almost never that. In

1962, as a single mother living in a foreign country, one who hadn't been steadily employed since 1958, that was no easy fix.

Hughes also wanted out. Plath wrote to Beuscher that Hughes told her he had felt trapped in their marriage for at least the last two years and he was done pretending. He was unrecognizable to her, more like the legendary "seducer" she had met in 1956. But there was more to this than simple sexual betrayal. The thorough pathologizing of Plath's creativity has left Hughes's mental health, and its role in the end of their marriage, largely out of this story. In summer 1962, Hughes's mother, Edith, wrote to Olwyn that she thought Ted was having a nervous breakdown; he had overdrawn his bank account, and the bank manager had come to see Edith and her husband, William, about it. If Hughes seemed like a different person to Plath in the summer and fall of 1962, he was also writing to his sister Olwyn, then, about "creating two other poets." "One," he wrote, was "experimental & lyrical, one very rigid formalist." Shortly after, he wrote to his cousin Vicky, ostensibly to congratulate her on her marriage, but also to enlist her in his creation of these new poets, which by then he was calling "a secret life." Hughes wanted a second address, one where he could send out poems from pseudonyms, which he believed would be received as "a rival poet, or perhaps two, one who will gradually become much better than me—then the people who resent me for one reason or another, will line up to support one of my rivals (i.e. me)."

He wanted Vicky to be his second address, in Yorkshire. He wrote to Olwyn that he had "written more perfect anthology pieces than anybody alive" and that he would "become the guiding taste at Faber's, when [T. S.] Eliot retires . . . an amusing coup." Plath, observing this strange behavior, wrote to Ruth Beuscher in exasperation that Ted planned to seduce the world: "he wants to be an 'international catalyst.'" In an unpublished letter to Olwyn from the summer of 1962, Hughes sounds unhinged: "I'm going to live . . . as if it were possible to please myself for 24 hours a day, and I'm going gravely to insult . . . the prisoners of wage-packets and emulation of

Wild ponies on Dartmoor, in Devonshire, where Plath wrote most of *Ariel*. She went horseback riding nearby.

souls ... I am not a nail to be driven into a door, and I am not a tooth to rot in a house of eating, so let me be. Kill flies and meditate on the imminence of things." Another letter to Olwyn from the same period is less cryptic. Hughes had ignored his desire to sleep with other women for the last six years "in a gentlemanly considerate way," but he was done with that now. To Beuscher, Plath wrote that although Hughes was in love with Assia Wevill, "he picks up Finns in coffee bars & takes them to hotels."

Plath drove Hughes to the train station on October 11, 1962. She wrote to Beuscher that after she returned, "I was ecstatic. My life ... seemed to be flying back to me from ... buried hidden places." She began horseback lessons, riding a horse called "Ariel" around the Devon countryside, a dramatic landscape that found its way into many of the poems she wrote that month. Over the next thirty-one days, she finished twenty-five poems. In the most famous of these, the canonical "Daddy," she wrote, "Every woman adores a Fascist," a line that has been largely misread as Plath's statement that either her father, her husband, or both were fascists. But Plath is placing her speaker in the position of any woman who has ever loved a man, someone whose existence is intended to blot the rest of the world from your vision. In a July 1970 interview, Aurelia told Harriet Rosenstein that "Daddy" was really about Ted Hughes; the villagers in North Tawton disliked Hughes as "a dark, brooding, long-haired enemy and alien," the inspiration for the line "And the villagers never liked you." Plath told the BBC in December 1962 that "Daddy" was allegorical, about a girl with an Electra complex whose father is a Nazi and whose mother is "quite possibly Jewish." (In Aurelia's interview with Rosenstein, she said that her grandmother was "possibly Jewish.") The girl has to "act out" the allegory "in order to be free of it," language similar to Plath's own letters of the time—*How can I ever get free?*

"Daddy" was one way that Plath answered her own question, in layered biographical, historical, and cultural allusions that encapsulate the suffocating violence of the family unit. "Daddy" offered art—specifically, poetry—as a possible escape. Every woman does not inherently adore a fascist in the poem. They learn to, from a teacher father and a passive mother. The poem's speaker stutters the German pronoun for I, *Ich*, unable to speak in her father tongue or, crucially, say anything on her own behalf. Later, she marries the man she makes in her father's image, but finds herself trapped in the same disaster as her mother. The only solution to this is indirect violence. She takes her phone off the hook and exposes her husband to angry villagers who put a stake through his heart.

"Daddy, daddy, you bastard, I'm through" is Plath's infamous last line, proof she was finished trying to learn this language. But "through" does not just mean "finished"; it also means "across." Plath had broken her link to the past to arrive in a strange place, where the language was brand-new and all her own. To get there, she had leaned gratefully on her friend Anne Sexton, who that August had sent Plath a copy of her 1962 book, *All My Pretty Ones*. Plath loved it, telling Sexton it was "womanly in the greatest sense, and so blessedly <u>unliterary</u>." Plath stole some of Sexton's clever syntax from "Letter Written on a Ferry While Crossing Long Island Sound" for her October 1962 poem "Fever 103": where the nuns in Sexton's poem are "as good as good babies," Plath's orchid is "hanging its hanging garden in the air."

Like many of her October 1962 poems, "Daddy" was heavily criticized because of Plath's identification as a Jewish victim of the Nazis. "Whatever her father did to her," Leon Wieseltier wrote, "it could not have been as bad as what the Nazis did to the Jews." The follow-up to this has been a fruitless search for any kind of Nazi activity in Plath's father's past. The FBI investigated Otto Plath during the First World War because he was a German immigrant who refused to buy war bonds, but their search turned up nothing except that Otto was an avowed pacifist. This focus on Plath's father's history has turned a blind eye to Hughes's interest in fascism, which, in the summer and fall of 1962, seems to have flourished. He wrote to Olwyn that he had left Sylvia and the children for good after Hitler came to him in a dream and ordered him to do so.

Writing about Hughes to Ruth Beuscher in the same period, Sylvia described Hughes's special fondness for a work of his that was "pure ego-Fascist, about a hawk." Plath's observation is keen. Hughes had long associated fascism with nature. Jonathan Bate, writing of Hughes's interest in ecology, describes Hughes's lifelong admiration of Henry Williamson, who wrote *Tarka the Otter*. Williamson so admired Hitler that he attended the 1935 Nuremberg Rally and then joined the British Union of Fascists. Bate cites Hughes's memorial address for Williamson, who lived near Hughes in Devon and whom he befriended later in life, which draws a close line between the strongman of fascism and the violent view Williamson (and Hughes) took of the natural world. The memorial address came later, when Williamson died in 1977, but Bate also reports that when Hughes went fishing on the river Taw for the first time in the spring of 1962, "an otter leapt from a ditch and led him to the river," and he felt that he had found "another spiritual home." That fall, as he dreamed of taking orders from Hitler, Hughes published an introduction to *Tarka the Otter* in the *Sunday Times Colour Supplement*.

The critical focus of Plath's fall 1962 poetry has long been its emphasis on the horrors of the Holocaust and Hiroshima and Nagasaki and the general understanding of her work as obsessed with suicide and death. But many of her poems of the time take on the problem of marriage, placing it historically as an institution as much in need of question as warfare, literature, or medicine, and using those institutions as a framework to better understand the gender dynamics of marriage, particularly the ways that power functions inside of a broken one. "The Detective," "The Courage of Shutting-Up," "A Secret," "The Applicant," "The Jailer," "Amnesiac," "Daddy"—these poems attempt to place the married woman into history and interrogate that place in a way no poet had done previously.

In "The Detective," Holmes and Watson investigate a crime scene in a lush English country home with "the smell of polish, . . . plush carpets." Although emptiness pervades it, no one is dead. In "The Courage of Shutting-Up," the body of the deserted wife is a battlefield, a site of wartime surgery and cannons, her brain a dangerous weapon, given the knowledge it possesses, her tongue "that antique billhook . . . Must it be cut out?" These poems turn the home and the married woman's body into a site of terror, with the greatest threat not to that body, which is always already at risk because of the violence of the home and the primacy of the husband. The threat is instead against the established order of the home, marriage, and the family, should the married woman choose to unleash what she has seen and lived in speech acts.

Plath ramped up all of these stakes in "The Jailer," the most potent, frightening poem of this group, in which she plays a risky, racist game of switched identity. Written October 17, Plath's speaker dons what Audre Lorde would later criticize as "white feminism in Blackface." The poem centers on a prison of a marriage, a stage set the jailer rolls in each morning, where he burns the speaker with cigarettes, "Pretending I am a negress with pink paws." In the poem's libidinal economy, the jailer recasts his white wife as a Black woman in order to justify her captivity, his desire to do her physical harm, and, importantly, to derive more, or differently charged, pleasure from these acts than he might if he saw her as herself—who, as Plath writes, "is not enough."

"The Jailer" explores marriage as an interpersonal version of what the writer Saidiya Hartman calls "the slippage between victims and sweethearts," her unforgettable description of the hold of the slave ship *Recovery*. But a white, twentieth-century marriage, gone however wrong, is not a slave ship. The poem's later importance to the second-wave feminist movement, which sometimes described a wife as a slave, as an emblem of the abused wife, forces us to reckon with reality. While Plath was certainly a victim of intimate partner violence and sexual assault, the idiom of marriage as slavery is a failure, blind to the sexual slavery Black women in antebellum America suffered in addition to the forced labor they endured in the daylight. Drafts of "The Jailer" heighten the fact that the speaker is one player in a sadistic game—Plath crossed out lines in which she goes from a Black woman in a cage to a "dead white heron" sitting under a bell jar. The cigarette burns the speaker suffers at the hands of her captor intentionally bring to mind images of Black flesh branded by slavers. But blackface can be wiped off, and stage sets rolled away. Eight days before she wrote "The Jailer," Plath closed her letter to Ruth Beuscher with the ironic, crushing observation that her early years with Hughes would mark her, "Like a Belsen label. Do write."

Plath's work from October and November of 1962 energized her tremendously, and she wanted to be in literary London to celebrate her success. Her publisher, William Heinemann, was going to bring out her first novel, *The Bell Jar*, on January 14, 1963, and the manuscript for the book was being considered by her American publisher, Knopf. She was working on a new novel called *Doubletake*, about the breakup of a marriage. Plath went shopping; she got a new haircut and a black leather handbag. In the first week of November, she visited London, where she was seeing the critic Al Alvarez, for whom she wrote the love poem "Letter in November," which proclaimed, "I am so stupidly happy." She wrote it in between sleeping with Alvarez and house hunting in her old neighborhood, London's Primrose Hill. Plath doubted she would find a home there, as it was an increasingly trendy place to live, but went anyway. There she saw a sign on Fitzroy Road announcing "Flats to let" in a building she had long coveted, a beautiful space on its own, also bearing a blue English Heritage plaque announcing that the poet W. B. Yeats, one of her favorites, had once lived there.

Plath put in an application for the flat and returned home to Court Green on the train, certain the house was an impossibility—probably there were hundreds of people in front of her with more money. She wanted a sign. She pulled Yeats's *Collected Plays* off her bookshelf and opened it at random to page 347, to his play *The Unicorn from the Stars*. She was startled to find the following lines: *Go, then, get food and drink, whatever is wanted to give you strength and courage. Gather your people together here, bring them all in. We have a great thing to do, I have to begin—I want to tell it to the whole world. Bring them in, bring them in. I will make the house ready.* Plath's edition of Yeats's *Collected Plays* is housed in her archive at Smith College. The lines I have underscored are the same ones she did that November day. She drew a star in black ink next to the first line, and at the bottom right-hand corner of the text, she wrote, "Nov. 13, 1962 the prophecy—true?"

Plath's bibliomancy did prove true. She signed a five-year lease for the top two floors of Yeats's House, at 23 Fitzroy Road, at the end of November. On the tenth of December, she moved the children and herself into the new flat. Although Plath was thrilled, initially, to be in London, she faced a series of challenges. First, famously, it was cold—the coldest winter in a century. The fountains froze. Plath's heat and electricity went off intermittently for the entirety of her time in London. She was still on the waiting list for a telephone at the time of her death, a state of affairs that, ironically, made her feel more isolated in London than she had at Court Green.

Hughes was in London, a fact that might have, at least in part, initially attracted Plath back to the city. But being in the same city as him disturbed her. By December, Hughes was having at least two affairs, one with Assia Wevill, another with a woman named Susan Alliston, whom he had met at his publisher, Faber & Faber, where she worked. Sylvia was barraged with gossip about her husband's affairs wherever she went. Throughout the fall and winter, Aurelia Plath entreated her daughter to return home. But in a bizarre coincidence, Alliston was the ex-wife of a man named Clement Moore, who had roomed with Sylvia's brother, Warren, at Harvard; the two were close. Plath had touted Hughes as the ideal husband to everyone she knew back home in Massachusetts, but now, he was sleeping with Moore's ex-wife. There was no hiding this disaster, she surely felt.

For this and other reasons, she stayed in London. By January, she was writing again, similar to her burst of creativity in October, but poems of a different nature. One was "Mystic," with its fusion of religion and domesticity, in which Plath asks, "Once one has seen God, what is the remedy?" Another was the famous "Edge," in which a Medea-like woman kills her two small children along with herself. Along with severe physical illness—cold and flu for both her and the children—Plath's depression had returned, as she wrote to Ruth Beuscher on February 4, 1963, a week before her death: "What appals [sic] me is the return of . . . my fear & vision of the worst. . . . Perhaps . . . accentuated by my seeing Ted once a week."

She wrote right up until the last week of her life, during which her doctor began to look for a place for her at an inpatient psychiatric hospital. It's possible that this was a tipping point. Plath had told many friends that she could not endure another stay in one, not after her time at McLean. She and the children spent the last weekend of her life with her friends the Beckers, but on Sunday, February 10, she insisted on returning home. She was distraught, and the Beckers tried hard to get her to stay. It is probable that she was planning suicide then, as she insisted on going. She put her head in the oven and gassed herself around seven o'clock the next morning. She was found dead several hours later by a young nurse who was scheduled to come help her with the children. Plath had protected the children by sealing off their nursery door from the gas with thick masking tape. She was thirty.

She left behind her flat at Fitzroy Road, for which she had paid a year's rent in advance, a small amount of money, and a large amount of unpublished writing. The output of her final year astounded her husband, who spent the weeks after her death reading it aloud to visitors, telling them he planned to "auction" it. Hughes recognized immediately that it would surpass artistic triumph to become a commercial and financial one, and by the 1980s, he reported making somewhere in the area of £150,000 a year from Plath's royalties. With the help of his sister, Olwyn, who left her job as a literary agent for Martonplay, in Paris, to represent Hughes and the Plath estate, he pulled Plath's books from her British publisher, William Heinemann Ltd., and published *Ariel* with Faber & Faber, his publisher, in 1965; they took over the publication of *The Bell Jar* the same year. The inside back jacket of the first Faber *Ariel* was wholly taken up with advertisements for books by Ted Hughes.

Plath's American editor, Judith Jones, wrote to Hughes that she "was not really prepared for the impact that the book, which Faber has just sent us in proof, made upon me. It is really . . . extraordinary . . . and . . . we are very anxious to publish it." Jones and Plath had had a strong working relationship on *The Colossus*, but Hughes refused her offer. He gave the book to his American publisher, Harper & Row, after the poet Donald Hall, then an acquisitions editor for Harper, sent him an airmail asking, "Can Harper's have *Ariel*?" Hughes's American editor, Fran McCullough, took over the editing of Plath's manuscripts, as well.

Later, in his 1971 essay "Publishing Sylvia Plath," printed in the *Observer*, Hughes wrote that Knopf "seemed nonplussed" about

Plath's poems and that "a deadlock dragged on." Actually, he appears to have stopped replying to Jones's letters, even as Jones held a spot for *Ariel* on Knopf's fall list and told him repeatedly of her admiration for his late wife's work. It is difficult not to wonder how we would have perceived a Sylvia Plath edited by Judith Jones, who in 1964 was on her way to becoming one of the most important voices in publishing, responsible for *The Diary of Anne Frank*, the cookbooks of Julia Child, and the novels of John Updike, among many other books. She counted Plath among these landmark American voices and had worked with the living Sylvia Plath, not the Plath of legend.

Plath had left her *Ariel* manuscript behind on her desk, with a typed table of contents, but Hughes excised nearly all of her poems about marriage from his version of *Ariel* and included, instead, poems she had written in the last three weeks of her life, when she was experiencing what her doctor, John Horder, later called "a psychotic depression." Hughes ordered "Edge" as the penultimate poem, giving it the air of a suicide note. The book was chosen by the Poetry Book Society as its Book of the Month, for which Hughes wrote an accompanying, explanatory note that said of *Ariel*, "It is her. Everything she did was just like this, and this is just like her—but permanent." *Ariel*, a book Hughes had put together in a way that looked nothing like Plath's intentions for it, became a literary mausoleum for the dead girl, speaking.

Almost as soon as Sylvia Plath became famous, she became infamous, and then iconic. Ted Hughes quickly blamed her fans for this state. But it was Hughes who couched repeated public references to Sylvia Plath in religious language. In 1966, he wrote that Plath's poems acted as "chapters in a mythology." "Every word is *Baraka*," he said—his first published comparison of Plath to Islamic divinity, but not his last. He wrote, "The world of her poetry is one of emblematic visionary events, mathematical symmetries, clairvoyance and metamorphoses. Her poetry escapes ordinary analysis in the way clairvoyance and mediumship do: her psychic gifts, at almost any time, were strong enough to make her frequently want to be rid of them." Hughes complained to Aurelia Plath in a 1966 letter that "teenagers at college set up [Plath's] corpse as a holy example," but he himself framed Plath's work in the language of Christian fundamentalists: If Robert Lowell "is a fine doctor, [Sylvia] is a miracle healer." Hughes continued to use the rhetoric of magic, mythology, and religion in his published descriptions of Plath's life and work until his death in 1998.

When Plath died in February 1963, Hughes waited more than a month to write to her mother in America. He excoriated himself in that letter, telling Aurelia Plath that he didn't ever want to be forgiven (in the margins of the letter, in shorthand, Mrs. Plath wrote, "You won't be") and that "if there is an eternity, I am damned in it." By the mid-1970s, reading, for publication, Plath's letters describing the breakdown of their marriage, Hughes rejected Plath's complaint that she had sacrificed a great deal for their marriage—her writing, her college teaching job, her homeland, a whole way of life. Hughes wrote to Mrs. Plath that actually, in their years together, Plath's writing took precedence. As for the marriage, it failed for mysterious reasons: "Sylvia's marriage hit an underwater rock. . . . The geology of the rock is nobody's business." The further Hughes traveled from his actual history, the easier it became for him to see his life with Plath as a story with characters whose actions were dictated by unseen forces, rather than human beings living in ordinary time. His Plath character had "No case" in her argument that she had made her writing career second to her husband's.

Forgetting became central to Hughes's philosophy of his life—and his wife's work. He claimed to have burned Plath's final journals, lost others, lost the manuscript for her second, unfinished novel. Despite this, he continued to publish heavily censored versions of her work, including, in 1982, about one-third of the text of her remaining journals. In the penultimate sentence of his short foreword to *The Journals of Sylvia Plath*, Hughes wrote that he didn't destroy Plath's last journals to hide his own behavior from the world. He did it to hide his own behavior from himself: "in those days I regarded forgetfulness as an essential part of survival." Plath was onto Hughes's will to forget, too, as seen in her October 21, 1962, poem "Amnesiac," about a husband who leaves his family: "No use, no use, now, begging Recognize!" But as the poet Kathleen Ossip reminds us in her Plath-inspired poem *"No Use,"* "Thanks to her habit of journal keeping and her resolve to memorialize her experience in writing, Sylvia forgot nothing."

What Plath recalled in writing, however, was not sufficient to relay her life's history and the focus of her work to a world that was hungry for both, at least for the first half century after she died. Hughes maintained a form of silence about Sylvia Plath, writing about her work, but rarely about their lives together, and enforcing a code of silence about the same to his and Plath's family and friends, one many of those closest to Plath attempted to refute, with varying degrees of success. In 1998, six months before his death from cancer, Hughes published *Birthday Letters*, a book of poetry "about" his marriage to Sylvia Plath, which many critics claimed "set the record straight." In fact, *Birthday Letters* continued the same mythologizing (and pathologizing) of Plath that began with *Ariel*, further cementing the idea of Plath as doomed to die by her poetry. A single poem in *Birthday Letters*, "Dreamers," acknowledged the existence of Assia Wevill, blaming her witch-like powers for the end of Hughes's marriage to Sylvia Plath, saying nothing of her daughter, Shura, with Hughes, or her 1969 murder-suicide of Shura and herself. By 1998, history had enshrined a legendary Sylvia Plath. But it had forgotten Assia Wevill altogether.

Loving
Assia Wevill

※※※◆※※※

IN 1967, ASSIA WEVILL, A GERMAN-JEWISH ADVERTISING copywriter who had been living in London for most of her adult life, began translating the work of the Israeli poet Yehuda Amichai. Wevill had met Amichai in July of the same year through Ted Hughes, who, by then, had been her on-again off-again lover for several years. Hughes had brought Amichai to England for a festival called Poetry International, which also featured Anne Sexton, Robert Lowell, and Zbigniew Herbert. Amichai wrote in Hebrew, and Hughes wanted his work to reach a larger, English-speaking audience. Wevill, who grew up reading and speaking Hebrew, was his obvious choice to do the translations. The poems were eventually published as Amichai's *Selected Poems* in both the United Kingdom and the United States, and some remain widely anthologized. Wevill chose to be credited in the book as Assia Gutmann, her Jewish maiden name. She and Hughes presented the translations on a BBC Radio 3 program, which they recorded on June 28, 1968. It aired December 12 of that year.

Assia Wevill shared a common history with Yehuda Amichai. Both were born Jewish in Germany and fled the Nazi regime with their families. Amichai's family left Wurzburg for then-Palestine in 1935, when he was twelve. Wevill's parents, Lonya and Elisabeth ("Lisa") Gutmann, chose to leave Berlin in 1933, landing first in Italy before moving to Tel Aviv in 1934. Lonya Gutmann was a successful doctor, a profession that hastened his departure from Germany. In their 2006 biography of Assia Wevill, Yehuda Koren and Eilat Negev explain that the medical profession was one of the first in Nazi Germany to be Aryanized:

> Nazi ideology described the Jews in metaphors of disease: as a bacillus, a parasite, or a malignant tumor in the body of the nation. Hitler was thus perceived as the Good Doctor who would remove the Jewish malignancy and cure the German patient. It was the task of the medical profession to join the effort, restore "hygiene" to the German nation and cleanse it of Jews.

Lonya and Lisa quickly surmised how much danger their young family was in and left Germany with Assia, who was just about to finish kindergarten, and her younger sister, Celia. In Pisa, Italy, Gutmann began to look for countries that would accept him as a practicing physician without requiring him to return to medical school; and so he brought his family to Palestine, then under British control. In Tel Aviv, Assia learned to read, write, and speak Hebrew, while also maintaining her fluency in three other languages. She spoke in Russian with her father and German with her mother. Of the four family members, the six-year-old Assia was the only one who gained conversational Italian from their time in Pisa, and the family loved listening to her speak as they established their Palestinian home.

The early histories of Yehuda Amichai and Assia Wevill reflect one of the central conflicts of the twentieth century—the expulsion of European Jews and the role this played in the establishment of Israel. But gender played a crucial role in how their stories diverged once they came of age in the burgeoning Jewish state. Amichai fought for the British during the Second World War, and then for the Zionists in the series of conflicts from 1947 to 1949 that established the nation of Israel. After he attended Hebrew University, where his talent for writing was quickly recognized, and he began to publish his poetry, much of which dealt with the political ramifications of his time as a soldier. This led in fairly short order to international acclaim, with teaching appointments at prestigious American universities, including Yale, where his papers now reside.

By contrast, Assia's parents understood her talent for languages and her looks as an entree into marriage and a possible avenue of return to Europe. They sent her to the Tabeetha School, a private, expensive prep school where the daughters of wealthy Palestinian families learned an English curriculum and British manners. While most of the young women were chauffeured to school, Assia took the bus. In addition to British poetry and a math course where money was taught in pounds sterling and weights measured in stones, Assia quickly became fluent in English, which, for the rest of her life, she spoke with the posh accent cultivated at Tabeetha. This would one day become a thorn in Ted Hughes's side. In 1968, when Assia Wevill's Amichai translations debuted to rave reviews, Hughes sent her a letter he called "Draft Constitution," outlining his expectations for her behavior, should the couple try once more to make a home together. At the time, Hughes was at Court Green with Frieda, Nicholas, and his aging parents, William and Edith, and Wevill was living in London with Shura, the daughter she had with Hughes in 1965. In a ten-point list of directives that included rules about when she could and could not sleep, what she could and could not wear, and what she could cook for the children, Hughes tells Wevill she must "be as German as possible, as Israeli as possible preferably," and "do all you can to rid yourself of English sophistications." Much later, he mocked her accent as a "Kensington jeweller's elocution" in his poem "Dreamers," which appeared in *Birthday Letters*.

"Dreamers" is about Assia Wevill's first-ever visit to Court Green in May of 1962 and describes her as a predatory animal with "tiger-painted nails" who "sniffed ... out" the happiness Hughes claimed to have shared with Sylvia then. In "Dreamers," Wevill's history as a displaced person is turned against her. She becomes a woman who is somehow simultaneously a "Sabra" (a Jewish person born in Israel) and an "ex-Nazi Youth," in an apparent nod to her mother's Teutonic background and her father's Judaism. The two elements combine to create a literal monster, a wolflike witch who touches Plath's children's hair as though plotting their demise.

In reality, Wevill's parents' mixed marriage was a cause of sustained trauma for her and her family. In 1941, while the Gutmann family were surviving the Second World War in Tel Aviv, the Nazi Field Marshal Rommel's North African campaign had his forces "within a week's drive" of Palestine. As reports of the Nazi atrocities made their way back to Tel Aviv, British officials began deporting German nationals to Australia, and the Gutmanns lived in terror that Lisa would be sent away from her young family. By that time, the Gutmanns also knew that a return to Germany as a family was impossible. In the summer of 1935, Lisa Gutmann had traveled back to Germany with her daughters to visit her parents and sister, with "her passport, issued by the British authorities in Palestine, serving as a political shield." There she witnessed how mixed marriages between Christians and Jews were actively persecuted by the Nazis under the newly instituted Nuremberg Race Laws. Lisa Gutmann saw firsthand what would have happened to her husband and their daughters had they stayed in Germany. She also permanently severed her relationship with her sister after seeing her nephews in their "Hitlerjugend" uniforms, a reality of Wevill's history that makes Hughes's description of her as "an ex-Nazi Youth" especially difficult to swallow.

The story of Assia Wevill is the story of the mid-twentieth century—the Second World War, the Holocaust, the subsequent refugee crises of both, and the establishment of Israel. She was born Assia Esther Gutmann on May 15, 1927, in an affluent quarter of Berlin. Within six years of her birth, the city would explode in the beginnings of the Second World War. She was part of the generation of women who reentered the workforce in the late 1950s. She made significant contributions to the advertising world that flourished in England and America in the 1960s and ushered in the so-called golden age of consumerism. She lived all over the world—in six countries, on three continents—and witnessed England, her longest adopted home, go from the dregs of postwar austerity to swinging London. She died in the earliest years of second-wave feminism, unaware that she would become symbolic of its aims to recover and reclaim women's lives and histories.

Most famously, of course, she was a major influence on the lives and works of Sylvia Plath and Ted Hughes, two people who in turn influenced Wevill's life and creative output. The reality of that shared influence remains a difficult one to tease out, since almost immediately after Wevill's 1969 suicide, in which she also killed her four-year-old daughter, Shura, Hughes began a campaign to obscure, and then erase, Wevill's existence from memory.

In their foreword to *The Collected Writings of Assia Wevill*, her biographers, Koren and Negev, write of their interview with Hughes two years prior to his death: "Publicly, Hughes continued to write Assia out of his life story, but she deeply occupied his poetry," a reference to Hughes's book *Capriccio* (1990), a twenty-poem sequence about his life with Wevill, and her death. Hughes probably also referred to the poems about Wevill in *Birthday Letters*, which debuted soon after the interview. Hughes "was relieved no reviewer or journalist had deciphered the autobiographical clues. 'People are so dumb they don't know I have given the secret away,' he told us."

For Hughes, "[giving] the secret away" meant publishing poetry in which Wevill was reduced to literary tropes rooted in anti-Semitism, racism, and misogyny. Jonathan Bate called Hughes's characterizations of Wevill in some of these poems "his most tasteless lines," while Katha Pollitt wrote in 1998 that they "[managed] to hit the nadir of taste and the zenith of self-delusion." Much like the Sylvia Plath of *Birthday Letters*, in *Capriccio*, Wevill's suicide and her murder of Shura are a fated, inevitable act, a die cast when she and her family managed to escape the Nazis. In "The Locket," Hughes's Assia wears a locket around her neck that contains an oven marked with a swastika. This Assia Wevill is so enamored of her narrowly escaped death that she "nurses" the locket like an infant against her breast. Hughes positions himself as trying vainly to save her by closing the locket, which refuses to stay shut, and then moves from his doomed lover's heroic savior to her victim. The locket transforms into a metaphor for a vagina (lips) and misogynist slang for the same (slit): "Its lips kept coming apart—just a slit." Hughes's speaker is helpless to close the deadly woman's locket, or legs. The poem ends with the phrase "*fait accompli*."

"The Locket" is one of several poems in *Capriccio* that insinuates that Wevill was sexually obsessed with Nazism, which was, in reality, a source of horror throughout her life. Her father's brother had been murdered by the Nazis, along with his wife and children. In 1954, Wevill traveled to Germany with her second husband, the economist Richard Lipsey, and tried to visit Dachau concentration camp but could not bring herself to move past the entrance gates. Several experiences during that trip—including a former SS officer mistaking her for a Nazi sympathizer and gifting her his swastika medal—convinced Assia that Germany could never again be her home. Later, she wrote to her sister Celia that she was certain Nazism would reemerge in Germany in the near future: "I still believe . . . we shall see some form of Naziism [*sic*] in full flourish in about 3–5 years."

In *Capriccio*, Hughes merges Wevill's cosmopolitan background and displaced history with her dark looks to reduce her to a literal password, a shibboleth. Derived from the ancient Hebrew word meaning "ear of grain," a shibboleth is a language test used to determine if someone is an imposter. In one of the many conflicts described in the Book of Judges, the word is used to distinguish between the Gileadites and the Ephraimites, two warring tribes of Israel. Gileadites pronounced the word with its "sh" sound intact, while Ephraimites dropped the *h*, saying "sibboleth." The Ephraimites were asked to speak it to prove their identity and were murdered when they said "sibboleth."

In Hughes's poem "Shibboleth," Wevill's authenticity as an Englishwoman is called into question. He writes that her mother bought Wevill her English accent "by mail" from "Fortnum and Mason," reducing Wevill's extensive study of English and her long history living in English-speaking countries to a cheap attempt to buy her way into Englishness, something Hughes sees as an impossible act for a foreigner. "Shibboleth" also points to the ways Wevill is a victim—in these poems as in life—of a catch-22: she is either a posh snob with a "Kensington jeweler elocution" or a crass imposter who can't get her accent right. Either way, in "Shibboleth," English is privileged over Hebrew, a haunted language that lives under Wevill's tongue, proof of a war-torn past Hughes characterizes as deliberately hidden.

In "Shibboleth," Wevill's accent betrays her during a long weekend away in posh Berkshire County, in England. Having tripped up in the pronunciation of an undisclosed English word, Wevill "Flushed sootier." In her otherness, Wevill's beauty becomes dirty, again echoing "Dreamers," which proclaimed her "filthy." As in "Dreamers," which exoticized Wevill as having hair as "Mongolian," Hughes ties Wevill's sullied beauty to her race, fantasizing that she is a Tartar, an antiquated word used to describe someone of Mongolian or Turkish descent. This metaphorical tying becomes chillingly literal as Wevill is dehumanized: "something pinioned" (meaning having one's legs or arms tied up) beneath the barrel of a gun. Her captors, knowing she is an imposter, "drawl" a dated racist idiom at her: "'Lick of the tar-brush?'"

This is not the only poem in *Capriccio* that denigrates Wevill for appearing to be other than a white woman. In the opening poem "Capriccios," a "bride" (a stand-in for Sylvia Plath) looks into a mirror and her double (a stand-in for Assia Wevill) stares back. The double's eyes have "cold / Epicanthic folds," referring to the way skin can fold over the corner of the eye, most commonly in East Asian people. The phrase marks Wevill as nonwhite and therefore threatening to Plath. The lines also reference the famous scene in Charlotte Brontë's *Jane Eyre* when Jane—so quintessentially English that her character gave rise to the phrase "plain Jane"—awakens in the middle of the night to see her fiancé's wife, Bertha Rochester, staring at herself in Jane's bedroom mirror, wearing Jane's wedding veil. Bertha, a Jamaican Creole, is seen by Jane as "'the reflection of the visage and features quite distinctly in the dark oblong glass.'" When Rochester asks Jane to describe the face she saw in the mirror, she tells him:

> "This, sir, was purple: the lips were swelled and dark; the brow furrowed: the black eyebrows widely raised over the bloodshot eyes. Shall I tell you of what it reminded me?"
> "You may."
> "Of the foul German spectre—the Vampyre."
> "Ah!—what did it do?"
> "Sir, it removed my veil from its gaunt head, rent it in two parts, and flinging both on the floor, trampled on them."

In "Capriccios," the Plathian bride sees the image of her double in the mirror before the wedding, a sign that the marriage is doomed, just as Bertha's tearing of Jane's veil portents the disaster of her aborted wedding to Rochester. Wevill's German-Jewish background and her monstrous characterization in *Capriccio* are on full display in "Capriccios" if you know what you're reading. Given that Ted Hughes grew up a stone's throw from Charlotte Brontë's childhood home, I think we do.

Capriccio is typically described as a book of poems "about" Assia Wevill and Hughes's relationship with her, the implication being that Hughes was giving away the story by writing the poems. While the poetry is frequently oblique to the point that without a dictionary of world mythology it would be impossible to pull a narrative from it, we should be wary of doing so in the first place, given Hughes's loose interpretation of Wevill's biography. The alleged event described in "Shibboleth," for instance, when Wevill's accent betrays her at a posh English home, has no apparent basis in Wevill's biography, while the poem "Snow," which is based on the last time Hughes saw Wevill alive, moves from actual events to—once more—imagining Wevill's corpse burning in Hitler's ovens, events that (obviously) did not take place.

Whatever its contents, we can argue that Hughes gave nothing away about his relationship with Wevill with the book's debut for one simple reason. He published *Capriccio* with the rarefied Gehenna Press in editions so prohibitively expensive that almost no one read them (two different editions debuted in 1990—the less expensive of the two was listed for £9000). Alternatively, anyone who may have been able to tell, or confirm, "the secret" of Assia and Shura—Hughes's family, friends, and influential literary figures like his confidants Seamus Heaney and Yehuda Amichai—remained silent about who Assia and Shura were, as well as about Hughes's role in their lives, deaths, and burials. Amichai's silence, though, must have been a troubled one. He and his wife Chana had been close to Wevill in the last two years of her life, and he worked intensively with Wevill on her translations of his poetry. In 1973, he published an elegy for her called "The Death of Assia G." Several long, intimate letters from this time exist between Amichai and Wevill—Assia's side of this correspondence was published as part of Wevill's *Collected Writings* in 2021. Wevill ends most of her letters to Yehuda by entreating Chana to write to her and—in words that only now can be read with heartache and hope—not to forget her.

I first learned of Assia Wevill's death during dinner with friends. It was January of 2000 and I was at a writing retreat over a holiday weekend, preparing to return to college for the spring term. One of our group was studying for her MFA in poetry and reading a lot of Sylvia Plath for her workshops. It was she who told us that Wevill had killed herself, too, and murdered the daughter she had with Ted

Hughes at the same time. It was almost not to be believed—because of the unimaginable horror of the acts themselves, of course, but also because by then I had spent a great deal of time with Plath's story and read multiple biographies and articles about her life and death. Most lightly touched on Wevill's role in the end of the Hugheses' marriage; none reported Assia's and Shura's deaths. For all I knew, before that dinner, Assia Wevill was still alive.

It was around this time, too, that I began reading the poetry of Yehuda Amichai in anthologies. I became enamored of his famous poem "A Pity, We Were Such a Good Invention." The poem was translated by Assia Gutmann, whom I did not associate, or think to associate, with Assia Wevill, Ted Hughes, or Sylvia Plath. It would be years before I realized it: poetry and biography, the two essential strands of my education that I was often taught were disparate and incompatible, were one woman with two names.

DISPLACEMENT, THE MOST COMMON THEME of Wevill's early life, plagued her until her death on March 23, 1969. In January of that year, she wrote to her father, Lonya, in the event of her suicide: "The prospect before me is so bleak . . . this life alone. . . . No husband. No father for Shura." In the same letter, she called Lonya "my colleague in exile and disaster." By the time of her death in London, the rest of her family were living across the ocean in Montreal. Only Lonya, who had always made Assia his favorite and had tried for a brief time to live near Wevill and Hughes to support his daughter and granddaughter, was able to fly over for her funeral.

Twenty years earlier, the Gutmanns had followed Assia to Canada. In 1948, she was living in London in an undesired and unhappy first marriage to John Steele, who she met when he was stationed in Tel Aviv during the Second World War. A member of the Royal Air Force, Steele was eventually transferred out of Palestine, but when the war ended, the Gutmanns paid for Assia's passage to England—ostensibly to attend art school, but with the express purpose that she should find and marry Steele. Although Assia was unsure about the marriage, her mother made it clear that she had sent her oldest daughter to England for marriage, not education or entertainment. If she did not marry John Steele and begin the process of taking her family out of Tel Aviv, where violent clashes between Zionists, Palestinians, and the British increased all the time, Assia could not stay in England. The couple married on May 17, 1947. Steele quickly decided that his financial prospects in London were dim and that he would move his new wife to Vancouver, British Columbia. Dismayed at the prospect of moving to a third continent in as many years, Assia tried to kill herself by swallowing an overdose of fifty aspirin, the first of at least three suicide attempts prior to her death.

Like Plath, Assia Wevill's suicide has frequently been reduced to an act of heartbreak, revenge, or simple pathology. In reality, it fits into the pattern of suicidality by Jewish survivors of the Nazi genocide who left Europe before being interred in a concentration camp. According to a 2018 article in *Psychiatry Research*:

> Reliable studies conducted in Israel among refugees who entered pre-state Israel, 1939–1945, and post–World War II survivors reaching Israel (1948 on), show a mixed picture: suicide rates among the former were higher than comparison groups, while the latter group shows evidence of resilience.

Assia's stomach was pumped and she survived, sailing with John Steele to Canada. By this time—1948—the Gutmanns were experiencing the kind of displacement that would haunt many European Jews in the postwar years. Lonya Gutmann was working as a doctor in Mozambique, Celia was doing her compulsory military service in Israel, and Lisa had left the newly established Israeli state to seek work in England. The Gutmanns were therefore scattered on three different continents, hoping to follow their oldest child to England, when Steele abruptly moved the couple to Canada; they had no choice but to go there, instead, if they wanted to reunite.

In Vancouver, the Steeles' marriage fell apart and they divorced, uncontested by either party, in the summer of 1949. Assia moved back in with her family and enrolled at the University of British Columbia under the name Pamela A. E. Steele. Pamela, the name of a lifelong close friend, Pam Gems, was Anglo and basic, a way, as her sister Celia later reported to Assia's biographers, to masquerade as Canadian, something Assia, with her ability to speak perfect English, could actually pull off. But Pamela was also the name of her first husband's deceased younger sister. The Steeles, hearing of her choice of pseudonym, accused her of trying to steal their child's identity. The reality was hardly so nefarious; anti-Semitism was rife in Vancouver and Assia's maiden name, Gutmann, was identifiably Jewish, so she continued to go by Steele. She stopped using Assia after her fellow students mocked her for having a name they said matched the size of her ass; her middle name, Esther, similarly gave away her Judaism, so both were reduced to initials.

At the University of British Columbia, Assia met Richard Lipsey, the renowned economist who became her second husband. They married in October 1952 and moved to London shortly thereafter so that Lipsey could complete his PhD at the London School of Economics. They lived on Lipsey's university stipend and what little money Assia could pull in from temporary secretarial work, and Assia angered her friends and in-laws by leaning on them financially. But if she was frustrating in regard to financial obligations, she was always a fascinating social companion, regaling her friends and husband with wild stories of her past lives across Europe and Palestine, performing Russian folk songs and dances, and dressing in exotic colors that were atypical for postwar London. Two years later, Sylvia Plath, moving to England to begin the first year of her Fulbright fellowship at Cambridge University and dressed in the bright reds and blues she was fond of, similarly stood out.

Assia's second marriage outlasted her first in duration and affection, but unraveled when she fell in love with a Canadian poet she met at dinner on board an ocean liner as she sailed back to England after spending the summer in Canada with her second husband and his family. At twenty-one, David Wevill was seven years younger than Assia, returning to England to complete the last year of his degree in English literature at Cambridge University. Assia's relationship with him seems to mark the first time she really fell in love. Her marriage to Lipsey was genuine, but also motivated by convention—the necessity for women of her age and class to marry—and a desire for independence from her family through marriage to someone with economic stability and social mobility. Lipsey loved Assia, but also told her biographers that above all, propriety dictated the marriage: "In today's terms, when I met her I would have said, come live with me, and we would have had six months of a crazy, intense wonderful affair, and then we would have split up."

Assia began an open affair with David Wevill that lasted three years, during which time she lived partly with him and partly with her husband. During this time, the Suez Canal crisis of 1956 created a need for people fluent in English and Hebrew, and Assia began a well-paid translating position with Reuters. At Cambridge, David became a member of "the Group," an influential gathering of poets and poetry lovers founded by the poet Philip Hobsbaum, a friend of Ted Hughes's, who was later common-law married to the American poet and expatriate Anne Stevenson, one of Sylvia Plath's biographers. Although Hughes was an occasional member of the Group, he and Plath had left England for America in 1957 and wouldn't return until the winter of 1959–60, so the couples did not meet during this time. Assia, too, began writing her own poetry (only a handful of her poems from this time survive) and painting. She was also hired as a secretary at Notley's, a high-end London advertising firm, where she eventually became a successful copywriter, a career she held at various agencies until her death.

In 1958, David Wevill took a two-year appointment with the British Council teaching history and British and American literature at the University of Mandalay in Burma. As Assia was still married, she had no choice but to stay behind. In spring 1959, Lisa Gutmann was diagnosed with cancer, and Assia traveled back to

Canada to be with her mother. In her absence, Richard Lipsey decided he wanted a divorce, which he informed Assia of when she returned to England. Divorce wasn't possible in England then without a party guilty of desertion, cruelty, or adultery, so Assia gave a detailed account of her affair with David Wevill. The couple submitted their petition for divorce, and Assia sailed to Burma in June 1959. She and David married on the sixteenth of May, 1960, in Rangoon, Burma, after a long, bureaucratic delay in her divorce from Richard Lipsey. Because of this, the Wevills had to live for almost a year as an unmarried couple, an impropriety that caused the British Council to turn down his application to continue teaching at the University of Mandalay. Devastated, the newlyweds sailed back to England two days after their marriage. Back in England, the Wevills happily discovered Assia was pregnant. She wrote to her parents in Canada, who shared her excitement. Unfortunately, she miscarried in September of that year.

As described in the previous chapter, the Wevills became involved with the Hugheses in 1961, when Sylvia and Ted made the choice to buy a large house in the southwest of England for their growing family, necessitating a sublet of their flat at 3 Chalcot Square; the Wevills took it over. Koren and Negev write that in the course of the flat transfer the Hugheses and the Wevills met for dinner quite a few times, but that Hughes was not yet interested in Assia Wevill sexually, and despite opportunities, neither Assia nor Hughes initiated an affair at the time. All published biographies of Plath and Hughes concur, reporting that the attraction between Hughes and Wevill began in May of 1962, when the Wevills made their infamous first visit to Court Green.

But in 2020, Hughes scholar Steve Ely published an article about Hughes and Wevill in the *Ted Hughes Society Journal* that calls this conventional wisdom into question. In "The Key of the Sycamore," Ely zeroes in on a list Ted Hughes made of his interactions with Assia Wevill when he was in the beginning stages of writing *Capriccio*:

A document in the *Capriccio* materials held at the British Library seems to refer to a prior meeting between the two. The document is a numbered list of Hughes's early encounters with Wevill that seems to be placed in chronological order. It begins with Hughes recalling that he and she had exchanged "a glance in the office" (possibly at Notley Advertising, where Assia worked for two periods, 1957–59 and 1960–61, alongside Edward Lucie-Smith, Peter Porter and Peter Redgrove, Hughes's friends from "the Group").

A letter from Hughes to Al Alvarez confirms this initial meeting. Held by the British Library and published in *Letters of Ted Hughes*, the letter is listed as having been written in "late 1961"; Hughes sent it to Alvarez from Court Green. In it, Hughes tells Alvarez that the Wevills "took over our flat—quite by chance. I'd never met him though I'd met her glancingly." The similarities in the language used—"a glance at the office" and "glancingly"—lend further credence to Ely's belief that Hughes and Assia had met prior to the Wevills' takeover of 3 Chalcot Square. Those same "planning materials" for Hughes's book of poems about Assia Wevill state how the "glancing" meeting between the two of them led to "a frisson of attraction" during the Wevills' initial visit to see 3 Chalcot Square. Hughes accords the "desperate maneuvers" he took to let the flat to the Wevills to this attraction—he pushed for them to have the flat so that he might have a reason to continue seeing Assia Wevill.

If the list is correct, he continued seeing her. According to the same "planning materials," Hughes and Assia slept together for the first time sometime in the summer of 1961, not July of 1962, as has been reported in every prior biography of Plath, Hughes, or Assia. Again, Ely:

A seed of attraction between Hughes and Wevill had begun to germinate as early as the summer of 1961, and indeed, point four in the list: "Sherry—the broken bed—the thick waist, relieved that there was an argument to defend his escape," may indicate in its sequencing (placed before the [May 1962] visit to Court Green) that he and Wevill met for an assignation earlier than is usually asserted, before he and Plath moved to Devonshire.

In the 1961 letter to Al Alvarez, Hughes also writes that he admires David Wevill's poems: "I'm sending you 3 which I don't imagine you'll have seen but which seem to me first rate," an evident attempt to place Wevill's work in the *Observer*, where Alvarez was poetry editor. This, too, resembles language and behavior Hughes engaged in when he began his 1962 affair with Assia. Diane Middlebrook writes of how, when Ted Hughes heard that David Wevill was devastated by Assia's infidelity, "[Hughes] promised to work behind the scenes to get some of David's work published in the *New Yorker*" as a way to atone for sleeping with his wife. Middlebrook's notes give the source of this as Nathaniel Tarn's diary from July 19, 1962, shortly after Hughes and Wevill slept together for what was likely the second time, on or around July 11, 1962. Tarn, another prominent London writer and friend of Assia Wevill's, liked to gossip with Assia about her affair with Hughes and then record the gossip in his diary, which has served as a valuable source of information for biographers of Hughes, Plath, and Wevill.

Hughes's chronology in the *Capriccio* "planning materials" is also consistent with what David Wevill reported to Koren and Negev in *Lover of Unreason*—that after the Wevills agreed to take over the Chalcot Square flat, the couples got together in London about six times in the next three weeks. During one of these London outings, Assia Wevill gifted Plath a carved wooden snake that she had brought back with her from Burma. Hughes's list reflects this. He writes that he and Assia Wevill slept together after the Wevills agreed to lease 3 Chalcot Square, but before Assia gave Sylvia "the wooden tinted cobra." Hughes also writes of "the glance in the office that turned poetry—in time, after eight years, to ashes." The glance in the office took place in 1961; eight years later, Assia Wevill killed herself, and Hughes had her cremated.

In *Lover of Unreason*, Koren and Negev report that while the Hugheses' marriage was under considerable strain by May 1962, the Wevills were still a happy couple, described by David Wevill as "equals, sharing most things . . . partners, lovers, friends, companions." If this was true, it can only have been because Assia had managed to conceal her liaison with Ted Hughes from David, who, upon learning of their affair the following year, attempted suicide. Sylvia Plath was seemingly unaware of Hughes's alleged infidelity with Assia in the summer of 1961, but for most of that year, she had been suspicious of his behavior, sure he was having, or intending to have, an affair. Their marriage was troubled throughout, which partly inspired their move to Devon.

Whatever the state of either marriage, by the time the Wevills boarded the train to Exeter in May 1962, Assia and Ted Hughes were probably about to resume, not begin, an affair.

SEVERAL STRANGE INCIDENTS ALLEGEDLY occurred that May weekend in Devon. According to Hughes's poem "Dreamers," Wevill told the group over Saturday breakfast of a dream she had about a pike, one of the fish central to Hughes's early poetry. Hughes attributes his falling in love with Assia to her dream—his dreamer had fallen in love with hers.

Diane Middlebrook was the first to report Wevill's dream as a biographical event, as opposed to an object of Hughes's poetic fancy. Middlebrook's treatment came with the caveat that if she actually told her hosts she had a dream about a giant pike, it was "a calculated act of seduction on Assia's part," since, by May 1962, one of Hughes's most famous poems was "Pike." "Pike" describes Hughes's lifelong obsession with pike fish, which are "in all parts, green, triggering the gold, / Killers from the egg," imagery supposedly echoed in Assia's dream. Wevill did tell three friends—Suzette Macedo, Julia Matcham, and Angela Landels—that she was going to Devon with the intention of seducing Ted Hughes. She told Suzette Macedo that she was going to Court Green "in war paint" for this purpose.

Biographers differ over whether or not Wevill really told her hosts about this dream of pike, which is to say, they differ over whether or not she is a seductress. In *Red Comet*, Heather Clark writes of the pike dream as an event that certainly occurred. Clark notes that Wevill surely knew the poem "Pike," since the Hugheses left a Gehenna Press broadside of it hanging in Chalcot Square when the Wevills moved in. *Red Comet* operates under the assumption that Wevill's telling of the dream was part of how she seduced Ted Hughes, but as with all books that do the same, her only source for this is the poem "Dreamers." Clark writes that Wevill's dream "unsettled Sylvia," but this, too, is taken from "Dreamers," where Hughes tells us that Plath is "astonished, maybe envious" when she hears of Wevill's dream. Clark's only other source for Plath being unsettled by Wevill's dream is retroactive—Plath's note in her journal entry of September 6, 1957, in which she writes that she is thinking of writing a story about a wife whose husband writes passionately about a dream woman, rather than his wife. Plath made no note about Wevill's dream in any letters or poems of 1962.

The Hughes scholar Mark Wormald further complicated the question of Assia's dream in his 2022 book *The Catch: Fishing for Ted Hughes*. Wormald draws on the fact that by the fall of 1957, Plath already *had* written a story about a newlywed couple and their dreams. Called "The Wishing Box," it describes the new married life of Harold and Agnes. Harold has extraordinary dreams, which he tells Agnes over breakfast. The story opens with him telling her about a dream in which he discussed his manuscripts with William Blake, a dead ringer for Ted Hughes's dreams. In his biography *Ted Hughes: The Unauthorised Life*, Jonathan Bate writes about a dream of Hughes's in which Shakespeare showed up at Court Green "in all his Elizabethan gear, like that portrait of Gloriana—jewels, ruffs, and the rest of it" to scold Hughes for trying to alter *King Lear*.

In "The Wishing Box," Agnes interrupts Harold to ask how he could possibly know it was William Blake, to which Harold replies, "Why, from his pictures, of course." Harold's dreams become a source of intense envy for Agnes, who can't get her own dream life going, and she kills herself at the story's end. Wormald notes two points about "The Wishing Box" that have been little regarded in the literature about the Wevills' famous May 1962 visit to Court Green. First, when they were briefly apart in the fall of 1956, Plath wrote a letter to Hughes about "The Wishing Box" in which she admitted writing a "humorous terrible little story" wherein she had "shamelessly plagiarized" some of the dreams he had told her about, including a dream Hughes had about fishing for pike.

Second, "The Wishing Box" was first published in a 1957 issue of *Granta*, then an exclusively student magazine out of Cambridge University, where, at the time, Plath was still studying on her Fulbright fellowship. In the same issue, David Wevill had published his first-ever poem—only five pages separated it from "The Wishing Box." As Wormald writes, "That month, Assia Lipsey, who had just met [David Wevill] on the transatlantic crossing from New York, was telling her second husband one thing while spending the weekends with David in his college room. And, whatever else they were doing, reading."

Did Assia Wevill, inspired by her reading of Hughes's poetry and Plath's short story, have the dream of the pike at Court Green and tell her hosts over that Saturday morning breakfast, with the intention of seducing Ted Hughes? Or did she make the dream up, whole cloth, solely to catch his attention? Did she know—not intuit but, as Wormald posits, *know*—that Sylvia Plath had a complicated, envious relationship with her husband's now-famous dream life because she had read "The Wishing Box" in *Granta*, and use this knowledge as a way to further disrupt the Hugheses' marriage?

A third possibility exists, one Koren and Negev endorse—that none of this happened the way Hughes reported it decades later in "Dreamers," that it was yet another way to mythologize Assia, Sylvia, himself, and the events of the weekend, and that, à la *Lover of Unreason*, "the claim of fatal attraction also served to exonerate Hughes of any responsibility." David Wevill says he has no memory of his wife describing this dream that weekend, a dream he said was unlike her: "That dream is not typical of her. It's loaded with mythic imagery, almost too much to go into." It's the kind of mythic imagery, of course, that made up much of Ted Hughes's work.

Jonathan Bate also doubts that Assia Wevill either had, or reported having, this dream of pike, saying that to believe it occurred as Hughes said it did in "Dreamers" is "to buy into the image of [Assia Wevill] as a ruthless seductress." Julie Goodspeed-Chadwick writes in *Reclaiming Assia Wevill* of the ways "Dreamers" in particular has gone far to fix Wevill in our cultural imagination as a "demon seductress:" " 'Dreamers' is the one poem among the eighty-eight of *Birthday Letters* that does the most damage to Assia. . . . Far more recognized than *Capriccio*, . . . *Birthday Letters* became a best seller and won [every major literary prize in England]."

In his *Birthday Letters* poems as in his life, dreams mattered a great deal to Ted Hughes. Read together, "Dreamers" and the *Birthday Letters* poem "Fairy Tale" name Assia Wevill as the chief cause of Plath's suicide. In "Fairy Tale," an Ogre representing Plath's death lives in her dreams, which Hughes says comprise "forty-nine chambers." The Ogre lives in the forty-ninth chamber, but Hughes can only access the first forty-eight chambers for most of their marriage. In this poem, Hughes's Plath is "love-[sick] for" the Ogre (that is, her death), but she manages to fend him off until Hughes unleashes him by opening the forty-ninth door "With a blade of grass" which he calls "a skeleton key." After the Wevills visited Court Green, Ted Hughes went to London on June 26, ostensibly to rehearse a program for the BBC, but also to drop by Assia's office. She was out; he left her a note that read, "I have come to see you, despite all marriages." In response, Wevill mailed him a single blade of grass, which he claimed in the poem "Chlorophyll" was "dipped in Dior perfume." He mailed her back a single blade of grass from Court Green, laid beside hers. In

Hughes's poetic mythology, Assia Wevill sent him the "skeleton key" that killed Sylvia Plath.

We have been taught to believe in Assia Wevill as a femme fatale, not only by Hughes's poetry but by the cultural scripts that cast women in such roles. But if we do, we cast our lot with a version of this story that lays blame for Sylvia Plath's death on two sexist pathologies, Plath's supposed predetermined date with death and Assia Wevill's wild, deadly beauty. We only have to scan the books on Sylvia Plath and Ted Hughes for evidence of this last: Wevill is described variously as "Babylonian," as having a face so beautiful it was "staggering," and as a woman who "killed" her first two husbands and would kill her third—the poet Peter Redgrove's comment when David Wevill first brought Assia to meet the Group. Here's how Hughes's friend Ben Sonnenberg described Wevill to Koren and Negev: "feral beauty, feral eyes, feral touch and feral movements. . . . What a seductive animal." Hughes wrote in his poem "The Pit and the Stones" that Wevill, rendered as a hunter who eats men as prey, thought of him "as one for your collection . . . / Of trophies digested."

Wevill is framed as having been responsible for the deaths of several men—all of whom outlived her. In the wake of the destruction of the two marriages, David Wevill found a university appointment in the United States and remarried, going on to live a long and happy life. Hughes married Carol Orchard within eighteen months of Wevill's suicide and was appointed poet laureate of England in 1984. As women of their time, alone in a country with no family to depend on and with children to provide for, Assia Wevill and Sylvia Plath were hard-pressed to find the avenues of personal and professional renewal available to David Wevill and Ted Hughes following divorce and tragedy.

In his work, Hughes assigned two people the power to meddle with fate and, ultimately, to kill. Both died.

THE WEVILLS' VISIT TO COURT GREEN accelerated Hughes and Wevill's affair. In July 1962, after they slept together again, Assia told David Wevill that Hughes had raped her. Nathaniel Tarn recorded Assia telling him the sex was "so violent and animal, he [ruptured] her." To the poet Edward Lucie-Smith, her work colleague, Wevill said Hughes "smelled like a butcher" in bed. Despite her unease with Hughes, she continued to see him, and they escaped together to Spain without the knowledge of either of their spouses in September 1962. By the time of Plath's suicide, Assia was pregnant with Ted Hughes's child. Asked by her colleague Julia Matcham if she felt responsible for Plath's death, Wevill demurred—she thought Plath's death had nothing to do with her, a line that has sometimes been held up as proof of her cavalier attitude as a femme fatale.

But was she wrong? They didn't know one another well, and Plath made it a point to be vicious when she gossiped about Wevill with her London friends, words that surely found their way back to Assia, affecting her feelings toward Sylvia. When we demand that Wevill castigate herself for Plath's suicide, do we follow the same cultural scripts for women, expecting more compassion from her, for instance, than we do from Ted Hughes, who moved Wevill, one of his lovers, into the home where his first wife died a scant month after her suicide? Julie Goodspeed-Chadwick, writing of representations of Wevill, says that she "could never emerge in our literature, scholarship, or classroom discussions as anything other than unimportant at best and despicable at worst until we problematize her presentations and legacy in the twentieth and twenty-first centuries and understand what is at stake in such representations."

Whatever the answers are to these difficult questions, Wevill quickly discovered how Plath's legacy would affect the rest of her life. In spring 1963, she moved with Hughes into 23 Fitzroy Road—which she memorably dubbed "the ghost house" in a short letter to her friend Jannice Porter that same year. Living in Sylvia Plath's house, Wevill had access to Plath's poetry, her journals, and her unfinished novel, *Doubletake*, in which she and David appeared as characters, "the Goof-Hoppers."

Assia was appalled by *Doubletake* and the vitriol with which Plath apparently wrote of her in her last journals, but astounded by the poetry of *Ariel*, despite the fact that she was also the subject of some of the more vicious poems from the collection. When, in August 1963, she went with Hughes to Court Green to help clean the house of Sylvia's things, she referred to Plath's study in her journals as "the holy study." As she stared out the window, she noticed "the church, the Elm, the yew trees," all features of Court Green that figure prominently in *Ariel*. Assia's capitalization of the word "Elm" indicates that the poem, not the tree, was on her mind as she stood in Sylvia's study: Plath's famous elm tree describes a toxic, elusive love, as though predicting Wevill's sense that she could never have with Hughes what he had with his first wife. While at Court Green, Wevill asked Plath's close friend Elizabeth Sigmund if she thought that she and Ted could ever be happy. Sigmund told her no—Sylvia's ghost would always be between them, a sentiment that recurs in Wevill's journals. Coming across Sylvia's copy of Eric Fromm's *The Art of Loving*, Assia "added her own stamp of ownership" beneath Sylvia's, writing "Sept. 63" under Plath's inscription of "Sylvia Plath, Court Green, 9 November 1962."

CRUELTY, WHICH PLATH NOTED HAD reemerged in Hughes's nature in the summer of 1962, was a continuing feature of Wevill's life with Ted Hughes in 1963. On May 20, the strain of living in a house haunted by Plath's presence is clear. In the midst of a long journal entry in which Wevill describes her face as "teary and watery with mascara," she also writes, "There's a bruise on my right bosom. Ted inspects it with pleasure. Like a P.I.D.A. [Pig Industry Development Authority] sheep stamp. It's dutifully purple. The pain's going slowly." In the next paragraph, she considers taking herself back to the Highbury flat she and David had shared prior to their separation, which he was temporarily living away from, and killing herself.

Three days later, she writes of "feelings of immense alienation between Ted and I . . . I hated him all night." Four days later, visiting

Hughes's family in Hebden Bridge, West Yorkshire, Wevill reports that Hughes said to her, "Have you ever thought . . . that if you made a £1 every time you made love, you'd be very rich by now." By June, Wevill had decided that Hughes only wanted her as a nanny for his children—"All this has been a summer job." Her real life, she felt, was back in London with David: "T is a long night of nightmares. Whatever the consequences for me, T. is unconcerned." By June 12, Wevill writes that after a long argument about their relationship on the train, the couple "lived in peace for 5 days now," which she says was the longest congenial stretch between them since Plath's death.

Already, in March 1963, Wevill suspected that Hughes was running cold on their relationship, writing to him while she recovered from her abortion—in Sylvia Plath's bed—"What do you want? What do you need? Why are you so relieved that I'm no longer pregnant?" "The list ended," write Koren and Negev, "with a statement in Hebrew: 'I'm just like Marilyn Monroe in the shape of a hot-water bottle.'" The line points to Wevill's sense of humor about herself and her situation, but also to her awareness of the truth of Hughes's interest in her, which, even years after her death, he characterized as frankly sexual. In his work on *Capriccio*, Hughes scholar Steve Ely quotes from an unpublished poem about Assia Wevill held by the British Library: "the mystery that fevers imagination / And makes the prick stand up willy nilly," lines Ely characterizes as "a case of the big head (capo) being led by the little head (prick)"—in other words, Hughes's lust for Wevill was his source of inspiration for the poetry he wrote about her, "capo" being one half of the etymology of the word "capriccio."

It was true that as their years together passed, Wevill lived in terror of losing her famous beauty, a fear that some biographers—and Hughes himself—have attributed solely to vanity. In his *Capriccio* poem "Fanaticism," Hughes writes that Wevill sacrificed her life at the altar of beauty, which he associates in the poem with the Greek goddess Aphrodite. In that poem, Wevill trades marriage "for the manic depression / Of the ovaries," a cryptic set of lines that seem

Assia and Shura Wevill in London, 1968. (Photograph by Martin Baker, used with his permission.)

to indicate that Wevill chose beauty and fertility over marriage, a strange description of a woman who was married three times and only had one child—stranger still, given Wevill's stated desire to marry Hughes and make a home with him, which he refused to do. Wevill's fear of losing her looks seems to have had much more to do with her understandable belief that if she lost her beauty, then "the animal thing between us," as she called her sexual chemistry with Hughes, would disappear with it, and she would lose him. As early as the spring of 1963, ill with an attack of cystitis that kept the couple from having sex, she wrote in her journal of her fear that Hughes would leave her if she couldn't sleep with him.

As Julie Goodspeed-Chadwick writes in *Reclaiming Assia Wevill*, "Assia valued that which she believed made her unique, worthy, important, and capable of being loved: apparently, she thought that beauty and youth made her desirable and lovable."

By March 1968, when she wrote of "the animal thing between us" to Ted Hughes, their romance was mostly over. But by then, Wevill also had a daughter to care for, one she wanted Hughes to claim as his own. March 1968 was precisely one year before her suicide, an event that seems to have been spurred partly by Wevill's knowledge that the possibility of a settled domestic life with Ted Hughes was impossible. Again, Goodspeed-Chadwick: "Unfortunately for her, there were no other pathways—readily apparent to her—that provided alternatives in allowing her to accept her aging female body or in finding value in her life as a middle-aged, separated/unmarried woman." In 1968, more than anything else, Wevill wanted a home with Ted Hughes, his children with Sylvia Plath, and with their young daughter, Alexandra Tatiana Elise, who Wevill called, simply, Shura.

SHURA WEVILL WAS BORN MARCH 3, 1965, at a time when Wevill's relationship with Hughes hung in the precarious balance of his emotional and psychological instability. This included his grief over Plath's death and his family's belief that Wevill was responsible for it. From 1963 to 1965, Hughes bounced back and forth with Frieda and Nicholas between London, Court Green, and West Yorkshire, where his parents still lived, eventually settling at Court Green with his sister Olwyn, who left her job in Paris to care for Frieda and Nicholas. When Shura was born, Assia was still living with David Wevill, who gave Shura his surname, despite Hughes's name being on the birth certificate. In this way, Koren and Negev write, the child belonged to both David Wevill and Ted Hughes—and, at the same time, to neither of them. She was, in a way, entirely her mother's.

In the *Capriccio* poems, Hughes reimagines Assia as a monstrous mother, one who is inhumanly cruel to her own child and to the children of others. In "Possession," for instance, she inspires men to kill their own children in her name, while in "The Error," Wevill sacrifices Shura (and other people) to "the offered-up flames." Hughes consistently associates Wevill with Lilith, who in Jewish

Shura Hughes in London, 1968. (Photograph taken by Martin Baker, and used with his permission.)

folklore steals infants in the night; in "Dreamers," Wevill strokes the hair of Sylvia Plath's children with the intent to steal them. If we believe, as Hughes wants us to, that Wevill killed herself because she was no longer beautiful, then it's easy to see her filicide of Shura as equally frivolous and to understand Wevill as a horrific mother. But all evidence points to the contrary. David Wevill spoke tenderly of Assia's love and care of Shura, and Assia herself wrote beautiful, humorous letters about the experience of having her daughter throughout the remainder of her short life.

Wevill's pregnancy and Shura's birth inspired a period of intense and productive creativity, which also indicates that it was a positive experience for her. She adapted the Russian novelist Ivan Turgenev's book *First Love* into a screenplay and worked with Ted Hughes on a number of projects, including filmscripts and a pack of elaborately illustrated playing cards with accompanying poems—Wevill did the illustrations, but none have survived. The most impressive and high-profile of her creative projects from this time was the short film *Lost*

Island, which she wrote as a long-form advertisement for the Sea Witch hair dye company.

Based on the popular James Bond films of the day, *Lost Island* was filmed on location in the Aegean Sea and cost a small fortune to produce. In it, seven men dressed all in black stalk an island littered with human bones, and a voice-over repeats Wevill's brilliant, hilarious copy: "The Sea Witches. The Greeks knew about them, the faces of mortal women, but their hair . . . their hair is legend." The men in black discover the Sea Witches, enthroned on rocks and dressed in long white togas, and battle them for their secrets: the hair dye, which they spirit away in a black briefcase, aboard a speedboat, as riotous jazz by Miles Davis plays in the background. "At your chemist. Four pence eleven," the voice-over says, switching from an ominous to a matter-of-fact tone as the commercial ends. Played in movie theaters before films, *Lost Island* was greeted with wild applause from the audience and later adapted for television. Its success raised Wevill's profile at J. Walter Thompson, the advertising agency where she then worked, as well as her salary, and she became known in the industry as "the Sea Witch Lady."

"Was this the real location of Eden? The banished descendants of Eve?" goes Wevill's script for this revolutionary advertisement, "invoking," write Koren and Negev, "the legendary Lilith," the mythical first wife of Adam, who abandoned him when he refused to allow her to be on top of him during sex. Lilith is associated in Judaism with wantonness, demons, and the murder of children, but in *Lost Island*, Wevill is clearly making light of the image of the seductress, while also portraying her astute knowledge of mythology and literature. In 1997, Lilith came back into the popular American lexicon when the singer-songwriter Sarah McLachlan organized an all-women summer music festival that she called the Lilith Fair. Six months later, Hughes published *Birthday Letters*, in which he describes Wevill as "the Lilith of abortions," a line that simultaneously references Wevill's invocation of her own cultural history, while disregarding her ironic approach. The travesty is that Hughes's casting of Wevill as Lilith has stayed with us, while her own clever ideas about the mythical woman some consider the first feminist have largely been lost.

Very few of Wevill's letters to Hughes from this period have survived, but many of his to her have, though most are still unpublished, with large sections of text removed from the handful in print. Their tone swings from deeply romantic (he has many pet names for her, including "Asseeke," "Asseenke," and "sweet love") to confusing and controlling. He implores her to be discreet in any communication with him, to use assumed names if she sends letters or telegrams, since he believes his neighbors are spying on him (this was a frequent refrain with Hughes, during and after Plath's lifetime).

Hughes posts his own letters to her under the name "F. Wall, Esq.," a tasteless private joke—he was the fly on the wall in the Wevills' marriage. And he tells her she should keep a journal, but that once she does, she should send the journal to him, a directive one can't help but read as a response to his having recently read Plath's last two journals, which so shocked and horrified him that he either burned them, lost them, or hid them so well they have yet to emerge. Given what he had found at 23 Fitzroy Road after Plath's death, Hughes seemed to want to control the narrative about him that Wevill, as a talented writer and professional copywriter, might put into the world.

And he did. In their foreword to *The Collected Writings of Assia Wevill*, Koren and Negev describe the intense challenge of tracking their subject down. Citing Janet Malcolm's famous denigration of the biographer as a "professional burglar, breaking into a house, rifling through certain drawers that he has good reason to think contain the jewelry and money," they respond, "Well, when we started our journey on the trail of Assia Wevill thirty years ago, we didn't know where the drawers were." This was not an accident. Hughes was keen on shutting down the story of his life with Wevill, and when he sold his archive to Emory University in 1997, it was "devoid of Assia's presence in his life," despite his having taken many of her belongings when she killed herself and Shura in March of 1969. This was not because Wevill left them to Hughes—in the will she made two years prior to her death, she pointedly and explicitly left him nothing—but she left the will unsigned, so its executor, a friend of Assia's named Chris Wilkins, could do nothing about it, despite his efforts.

Early biographers of Sylvia Plath were aware of Assia and Shura Wevill. Harriet Rosenstein discussed Assia repeatedly in her notes and talked about her in her recorded interviews, but Rosenstein's book was never published. Edward Butscher, whose 1976 book *Sylvia Plath: Method and Madness* was the first Plath biography to be published, notes Wevill's presence in Hughes's life, but not her death, and calls her "Olga" rather than Assia. Lois Ames, who was appointed Plath's official biographer by the Plath estate but, like Rosenstein, never wrote or published her book, met both Assia and Shura when she visited England with her good friend Anne Sexton in 1967, for the same Poetry International festival in which Wevill met Yehuda and Chana Amichai.

In the 1980s, two high-profile biographies of Plath were published—an unauthorized one by Linda Wagner-Martin and the only biography ever authorized by the Plath estate, *Bitter Fame* (1989), by Anne Stevenson. Neither book mentions Wevill's death or Shura's existence. Wagner-Martin's efforts to do so were stymied. Discussing *Bitter Fame* with Janet Malcolm, Anne Stevenson told her that Assia and Shura's deaths were an open secret among "the poets" in England, one you simply did not write about. You just didn't say no to Ted Hughes, Stevenson told Malcolm. "He always says, *please.*"

For a brief moment in the early 1970s, however, Assia's and Shura's deaths, and the ways they contextualized Sylvia Plath's experience as a survivor of domestic and sexual violence, as well as her suicide, came to light. In 1972, Robin Morgan, then a high-profile activist and poet, published her controversial poem "Arraignment." Morgan, a self-proclaimed radical feminist, believed that Hughes's violence in his relationships had direct bearing on Sylvia Plath's and Assia Wevill's deaths, and she says as much in both the poem and a later essay she wrote about the experience of trying to publish it. In

"Arraignment," Morgan calls Assia "Assia Gutmann Wevil [*sic*]" and describes her as a heroic Jewish mother for her decision to kill Shura.

Koren and Negev doubt this contextualization, which ties Wevill's actions to Jewish mothers' "mercy killings" of their children during the pogroms of the nineteenth century and later the Holocaust, to save them from a worse fate. Wevill did not consider herself religious, and her biographers doubt she made this choice with this history in mind. But this doesn't necessarily change Morgan's reading of her actions, which views Wevill's filicide of Shura as a choice made out of terror of what might happen to the child if she was left alone with Ted Hughes. By 1969, Wevill viewed Hughes with fear and contempt. The novelist Fay Weldon, Assia's friend, witnessed Hughes giving Shura wine to drink around this time, when she had not yet turned four—Shura "danced and danced until she dropped into sleep." Weldon called the act "very sadistic" and attributed it to Shura's being the daughter of his mistress—he would never have done something like that to Frieda or Nicholas, she thought.

In 1967, Wevill met Aurelia Plath when Aurelia came to visit her grandchildren in England. Despite her apprehensions about meeting Sylvia's mother, she enjoyed her company, writing in a letter to Anne Sexton that she found Aurelia to be "a remarkable woman," a "near-genius." Assia began writing to Aurelia during this period, letters that for many years were thought to be lost. Richard Larschan, a retired professor of English at the University of Massachusetts, who became Aurelia Plath's confidant in the last years of her life, read them and told Koren and Negev that the letters were "'very much [those] of a daughter seeking parental support'" and that they "complained that Ted was brutalizing her, with 'frequent mentions of emotional and physical abuse, some of it, I seem to recollect, sexual.'" These letters have recently resurfaced but have yet to be read by anyone outside of Aurelia Plath's estate.

Assia Wevill did begin a journal in 1963, but if she ever sent it to Hughes, there is no evidence of it. She probably didn't, since much of it is concerned with their troubled relationship and his mounting obsession with his dead first wife—by 1965, Plath was famous and Hughes was her editor and promoter. Wevill wrote about the deleterious effect this had on their relationship in unforgettable lines like "He's busy espalliering [sic] Sylvia," which is startling in its absent contrast. With Plath dead, Hughes believed he could prune her work and train her image into his desired shape. Assia, living, and ultimately refusing to conform to the demands he made about the size and shape of her body, the way she spoke and dressed, and the role she played in his life, could not be espaliered.

Living women are troubling that way; they are easier to morph, or disappear, in death. "1. So—they—will have clear notion of me—you will not be known, shadowy," Hughes wrote in another list for his *Capriccio* "planning materials." In trying to give us a picture of Assia Wevill, biographers of Plath and Hughes tend to follow the same sexist pattern of describing her body in derogatory terms as a point of contrast to her face or as a point of contrast to her famous rival, Sylvia Plath, who was taller, with longer limbs. In this, they seem to take their cues from Hughes, who, writing about their first-ever sexual encounter, said he was glad to have an excuse to escape once he discovered her "thick waist."

Jonathan Bate, at least, couches his descriptions of Assia's physical body within her own stated insecurities about it, but Paul Alexander, who wrote the 1991 Plath biography *Rough Magic*, quotes a friend of hers who said Assia had "hips like the rear end of a 158 bus." Al Alvarez makes similarly derogatory comments about her body in his memoir *Where Did It All Go Right?*, writing that Assia "had a delicate, sultry face that seemed out of proportion with her heavy figure." Alvarez, though, had once been in love with Assia, had proposed to her and been turned down, something he conveniently leaves out of his memoir.

Efforts to recover and reclaim Assia Wevill in recent years by Koren, Negev, and the feminist scholar Julie Goodspeed-Chadwick have met with resistance from scholars of Hughes's work. Reviewing Goodspeed-Chadwick's *Reclaiming Assia Wevill* for the *Ted*

Hughes Society Journal in 2020, Terry Gifford wrote that he doubted the validity of Wevill as a subject and questioned Hughes's paternity of Shura, despite the fact that Hughes openly claimed Shura as his biological child, and his name is on her birth certificate. In the same review, Gifford wrote that he doubted whether Wevill had translated Amichai's poetry: "at present, we cannot know how much of Hughes is in [the Amichai translations]." In her lifetime, Hughes gave full credit to Wevill for these translations in his letters to Amichai, but somehow, over the years, that credit has strayed to Hughes. Amichai scholar Chana Kronfeld, however, is firm in her belief that Wevill was his first successful English translator. She writes about this in her book *The Full Severity of Compassion: The Poetry of Yehuda Amichai*. And it was Amichai's 1973 poem "The Death of Assia G.," which begins, "I want to publicize / your death" that first brought Wevill to the attention of Koren and Negev, who are Israeli.

When Assia Wevill died, Hughes was involved with three women—Assia, Brenda Hedden, and Carol Orchard. In his journals, he refers to them as "A, B, and C." In the late 1960s, he would send all three of them the same love poem, claiming to have been singularly inspired by their beauty to write it. Although he married Carol Orchard, he continued an affair with Hedden for several years after Wevill's death. In an interview conducted by Harriet Rosenstein, midwife Winnifred Davies talks about the curious fact that Brenda's two children are the spitting image of Shura. For a while, Hughes lived a double life, splitting his time between Brenda Hedden and her children, and Carol Orchard, who took over the care of Frieda and Nicholas. In an interview many years later, Hedden said:

> He was a real hunter. The moment I drew away from him and became independent, I was more attractive in his eyes, and he chased me. . . . It was the same with Assia . . . when they were together, he did terrible things. I feared I would end up like her, and resisted his temptations. Her terrible suicide saved my life.

Nota Bene

The Dead Girls

---·-≪≪◆≫≫-·---

IN NOVEMBER OF 2019, WHILE IMMERSED IN TED HUGHES'S papers at Emory University's Rose Library, I came across an October 26, 1984, letter to Hughes from the writer Susan Fromberg Schaeffer. Schaeffer, a prolific American novelist who died in 2011, became close with Ted and Olwyn Hughes after she met Hughes while he was visiting New York City in 1971. They dined with her friend Erica Jong, who later wrote of Hughes's "vampirish warlock appeal," which "he tried . . . on me full force. . . . He was a born seducer and only my terror of Sylvia's ghost kept me from being seduced."

Schaeffer became Ted Hughes's lifelong friend. She was also close to Olwyn Hughes until she published *Poison* in 2006, a novel that made no attempt to disguise its fictional portrayals of Ted Hughes, Olwyn Hughes, Sylvia Plath, Assia Wevill, and many other people involved in the Plath-Hughes drama, including Dido Merwin and Hughes's friend, the poet Elaine Feinstein. *Poison* disclosed intimate partner violence between Plath and Hughes, and Plath's resultant 1961 miscarriage, eleven years prior to the emergence of Plath's letters to Ruth Beuscher. But in 1984, Schaeffer wrote the following to Ted Hughes:

> I don't know if you're aware of it, or want to be aware of it, but there's a very good scholar here named Linda Wagner . . . who seems to be writing a biography of Plath and who has been writing to you for permissions for something or other. For what it's worth, I have great faith in her. She's not your standard academic type, either. I think, at the moment, she's trying to get married with her three kids to a man who has four of his own. Is Olwyn looking for someone who has his own reputation as a literary person or someone very good at critical things? This lady is the second . . . Mission accomplished: I will change the subject.

Linda Wagner-Martin's 1987 biography of Sylvia Plath was published by Simon & Schuster. Dismissed by Janet Malcolm in *The Silent Woman* as having a style "as blandly unpretentious as a young girl's diary," it became one of the "bad" biographies of Sylvia Plath, hated by the Hughes family despite its excellent reviews. Schaeffer's letter surprised me because I was unaware of a connection between the two women, much less an endorsement of Wagner-Martin, whose work I assumed Schaeffer, so close to Ted and Olwyn Hughes, would disavow. Wagner-Martin is still writing (she is Frank Borden Hanes Professor of English and Comparative Literature emerita at the University of North Carolina, Chapel Hill, and coedited *The Bloomsbury Handbook to Toni Morrison* in 2023), so I wrote to ask about the letter. She was unaware of its existence. We arranged to speak on the phone the next day and spoke for an hour, after which she asked me for my address so she could send me a "box of treasures." A week later, on a rainy Monday, a large envelope arrived in my mailbox, stuffed full of the noisy dead.

THE YEARS IMMEDIATELY FOLLOWING Sylvia Plath's death were an open series of wild questions about her life and the circumstances of her suicide. "The rumor was at first that Plath had died of flu or pneumonia," Sandra Gilbert wrote in 1978, until "finally the violence seeped in, as if seeping from the poems into the life, or rather, the death. She had been killed, had killed herself, had murdered her children, a modern Medea."

"Why did she die?" Erica Jong wondered. "Who was responsible? How could she have left these driven, hurtling lines and, as we later learned, two helpless children? What did her husband, the rugged Heathcliffian poet Ted Hughes, have to do with it?" In 1971, Harper & Row published *The Bell Jar* for the first time in the United States and included "A Biographical Note" at the book's close by Lois Ames, who had been contracted by the estate to write a biography of Sylvia Plath. The "Note" confirmed the date of Plath's suicide in London but offered few details: recurrent sinus infections, a cold London winter, poems Ames said were written as though "all relationships were puppetlike and meaningless." The same year, Al Alvarez published *The Savage God: A Study of Suicide*, which opened with a prologue that he called, simply, "Sylvia Plath."

A prolific literary critic who had known Sylvia Plath and Ted Hughes well in the last two years of their marriage, by 1971 Alvarez had established himself as the leading authority on Plath's poetry. He began to publish about her within a week of her death and never really stopped, giving interviews about her as late as 2013 (he died in 2019, aged ninety). Alvarez came from the school of New Criticism, which held that a biographical reading of a poem was a poor frame to read through, since everything a reader needed was present on the page. Alvarez seemingly abandoned this concept with his readings of Sylvia Plath in the 1960s, claiming Plath's suicide as the singular lens to read her poetry. "Lady Lazarus" was about "the total purification of achieved death," death itself "an unavoidable risk in writing [Plath's] kind of poem," which could be "read posthumously," as though Plath was already dead when she composed it. Much later, Alvarez wrote that Sylvia "went down into the cellarage" to write her *Ariel* poems. Given his ideas about Plath, he seemed determined to keep her there.

The first half of Alvarez's prologue about Sylvia Plath was serialized in the *Observer*, where he was the longtime poetry editor. It describes in fond detail how Alvarez met Plath in London in early 1960, when he became friends, first, with her husband. Alvarez's relationship with Plath begins when she tells him that she is not who he thinks she is—she is Sylvia *Plath*, the poet whose work he has been publishing in the *Observer*. He knows her as Mrs. Hughes, "bright, clean, competent, like a young woman in a cookery advertisement."

In the spring of 1961, Alvarez senses trouble in the Hugheses' marriage, which spurs their move to the rural village of North Tawton, where he visits them at their country house, Court Green, in spring 1962. There, he writes, Plath took center stage in a marriage once dominated by her husband. Alvarez initially attributes this to her having given birth to a son, but is clued into its actuality when Plath pulls him aside to tell him she is "really writing" and wants to show him some of her work. By October, the Hugheses' marriage has ended; Plath shows up on Alvarez's London doorstep with a folder full of new poems. There, drinking whiskey by his fireside, she reads aloud from "Daddy" and "Lady Lazarus," poems she had drafted that month. The two flirted with the idea of a romance, but, at least in the prologue, it never happens. Alvarez goes to see Plath at Christmas, by which point she has moved back to London. He is disturbed by her appearance and demeanor—she has lost a great deal of weight and seems not to be taking care of herself. Although she tries to contact him again in the last month of her life, he ignores her. Then she kills herself. Alvarez accompanies Ted Hughes to the London morgue to see Plath's body, and then to the coroner's inquest.

The prologue is a memoir of Sylvia Plath in every sense, but Alvarez invited Ted Hughes's ire when he published it, in part because he referred to it as a case study, as though Plath were his patient or the subject of his dissertation. In a series of angry letters between the two men, Hughes tells Alvarez that he was misinformed about many of the details surrounding Plath's suicide, which he has now broadcast to the world of Plath's fans. Hughes characteristically calls her readers "a sensation-watching and half-hysterical congregation. . . . Now there actually is a body. The cries drew the crowd . . . they can smell its hair and its death." His letters to Alvarez are shot through with betrayal, informed by his belief that Plath's life and death were his alone to write about.

There is also the not so subtle hint of sexual jealousy. In *Ted Hughes: The Unauthorised Life*, Bate writes that "Ted and Olwyn knew rather more from what they had read in Sylvia's last journal. . . . 'Alvarez,' she scribbled on her calendar for . . . the night she read her latest poems to him . . . they were engaged in a certain activity when the telephone rang. She put her foot over his penis so that, as she phrased it, he was appropriately attired to receive the call." In June 1988, Olwyn Hughes wrote to ask Alvarez to come forward about his relationship with Plath. He refused, as he would for the rest of this life, maintaining his stance in *The Savage God* that he loved Plath as a friend and nothing more, despite her interest in a romance.

In his letters to Alvarez about the prologue to *The Savage God*, Hughes also pins his rage to the fact that he will now have to tell his children the truth about their mother's death, which, until that point, they believed was from viral pneumonia (Frieda was eleven, Nick, nine, at the time of publication). Hughes feared that their school friends would read about Plath's suicide in the *Observer* and gossip to them. Whereas before, Plath was their "guardian angel," Alvarez had "made a public statue of [her suicide]. What your memoir supplies is not just facts . . . but poison. Poison is no less poison for being a fact."

The problem, then, was not simply moving Sylvia Plath's suicide into the public realm, since, by 1971, it already lived there. The problem was the suicide itself, a poison that, until the publication of *The Savage God*, Hughes believed he had bottled up on a faraway shelf in the "ghost house" at 23 Fitzroy Road. Alvarez had broken into the house and uncorked the bottle, and its vapors would inevitably make their way to Court Green. Alvarez had forced his hand. Hughes would have to tell his children the truth about their mother's death.

Susan Fromberg Schaeffer's novel *Poison* opens with Sigrid Grosvenor speaking these lines to her brother, Peter: "The story's out in the papers. You can't escape it. The children will hear about it in school." Sigrid and Peter are closely based on Olwyn and Ted Hughes, with Sigrid acting as her brother's ferocious protector and the literary agent for the estate of his first wife, the fictional poet Evelyn Graves. Peter's children, Sophie and Andrew, are brought home from boarding school and placed around the fire in the parlor of their home, Willow Grove, an evident stand-in for Court Green. There, Peter tells Sophie and Andrew a fantastic story about a handsome giant who "is put under a spell—well, a curse, really—and the result was, everyone came to believe that he was the most handsome man in the land." This giant, Peter tells his children, is poison to the women who love him. They won't go away, and their love for him kills them—with gas, which Peter describes to his children as "something in the stove that can make people stop living."

"Well, what was the giant to do?" Peter asked.
"Give them a cookie and send them back," Sophie said.

Poison also treats the long-standing rumors that Carol Hughes, Ted Hughes's second wife, whom he married in 1970, had a history of suicidal threats. Peter Grosvenor's third wife is named Meena in the book, and she is the architect of its conflict, which begins in the second chapter when Grosvenor dies and leaves behind fishy instructions about the divvying up of his estate among his wife, children, and sister (this closely mirrors what happened after Ted Hughes died in 1998). Meena seizes control of the confusion and attempts to take everything as her own, compensation for decades of misery during which her famous husband carried on affairs while she sat home in the country. In *Poison*, Meena hovers at the top of the stairs as Peter tells his children about their mother's death and the subsequent deaths of their second mother, Elfie, and their infant sister, Petra, also by gas poisoning. The telling triggers a memory in

Sophie of her father and Meena having a terrible fight, and Meena yelling, "If you keep carrying on like this, Peter, you will have to buy an *electric* range."

In *Poison*, Meena keeps a bottle of potassium pills in her bathroom cabinet as a threat to keep her husband in line—"the pills frightened him; he knew that swallowing those pills would have stopped her heart. And then he would have three women dead." Writing about *Poison* in *Ted Hughes: The Unauthorised Life*, Bate wrote that Meena was "a monster of the imagination." But Bate's biography predates the availability of Harriet Rosenstein's archive, with its lengthy interview with Elizabeth Sigmund, who lived in North Tawton and knew Sylvia Plath and Ted, Olwyn, and Carol Hughes well, often babysitting for Frieda, Nick, and, in 1967, while Assia Wevill lived at Court Green, Shura. In an interview that spanned multiple days and more than six hours of tape, Sigmund told Rosenstein that Carol would threaten suicide to force Hughes home from London, where she knew he was having affairs. An undated letter from this period from Ted to Olwyn Hughes, which Frieda Hughes made available for the first time in 2021, confirms serious trouble in their marriage, the first to do so. In it, Hughes tells Olwyn that the couple have separated and that Carol wants a divorce. He laments not separating and initiating a divorce when he wanted to do it, first, and giving Carol the upper hand. "Please," he asks his older sister, "no reproaches."

A key tenet of Alvarez's memoir of Sylvia Plath—you could call it his thesis—is that her suicide was accidental, a word he uses repeatedly but which does not exactly explain his beliefs about Sylvia Plath's suicide. In the prologue to *The Savage God*, Alvarez writes that Plath's suicide was accidental but only because she planned it badly. It was his belief that Plath wanted to be saved and had set her "death" up so that her new au pair, who was due the next morning by nine, would find and rescue her. As evidence of this, he includes Plath's suicide note with its instructions to call her doctor (the doctor's phone number was included). Alvarez believed that Sylvia Plath used the gas oven as an escape hatch from the poetry she had written in the last six months of her life, with particular emphasis on the poems of her final two weeks: "Kindness," "Contusion," "Edge," "Words," "Mystic." He believed that Plath had kept her depression at bay by writing poems about death and dying:

> The end came when she felt she could stand the subject no longer. She had written it out and was ready for something new. . . . The only method of stopping it she could see, her vision by then blinkered by depression and illness, was that last gamble. So having, as she thought, arranged to be saved, she lay down in front of the gas-oven almost hopefully, almost with relief, as though she were saying, "Perhaps this will set me free."

Alvarez seized on a couplet from Plath's poem "Kindness," which she finished ten days before she died. In it, she calls poetry an unstoppable "blood-jet." In the first ten years after Plath's death, these were some of Sylvia Plath's most quoted lines (*Time* magazine called them, characteristically, "her last clouting couplet"), held up as proof that poetry was metaphorically bleeding Plath out at the end of her life. Alvarez's use of the couplet seems in line with these readings; suicide, for him, was Plath's attempt to stanch the bleeding with the deepest cut.

Other writing by Alvarez confirms this. In unpublished letters between him and Olwyn Hughes, held by the British Library, both refer to Sylvia Plath's suicide as "Russian roulette." "I wonder if you know her doctor, John Horder, firmly believes this was Russian roulette indeed but with the odds well weighted in favour of rescue—and with persuasive evidence," Olwyn wrote to Alvarez on June 22, 1970. This identification of Plath's suicide as a gamble with her life for the sake of her art expanded the mythology of Sylvia Plath rather than ending it, which, from his prologue to *The Savage God*, as in his letters to Olwyn Hughes, seems to have been Alvarez's intention.

The publication of *The Savage God* coincided with the height of Plath's literary and mass-market fame. *Ariel* had sold extraordinarily well for a book of poetry, but *The Bell Jar* stayed on the *New York Times* bestseller list for twenty-four weeks when it made its American debut, and was later made into a major motion picture. This popularity guaranteed a wide readership for Alvarez's memoir, with its revealing details about the last weeks of Plath's life, and cemented her poetry as the key player in her death, deriding the role of depression, Plath's personal history of suicidality, and the pain she felt living without Hughes but with his public infidelity. It was another way that Alvarez erased his presence from helping to design the mythology of Sylvia Plath. "It was a mistake, then, and out of it a whole myth has grown," he wrote in the passive, third-person voice, as though he had not planted those seeds himself with ongoing published descriptions of Plath's poetry as a deadly form of apotheosis. As though suddenly struck with amnesia about all of his previous work on *Ariel*, Alvarez accused Sylvia Plath's fans of creating "a myth of the poet as a sacrificial victim, offering herself up for the sake of her art, having been dragged by the Muses to that final altar through every kind of distress."

In the same June 22, 1970, letter, Olwyn Hughes told Alvarez that she had heard that Sylvia Plath's suicide was a gamble from Dido Merwin, who claimed to have heard it from John Horder, who treated both Dido and Plath. Dido had made the initial introductions between Plath and Horder when Plath was pregnant with Frieda in London, in 1960, and looking to be set up with the British National Health. Dido Merwin's hostility to Sylvia Plath is well known. She concluded her memoir about Plath by saying her suicide was "inevitable, sooner or later," and referred to Plath's visit to the Merwins' French farmhouse as "a reign of, if not terror, then tiresomeness every bit as effective." That hostility extended to unverified rumors about Plath's death, since wherever Merwin discovered the story of Plath gambling with her life in the hope of being rescued, it could not have been from Doctor Horder, whose notes to biographers and critics are remarkably consistent. His patient intended to die. Moreover, he believed that she did so in a psychotic state that, as he wrote to Linda Wagner-Martin, "seems to me to take away most of the blame for depriving two young children of their mother."

In the same handwritten letter, John Horder told Wagner-Martin that Plath could not have survived, even if she had been rescued, which Alvarez claimed was her plan in *The Savage God*. "I do not think that it should be implied that Sylvia might have been saved if the nurse had arrived earlier," Dr. Horder wrote. "That is improbable. At best, she might have been found in extremis and survived with brain-damage from the sleeping pills." Above the word "best" he wrote "worst?" He signed the letter with two short sentences, each comprising its own paragraph.

> I think my information helps, rather than hurts, Sylvia's memory.
>
> I decide to risk criticism.

John Horder's letter to Linda Wagner-Martin implies that Sylvia Plath took an overdose of sleeping pills when she gassed herself, enough that, had she survived, it would have damaged her brain, forcing her to live, as Horder writes, "in extremis"—a painful coincidence of language, given that two essays on Plath of the same name exist, one by George Steiner and one by Alvarez, both crediting poetry as Plath's real killer. Steiner's essay follows similar logic used by Alvarez, Lowell, and other critics who believed that Plath's death was the tragic lark of an irresponsible, wildly gifted artist who gambled her life for her art, and lost. In his letter to Wagner-Martin, Dr. Horder addresses this trend, calling it "so limited an explanation as to be nearly ridiculous."

John Horder's letter makes clear that Sylvia Plath's story is still, despite so many years and so many retellings, incomplete. The presence of an overdose of sleeping pills makes Plath's suicide complex, the clinical term used to describe a suicide where the victim has used two methods to ensure their death. Complex suicides are rare. In their 2009 article "Complex Suicide versus Complicated Suicide," researchers Klara Toro and Stefan Pollak write that only 5 percent of suicides are complex, but that of these, almost half involved a history of suicidal behavior or attempts. Plath survived her 1953 suicide attempt because she took too many pills and vomited them up. In 1963, she took enough to ensure her death. There was no escape hatch. That was the point.

WHEN I WAS TWENTY and she was twenty-one, a childhood friend died suddenly in her family's finished basement. I never learned exactly how. Like Sylvia Plath, there was a love affair gone wrong—another girl and my friend's resulting despair. I was left with the sense that love had killed her, as we are also sometimes led to believe of Sylvia Plath. Love went off the rails and collided with youth and beauty, *eros* into *thanatos* in one dread turn. The day she died, I watched as her mother called her own mother with the news that her granddaughter was dead. *Every time she tells someone*, I thought, *it's like its happening again for the first time.* That fall, in a playwriting class, I wondered, *What if you didn't tell people? What if you pretended it never happened?*

That thought returned to me when I read through the notes of a July 3, 1970, interview Harriet Rosenstein conducted with Aurelia Plath. In it, the chain of language about her daughter's suicide breaks down and lets us through to an open field of questions and errors. Ted Hughes didn't tell Aurelia Plath about his wife's death, sending, instead, a telegram to her sister, Dot, the day after Plath's suicide. It read, "Sylvia died today." There were almost no obituaries in America, and one of the few that did run, in the *Wellesley Townsman* sixteen days after Plath's death, listed the cause as viral pneumonia.

By 1970, seven years had passed, years in which, Aurelia confided to Harriet Rosenstein, she had kept her daughter's death from multiple family members, including Sylvia's uncle, who only learned of her suicide two years later, in 1965. He died shortly after, an event Aurelia attributed to shock. "SPEAKING OF DADDIES," Rosenstein wrote in all capital letters, "SHE NEVER TOLD HER OWN FATHER THAT SYLVIA WAS DEAD." Did Sylvia's grandfather die believing Sylvia was alive in England? On the last line on the penultimate page of her notes, Rosenstein wrote, "Did she once use the word 'suicide'?"

Sylvia Plath's suicide was therefore both extraordinary and utterly common. It helped to vault her into literary infamy, becoming the most recognizable event of her short life; in England, where she died, Plath's suicide was the near-immediate property of the public. But a 2013 *Atlantic* article by Ashley Fetters, marking its fiftieth anniversary, called Plath's suicide "unusually quiet," pointing to the ways it was initially, in America, covered up, euphemized, and kept from some who knew Plath at her most private and domestic. (Her grandfather lived near or with her for all of her childhood; in *The Bell Jar* she wrote adoringly of his having introduced her to avocados and gourmet food like caviar.) Thus we see a paradoxical combination of domestic silence and very public speech in the years immediately following Plath's suicide: Ted Hughes's rush to publish the poetry of her last year while refusing to publicly acknowledge her suicide, and her mother's attempts to keep her death private and quiet. This led not only to a misreading of Plath's poetry, but of her life.

Al Alvarez's work is, once more, key to understanding the creation of this mythology. Writing about "Lady Lazarus" in March of 1963 for the BBC Third Programme, Alvarez said that the poem was "far more intimately concerned with the drift of Sylvia Plath's life. The deaths of Lady Lazarus correspond to her own crises: the first just after her father died, the second when she had her nervous breakdown, the third perhaps a presentiment of the death that was shortly to come." Plath's recording of the poem accompanied this analysis. The combination of the two is the first instance of one of the stranger tendencies in the public's interest in Sylvia Plath, in which people began to look for events in her life that corresponded directly with her poetry, in ways that mirrored Alvarez's claim that "Lady Lazarus" predicted Plath's death by suicide.

The reality was far different—Plath wrote "Lady Lazarus" in a state of elation four months before her suicide—but the idea took root so firmly that people still interpret the poem this way today. In 2016, writing for the British Library's website, Mark Ford wrote, "['Lady Lazarus'] anticipates yet another dicing with death, 'Number Three', from which, she predicts, she will again emerge like the phoenix from the ashes, though this time as a vampiric, female avenger. . . . In fact her next suicide attempt, in the early hours of 11 February 1963, would succeed." Like Alvarez before him, Ford has Plath "dicing" with suicide through the act of writing, as if the two acts—writing poetry and killing oneself—are a gamble, and one and the same.

The tendency to obscure the suicides of young women, or ascribe them to poetry, fate, or unspecified supernatural affairs, is explored by Shirley Jackson in her novel *The Haunting of Hill House*. Like Sylvia Plath, Jackson's protagonist, Eleanor Vance, who goes by Nell, dies by her own hand as the book ends. A lonely young woman trapped by circumstance in an unhappy life, Nell is invited to spend a week at Hill House, a remote haunted house, as part of a research project by an anthropologist named John Montague. Nell is both literally and figuratively haunted. As a child, she and her sister experienced a haunting with biblical overtones when, for three days after the death of their father, the sky rained stones upon the roof of their home. This event is recalled by their neighbors to Dr. Montague, inspiring him to include Nell in his experiment. But Nell is also haunted by the life she is trying to escape, one of forced servitude, first to her invalid mother, then to her sister's children, a life she pretends doesn't exist when she joins her fellow subjects at Hill House.

Once there, her effort to style herself as a fashionable, carefree young woman appears to briefly win her friends and the possibility of a new life. But Hill House and her past are too strong. In the middle of the night, Nell is mysteriously compelled to climb to the top of a winding staircase, rotting from age, risking her life and the life of another housemate, Luke, who saves her while also threatening her: "Perhaps I will just push you over the edge," Luke says. "Let you smash down there on the floor. Now behave yourself and move slowly." As a result of this event, Nell is forced from Hill House by the people she believed were her friends. She drives into a tree on the property as the group at the house watches from a distance. Her last thought is, "*Why* am I doing this? Why am I doing this? Why don't they stop me?"

I don't mean to imply that we should read Plath's suicide in the context of fiction. What I am saying, instead, is that Plath's suicide has always been read that way, as if she were the author and heroine of her own life. This has worked as an effective censor of the actual circumstances of that life. The fictional conditions of Nell Vance's suicide (intergenerational haunting, fated inevitability, engineering one's own death through art) are, instead, applied to Sylvia Plath. The most famous example of this comes to us from Elizabeth Hardwick, whose long and influential essay about the correlation between Plath's history and her poetry was initially published in the *New York Review of Books* and later included in her now classic book *Seduction and Betrayal: Women and Literature*. In it, Plath "is both heroine and author; when the curtain goes down it is her own dead body there on the stage, sacrificed to her plot." Anne Stevenson later used this as the penultimate quote in her biography of Plath, which claimed to "dispel the posthumous miasma of fantasy" of Plath's mythology. It was later picked up by Janet Malcolm, who extended it to Plath's journals when she referred to them as a bildungsroman, further reinforcing the idea of Plath as the unreliable narrator of her own fated life.

In the Netflix adaptation of *The Haunting of Hill House*, Nell and Luke are portrayed as young fraternal twins, Nell and Luke Crain. The twins are grimly haunted by a series of hellish ghosts at Hill House, where they are temporarily living while their parents renovate the house for resale. When they try to tell their parents about the ghosts, they don't believe them. But no one can talk the twins out of their haunting; they know, even as they grow into adults, that one day the ghosts could return and kill them.

The family eventually leaves Hill House, but Nell, like the character for whom she is named, later dies there when the ghost that haunted her as a child, "the Bent-Neck Lady," comes back. We see her in shadow: a fall of spiky hair and some gray-blue skin, a woman-shaped ghost with a gruesome broken neck. It's not until the final scenes of Nell's adult life that the Bent-Neck Lady's identity is revealed. In a stunning single shot, we see that the Bent-Neck Lady is Nell herself, dead, as a grown woman; this image transforms to the adult Nell, climbing over the balcony railing at Hill House. She becomes tangled in a rope her father left hanging there when he fled the house, decades earlier. The rope, predictably, catches around her neck. She slips, falls, and dies. Her death is ruled a suicide. She had spent the day calling each member of her family, with no response.

If most supernatural horror is in effect a way to describe unspeakable trauma, then it stands to reason that the trace of that unspeakable trauma cannot be fully recast as ghosts. In this way, while in the straight narrative of both Jackson's novel and its adaptation, Nell is not the victim of anything *but* ghosts, the responses and subsequent actions of her fellow characters are that of survivors who cannot name the realities of trauma. Nell Crain, haunted as a child by her own death, represents the power and terror of intergenerational trauma, and the lengths we go to deny it. According to her parents, when she saw a ghost, Nell must have been sleeping, dreaming, or sleepwalking, and not, as she actually was, fully cognizant, aware, and describing her experience in perfect detail. And although the viewer is led to believe that in the end things resolve—the family who disbelieved Nell's haunting come around to her way of thinking—what is really any better? When yet another young woman is haunted, or hunted, by a danger so keen she dies of it, what story do we tell ourselves about it so that we can move on? The house killed her. The devil made her do it. What stories do we still tell about Sylvia Plath? It was Yeats's house. It was black magic. Her poems killed her in the end. They made her suicide "inevitable, even justified, like some final unwritten poem."

Nell Crain's childhood trauma—the Bent-Neck Lady—is caused by her magical knowledge of her future suicide, which is in turn caused by the return of her childhood trauma. Literature about Plath's suicide is similarly infused by this kind of circular haunting, with Plath haunted by her suicide before it actually occurs, but also able to cause it by calling up her childhood trauma, usually located in the sudden death of Plath's father when she was eight. "I understand"—Ted Hughes wrote in his poem "A Picture of Otto"—"you never could have released [Sylvia]," giving the reader the impression that instead of "[releasing]" Plath from the grip of his death, the ghost of Otto Plath "killed" her instead. In an unpublished poem about Sylvia Plath's suicide, Hughes wrote that Plath's suicide was caused by her own childhood self, "Little poltergeist girl, who lived in death," with the child Plath held responsible for the adult Plath's death. Plath, like Nell, has been dead *the whole time*, her writing the sustained cry of the underworld from which the adult Plath could never hope to escape.

There is not only, in this version of events, no hope for Sylvia Plath. There is also no responsibility, or blame, for her suicide on any of her survivors, a concept that critic and Stanford professor Terry Castle seized upon and expanded in 2013, reviewing a series of Plath biographies for the *New York Review of Books*. Plath, writes Castle, "seems never to tire of creating tragic inhuman mischief from beyond the grave," and is responsible for the tragic suicide of her son, Nicholas Hughes, in 2009—"Lady Lazarus caught up with him at last." Rather than blaming intergenerational trauma, basic genetics, or the potent combination of both that likely brought on Nicholas Hughes's suicide, Castle blames the ghost of his mother. By then, Sylvia Plath had been dead almost fifty years. "Yet even so," Castle finishes her review, "I couldn't help wanting to kill her."

Despite death being understood as Sylvia Plath's primary subject, our understanding of her suicide over the years has been as much a mythology as Nell Vance, driven by a haunted life and a haunted house to drive her car headlong into a tree. As the ultimate dead girl, Plath's suicide has long been presented as her singular subject, "the surprise, the shimmering, unwrapped birthday present, the transcendence 'into the red eye, the cauldron of morning,' and the lover . . . always waiting for her, are Death, her own abrupt and defiant death." This singular identification of death with Sylvia Plath's entire biographical and creative oeuvre has led to the belief that, had she not killed herself, her work would have gone unrecognized—we only love it as we do *because* she died.

The same faulty logic that says that Plath's poems were responsible for her death also holds that Sylvia Plath's death caused the success of her poetry. In *The Silent Woman*, Janet Malcolm writes that Plath's poems work only because we know Plath killed herself: "It has frequently been asked whether the poetry of Plath would have so aroused the attention of the world if Plath had not killed herself. I would agree with those who say no. The death-ridden poems move us and electrify us because of our knowledge of what happened." But what really happened? The conditions of someone's death shape our understanding of not only the death itself, but the life. In *The Haunting of Hill House*, Shirley Jackson presents us with a young woman whose suicide is nothing if not preventable, who wonders, as she drives her car into a tree, why the people she begged to save her do not. The reader questions not only their complicity, but also Nell Vance's life, which has trained her to see her own needs as worthless, her own voice impossible to use or hear. The immediate correlation of Plath's suicide with her poetry has trained us to hear the many voices she left behind as coming from beyond the grave, rather than as the record of her life—a unique form of censorship.

"I am content to live in silence / with the dead," the poet Linda Gregg wrote in "Hearing the Gods." To live with Sylvia Plath is to live in congress with the dead. But to believe in her silence is to be lulled into complacency, or hubris, the idea that this is my story to tell, that I know better than her. The dead remind us: this is a ghost story you coaxed from our mouths, though our lips are sewn shut.

They don't speak suddenly. Instead, I sometimes failed to listen as carefully as they needed, returning me to letters and poems hundreds of times. I wondered: How many of you require an attention I lack? How many speak a language I can't hear? How many of you will I fail?

The Haunting of
Ted Hughes

※

TEN DAYS BEFORE TED HUGHES DIED, ON OCTOBER 28, 1998, of cancer, he published the last poem of his lifetime, in the London *Sunday Times*. Taken from his limited-edition book *Howls & Whispers*, "The Offers" is a ghost story in which Sylvia Plath's specter visits him three times. According to his biographer Jonathan Bate, Hughes revised and reworked the poem many times over a series of years. The first time Plath's ghost appears to him, he is riding the Underground, the Northern Line, which carried the Hugheses home to their Primrose Hill neighborhood when they lived together in London from 1959 to 1961. It's two months after Plath's suicide, and her ghost bears the scars of her death. Sitting across from him on the Tube, Plath seems yellow and aged. The second time, Plath's ghost is sitting at home in her flat at Fitzroy Road, as if she had never died. Hughes writes that she is unaware of her own identity, and calling herself by the wrong name, that of her "oldest rival." The visions decrease in ghastliness until, by the third visit, Plath is young and shining, her face like a blue jewel. Hughes is about to step into the bath. Plath, "Younger than I had ever known you," speaks to him. She will not come back to him again; this is the last time: "Don't fail me."

Like many of the poems in *Howls & Whispers* and its companion *Birthday Letters*, published the same year, "The Offers" converses with Sylvia Plath's poetry—in this case "Purdah," which Plath wrote the same day she drafted "Lady Lazarus." Both "The Offers" and "Purdah" end with an allusion to Aeschylus's tragic heroine Clytemnestra. Clytemnestra's husband, Agamemnon, betrayed her by sacrificing their daughter, Iphigenia, and by bringing home a concubine, the princess and seer Cassandra, from the Trojan War. In *Agamemnon*, the first play in Aeschylus's *Oresteia* trilogy, which Hughes translated in the last year of his life, Clytemnestra kills her husband offstage by trapping him in nets as he enters the bath and then stabbing him. In "Purdah," a veiled bride characterized as doll-like, with a narcissistic husband, closes out the poem by telling us she is planning to do the same. Her speaker "[unlooses]" a "lioness," "The shriek in the bath, / The cloak of holes."

"Purdah" is in dialogue with Plath's other poems of this period, which engage in a sharp critique of the institution of marriage. In "The Applicant," marriage is a sales job and the wife a shiny product. Plath's speaker is a fast-talking huckster interviewing the husband to see if he has the goods worthy of "A living doll, everywhere you look" who can "sew," "cook," and "talk, talk, talk." By the time she wrote "Purdah" two and a half weeks later, the "living doll" has transformed into the "lioness," another recurring theme in *Ariel*. In "Purdah" the lioness is the "[unloosed]" mother who avenges the death or abandonment of their children by her faithless husband.

In "The Offers," Hughes subverts this powerful act of revenge to strip Plath's ghost of her literary birthright. Instead of the lioness, she becomes the agent of her husband's legacy and absolution. Or, as Jonathan Bate puts it in "The Legacy," the epilogue to his Hughes biography:

Whereas Clytemnestra kills unfaithful Agamemnon in his bath, Sylvia gives Ted one last chance as he is entering his bath.... He honours Sylvia's ghost, the sorrow of the deer and the jewels that were her eyes.... It is a poem of longed-for redemption.

Diane Middlebrook similarly reads "The Offers" as the poem that "marks the turning point in [Hughes's] creative life," when he overcame the inertia that crushed his poetry after the suicides of Sylvia Plath and Assia Wevill and Assia's killing of Shura. She believes that Hughes had created *Howls & Whispers*, in its prohibitively expensive, limited print run, like "a winemaker [who] sets aside the choicest vintage for special labeling," and that "The Offers" was the collection's "keynote poem." For Middlebrook, when Plath's ghost tells Hughes, "This time, don't fail me," she forces him to answer for his failures in their marriage with his poetry. By making writing the central act of his life, Middlebrook says, Hughes stayed married in spirit to Sylvia Plath until his death. Since he and Plath had set off to be great artists together when they married in June 1956—a journey that, in 1962, he abandoned—poetry was the way Ted Hughes was faithful to Sylvia Plath. Jonathan Bate expanded on this argument in *Ted Hughes: The Unauthorised Life*, discussing it on National Public Radio's *Weekend Edition Saturday* with Scott Simon. Simon made the frank critique that Hughes's dishonesty and infidelity ruined the lives of Sylvia Plath and Assia and Shura Wevill. Bate replied, "Infidelity to others is a form of fidelity to the true love that you've lost." Or rather: the "double life" Hughes led from the time he and Plath split in 1962 until his death was another way, alongside his poetry, of being faithful to Sylvia Plath.

Ted Hughes: The Unauthorised Life helped secure a literary universe of paradox where cheating on your living wife was a form of cosmic fidelity to your dead one, and all of this could be atoned for with poetry. Like Diane Middlebrook, Jonathan Bate believed that Hughes used poetry to "[turn his] marriage [to Sylvia Plath] into a resonant myth." Writing of the last years of Hughes's life, Bate focuses on Hughes's translation of Euripides's *Alcestis*, a tragicomedy about Admetus, a husband granted the ability, by Apollo, to cheat death, but whose wife, Alcestis, must die in his place. For Bate, "The Offers" is Ted Hughes's "*Alcestis* moment." Writing of Hughes's *Alcestis* drafts in the British Library, Bate quotes lines that Hughes left out of his final version of the play, "perhaps because they were too painful." "Is this why we were given our life?" Alcestis wonders—to have to bear the unbearable?

"Through the act of translation," Bate writes, "Hughes comes to terms with the fact of his own destiny: that he was given life so as to be tested by the unbearable." This is tough logic, considering that "the unbearable" that "[tested]" Ted Hughes is here understood as the lives of the mothers of his children and one of his children. Did their agony exist solely to test him, which, so says this logic, created great poetry? Is that why they were given a life?

THE RESONANT MYTHOLOGY OF TED HUGHES'S marriage to Sylvia Plath ended with "The Offers," but it began with *Birthday Letters*, a book in which Sylvia Plath is a figure capable of powerful and lasting destruction, one who can, in the poem "The Shot," turn herself into a bullet and aim for Ted Hughes. In the poem "Trophies," Plath becomes a "big predator" who, when she bites him, "numbs" Hughes "Into drunken euphoria." Hughes, by contrast, presents himself as a figure who doesn't make choices. They are made for him, a condition that shows up in the poems' grammatical DNA: "the solar system married us," he writes in "St. Botolph's," a poem about the couple's first meeting.

"St. Botoloph's" is imbued with the language of astrology, predicting "disastrous expense" from the evening, "Especially for me." Even though Plath will lose her life, Hughes is the one who will suffer the greatest "expense." He writes that at the time (he was twenty-five, Plath, twenty-three), he was "a wait-and-see astrologer," and so shrugged off the stars' bad omens for the evening. Chaucer and Dante, he writes, would have been smarter and stayed home. Chaucer, in particular, would have told the young couple that the stars married them, another way Hughes links the couple's fate to astrology and poetry—both had the power to control their destiny.

In the last line of the poem "Flounders," Hughes writes, "And we / Only did what poetry told us to do." "Flounders" describes an event that took place during the Hugheses' second honeymoon on Cape Cod in the summer of 1957. They went out for a day of fishing, but, as Diane Middlebrook writes, "the wind shifted and the tide turned, and they rowed helplessly while their boat was slowly being pulled out to sea."

The couple was terrified, but thankfully, a family in a speedboat found them and towed them "into a quiet channel, where they ended the day happily making a fabulous catch of flounder." Middlebrook reads the poem as a fight for "the hearts and minds of the young couple" between a "New World" "goddess . . . of American abundance" and the goddess of poetry, Robert Graves's White Goddess, who wins the day. The couple turns their back on American abundance, and on America, devoting their lives to poetry and moving back to England. But the White Goddess is, as Middlebrook points out, "a jealous, marriage-hating deity"; she will grant the couple poetic greatness, but at great personal cost. Once more, in "Flounders," the marriage of Sylvia Plath and Ted Hughes is fodder for a mythology that casts the end of the Hugheses' marriage, and the death of Sylvia Plath, as the inevitable result of fate and poetry.

In *Birthday Letters* and *Howls & Whispers*, Ted Hughes constructed two distinct marriages, his historical one to Sylvia Plath and his poetic marriage to her ghost. He marked the first with poems like "A Pink Wool Knitted Dress," which reconstructs the scenes of the couple's wedding and honeymoon. They married in London on June 16, 1956, at the church of St. George the Martyr, in Bloomsbury. Aurelia Plath was visiting at the time and she lent Plath the titular dress to be married in: "So slender and new and naked, / A nodding spray of wet lilac." Hughes recounts how he had no best man, and the sexton had to stand as witness. The couple went first to Paris, then Spain, for a summer-long honeymoon. In "Your Paris," Hughes contrasts his continental understanding of Paris as the all too recent site of the Nazi occupation with the naive American Plath's as "Street after street, of Impressionist paintings." "Your Paris" shows us Hughes's retroactive application of gloom to everything he did with Plath. Although the poem begins with his patronizing Plath's joy at being in her favorite city, wanting to humor her whenever she exclaims with joy at seeing the Parisian streets, it devolves into his belief that this joy is false and disguises her "underground . . . chamber" where she waited for a "torturer." Somehow, this misery extends to the entirety of Paris in June, and the advertisements papered to the city's ancient stone walls are Plath's "own flayed skin."

"You Hated Spain," the first of four poems that recount events from the couple's six weeks in Spain, describes Plath's discomfort there, her inability to speak Spanish (she was conversational in French), and the way the country's frank embrace of death (what Hughes calls "the Goya funeral grin") was recognizable to Plath, a woman whose first, near-deadly suicide attempt was then only three years in the past. But rather than offering an entrée into Spanish life, this recognition brings Plath face-to-face with demons she has yet to banish and terrifies her, inspiring her to panic and "[Clutch] back towards college America." In "Moonwalk," Hughes tells of an unhappy moonlit walk in which Plath's words are "Like bits of beetles and spiders / Retched out by owls." The language echoes his earlier poem "Shibboleth," in *Capriccio*, which says that Assia Wevill's knowledge of the Hebrew language "Survived on bats and spiders."

In "Drawing," Plath's practice of sketching her surroundings is cast as a form of "infernal . . . branding," where whatever Plath draws is "Suffered into their new presence, tortured / Into final position." Ironically, during Plath's diabolical bouts of drawing, Hughes feels better—the reader assumes because for once she isn't torturing him into his final position as her husband. Even the local, medieval marketplace is an occasion to remind the reader of Plath's terrible fate:

it disappears as Benidorm, the small fishing village where the couple stayed for most of their time in Spain, is modernized into a dazzling, modern resort, just as Plath, too, is entombed. The sequence closes with the poem "Fever," in which Hughes tries to nurse an hysterical Plath, burning up with fever, back to health with a soup he makes that supposedly "saved Voltaire from the plague." He thinks his new wife is exaggerating her illness: "Stop crying wolf."

Reading "Your Paris" back-to-back with the four poems about Spain is an interesting exercise in watching Hughes turn Plath into an unreliable narrator—or else contributing another series of tropes to existing literature that already painted her as one. In "Your Paris," Hughes can't take Plath's happiness at face value and transforms her exuberance about the city into a mask for a hidden misery that so affects *him*, he sees it reflected in the structure of the city itself. Plath's gushing about the city's beauty has to be "decoded" by Hughes so he might understand the ways his new wife, rather than her surface state of enjoying Paris, is actually trapped in a labyrinthine hell. By contrast, when Plath discloses her unhappiness and her physical illness to Hughes, she is "crying wolf," and he wants her to stop, or he won't be able to tell "'When things get really bad.'" This becomes another way to explain his actions—or lack thereof—at the end of Plath's life when things had, indeed, gotten "really bad."

In Hughes's poem "The Hands," Plath's suicide, the writing of poetry, and Hughes's infidelity are the result of two giant hands that wear the couple "like gloves." Eventually, they merge into one person: "The fingerprints . . . inside your poems and your letters . . . Are the same." That he and Sylvia Plath were one person was an idea not unique to this poem. Hughes spoke publicly during the marriage about the notion that he and Plath shared a brain. In the couple's 1961 interview for the BBC's "Two of a Kind: Poets in Partnership," Hughes told the host, Owen Leeming, that he had access to "all the experiences [Sylvia's] had in the past. It's like, um . . . two people that are sympathetic to each other . . . make up one person, they make up one source of power which you both use and you can draw out material in incredible detail from this single shared mind." Responding to Hughes's statement that she felt the same way, Sylvia demurred. She didn't think she and Hughes shared a brain: "I think perhaps I'm a little more practical about it, not quite so abstract."

Hughes's declarations that he and Plath shared the same mind, body, and a fate that put circumstances beyond their control reduce her to less than adjunct to her famous husband, a condition she felt keenly in her lifetime. Subsumed completely by his identity, in Hughes's *Birthday Letters* Plath lacks even her own fingerprints, much less her own mind. When Hughes tells Leeming he can access what Plath is thinking not just *now* but in the life she had prior to knowing him, we can read in this a classic sign of intimate partner violence, almost always rooted in a desire to know everything about one's spouse so that one can wield power over that person. Many contemporary practitioners of psychology and social work use a tool called the "Power and Control Wheel," developed by the Domestic Abuse Intervention Project, to help victims diagnose the ways in which they have experienced economic, physical, behavioral, and sexual coercion, including through mind games and the minimizing or denial of physical abuse and repeated infidelity. We can call this a marriage of poetry, a resonant myth. Or we can call it a bid for control.

Whatever we call it, the poetic marriage survived both Plath and Hughes. In 2017, their daughter Frieda wrote in her brief foreword to her mother's first volume of letters that her parents were "as married in death as they were in life." She explained her "conviction": "The reason my mother should be of interest to readers at all is due to my father," whom she credited with bringing her mother's work into the world. Historically speaking, this is a misreading of her mother's career: by the time of Plath's suicide, she had already published two books. But it also shows that while this poetic marriage may have outlasted death, it's saddled with the same bleak terms as its historical twin: in their daughter's reading of their posthumous life together, Hughes didn't just marry Plath, he created her. So it is that on the first page of a book that encompasses more than one thousand pages of her letters, preserved by her friends and family and the collaborative work of libraries and archivists over the course of half a century, Sylvia Plath is not a writer. She is written: a corpse bride in her husband's perpetual romance.

In reality, their marriage lasted less than seven years before Hughes blew it up and Plath killed herself. Hughes would later tell Frieda that he and Plath were trying to get back together: "We were working toward it when she died." In his *Howls & Whispers* poem "The Laburnum," Hughes writes that in the last days of her life, Plath extracted a promise from him. By the summer, they would sit together under the laburnum at Court Green. "Yes," Hughes tells her, "yes yes yes." Hughes recasts his 1962 self as the Molly Bloom of the couple's marriage (given their Bloomsday marriage, this is not an accident). He offers us a glimpse of a rosy counter-history where Sylvia lives and they return to Court Green with their children in tow. Where Sylvia herself publishes *Ariel*: a different book, full of bumblebees and babies, in which the promise of love—romantic love, not the fierce love of the resurrected self—is renewed. Where she is pregnant again by summer, writing a new novel by fall. Had Plath not killed herself, this logic goes, the couple would have made it.

"I *told* her," Hughes said to Plath's friends Jillian and Gerry Becker at her funeral, "that by summer we'd all be back together at Court Green." Even a week after Plath's death, Jillian Becker knew that was impossible, writing in her memoir of Sylvia Plath that moving back and forth between Sylvia and Assia would have destroyed both women's lives. Becker hits on the impossibility of the marriage being repaired after the advent of Hughes's affair with Assia Wevill, but the cracks showed long before that. The Hugheses hadn't lived in the country for a full year before Hughes resumed his affair with Wevill, after a freezing winter in a house so poorly heated that Plath developed chilblains, a disease she called "Dickensian." She said that it was not so much the chilblains that had "demoralized" her, but "the cold . . . secretly got . . . me when I thought I was winning out," a grim prediction of Plath's response to the winter of 1963. Tensions in the marriage were high by May 1962. By July, Plath was writing to Ruth Beuscher that Hughes was unfaithful, telling Beuscher that Hughes said he had finally woken up, having been sleeping "all the time we were married." They had hardly shared an idyll, much less an idyllic season, at Court Green before their marriage ended.

In 1970, interviewing Aurelia Schober Plath, Harriet Rosenstein asked about the couple's breakup. Hughes never wanted a divorce, Mrs. Plath told her: "He wanted to have a homebase yet be permitted to roam." In 1962, as their marriage disintegrated, Plath had already written plainly that she could never live that way: "I can't be [a] sweet homebase." "This would have been a far crueler alternative, clearly," Rosenstein wrote in her interview notes, and it was—for Hughes's second wife. In Hughes and Plath's poetic marriage, Plath is conveniently gone from the earth, freeing him to behave as he pleases with Carol Hughes, his actual wife, alive to bear the burden of the myth.

In 1970, seventeen months after the deaths of Assia and Shura Wevill, Ted Hughes married Carol Orchard. She was twenty-two and he was forty. He left her on their wedding night to be with Brenda Hedden. This was the double life that Hughes was already leading by the time of Plath's death. For Plath, it was intolerable. By February 1963, the only possible marriage left to them was Middlebrook's resonant myth, where Hughes was Orpheus and Plath was dead.

BIRTHDAY LETTERS HAS MOSTLY BEEN praised as a sustained love song. When it was published, Michiko Kakutani called it "a deeply affecting portrait of the couple's marriage . . . attesting to Hughes' own impassioned love for Plath." Bate ended his biography of Hughes with the declaration that "[Hughes] loved [Plath] until the day he died." *Howls & Whispers*, with its extremely limited release of 110 copies at an impossibly high price, received less attention than

Birthday Letters until critics like Middlebrook and Bate made "The Offers" a centerpiece of their biographical work on Ted Hughes. Bate believed that the two books were more like a sustained cry of agony than a love song, but praised "The Offers," writing that his use, in the poem, of the phrase "the gas / Of the underworld" "took enormous courage," given the way Plath killed herself. *Publishers Weekly* said that *Birthday Letters* "may lead some to accuse [Hughes] of an elaborate attempt at revisionism. But the strength of the poems simply renders the charge moot."

Reading *Birthday Letters* as a love story depends on your definition of love. As in much of his work, Hughes's *Birthday Letters* women are monstrous, often armed with supernatural abilities. Jillian Becker's *Giving Up: The Last Days of Sylvia Plath* is mostly cited for its descriptions of Plath's last weekend. But Becker also writes astutely about Hughes's treatment of Assia in his later work, offering a chilling analysis of his *Birthday Letters* poem "Dreamers," which she called "sickeningly anti-Semitic":

> Some of its vocabulary could have come spitting out of an issue of the *Völkischer Beobachter* . . . : "greasy" (was Assia's speech); "filthy" (she was, though only "slightly"). . . . Some of the ideas could have dripped from a medieval text on witchcraft. . . . And there [is] a hint of both Dr. Mengele and the ancient blood-libel [in "Dreamers"].

Hughes's description, in "Dreamers," of Assia Wevill's face when she met Sylvia Plath calls to mind propagandistic images of Jews from the turn of the last century, including, famously, one James de Rothschild produced for the anti-Semitic "Musée des Horreurs" in 1900. Plath is similarly monstrous in "The Ventriloquist," capable of splitting off into a homunculus, a ventriloquist's dummy screaming about "Daddy," which breaks into their home and kills the real Plath in the night as Hughes tries to flee through the woods with Plath in his arms.

Much like "The Offers" did with "Purdah," "The Ventriloquist" appropriates Plathian imagery to subvert the voice and project of her poems as illegitimate, since, in *Birthday Letters* and *Howls & Whispers*, the poems are often to blame for Plath's suicide. Dolls and homunculi appear in *Ariel* as shells the speaker breaks out of to cast off what is false or damaging—marriage or, in the poem "Cut," an illness that makes the speaker feel "thin" as paper. In "Cut," the homunculus is a tiny version of the maimed speaker. She has run off with the speaker's lost blood from the cut of the poem's title. The speaker has to fill the paper with words to reestablish herself as whole, just as, in the poem's parallel world, she fills the gauze wrapping her "thumb stump" with her own dirty blood. In "The Ventriloquist," the voice of "Cut" is reduced to a disembodied doll who writes a histrionic "Daddy" and, in another verse, pens Plath's poem "Medusa," referenced in "The Ventriloquist" as "your Mummy on show / The Kraken of the seas." This last will turn out to be more significant than it might appear here; as we will see, Ted Hughes told several people that the poem "Medusa," read correctly, had the power to kill Aurelia Plath.

By contrast, in *Birthday Letters*, the living Hughes is the powerless victim of Assia and Sylvia, a loving, passive figure who is sometimes a sleepwalker, sometimes a nurse, and sometimes a loyal dog, with Plath as his master, in a reversal of the actual power structures in his relationships with these women. In "The Error," Hughes writes that he "sleepwalked [Plath]" to the southwest of England, where they purchased Court Green together. Once there, though, it is not Hughes's infidelity or neglect that harms Plath but, instead, women. Hughes calls the local women "loamy badgers" who "[paw] at [Plath's] dreams." Given that in other *Birthday Letters* poems like "Dream Life" and "Fairy Tale" Hughes has the ability to enter Plath's dream life and rescue her, it is significant that here, local strangers, all women, do her harm in her dreams.

Poems and dreams aside, this is also a gross subversion of Sylvia Plath's experience of the women of North Tawton, the village where the Hugheses lived. Plath became close friends with many of the local women there. She dedicated *The Bell Jar* to her Devon friend Elizabeth Sigmund and wrote movingly in her letters of her admiration and love for her Devon midwife, Winnifred Davies, who delivered Nicholas in January 1962, and included Davies in her poem "Wintering": she is the midwife who helps Plath learn to keep bees. Writing of Davies to her mother after Nicholas's birth, Plath praised "her immense moral force and calm." Plath's relationship to Davies was close enough after Nicholas's birth that Aurelia stayed with Davies during a visit to England the following summer and remained close to her after Sylvia's death. Yet it is Hughes, in the *Birthday Letters* poem "The Blackbird," who is Plath's nurse: "I was your nurse and your protector."

"The Blackbird" is also a bland and moralizing reread of "The Jailer," which Plath included in *Ariel* but Hughes removed. "The Blackbird" begins, "You were the jailer of your murderer" and misappropriates Plath's poem throughout. In "The Jailer," Plath explodes simplistic ideas of what makes a prison a prison: psychic states, like identity (a husband, a wife), and physical ones, like being drugged and assaulted, are explored as prisons, as well as the home, portrayed as a stage set that the jailer rebuilds daily to keep his prisoner fixed in place. By contrast, "The Blackbird" resorts to stereotypes, describing a prisoner trapped in a dungeon, eating scraps through a keyhole. Both poems employ the metapoetic. As in "Cut," Plath's speaker in "The Jailer" exists in a universe made of paper that she must fill to restore herself. These holes are also reflected in the body of the speaker herself, who has been burned by her jailer's cigarettes and stabbed by his "little gimlets." The jailer, in turn, depends on the speaker's permeable body for his very existence: he cannot live without her.

In "The Blackbird," this same paper motif is used with none of Plath's complex deconstruction of the relationship between the body and writing, or one body's sadomasochistic dependence on another in a relationship that is both a marriage and a jail. Plath's poem invites us to question the complicity of the prisoner in this relationship and offers the reader no easy answers—no answers at all—for how the two have arrived at this place or how they might escape it. In attempting to imagine her jailer, who is also her prison, "dead, or away," the speaker declares this an "impossibility." That is the crux of the problem—the power imbalance in the relationship is in fact the jail and, given its reflection in the larger world, inescapable. In "The Blackbird," these metapoetics are reduced to a suburban lawn that waits like the crisp, empty page "Of a prison report." Plath would eventually write what Hughes, in "The Blackbird," reads as a prison report, her poem "The Jailer," which "The Blackbird" pronounces a moral failure: "Wrong is right, right wrong."

IN "THE OFFERS," SYLVIA PLATH'S ghost screams to be heard, flares up like a jewel to be seen, and disguises herself to sneak into her own home, where she is now read as trespassing. I envision the ghost of Sylvia Plath haunting her husband three times like a feminist Jacob Marley, with three distinct messages that, unlike Ebenezer Scrooge, Ted Hughes can't hear. When Sylvia Plath haunts Ted Hughes for the second time in "The Offers," he makes a point to tell the reader that Plath is in her own home, as opposed to their own home.

Houses figure greatly in the mythology of Sylvia Plath and Ted Hughes, and for good reason. In less than seven years, the couple inhabited five different homes across two continents. For fans wanting to visit the sites of their romance and its end, there is no shortage of locations—in Cambridge, Northampton, Boston, and London. When their marriage ended, they were both living at Court Green; Hughes left permanently in October 1962. Plath and their children stayed behind until December 10, when she closed up the house for the winter and rented her own flat, back in Primrose Hill—the top two floors at 23 Fitzroy Road, around the corner from the couple's old digs.

The house at 23 Fitzroy Road has a special significance for Plath fans because she died in the kitchen there. But we should recall how significant the house was for Sylvia Plath in her lifetime, too. It was a symbol of independence, financial and otherwise, a place where she wrote some of her greatest poetry and watched *The Bell Jar* debut on January 14, 1963. It was a place where she believed she would soon host literary salons. During her short time there, Hughes was living a bachelor life and visiting Plath once a week. But he moved himself and, in March 1963, Assia Wevill into Fitzroy Road when Sylvia died, since Plath had paid a year's rent in advance. Small wonder that Plath's ghost, coming to the home where her husband was now sleeping in her recently purchased bed with one of his mistresses, would come in disguise.

In "The Offers," Plath is confused during this second haunting, rather than deliberately incognito. She even calls herself by the wrong name, that of "her oldest rival"—Shirley, the name of Hughes's Cambridge girlfriend, who was present at the famously raucous party at the Women's Union where Plath and Hughes first met. Two years later, married and living in Massachusetts, Plath recalled anxiously waiting in her Cambridge dorm for Hughes to show up and wanting to "murder his pale freckled mistress called Shirley. Let all rivals forever be called Shirley." Disguising herself as Shirley was a smart bet for Sylvia's ghost—Shirley was quiet, English, unobtrusive, the kind of wife Hughes's friends, and his sister, Olwyn, always wished he had taken. They despaired when he left Shirley for Sylvia Plath, who they saw as a rich and flashy American. Diane Middlebrook claims they even wrote a song about it at Cambridge, which they used to sing at The Anchor, the pub where they gathered to drink and talk poetry, after Hughes fell in love with Plath: "I'd rather have my Ted as he used to be / Than Sylvia Plath and her rich mommy."

In the time Ted lived in Yeats's house after his wife's suicide, it was full of Sylvia's rivals for her husband's affection. But rivalry, as a subject, was Sylvia Plath's, not Ted Hughes's. She wrote a lasting poem about it called "The Rival" in July of 1961: "No day is safe from news of you." In "The Offers," Hughes tells us that Plath seemed not to know herself, but it's possible that Hughes didn't recognize what his wife was up to. In the complicated web of private signals both made public in their writing, rivalry was Plath's way of signaling her power. "He can have . . . only one wife. . . . And that's me," she wrote in a fall 1962 letter to Ruth Beuscher. Or, as her poem "The Rival" puts it: "[You're] walking about in Africa, maybe, but thinking of me." In 1963, "The Rival" would shortly be published in *Ariel*, the most famous poetry collection of the decade. During their marriage, Hughes's star rose while Plath wrote quietly in the background as Mrs. Ted Hughes. Disguised as her "oldest rival," she snuck into her own home to telegraph news from beyond—she was his greatest rival now.

In his prologue to *The Savage God*, Al Alvarez suggests a rivalry between Hughes and Plath that he observed during his visit to Court Green in June 1962, when he noted a change in Plath and the marriage's dynamic. In 1960, Plath had hovered in the background, a housewife who "seemed effaced." Now, Alvarez writes, "Sylvia had changed. No longer . . . a housewifely appendage to a powerful husband, she seemed made solid and complete, her own woman again." Alvarez sensed the reason for the change when Plath told him she was writing again, "Really writing." He either did not sense, or politely does not say in the prologue, the other reason for the change in the marriage dynamic—that Hughes had fallen in love with another woman. Alvarez believed that the marriage was "a strong, close" one and that Ted was therefore "unconcerned that the balance of power had shifted for the time being to [Sylvia]." When Hughes read this, he was enraged and wrote to Alvarez, "Not even temporary insanity would explain your completely false remarks implying that there was some sort of artistic jealousy between Sylvia and me."

But Heather Clark argues that it was exactly this that helped to blow up the marriage in spring 1962: "fame and its legendary temptations." Hughes's strange statement after Plath's death, "It was either her or me," which he repeated at her funeral and, Clark writes, told to Plath's friend Suzette Macedo after the coroner's inquest, hints at a rivalry with the highest possible stakes: "Was the relationship so dysfunctional that he felt only one of them would survive it?"

In any case, only one of them did.

THE FEMINIST THEORIST GAYATRI SPIVAK, writing about women trying to produce philosophical discourse within affirmative deconstruction, warns them: beware of becoming Athena, who, armed with the law and "Justice,"

> [ruled] against Clytemnestra by privileging marriage, the Law that appropriates the woman's body over the claims of that body as Law. To the question: "Where is there a spur so keen as to compel to murder of a mother?" the presumed answer is: "Marriage appointed by fate 'twixt man and woman is mightier than an oath and Justice is its guardian."

Clytemnestra, the fiercest of mothers, privileged the female body as its own sovereign law. Sylvia Plath's late poems are the embodiment of Clytemnestra's rage, her refusal to bow to politesse, to do what was expected of her, to go quietly away, to show deference to her husband by placing his desires, his law, above that of her own body. Writing of the initial break in her marriage in July 1962, Plath says that she knows that Beuscher, along with many of her friends and family, will tell her to let Hughes get the affair out of his system:

> Well, what about my system? How do I get this other It out? This jealous retch, this body that comes, laughing, between my body & his body.

For Clytemnestra as for Plath, the body was a law unto itself, a place marked by terror that cannot be erased into beauty and compliance by the vengeance of the son. Or, in Plath's case, the daughter. When writing about her mother and father, Frieda Hughes has discounted her mother's accounts of her father's violence and credited her mother's creative success to her father. Sylvia Plath may have famously associated herself with Electra, haunted by her dead father, but her daughter reads like a modern-day Orestes, working with the law to transfigure her mother's rage in the name of her father.

"I am the ghost of an infamous suicide," Plath wrote in "Electra on Azalea Path," as though to prompt us to ask—where are Sylvia Plath's Furies, those bloody hell-goddesses weeping pus and shit in the name of the mother? "Red was your color," Hughes wrote in the last poem of *Birthday Letters*, "but the jewel you lost was blue," as though Plath's red rage wasn't stolen from her, her Furies transfigured into Eumenides as she stands there, screaming. "Don't fail me," Plath's ghost says to Hughes in "The Offers" as he lowers himself into the steaming bathwater. But she doesn't say, "Don't fail *you*"; she says, "Don't fail *me*": Don't squander my rage, don't light up my bloody face until I shine like a sapphire. Why would the ghost of Sylvia Plath be young and beautiful and satisfied with Ted Hughes? Why would her only concern, her only message from the underworld, be "Go—be the poet we always knew you could be"? Why would Sylvia Plath cross the River Styx to watch Ted Hughes lower his toe into his bathwater, without carrying a shiv and a net?

How Reliable a Witness?

※

"HE SAID, SHE SAID" IS THE OLDEST ARGUMENT ON RECORD about intimate partner violence (IPV) and sexual assault. When we ask who is telling the truth in varying accounts of these events, these are the words and the power dynamics we fall back on, despite the generations of proof that they are dangerously inadequate. In the case of Sylvia Plath, Ted Hughes, and the existence of violence in their relationship, this tends to be solely a question of what she said. At least in his writing, Hughes was mostly silent about interpersonal violence in his romantic relationships, and instead wielded threats as a weapon against Plath's claims and against those who tried to write about those claims. This was especially true in the case of Paul Alexander's 1991 biography *Rough Magic*, one of the few in Hughes's lifetime to report outright an incidence of violence between Plath and Hughes. Ted Hughes, aided by his wife, Carol, tried and failed to block publication of the book in the United Kingdom under the country's libel laws, writing to their lawyer Katy Baldock, "We would like you to send Penguin USA a list of the page numbers I enclose with this letter with the comment that these pages contain untruths, totally unfounded allegations of gross conduct by Hughes, and defamatory libel."

Ted Hughes also threatened Anne Stevenson with a lawsuit after she used the phrase "the cruelty of the husband" in a discussion of her book *Bitter Fame* on a late-night British talk show. In a November 1989 letter, Hughes wrote, "Also, Anne . . . you let 'the cruelty of the husband' trip off your tongue . . . My only thought was, is that actionable or isn't it?" In the same letter to Stevenson, he describes threatening "an old friend of mine (female)" with a lawsuit when she asked his permission to write about their relationship: "She was damned if I was going to gag her." To "[retrain]" her, Hughes writes, he sued two major British newspapers.

By contrast, "she," Sylvia Plath, talked. In her public writing, her poetry and her one published novel, and in her private journals and correspondence, Plath described or adapted repeated incidents of violence between her husband and herself. During at least one alleged conversation with a friend, Plath told of an incident in which Hughes nearly killed her. In her journals, she wrote about violent events she later adapted into fiction for *The Bell Jar*, and the power dynamics of IPV are at the heart of much of Plath's *Ariel* poetry, including "The Jailer," "The Rabbit Catcher," and "Daddy." One of Plath's 1962 letters to Ruth Beuscher makes a frank claim of IPV, which Plath also connected to her 1961 miscarriage. While I will discuss many of these examples in this chapter, in doing so, I am not trying to "prove" that Sylvia Plath was telling the truth when she described IPV. To do so would turn the conversation about her relationship with Ted Hughes back to the same stuck place it has been since it began, in the he said/she said binary that dead-ends so much discourse about IPV and sexual assault. Instead, I want to offer a new reading of Plath's accounts, and the public response to them, through the framework of the feminist analytic philosophers Miranda Fricker, Kristie Dotson, and Kate Manne.

Miranda Fricker's 2010 article "Epistemic Oppression and Epistemic Privilege" served as a foundational text for Dotson's and Manne's work on IPV. Fricker defined the concept of "hermeneutic injustice," which says that when forms of adverse social experience for oppressed groups are repeatedly misinterpreted by the privileged, we develop no language to interpret, or describe, these adverse social experiences. We therefore necessarily misinterpret that group of people's lived reality when they describe it, or attempt to describe it. It is possible, she says, to point to individual hermeneutic failure—the inability to understand or describe an interaction without the knowledge that one participant in the exchange has the ability to fire another, or fail them on an exam, or beat them in a physical fight. But individual hermeneutic injustice can also, Fricker says, result in "*collective* systematic cognitive failings." Fricker's primary example of this is someone who has lived under "long-term domestic violence":

> Where a given misinterpretation stems from a collective failure to understand the nature of some type of social experience—what it's like, for example, to be the victim of long-term domestic violence—then a correct interpretation can appear to be irrational or outrageous. Perhaps it is only once the experience of long-term domestic violence is properly understood that we are collectively in a position to see the reasons in favour of extending the legal notion of provocation, so that in a murder trial the defensive claim "she was provoked" may no longer appear outrageous, as it once would have.

In the case of Sylvia Plath and Ted Hughes, there was, of course, no murder, but there was a death, one that has, over the years, taken on the elements of a murder mystery. The couple's breakup, and Plath's suicide, have frequently been discussed in terms of detective fiction, notably by the writers Sarah Churchwell and Jacqueline Rose. Rose writes in *The Haunting of Sylvia Plath* that Plath's survivors "have turned this story into a case of what psychanalysts Nicholas Abraham and Maria Torok term 'transgenerational haunting,' by repeatedly conducting themselves *as if* they were the perpetrators of a crime." For Churchwell, "it is hard to determine what crime precisely is said to have been committed in the struggle between Plath's and Hughes's words (adultery, abandonment, murder, slander, libel). The question is less 'whodunit' than 'what was done?'"

Both Churchwell and Rose take their cues from Plath's October 1962 poem "The Detective." "The Detective" could serve as a description of biographical inquiry into Plath's life and death. "This is the valley of death, though the cows thrive," Plath's speaker declares, as though predicting the experience of visiting her Heptonstall grave while the cows graze in the distance. Plath's speaker reminds us that this "case" has no body; the body in question has slowly been "[vaporized]," piece by piece: in the second year of the marriage, the "insatiable" mouth is "hung out" in punishment. Has this "insatiable" mouth been punished for the desire to kiss its beloved? Plath wrote rapturously of kissing Hughes in her journals—"a hundred times [I] sniff his smell of bread & grapes and kiss his delectable places." Perhaps the "[vaporization]" of the mouth in "The Detective" means that the beloved cooled on the marriage two years in and wanted to be kissed less, or not at all. Plath wrote to Ruth Beuscher on October 9, 1962, eight days after she wrote "The Detective," "[F]or at least the last 3 years . . . I have been eating not real bread but a delusion of love."

One notes, of course, how Hughes's body, which in its delight smelled of bread to Plath as she "[ran] about" to kiss him has now turned false, and can no longer sustain her. Plath had a famously voracious appetite (remember Dido Merwin's description of her eating the foie gras), but reported to Ruth Beuscher in the same October 9 letter that in his absence, Hughes wanted her to get by without "sherry . . . or roast beef." Plath clearly viewed this as a sadistic punishment on Hughes's part, writing, "I feel this . . . desire to torture me of my last sense."

We can also read the lines about the mouth disappearing "In the second year" as Plath's uncanny prediction of the posthumous conditions for her own poetry. Hughes initially published "The Detective" in the British magazine *Encounter* in October 1963, about eight months after Plath's suicide. But by the time he published *Ariel* with Faber & Faber in February 1965, "The Detective" had been removed from the collection. The year 1965—two years after Plath's suicide—was also, then, the year Plath's posthumous mouth was quieted. If we read Hughes's excision of Plath's "more personally aggressive" poems from *Ariel* as both a cover for his reputation *and* a punishment for Plath's excessive and revealing speech, we have another mirror of the conditions Plath describes in "The Detective." There, silencing, as opposed to mere silence, is a punitive act: an "insatiable" mouth is "hung out" as punishment for its endless desire. In "The Detective," the speaker indicates that the woman's mouth, after "the second year," was punished for its insatiable desire to, among other functions, speak, a theme she took up again in "The Courage of Shutting-Up," written the very next day. The images of the woman who is vaporized are all silent—she listens quietly by a window—or else dead and being "[tamped] into a wall."

This last is a clear reference to Edgar Allan Poe's short story "The Black Cat," in which a husband murders his wife because she interferes with his attempted murder of a black cat. He bludgeons her with an ax—she falls "dead upon the spot, without a groan"—and buries her body, standing straight up, behind a brick wall in the cellar. But the black cat in question manages to brick itself in with the corpse of the wife without the husband noticing. When the police arrive several days later to search the home, the husband, believing his hiding place foolproof, invites the detectives into the cellar to search. In his arrogance, he brags to the detectives about how well built the house is and raps on the spot where his wife's body is with his cane. The cane alerts the cat, who begins to yowl in a voice the murderer takes as his wife's: "a voice from within the tomb!—by a cry, at first muffled and broken, like the sobbing of a child, and then quickly swelling into one long, loud, and continuous scream." The husband is caught and sentenced to death.

Both Sarah Churchwell and Jacqueline Rose correctly argue that in the case of Sylvia Plath versus Ted Hughes, we are typically arguing over Plath's other corpus, her enormous body of writing, which was mostly read after her death and under Ted Hughes's heavy editorial hand. This will be true here, too; given that Plath died before any of the claims of intimate partner violence we will examine came to public light, it is her body of writing that will have to serve as evidence. Hughes famously wrote that the poems of *Ariel* were "just like [Plath], but permanent," a comparison that, in an earlier chapter, I likened to the construction of Plath's poetic mausoleum. Hughes's *Ariel*, which removed so many of the poems Plath wrote that treated their violent marriage and its violent end, acted, then, as a textual version of Poe's brick wall.

We can imagine feminist critics as the very detectives to whom Poe's murderous husband says, "By the by, gentlemen, this—this is a very well-constructed house," just before the yowling cat alerts them to the presence of the body—or, to be more precise, to Plath's *other* body, the writing Hughes excised from his various publications of her work. In listening for Plath, we must be attentive to Miranda Fricker's claims in "Epistemic Oppression and Epistemic Privilege" that we can perform "a kind of hermeneutical affirmative action" by reading Plath's work, on one level, as the testimony of a survivor of intimate partner violence. As if on cue, I turn back to Sylvia Plath's detective, who ends by telling us, "Make notes."

PLATH'S TEXTUAL BODY IS GREATLY concerned with her physical one, just as her physical body creates her textual corpus. As Jacqueline Rose points out in her chapter "The Body of the Writing," Plath obsessively cataloged her body's functions. The production of mucus, the washing and shedding of hair, even her apparent lifelong fascination with picking her nose—in her journals, Plath turned her physical body into a body of text while at once making that body of text reflect the physicality of her self. "In this figuring of writing," Rose tells us, "Plath runs back and forth across the passage of the body into words ... the connection between the body and language knows no limit." This is also true in her poetry and in *The Bell Jar*, both of which showcase the body's cuts, bruises, and functions. Plath didn't limit this cataloging of the body to personal hygiene or illness. She included in it sex and violence, two acts that often met in her relationship with Ted Hughes and subsequently in her writing about that relationship. Plath's first meeting with Hughes, and her description of it in her journal, is now so famous that it feels redundant to quote it. But I will, because it foreshadows the whole of what came in its wake: "and then he kissed me ... ripped my hairband off ... and my favorite silver earrings ... when he kissed my neck I bit him long and hard on the cheek, and ... blood was running down his face." Hughes left the room, presumably to retrieve his girlfriend Shirley, who was (also presumably) not thrilled with this turn of events.

Excerpts of this passage appeared in the first, heavily abridged edition of Plath's *Journals*, published in America in 1982—the book that familiarized the world with her description of the couple's dramatic meeting. In it, she meets Hughes on February 25 and does not see him again before she goes to Paris over her spring break to meet with another lover, Richard Sassoon. She spends a short time in France, then goes to Italy and Germany with an old boyfriend, Gordon Lameyer, before talking herself into going back to London to see Hughes. Nearly all mentions of Hughes during Plath's time in Europe are cut from the text, save in the last entry prior to her return to England, when she references, twice, his calling her by the wrong name: Shirley, the name of his girlfriend when he met Sylvia at the party in Cambridge. When the reader turns the page, Plath is suddenly married to Hughes, and the two are honeymooning in Spain. This would have left any reader wondering—what happened in between?

In reality, about a month passed after the couple's first meeting, on February 25, before Plath met with Hughes in London on Friday, March 23, just prior to her trip to Paris and Italy for her spring break.

It was during this encounter that Plath and Hughes slept together for the first time, in her London hotel. Plath did write a journal entry about this meeting, on Monday, March 26, in Paris, which included the following passage: "Arrived in Paris . . . exhausted from sleepless holocaust night with Ted . . . I . . . washed my battered face, smeared with a purple bruise from Ted and my neck raw and wounded too." But this passage, along with several others describing violence between the couple, was wholly cut from the 1982 edition of Plath's published *Journals*.

Plath also wrote about her first sexual encounter with Hughes in an unfinished novel that she called, alternately, *Venus in the Seventh* and *Falcon Yard*, an apparent celebration of her married life with the artist of her dreams. The surviving passages from the novel are unpublished, but include descriptions of violent sex between the couple. In them, a young woman protagonist named Jess sleeps with Ian, who is obviously based on Hughes. Discussing their first sexual encounter, Jess says to Ian, "I went to Paris all scarred. Black and blue." "But you liked it?" Ian replies. "Yes," Jess tells him. "I was furious with myself. I don't know what happened to me," Ian says. It seems evident from both passages that Plath was writing about actual bruises. But in *Ted Hughes: The Unauthorised Life*, Jonathan Bate dismisses this as wordplay. "Love bites," he writes cleverly: "For Plath, desire was always a purple bruise; for Hughes, poetry was the healing of a wound." Maybe. But sometimes a purple bruise is actually a purple bruise, a contusion like the one Plath wrote about in one of the last poems of her life: "Color floods to the spot, dull purple."

Bate's analysis of *Falcon Yard/Venus in the Seventh* returns us to Miranda Fricker's concept of hermeneutical injustice as it applies to women who experience repeated incidents of IPV. Fricker, to be sure, is writing about the law: the ways in which judges and juries are frequently incapable of understanding the testimonies of "long-term domestic violence" survivors. But Fricker is also using hermeneutical injustice as the basis for the broader idea of what she calls "epistemic oppression." For Fricker, "a case of hermeneutical injustice will be a case of epistemic injustice, so long as the hermeneutical practice in question is one through which we gain knowledge." It is here that Plath's situation—in her chronicling of her own life, in the history of literature and the making of the twentieth-century literary canon, the history of second-wave feminism, and the history of popular culture—is thrown into sharp relief. Because Sylvia Plath is one of the most famous writers of the last century and remains a vital part of the literary, feminist, and cultural conversation in America and Europe. Her work and life transcend the boundaries of high and popular culture and art, and both are taught, and studied, at nearly every level of school in the United States and abroad. As poets, writers, artists, and feminists, we understand learning about Sylvia Plath as a vital way of gaining knowledge about multiple subjects.

If we therefore read and interpret Plath's accounts of violence at the hands of her spouse as mere poetic symbols or, as they are sometimes read, as outright lies, then we necessarily practice a form of epistemic injustice against Plath and other survivors of intimate partner violence. This is evident in Bate's reading of Plath's work as a wound that is both a preface and an epilogue to her suicide, which Hughes alone has the ability to cure, a thread Bate carries through to the end of his biography. It positions Hughes as Plath's good doctor, about a piece of writing where she characterizes him as someone who does her intentional physical harm. In this way, Bate—and therefore we—don't read *Falcon Yard* as one of Plath's attempts to find language for a pattern of violence, including sexual violence, within a romantic relationship. Instead, this violence is presented as a symbol of Hughes's emotional impact on her psyche, rather than a literal mark on her body.

Fricker goes on: "If someone or some group suffers epistemic injustice in a systematic way, then it will be appropriate to talk of epistemic *oppression*." Plath suffers epistemic injustice in two systematic ways—first, in the past tense, as a woman who made multiple accounts of being beaten, sexually assaulted, and strangled by her husband, Ted Hughes, during her lifetime, but who nonetheless ended her life in an act I would argue was, at least in part, a result of the isolation and despair she suffered from an abusive marriage. The question of whether IPV leads to an increased risk of suicide has long gone unanswered. This is not least because, as Fricker points out, we lack the proper hermeneutic and epistemic tools to understand and learn from its victims' experiences and their accounts of those experiences and have chosen, instead, to ignore some elements of them.

Thankfully, this has very recently begun to change. In 2022, the Agenda Alliance, a consortium of women's advocacy groups located within the United Kingdom, conducted one of the first major studies of the relationship between experiencing IPV and suicidality. Their findings, published in February 2023, speak directly to Plath's experience: women who had experienced IPV were three times more likely to attempt suicide than women who had not. In the case of women who experienced sexual IPV, the number rose to seven times more likely to attempt suicide. The high-profile nature of Plath's suicide and the way it has, in past literature, been accredited to either simple heartbreak or revenge, and the fact that no one has yet looked at IPV, or sexual IPV, as one of its causes, are further proof of the epistemic injustice surrounding her relationship with Hughes and her death.

Plath also suffers epistemic injustice in her "literary afterlife" as the literary and cultural figure "Sylvia Plath." We simultaneously venerate "Sylvia Plath" as a "high priestess" of her art and condemn her as an unreliable narrator who conjured a fantasy of her own life, rather than lived it. In the 1999 "New Preface" to *Bitter Fame*, Anne Stevenson writes that Plath's poetry was "the life after death that she demanded for herself and, at the cost of her reason and happiness, did achieve," driving home once more the absurd idea that Plath's poetry of 1962–63—not her depression, her isolation, or her abuse—was not only the cause of her death but that which robbed her, here, of "reason and happiness." This second form of epistemic injustice not only rises to the level of epistemic oppression, it perpetuates it. If Plath, with her extraordinary staying power as a writer and cultural touchstone and her continued acknowledgment as a genius by critics as powerful and varied as Helen Vendler, Janet Malcolm, and Jonathan Bate can be called a liar when testifying about experiencing IPV, what chance do any of us have of being believed? Moreover, if we read Plath as a writer *not* writing about her experience of IPV, we lose out on a valuable epistemic source on this topic, since she left behind such a varied and voluminous account of her marriage to Ted Hughes.

Whether or not Plath was a victim of IPV became something of a cause célèbre when her letters to Ruth Beuscher reemerged in 2017. As touched on in the introduction, Plath's letters to her therapist were written up in the *Guardian*, the *Irish Times*, the *New Statesman*, and a number of other major newspapers. All of the articles used similar language: the claims were "shocking," "stunning," words that indicate that prior to the discovery of the Beuscher letters, we lived in a world where no such claims against Ted Hughes had ever been made. As we have already seen, this wasn't true. In addition to Plath's journal entries citing violence by Hughes, other such claims appear in Sylvia Plath biographies, notably Paul Alexander's *Rough Magic*. In it, Alexander writes that Plath told a friend in the fall of 1962, when her marriage was under great strain, that on their summer 1956 honeymoon in Benidorm, Spain, Hughes began to abruptly strangle her until she almost lost consciousness; then, just as abruptly, he stopped. This episode, Alexander writes, made Plath "question the wisdom" of her marriage to Hughes.

This incident gives considerable context to several pieces of writing by Plath and Hughes and to the treatment of their honeymoon in *Bitter Fame*, where Stevenson puzzles over Plath's sudden descent into a black mood in Spain:

> Things improved after they moved inland, away from the seafront, yet her moods seemed to soar and sink with alarming

> rapidity. Sylvia recorded in her journal her volatile and intense reactions to some unmentioned incident, possibly arising out of her husband's surprise at the rancor she displayed in a running tiff with the house owner, who wanted to raise the rent, or perhaps arising out of an evening when they had drinks with some English people who upset Sylvia. These moods, Ted found, were largely unaccountable: they began and ended like electric storms, and he came to learn simply to accept their occurrence.... One side of her reached back for a harmonious home life and commercial success; another abandoned itself to moony fantasies, black, silent furies, or *imaginary scenes of violence* [my emphasis].

Stevenson quotes at length from Plath's journals of the time, including a passage describing a growing distrust of Hughes. In the dark, the couple goes out for an angry walk, during which, Plath believed, "all could happen: the willful drowning, the murder, the killing words." Stevenson tells the reader, "Suddenly, Sylvia found herself at the center of a melodrama." She fails to record that there are pages torn out of the journals that might have recorded an "unmentioned incident" that caused Plath distress. Instead Stevenson attributes her subject's discomfort to cranky English tourists and a rise in the Hugheses' rent.

Similarly, in Hughes's *Birthday Letters* poem "You Hated Spain," Plath's sense of distrust and unease is blamed on the fact that the country reminded her of death, "the dust-red cadaver." In the poem, as in Stevenson's analysis of her journals, Plath's discomfort lies in character faults and a pathological obsession with suicide. Plath was uncomfortable in Spain for more ordinary reasons—she wrote to her mother of her dislike of the bullfights. She and Hughes did fight over "some English people who upset Sylvia." But it is probable that Hughes strangled her on a Benidorm hillside. Paul Alexander thought his source credible, and he stood by the story. He also stood by his protection of his source, a woman who feared retribution from

Ted Hughes. The story was reported in Janet Malcolm's widely read *The Silent Woman*, which ran as a serial in *The New Yorker*.

Why, then, this tendency to react to reports of Ted Hughes's violence as though this were new information and that Plath might not be telling the truth? To better understand this response, we turn back to *Down Girl: The Logic of Misogyny*, in which Kate Manne expands on her theory of misogyny with an analysis of the role strangulation plays in IPV. In her introduction, "Eating Her Words," Manne writes that strangulation is gendered, "paradigmatic of misogyny," and meant as a show of "authority and domination" against its victims. Moreover, its deadliness is often unknown or underestimated by the general public and the police, which leads many of its victims, says Manne, to "minimize" their experience—if they are not "gaslit." In Plath's case, we see this last in the characterizations of her responses to Spain, which are all portrayed as internal problems she could never resolve—*It's all in your head, Sylvia*.

Despite the deadly nature of strangulation, it has only recently been categorized as "its own felony" in 48 states; in Ohio and South Carolina, it is still not considered a separate crime from assault. According to Manne, this, along with our indifference to and dismissal of the crime, has led to a walking back of the language we use to describe it. In Paul Alexander's account of the alleged Benidorm incident, for example, he uses the term "choke," which, as Manne points out, occurs when a foreign object has entered and lodged in the throat, and is typically accidental. Strangulation is deliberate. It is performed with one's hands, or with an object called a ligature, like a rope or a belt. It is also one of the most common forms of IPV. When questioned about it, however, its women victims often downplay the incident or deny it altogether: "You can train her not to say 'strangle' but rather 'choke,' . . . or best of all nothing." I am compelled to remind the reader of Ted Hughes's language to Anne Stevenson about stopping his friend from selling her story about their "friendship" to the newspapers, a woman who had to be "[retrained]," he wrote, and "was damned if I was going to gag her."

These are two examples of what Manne, reading the philosopher Kristie Dotson, calls "eating her words." Dotson defines the concept of "testimonial smothering," or self-silencing by a speaker, which occurs because "the speaker perceives one's immediate audience as unwilling or unable to gain the appropriate uptake of proffered testimony." Dotson identifies three circumstances that routinely exist in testimonial smothering: "1) the content of the testimony must be unsafe and risky; 2) the audience must demonstrate testimonial incompetence with respect to the content of the testimony to the speaker; and 3) testimonial incompetence must follow from, or appear to follow from, pernicious ignorance." She defines "pernicious ignorance" as a form of willful ignorance "that . . . causes or contributes to a harmful practice, in this case, a harmful practice of silencing." She distinguishes between what she calls "an instance of silencing and a practice of silencing" to help us understand the difference between "reliable ignorance" and "pernicious ignorance." Reliable ignorance occurs when people simply do not know something, for any number of reasons—Dotson gives the example of a three-year-old in Michigan who is unaware of the state's voting laws. She also uses this to point out that not all ignorance is bad. Ignorance, for instance, calls us to learn new things. But "a practice of silencing . . . concerns a repetitive, reliable occurrence of an audience failing to meet the dependencies of a speaker that finds its origin in a more pervasive ignorance."

In a grimly poetic analysis, Manne applies this concept specifically to victims of IPV who have survived strangulation. Strangulation silences the victim in the moment, since one requires oxygen to speak; this becomes a metaphor for the ways its victims, perpetrators, and the criminal justice system downplay the crime by using benign language to describe it, ceasing to discuss it, or forcing victims to redact their story. Manne gives two high-profile examples of this phenomenon. First she talks about a woman named Lisa Fierstein, who was once married to Andrew Puzder, Donald Trump's nominee for labor secretary. Prior to their divorce, Fierstein had appeared, in 1990, on *The Oprah Winfrey Show* in glasses and a wig, under a pseudonym, to describe her experiences being battered by Puzder, which included being "choked." Once Puzder was nominated for labor secretary, however, Fierstein revoked her original statements, twice claiming in a 2016 email to Puzder that he was not abusive.

Manne also recounts the case of a woman named Mary Louise Piccard, who was once married to Steve Bannon. Piccard filed a police report in 1996 in which she described Bannon "choking" her during a fight. The police—whom Piccard presumably called to the scene by dialing 911, which received a hang-up call from that address—photographed her neck, which was covered in red marks, and described in the report that for four minutes after they arrived, Piccard was unable to speak, which is consistent with strangulation. Bannon was charged with domestic violence and battery, but the charges were eventually dropped because Piccard didn't appear in court to testify, because, as Manne explains, Bannon had threatened her through his attorney, who told Piccard that if she went to court, "[they] would make sure that I would be the one who was guilty." Manne ends her description of Piccard's case by quoting Bannon's spokesperson from 2016, who claimed that Bannon and Piccard had "a great relationship."

Manne calls the difference over time in these women's characterization of their experiences and relationships with their former spouses "Vocal Changes" and notes how, reading the various accounts over time, it is as though you're hearing from two different women. In the case of Piccard, the change occurred when others spoke on her behalf. This is also necessarily what happened to Sylvia Plath, given her death at the age of thirty. Plath's private claims of IPV in her journals were stricken from the original publication of her journals, and Alexander's claim that Hughes had "choked" her in Spain is criticized as defamatory against Hughes in Janet Malcolm's *The Silent Woman* (a charge we will look at more closely). Heather Clark leaves the strangulation story out of her high-profile 2020 biography of Plath entirely. Jonathan Bate includes it in his biography of Ted Hughes but performs his own version of making Plath eat her words. Bate writes that it occurred while the couple was "[making] love in the open air" and that Plath "nearly choked." He calls the story "unverified," which recalls language Clark used in her keynote address at the 2022 Sylvia Plath Literary Festival, when she said she was conscious, writing about Plath and Hughes, that she wasn't "there" for anything that had happened between Sylvia Plath and Ted Hughes.

This is true—but who, usually, is "there" for incidents of IPV? Who could verify this story except Plath or Hughes themselves? Bate's note for the source is Alexander's biography, but he writes that "[t]he friend . . . is not an entirely reliable source." In her journals, Plath appears to describe strangulation as part of her first sexual encounter with Hughes ("my neck raw and wounded too"). In later poems—"The Rabbit Catcher" and "Kindness"—written as her marriage dissolved, she employs images of strangulation, often tangled with images of sexual intimacy, murder, and children. Yet there is scant literature connecting these poems to Plath's aforementioned journal entry, and with one exception, which we will look at momentarily, no literature connecting Alexander's claim that Hughes strangled Plath to either of these poems. Ironically, then, Plath is being made to eat the very words she used to describe this act of violence. Given all of this, it's worth returning to Paul Alexander's account in *Rough Magic*:

> [One] afternoon while she and Ted sat on a hillside, Ted was overtaken by an inexplicable rage. As Sylvia had described it, his face whitened, his body contorted, his gaze intensified. And, according to Sylvia, before she knew it, he was on top of her—not kissing her, as he usually did, but choking her. At first, she said, she fought him. Then, eventually, she merely gave in and allowed his superior strength to dominate her, his fingers to tighten more and more around her neck. Finally, at the moment when she began to lose consciousness—the

moment she said she resolved herself to die—Ted released his grip and stopped his assault as abruptly as he had started it. When Sylvia told this story, her marriage to Ted was under enormous stress, and she claimed that this episode had made her question the wisdom of her decision to marry him. Whatever the case, whatever happened on the hillside in Benidorm, Sylvia did nothing.

Two things are worth pointing out here. First, although Alexander wrote his account twenty-six years before Manne's work on strangulation, the language he uses is remarkably consistent with Manne's characterization of strangulation as a misogynistic crime, one used to assert dominance over another. In Alexander's version of this story, Plath fights and then gives in to what Alexander calls Hughes's "superior strength." (Manne writes that there is "a ten- to fifteen-second window when an adult being strangled will usually instinctually fight hard before losing consciousness.") Second, Bate claims in his biography that the couple were making love during the incident, which Alexander does not say. It seems unlikely that Bate, who is a careful and esteemed scholar, would mistakenly alter Alexander's account in his biography. Which begs the question— did Bate hear this story from a different source? He did not hear it from Paul Alexander, who confirmed to me that they never spoke.

When Janet Malcolm refers to the Benidorm strangulation story in *The Silent Woman*, she writes that the "chief aim" of Alexander's biography of Plath "seems to be to see how outrageously it can slander Hughes and still somehow stay within the limits of libel law." She is also heavily critical of Alexander for protecting his source: "This is a horrible story. Who is this 'close friend' who can charge Hughes with nothing short of attempted murder? How reliable a witness? We will never know. 'The information for this paragraph comes from my interview with a confidential source,' Alexander calmly writes." In another example of forcing Plath to eat her words, Malcolm can only understand this as a "horrible story" because she believes it libels Ted Hughes. Its horror as an example of potentially deadly interpersonal violence does not register with her, and the strangulation story is presented by Malcolm as if it couldn't possibly be true—another irony, given Malcolm's acknowledgment of the danger of strangulation, something many people, and the American legal system, discount.

In an interview he granted me on February 12, 2020, Paul Alexander revealed that Clarissa Roche, Plath's close friend, was the source for this story, which she said Plath told her when Roche visited her at Court Green in November 1962, after Hughes had left the marriage and was living in London. Like Paul Alexander, Janet Malcolm also interviewed Clarissa Roche at length and even stayed as a guest in Roche's home in Somerset, England, for several days, an experience she detailed in *The Silent Woman*. Malcolm was famously tricky to talk to. Jillian Becker describes the experience of being interviewed by her as "like standing in a room lined with distorting mirrors." In *The Silent Woman*, Malcolm intersperses descriptions of her visit with Clarissa Roche with her excerpts, and critiques, of Alexander's book. In a glancing back-and-forth, Malcolm moves between an alleged strangulation on a hillside in Spain and a warm English home where Roche serves Malcolm a delicious lunch. Did Roche tell Malcolm Plath's story of Hughes strangling her during this visit? Is it possible that Malcolm, by juxtaposing her time with Roche against her mockery of the strangulation story, was trying to make Roche, and therefore Plath, eat her words, while also hinting to the reader that Roche was Alexander's anonymous source?

I suspect so. Malcolm's taped interviews with Roche are available at Yale's Beinecke Rare Book & Manuscript Room. There are three tapes, each about forty-five minutes long; the archival notes state that they "[begin] abruptly." In the tapes, Roche repeatedly brings up the Hugheses' honeymoon, dropping her voice meaningfully each time she says the word "Benidorm." Roche makes a point of telling Malcolm that Plath's diaries from Benidorm have pages torn out. Moreover, Jonathan Bate never spoke to Clarissa Roche—

but he did speak to Janet Malcolm, who he gratefully acknowledges in *Ted Hughes: The Unauthorised Life*.

Sylvia Plath was not the only survivor of Ted Hughes who would end up having to eat her words. In 2020, I read the late Scottish writer Emma Tennant's memoir *Burnt Diaries*, a book about the years she spent, in her own words, as Ted Hughes's "sub-mistress." Tennant writes of seeking Hughes out because of her obsession with Plath; she seems to engage in an affair with him almost by accident. At the time, Hughes was already married to his second wife, Carol Orchard, and having another affair with the Australian journalist Jill Barber. The book chugs comically along about as I expected, until Tennant describes her last tryst with Hughes. They were in a secluded, wooded area of a London park, when suddenly,

> Ted leans down, and his hands go round my neck, and as they tighten, I am a tree, held by metallic twine in the cruel shape ordained for this arboreal amphitheatre in the Blue Garden. I am offered up in the deep shade of the hedge, and have no more life in me than the foliage, parched from lack of light, that runs raggedly between the espaliered trees. I could die here—and float away like the last of the cherry blossom that dances over the heads of the actors in Regent's Park. But this is no play: I feel my ears sing; my eyes blur as I look up into a face that grows from the pagan roots of the trees, a Green Man killing with his bare hands in the forest's depths. Then, with no more sense of time than *The Blind Owl* visionary's dream, we have walked out of the shade together and through the garden, to our car parked alone in the forecourt of Regent's College. There are no students to be seen.

A comprehensive search of the reviews of Tennant's memoir, which came out eight years after Paul Alexander's biography of Plath and six years after *The Silent Woman*, reveals no mention of this corroborating account of a violent pattern. Many of the reviews abound with one critical theme—that Tennant was in the wrong for airing the dirty laundry of Ted Hughes. In the *Irish Times*, John Banville questions "whether she should have revealed the details of her affair with a fine poet and complicated man" and postulates that Tennant would have done better to burn, rather than write up, her diaries from the time of her affair with Hughes. In the *Herald*, Lesley McDowell, like Anne Stevenson before her, reads Tennant's descriptions of Hughes as bearing no relationship to reality: "Tennant indulges in fantasies over her own possible self-destruction as a result of their affair." "Calm down," McDowell advises. Emma Tennant called her book *Burnt Diaries* as an homage to Plath's famous last journals, which Hughes claimed to have burned. Perhaps Tennant thought, in telling her story, that she was giving voice to Sylvia Plath. But she, too, ate her words.

SYLVIA PLATH SEEMS TO HAVE anticipated eating her words in her now-famous poem "The Rabbit Catcher." Begun May 21, 1962, after the Wevills' visit to Court Green, the poem details a series of images of strangulation and asphyxiation. Plath's speaker walks on a hillside with the sea in view. As she walks, she sees rabbit snares, which kill by crushing their necks, the first of many images that allude to the crushing or breaking of a neck or suggest strangulation. The speaker imagines the rabbit catcher himself, whose actions mirror the traps', as his hands go around a mug of tea, at which point the speaker is transmuted into the tea mug: "I felt hands round a tea mug, dull, blunt." Importantly, this place where she walks is not merely silent—it is "[absent]" of the sound of someone's screams. The speaker might want to scream, but she can't, as the wind blows her hair into her mouth, gagging her, another image of, importantly, not silence, but speechlessness.

Plath contends in the poem that "little deaths" "waited like sweethearts" for the rabbit catcher, but "little deaths" is also, of course, a well-known, highly literary euphemism for an orgasm. It is necessary to consider the possibility that this is a rendering of a violent sexual relationship that includes strangulation. Jonathan Bate wondered if, writing the poem, Plath wasn't recalling the incident in Benidorm. "The Rabbit Catcher" ends with "constriction" killing the speaker. This may well refer to a metaphorical tightening, but throats, too, constrict—from external forces, from illness, and from weeping, a condition we often describe, in its initial phase, as being "choked up."

"The Rabbit Catcher" takes as its most obvious referents two D. H. Lawrence poems, "Rabbit Snared in the Night" and "Cruelty and Love." Plath read Lawrence extensively at Cambridge, once writing in her journal, "Love, love: why do I feel I would have known and loved Lawrence?" She taught his novels to her freshmen at Smith and attended part of the *Lady Chatterley's Lover* obscenity trial when she was living in London in 1961, making notes about it in her journal. Diane Middlebrook writes in *Her Husband* about the exchange of Lawrentian imagery in Plath's "The Rabbit Catcher," calling it "an elegy for everything that had to be outgrown in [Plath's] femininity to acquire such clarity, such mastery within the medium of the distinctive poetic method and subject matter that would make her name."

Writing of Lawrence's work in 1958 as she tried to write her own novel, Plath said that his prose inspired her to write something great. In July 1962, upon discovering Hughes's infidelity, she wrote to Ruth Beuscher that her work "[was] killed by this mess. I write, not . . . out of sorrow, but . . . joy." But this, as Middlebrook points out, turned out to be, if not wrong, then slightly off, at least in terms of Plath's *Ariel* poems, which are animated by a rage so huge and articulate, it can feel like triumph. Plath believed, and wrote, for a long time that any great work she produced would surely be one that addressed her domestic bliss. But much of it turned out to address domestic violence.

Ted Hughes bought Sylvia Plath *The Complete Poems of D. H. Lawrence* in 1960 to celebrate her signing her first book contract; Plath had certainly read "Rabbit Snared in the Night" and "Cruelty and Love" before she wrote "The Rabbit Catcher." In the first, Lawrence uses the image of the rabbit caught and killed by the trapper as a metaphor for a sexual object who has "a hot, unthinkable desire" to be captured and killed by the poem's speaker. The speaker wonders, "Why should I want to throttle / you, bunny?" "Throttle" means to attack and kill by strangulation, but it is also an archaic word for throat. Ted Hughes wrote no notes in his edition of Plath's *Collected Poems* for "The Rabbit Catcher" and later claimed, in his poem of the same name from *Birthday Letters*, that Plath's poem was inspired by a May 1962 walk along a seaside cliff the couple took in which Plath was enraged by the presence of rabbit snares and tore them out of the ground. Given Lawrence's use of "throttle," and Plath's obsessive repetition in "The Rabbit Catcher" of images of a neck or throat being strangled, the other, equally strong influence here is clear.

It is even more so in "Cruelty and Love," in which a woman in the country waits for her trapper to return to her, which he does, having killed a rabbit. The woman can smell the dead rabbit on the trapper's fingers as he runs them down her face, in an act that appears to end in strangulation: "God, I am caught in a snare! I know not what fine wire is round my throat." Where Lawrence speaks first as the rabbit catcher and then as his lover, Plath's speaker blurs the line between the woman and the prey. Lawrence's first speaker convinces himself the bunny wants to be strangled—why else, he seems to say, would you sit on my lap? He talks himself out of his guilt in an escalating anaphora, an obsessive repetition of "not me, but *you*." His second speaker tells us that she "[dies], and [finds] death good," a signal that she takes great pleasure in exchanging her power. Plath's speaker seems to want to escape "a relationship," but she is trapped in it by "pegs too deep to uproot" and literally unable to voice her protest, being gagged "by [her] blown hair." *You / I wanted this*, say Lawrence's speakers. Given the choice, Plath's speaker might say, *I did*—it was she, after all, who proposed to Hughes—but she can't speak.

Plath's poem "Kindness," written in the last two weeks of her life, continues this interplay of imagery from Lawrence's poetry, with the added element of conversing with the work of her husband. On January 21, 1963, the BBC broadcast one of Hughes's plays, *Difficulties of a Bridegroom*, which he began composing in the spring of 1962. The play has never been published. Hughes's friend Daniel Huws speculated that Hughes gave other, published works the same title to distract people from reading it.

Hughes's protagonist in the play, a young man named Sullivan, runs over a hare with his car. A woman called "She" appears, and they have a dreamlike conversation about the nature of love, truth, materialism, and conformity. By that time, Hughes had come to see Plath as representing middle-class conformity and loveless marriage. "She" attempts to force Sullivan to marry, find a job, and wear decent clothes. "Truth is in the heart, the heart is a beehive," she tells him; when Hughes began writing the play, Plath had begun to keep bees, a powerful symbol in her personal history and her poetry.

Hughes later told Plath's friend Elizabeth Sigmund that he believed that hares were Sylvia Plath's "shamanic animal" and that he had said as much to Plath. The hare in *Difficulties of a Bridegroom* is said to be as large as a human, with "big inspired-looking golden eyes, even when it was dead," words similar to Hughes's descriptions of Plath's eyes in *Birthday Letters*. After Sullivan kills it, he sells it to a butcher for five quid. He drives to London to see his mistress, who calls his five quid "blood money." He uses it to buy roses for her, and the play ends. The symbolic death of the hare, sold for "blood money" to give Sullivan's mistress roses, would have been seen by Plath as Hughes's public declaration of the death of their love and marriage, and deeply humiliating. And yet, "Remarkably," Heather Clark writes, "Sylvia invited Ted to Fitzroy Road for sherry to celebrate the official January 14 release date of *The Bell Jar*." One week later, on February 1, Plath drafted "Kindness." In the top right-hand corner of the handwritten draft of the poem, she scrawled "Feb. 1, 1963," and circled it. It was the first day of the last month of her life.

Plath writes ironically of "Dame Kindness," who has come to

offer futile help for yet another inescapable quagmire. In "The Rabbit Catcher," the speaker and her predator/lover are strung together by "tight wires" and "pegs too deep to uproot," a relationship the speaker can never escape. In "Kindness," the relationship has been severed, but the speaker remains trapped, presumably by their children, whose happy faces are reflected all through house's mirrors. "What is so real as the cry of a child?" Plath's speaker demands. A purely biographical read of this line has Plath wondering why Hughes can't hear the cries of his own children: in a January 22, 1963, letter to her friend Olive Higgins Prouty, Plath writes that Frieda's tears each time Hughes leaves after a visit are like "a kind of mirror, utterly innocent, to my own sense of loss."

"Kindness" is shot through with imagery from Hughes's play. Picking up Sullivan's interaction with "She," in which he views "A pleasantly coloured land" through "A crystalline grain . . . of sugar," Plath's speaker in "Kindness" watches the colorful jewels of "Dame Kindness" reflected in the windows, as they become the proverbial rose-colored glasses she can no longer wear. Sugar, Dame Kindness tells her, is a cure-all. But sugar cures nothing. This is the point. Dame Kindness brings the speaker a cup of steaming tea, returning us to the rabbit catcher's hands, wrapped around a mug of tea while he waits, excited. Is the speaker being served a "little death"? Poetry pours from this speaker like blood; in exchange, Plath writes in the next lines, "You hand me two children, two roses." The blood/poetry that jets from Plath's speaker calls back again to Lawrence's penultimate stanza in "Rabbit Snared in the Night":

> It must be you who desire
> the intermingling of the black and monstrous
> fingers of Moloch
> in the blood-jets of your throat

Meanwhile, the juxtaposition of the two roses with the two children points back to the speaker, who is once more a rabbit (a hare?)

in a snare. Roses are symbolic, easily discarded by a mistress who can come and go as she likes. Children in "Kindness" transcend the symbolic to become the thing itself: there is "nothing so real" as their cries, cries the trapper can't hear, seduced, instead, by trapping, and impossible for the speaker to ignore. These are the "pegs too deep to uproot"—this is what ties the speaker forever to an impossible life.

"Kindness," however, was not the first time Plath transmuted Hughes's imagery from *Difficulty of a Bridegroom* into her own work. Hughes began drafting the play in May 1962, while he and Plath were still living together; that same month, Plath wrote "The Rabbit Catcher." At the time, Plath was also still making corrections to her novel *The Bell Jar*. On its surface, *The Bell Jar* appears to have nothing to do with Plath's marriage, or violence within it—it's the lightly fictionalized account of the summer of 1953, when Plath, having spent the month of June in New York City as a guest editor at *Mademoiselle* magazine, had a nervous breakdown and attempted suicide in August. The book begins in New York City, where Plath's avatar, Esther Greenwood, is struggling to get through a month she imagined as "a real whirl." Instead, she finds herself in scenes of repeated violence.

In one, Esther accompanies her friend Doreen on a spontaneous date with Lenny Shepherd, a famous disc jockey. Esther follows the couple back to Shepherd's apartment, where she watches Shepherd tear Doreen's dress off and assault her. The scene is a disturbing mirror of two entries in Plath's journals: the first entry details her first meeting with Ted Hughes, in which kisses are exchanged for bites, and Plath's hairband and earrings are torn from her head and ears. As Lenny and Doreen dance, Plath writes, "There is something demoralizing about watching two people get more and more crazy about each other, especially when you are the only extra person in the room." She compares the experience to "watching Paris from an express caboose heading in the opposite direction." Remember that Plath left for Paris the morning after she slept with Hughes for the first time—here she has written herself into the scene of her first encounter with Ted Hughes as a cool observer. The scene in *The Bell Jar* goes on:

> Then Lenny gave a terrible roar. I sat up. Doreen was hanging on to Lenny's left earlobe with her teeth.
> "Leggo, you bitch!"
> Lenny stooped, and Doreen went flying up on to his shoulder, and her glass sailed out of her hand in a long, wide arc and fetched up against the pine-panelling with a silly tinkle. Lenny was still roaring and whirling round so fast I couldn't see Doreen's face.

The scene mirrors a journal entry from June 11, 1958, describing a violent fight between the couple after an escalating series of disagreements. "I had a sprained thumb, Ted bloody claw-marks, for a week. . . . I remember hurling a glass . . . instead of shattering the glass rebounded and remained intact: I got hit and saw stars." Plath is certainly adapting violent scenes from her own life for the purpose of fiction. But she also seems to be mocking Hughes's characterizations of desire, love, and masculinity as he now saw them, in the late spring and early summer of 1962. In the second chapter of *The Bell Jar*—the drafts of which are absent from the archive at Smith College—Esther Greenwood watches as Doreen experiences the kind of violence Plath herself would claim, in letters and journal entries, at her husband's hands. Just then, Esther notices a jackrabbit mounted on Lenny Shepherd's wall. "Ran that one over in Las Vegas," he tells her, in a comical send-up of Hughes's gravely serious play where Sullivan runs over the hare.

Plath once wrote that the name Leonard would be a good choice for a character in her novel based on Ted Hughes—she found the name strong and sexual, just as she then found Hughes: "Leonard: Hero. God-man, because spermy." By the time she was revising *The Bell Jar*, she shrunk his mythological hare from *Difficulties of a Bridegroom* to a Las Vegas jackrabbit. "Spermy" Leonard became grimy, fast-talking Lenny, shepherding in a new era in Plath's work in which her colossal husband became a jailer, a vampire, a gigolo, a DJ.

THROUGHOUT HIS CAREER, HUGHES WAS afforded the luxury of what Diane Middlebrook lauds as his ability to "[lure] us into this labyrinth by hiding his secrets in plain sight." Plath hides almost nothing, and yet somehow, we are too often deaf and blind to what she reveals. This returns us, finally, to Miranda Fricker's idea that our "identity and social experience" are the things that create the lens through which we see the world. Fricker says that this is "an uncontroversial and even mundane point," but a radical one, nevertheless, when we consider the ways it affects women's interpretations of social experiences. In her footnotes to "Eating Her Words," Kate Manne writes that when the TV show *Big Little Lies* premiered, her friends had a debate about a central plot point, where a young boy strangles a young girl: would someone so young really do this? Manne knew that this act was possible. At the age of five, she reports, a male classmate strangled her with a piece of yarn. When she came back to consciousness, she was told that he strangled her because he was angry that she had beaten him in a spelling bee.

Manne's experience of having been strangled *because* she came out ahead of a boy she was competing with serves here as the foundation of her ability to read an experience of violence into women's masked language, or silence, about strangulation. Surviving intimate partner violence was, for me, the reason I returned to Plath's story, able to recognize elements of it I could never have otherwise seen. And yet misogyny, Manne reminds us, is "self-masking"—"trying to draw attention to the phenomenon is liable to give rise to more of it." I fear the same could be true here, that in trying to draw attention to Hughes's violence against Plath and Tennant, both women's accounts of it will be silenced, and I will eat my words. But silence, Manne reminds us, "is golden for the men who smother and intimidate women into not talking. . . . So, let us break it."

Let us tolerate no bystanding. Let us shriek.

Harriet the Spy

―⋘◆⋙―

"I want to know everything, everything," screeched Harriet suddenly, lying back and bouncing up and down on the bed. "Everything in the world, everything, everything. I will be a spy and know everything."

"It won't do you a bit of good to know everything if you don't do anything with it."

—Louise Fitzhugh, *Harriet the Spy*

HALFWAY THROUGH "THE DESCENT OF ARIEL," A 1977 THESIS by a woman named Elizabeth Hinchcliffe, there is a startling image. Xeroxed onto a page that also includes an image of the exterior of 23 Fitzroy Road is Sylvia Plath's suicide note. It reads "Please call Doctor Horder at PRI 3804." While reports of the note exist in every Plath biography on record, only Hinchcliffe's thesis contains an image of it. It is incontrovertible proof that Elizabeth Hinchcliffe made considerable progress toward an early, completed biography of Sylvia Plath.

She wasn't alone. In the 1970s, two other young women were conducting concurrent research alongside Hinchliffe. Lois Ames, a writer and close friend of Anne Sexton, had been appointed the official biographer by the Sylvia Plath estate and given a contract by Harper & Row, Plath's American publisher, but she seemed unable to make any progress. By contrast, Harriet Rosenstein, a newly minted PhD in literature from Brandeis University, was working throughout the 1970s to expand her dissertation on Plath into what she called a "critical biography." Where Ames was stymied in her work, Rosenstein flourished, tracking down interviews with Plath's mother, therapist, and closest friends.

And yet, none of their books were ever published, or even, to the best of our knowledge, completed, leaving behind three unfinished stories and the irrevocable sense that Plath's story is simultaneously over and endless, an open door in the universe that we can never quite click shut. What remains of the three women's work gives us something like a biography and a partial history of what it meant to work on Sylvia Plath at the height of her fame in the 1970s.

Hinchcliffe's thesis is the longest piece of sustained writing from the three, but it is all we have of her work. There are no research notes, leaving the question of whether or not she taped her interviews with Plath's friends and family a mystery. It seems likely that she did record the interviews, given the wealth of intimate details she includes about Sylvia Plath's relationship with Trevor Thomas, Plath's downstairs neighbor in London at the time of her death and the last person to see her alive. Thomas, whom Hinchcliffe calls "Phillip Evans" in her thesis, is described as "prim and rather fussy." He offers extensive observations about Plath's state of mind in the last months of her life, including the doubtful tidbit that Plath, who had lived independently since she was eighteen, "had never even heard of a plunger, so he found the plumber for her" when the pipes burst from the cold. Thomas describes the contortions of Plath's face when she was angry and the specific phrases she used when distressed. Once, he tells his young son, "That woman. . . . She's just becoming a nuisance. I'm through with her." His son replies, "She's very sad, Daddy, can't you see? She's so sad. It's in her eyes."

Hinchcliffe also wrote a play about Sylvia Plath, called *The*

Descent of Ariel. The play was performed at Cambridge University in the 1970s, and two copies—possibly the only in existence—are in the British Library's special collections. Much of the action consists of Sylvia Plath at her desk, shortly before her death, writing letters to Ruth Beuscher. Hinchcliffe's inclusion of material in Plath's actual letters to Ruth Beuscher—that she wanted to grow old and have purple hair, that she wanted Beuscher to fly to England to be with her—strongly suggest that Hinchcliffe interviewed Plath's psychiatrist. Other moments in the play indicate her intimate knowledge of Plath's life and death: at one point, the Plath character writes to Beuscher that Doctor Horder has given her sleeping pills, and she needs to know the correct dosage; she doesn't want to overdose.

Of Lois Ames's work, we have almost nothing. There is a letter in Ted Hughes's business correspondence with Harper & Row in which she justifies her lack of work on the biography she had been contracted to write, with the apparent blessing of the Hugheses, and another she wrote to Olwyn Hughes almost ten years later, which is a version of the same. Olwyn Hughes used Ames's name throughout the early 1970s as she turned down repeated requests for interviews from Harriet Rosenstein, telling her (and others) that the Plath estate had hired Ames as the official biographer and would only work with her. Ted Hughes, however, wrote to Aurelia Plath in 1966, telling her, "A full biography could not be attempted without your full cooperation and mine, and I refused mine."

Mrs. Plath underlined multiple sentences in this letter, as if to emphasize her agreement with Hughes that it was too soon for a biography. But Olwyn's letters indicate that Hughes was speaking out of both sides of his mouth. She fully endorses Ames, calling her a charming person, and for a time staunchly refuses to work with anyone else. Moreover, Ames visited England with Anne Sexton in July 1967 and met with Ted Hughes and Assia Wevill at Court Green. In a joint letter from the two of them to Sexton, Wevill tells her, "It was delightful to have you here, and Lois." Hughes writes, "It was so nice having you come down here—it completely redeemed the general unease I felt about Mrs. Ames."

Lois Ames was the daughter of Elizabeth Ames, the longtime director of the artists' colony Yaddo. Like Plath, Sexton, and Hinchcliffe, she grew up in Wellesley, the tony suburb of Boston where Aurelia moved her family when Plath was ten. She was Plath's classmate at both Wellesley High School and Smith College and one of Anne Sexton's best friends. At the time she was contracted to write the Plath biography, she was also appointed to work on a book about Sexton (Ames and Sexton taught together at McLean Hospital, where both Plath and Sexton were treated in their lifetimes). Despite a seven-year contract from Harper & Row and the stated full support of the Plath estate, she produced only the short "biographical sketch" of Plath published as an appendix to the first American publication of *The Bell Jar*. By 1973, Frances McCullough, Ames's editor, wrote to Ted Hughes that she had "completely given up on" her and that she "gathered" that Ames, on a research trip to England, had decided not to interview him. Ames died in 2022 at the age of ninety-one, having revealed little about her experience of working on a biography of Sylvia Plath, with the exception of one interview. In it, she told the poet Doug Holder:

> I was the first one to be asked to do the biography of Sylvia Plath. I had a contract with the family. Harper and Row was my publisher. It became increasingly difficult for me to do this, as other biographers have found out. And I finally decided for the sake of my own sanity and my family; that it was better to pay back the advance to Harper's. I always felt it was a wise decision.

By 1978, Olwyn Hughes, who by then was the face of the Sylvia Plath estate, had given up on Lois's book. As the expiration date for Ames's contract approached, Olwyn wrote to the person she considered the best choice, Harriet Rosenstein. Olwyn Hughes had met Rosenstein when she visited England on the first of at least two research trips related to her work on Sylvia Plath. At the time, Rosenstein was working on a dissertation for her PhD in literature at Brandeis University, and Olwyn was happy to assist her.

Once the dissertation became a biography, Olwyn changed her tune. But she remained impressed by Rosenstein's intelligent approach to scholarship and her work on Plath. She considered Rosenstein the logical choice to pick up where Ames had left off. In a series of letters from the summer of 1978, Olwyn's tone is—for her—unusually empathetic and generous. She tells Rosenstein, "After all the solid work you have done I am sure you will want to go back and finish it sometime. I do hope so." In the same letter, she invited Rosenstein to come and see Sylvia's notebooks. Olwyn's 1978 letters to Rosenstein asking her to take over the project are held by Emory University; with one exception, they appear to have gone unanswered.

Rosenstein's archive was purchased by Emory and became available for research in January 2020, after Smith College was declared the legal owner of the crown jewel of her Plath research, Plath's fourteen letters to Ruth Beuscher. Yet the remainder of Rosenstein's research is an equally fascinating view into learning about Sylvia Plath from those who knew her best, as well as proof that the art of biography leaves us, minimally, with two stories—the life of the biographer's subject and the story of how the book gets written. Or, in the case of these three women, doesn't.

Rosenstein talked to everyone she could and by the early 1970s had gone rogue, ignoring Olwyn's requests to stop her research. Having completed her dissertation, she published a long article on Plath in *Ms.* magazine and was seized on as the new It-girl of literary journalism. Despite the Hugheses' refusal to back her, other people, equally powerful in the publishing industry, did, and before long, Rosenstein had a contract with Knopf to write a biography of Sylvia Plath. She bought a reel-to-reel tape recorder and began recording long interviews with Plath's friends, including luminaries like W. S.

Merwin and, according to chatter at the end of her recording with Merwin, Adrienne Rich—the latter interview is, sadly, missing from the archive.

The taped interviews comprise much of Rosenstein's archive, a time capsule of writers, scholars, doctors, and artists in 1970s England and America. Children flit in and out of the interviews with Plath's friends Clarissa Roche and Elizabeth Sigmund and her former psychiatrist, Ruth Beuscher, and are sent to the shop for cigarettes and cans of tuna. Beuscher begins her interview by telling Rosenstein, "I never met a Smith girl who didn't have something wrong with her." W. S. Merwin—who later wrote to Hughes that he never spoke to a single biographer except "a very ambitious rather heady young woman from Cambridge"—chats quietly with Rosenstein in his Manhattan apartment as the train grumbles by. Al Alvarez gets drowned out by a jet passing through the London sky.

Rosenstein gathered hours of taped material from Plath's London doctor, John Horder, who saw Plath on the last night of her life and pronounced her dead the following day. She spoke at length to Aurelia Plath and Ted Hughes and stayed at Court Green. No records of the stay exist, except for a brief moment when Rosenstein, speaking alone into her tape recorder, says of Ted Hughes, "I'm angry . . . he wasn't nice to me . . . why did he mislead me? He did, too." Plath's Devon friend Elizabeth Sigmund tells Rosenstein that Olwyn has "trunks full of Sylvia." Sigmund trusted her enough to tell her stories about Ted Hughes and Sylvia Plath so intimate, damaging, or both, that the tape recorder suddenly shuts off—the *click* of the gap in the archive before it resumes and Sigmund tells Rosenstein another charming story of her beloved friend Sylvia Hughes. When Sigmund turned thirty-four, she says, Sylvia arrived at her house with a homemade cake bearing thirty-five candles. *One to grow on*, Plath told her, a story that sheds warm light on Plath's "Ariel," a poem with thirty-one lines, which she composed on her thirtieth birthday.

None of these women ever spoke about their experience doing

pioneering early research on Sylvia Plath, and their research was, for the most part, lost. Rosenstein sat on her work until she put it up for sale in 2017 but has never spoken publicly about it. With the exception of the brief biographical sketch of Plath, Ames's work is either held privately by her family or gone. Hinchcliffe's thesis is in the world, as are her letters with Al Alvarez, which are in the British Library, but as to the rest of her research and writing, there is nothing but rumors—it was lost, depending on the source, in a fire or a flood. Where her notes to her thesis should be, there is a résumé instead, which you read with what Sylvia Plath called "the shock of recognition": Hinchcliffe is not just, like Plath, from Wellesley. Her academic life is a mirror of Sylvia Plath's—Smith College, then Newnham College, Cambridge, for graduate study in English literature. Like Plath, Hinchcliffe won a guest editorship at *Mademoiselle*, the event that inspired *The Bell Jar*. While at Newnham, like Plath, she joined the Dramatical Society and acted in plays. While living in Wellesley, like Plath, she wrote for the local paper.

Like Plath, these women all started off on a narrow path. But Plath broke away from it. She married an English poet, left academic life, and journeyed underground to write "the best poems of [her] life," and died a lonely death that has been transformed into a spectacular one, designed, according to hostile sources, to garner her work incredible attention and inflict agony on Ted Hughes. It's possible that Hinchcliffe, Ames, and Rosenstein saw the writing of a great biography on Plath as the pinnacle of that narrow path. They also may have realized that to write that book, they themselves would have to break away from the path and journey underground. Like many of Plath's fans, they may have understandably believed the foolish story they were told, that it was poetry that killed her, and they can hardly be blamed for this—the people telling it were powerful men, some of whom these three women met, and dined with, and exchanged letters with, and accepted favors from, and were made, briefly, confidantes. They met their children and their second wives. They stayed in their London and New York City flats and their country homes. They learned, maybe, in body and spirit, what killed Sylvia Plath.

THE ABSENCE OF A FINISHED BOOK from the period less than a decade after Plath's death constitutes a massive gap in the Plath archive, the largest that exists outside of her missing diaries and her novel-in-progress, *Doubletake*, which she was working on at the time of her death. The voices of Ames, Hinchcliffe, and Rosenstein are, for the most part, swallowed into history. But Plath continues to speak. Like her heroine Lady Lazarus, she calls and calls, moving through time. We go back and back, looking for more of her to bring into our present moment. But the history of Plath can no longer be, if ever it was, only hers. When we go back to Plath, we go back to these three women. We are more like them than we are like Sylvia Plath—or anyway, I am. "I shall be a heroine of the peripheral," says the Second Voice in *Three Women*, Plath's 1962 radio play about three women who experience different pregnancies: a desired one, a miscarriage, and one that results in a young woman at university giving up her child for adoption.

To be fully immersed in her life was Plath's greatest pleasure and aim, especially since she knew so well the other side of that particular coin—to want, as Esther Greenwood says so memorably of her breakdown in *The Bell Jar*, "to do everything once and for all and be through with it." Writing about her, we become the heroines on the periphery and stand, "accused by . . . the white mute faces / Of unanswered letters, coffined in a letter case." Plath did not only love to be immersed in her daily life, she committed as much of it to paper as she possibly could and dedicated her life to transforming that record into a poetics that changed the way we understand the art. As writers on her, we hang in the balance of that transformation, struggling to reconcile the domestic "holes in the heels of socks" with the acts of flight she executed, in her last months, with seeming ease.

This is the terror in writing about Plath—you have to get everything right, but there is so much to get wrong. And there is the risk of becoming the woman in the unanswered letter, the one who gave up the writing, whether, like Ames, in an act of self-protection or for reasons we may never understand. The temptation to believe that the world needs one less book on Sylvia Plath is strong. But like my predecessor Jacqueline Rose, like the Third Voice in *Three Women*, I am haunted by this work. It will not give me up:

> I see her in my sleep, my red, terrible girl.
> She is crying through the glass that separates us.
> She is crying, and she is furious.

I first read about Harriet Rosenstein in Carl Rollyson's 2013 Plath biography *American Isis: The Life and Art of Sylvia Plath*, the first book to discuss her work at length. Janet Malcolm mentions Rosenstein in *The Silent Woman* in a single passing reference to her work on Plath's relationship with her mother. This belied Malcolm's real interest in talking to Rosenstein. In her recorded interviews with Clarissa Roche and Al Alvarez from the early 1990s, Malcolm pumps them for information about Rosenstein, but they have none, except to say that she was brilliant, the most astute researcher they spoke to in the years since Plath's death and ensuing fame. Rollyson describes Rosenstein, whom he became familiar with by reading letters about her in Frances McCullough's papers, as "securing Sylvia's letters on the sly, interviewing Dr. Beuscher, hiding recording devices under a sofa, and in general 'running circles' around Lois Ames." Rollyson, a retired professor and literary and political biographer with over twenty-five books to his name, including four on Plath, writes that Rosenstein, who had a cool critical stance on every faction of Plath's life and work, was in "a prime position to write a truly independent biography."

Rosenstein became a focal point of my work on Plath in the spring of 2017, when she attempted to sell Plath's letters to Ruth Beuscher for almost a million dollars. The *Guardian* ran an article about the sale, "Unseen Sylvia Plath Letters Claim Domestic Abuse by Ted Hughes," by a writer named Danuta Kean. Full of inconsistencies, most of which are easily fact-checked, Kean's article seems intended to discredit Plath's claims in the letters, which Kean had not read beyond the snippets available on the book dealer's website. A casual reader of Kean's article would not only doubt Plath's claims of violence; they would come away with the idea that, well before she wrote the letters, Sylvia Plath was always an unstable liar, an unreliable narrator par excellence. Of Plath's October 21, 1962, claim that Hughes openly wished her dead, Kean writes:

> The extent of [Plath and Hughes's] estrangement during this period is revealed in another letter in the collection, dated 21 October 1962, in which Plath claimed to Barnhouse that Hughes told her directly that he wished she was dead. Though Plath had a history of depression and self-harm, and had attempted to kill herself in 1953, she didn't reveal the full extent of her struggles with mental health to Hughes until some time after their marriage.

Here, apparent straightforward reporting ("Plath claimed to Barnhouse that Hughes told her directly that he wished she was dead") precedes an immediate move to Plath's history of suicidality—a strange transition unless you are of the mindset that Plath's mental health "made" Hughes want her dead, "made" her lie to her therapist about Hughes's behavior, or both. And if we believe Plath was dishonest with Hughes in the past ("she didn't reveal the full extent of her struggles with mental health"), well, what else would she lie about? Because the story of Hughes and Plath is so famous, so widely known, and Hughes is widely understood as the ferryman who braved the River Lethe to bring it to us—remember Frieda Hughes's note at the start of her mother's first volume of letters that it is only because of her father that anyone is interested in her mother in the first place—any dishonesty Plath might have shown toward

Hughes is understood by extension as dishonesty with her readers. If she was dishonest with him once, Kean seems to ask, why should we believe her now?

This line of discussion about Plath's dishonesty with Hughes was picked up almost verbatim by the *Irish Times*. But this claim of Plath's dishonesty was itself false. According to Ted Hughes's own accounts, Sylvia Plath told him the story of her 1953 breakdown the first time they slept together, during their second meeting in March of 1956. Plath had a visible scar on her face from her 1953 suicide attempt, which people often asked her about—and almost as often, she was forthcoming about its origins. Peter Davison, the longtime poetry editor at the *Atlantic* and one of Plath's boyfriends in the summer of 1955, writes about the night Plath told him of her breakdown in his memoir, *Half-Remembered*. Hughes refers to a similar incident in the poem "18 Rugby Street," one of the first poems in *Birthday Letters*, writing, "In the roar of soul your scar told me— / . . . How you had tried to kill yourself." Jonathan Bate notes the same, writing that on the night of their first sexual encounter, Plath told Hughes about her 1953 suicide attempt.

Kean's article describes Plath's claims of abuse as novel, and shocking, but by the time of its publication, Plath scholars Gail Crowther and Peter K. Steinberg had already published their book *These Ghostly Archives*, in which they analyze different mysteries surrounding Plath's work in archival collections. One such collection is Frances McCullough's papers at the University of Maryland. It includes documents from the summer of 1974, when McCullough spent time in Devon with Ted and Carol Hughes, working on *Letters Home*. A short handwritten note by McCullough describes a night when Hughes, discovering that Aurelia Plath had included letters in the book about Hughes's behavior at the end of his marriage to Plath, became distressed and insisted on taking McCullough out to dinner. On the way to the restaurant, he described to McCullough how he would have to "[slap Plath] out of her rages." But slapping Plath was "no good," McCullough writes with no apparent guile, as though slapping an angry woman was a standard cure, with Hughes the savvy film noir hero. "And once," during one of these episodes, McCullough continues, Sylvia "got herself a black eye."

The day after the *Guardian* ran Kean's piece, they added an addendum from Carol Hughes, Ted's widow, on behalf of his estate:

> The claims allegedly made by Sylvia Plath in unpublished letters to her former psychiatrist, suggesting that she was beaten by her husband, Ted Hughes, days before she miscarried their second child are as absurd as they are shocking to anyone who knew Ted well.

One could argue that Sylvia knew Ted as well as anyone. But what the Beuscher letters made clear was that the image we had of Ted Hughes was at least as distorted as the one we had of Sylvia Plath. Rosenstein's archive would force a reevaluation of the famous couple's relationship and the last six months of Plath's life, for which her letters to Ruth Beuscher now stand as one of the only primary sources available to us, since Plath's journals from the time are gone. How was it, I wondered, that they had disappeared for so long?

As relayed in the *Guardian*, Ken Lopez, the antiquarian bookseller in question, was selling an archive from Rosenstein, a woman he called Plath's "putative" biographer. The collection was blocked from sale when Smith College, Plath's alma mater and home to the world's largest collection of her work, sued, claiming the letters in the archive belonged to them. It seems that Ruth Beuscher, Plath's psychiatrist and the recipient of the letters, had willed her papers to Smith College. But the copyright of the letters would always, by law, go to Frieda Hughes, Sylvia's daughter and only living descendant. Smith College settled the suit, and the letters were deposited there for research use by the general public. Frieda Hughes agreed to publish them in Plath's second volume of *Letters*, a process she detailed in her foreword to that book. What was left of the archive went up for sale.

As for Rosenstein herself, she is still living in Massachusetts. For the majority of her life, she practiced clinical psychology and social work, despite completing a PhD on Sylvia Plath at Brandeis University in 1973. Her dissertation is called *Sylvia Plath, 1932–1952*. It is described in archival documents as a "critical biography" and seems to have been work that synthesized biographical research with readings of Plath's poetry and prose. I say "seems to have been" because the dissertation has never been made available to the public. Carl Rollyson, in his notes to *The Last Days of Sylvia Plath* (2020), writes that Brandeis University archivist Maggie McNeely told him she "[guesses] Harriet asked for that status." In the same 2017 email, she told Rollyson, "I happen to have heard from Harriet last week," and her dissertation "contained a lot of personal information and therefore was allowed to be seen by permission only." McNeely concluded by telling Rollyson that no further records exist of how, or why, Brandeis allowed this status or allowed Rosenstein to remove her work from the university altogether.

In 2020, Harriet Rosenstein sold the remainder of her archive to Emory University. It includes, as far as we know, most of what she had gathered when she was working on her dissertation and, later, her biography of Plath, with notable exceptions. The most notable of these exceptions are described in emails, included in the archive, between Harriet Rosenstein and Frieda Hughes. In them, Rosenstein and Hughes, who have evidently just spoken on the phone, discuss their prior meeting forty-six years earlier, when Frieda Hughes was a child and Rosenstein visited Court Green as part of her research. Rosenstein tells Hughes that she will type up a transcription of the notebook she kept during the Court Green visit and give it to Hughes. Hughes never confirms receipt of the Court Green transcription, but does tell Rosenstein she received "my mother's taped interview."

As strange as it is that Hughes is in the position of thanking a stranger for her mother's letters and psychiatric records, reading the drop-down list of file folders on the left-hand side of Harriet Rosenstein's printed emails is stranger. The folders are titled "Plath" and "Plath edits #7"—names not dissimilar to the folders I maintain on my own desktop. It is impossible to look at these images and not wonder if Harriet Rosenstein is still at work on a book about Sylvia Plath. Working closely with Rosenstein's archive, a twin mystery emerges: First, who was Sylvia Plath? Second, who is Harriet Rosenstein, and why didn't she finish her book?

Any evidence of the scholarly dissertation swiftly gives way to personal, highly subjective biographical research about a woman few people seem to have known well, but everyone knew a little. This foreshadows our own contemporary understanding of Plath—a handful of experts know who she was in reality, while the world over understands her via the shorthand of cultural signs: a witch, a myth, a Zombie Queen heralding the darkness inherent to man—or, more accurately, woman.

Rosenstein's long-forgotten archive has no lack of fuel for this mythmaking. Despite her stated intent to, as she wrote in a 1972 article in *Ms.* magazine, "demystify" Sylvia Plath, she has spent a great deal of time discussing witchcraft and astrology with Plath's contemporaries. Rosenstein's archive contains a marble composition notebook about her time with Ruth Beuscher, dated "Jan.-June '74" on the cover, and Rosenstein has inserted a typed note describing their time together, during which Beuscher taught her Tarot cards and took her to see a "professional astrologer to help me 'find' Sylvia Plath"—"I figured it was worth a shot." According to the note, obviously typed many years after the notebook was kept, Beuscher told Rosenstein she was a "white witch." At one point during the second hour of her interview with Elizabeth Sigmund, Plath's best friend from Devon, Rosenstein leans into the microphone and says, in a hushed tone I can only describe as deadly serious, that she knows of several people who believe Sylvia Plath is speaking through them from beyond the grave.

When Rosenstein's *Ms.* article was published in September 1972, she became something of a (now-forgotten) sensation, as the article

Harriet Rosenstein at the home of the photographer Elsa Dorfman, 1974. Dorfman photographed Rosenstein for her book *Elsa's Housebook: A Woman's Photojournal*. (Used with permission of Elsa Dorfman's estate.)

went the 1970s version of viral. Anne Sexton wrote to Rosenstein, "I was absolutely stunned by your piece in MS. . . . so beautifully felt and so well-written, I wanted to write you a fan letter." Rosenstein's correspondence from this time is filled not just with fan letters, but with letters from high-profile editors and publishers dangling financial carrots. John Leonard, then editor of the *New York Times Book Review*, sent Rosenstein an October 1973 telegram asking her to review several books "immediately." Michael Denneny, of Macmillan, wrote to Rosenstein's editor at *Ms.* in October 1972, "If [Rosenstein] needs a book publisher, I would be very interested." Peter Davison, who Rosenstein met during her research, began working with an editor at Little, Brown to try to offer a contract for her biography of Plath; it's not clear exactly why, but eventually, Rosenstein passed on their offer and signed with Knopf. Her contract there, with a delivery date of 1975, is included in the archive. According to her tax forms, Knopf gave Rosenstein an advance against royalties of $12,500—an incredible sum, back then, for an unknown author with nothing but one article to her name.

The Hughes family quickly viewed Rosenstein as suspect. Frances McCullough called her "Harriet the Spy." Olwyn Hughes acted in characteristic fashion to try to stop her from gathering any further information about Sylvia Plath, writing to Rosenstein on October 13, 1970, that while she had "enjoyed our pleasant meeting . . . Ted Hughes has already agreed that Lois Ames will be Sylvia Plath's biographer and that she has exclusive right to our help and also exclusive access to unpublished material." The problem was, the Hugheses seemed unaware of just how much unpublished material there was. Traces of Plath's life already resembled the decentralized archive described by Crowther and Steinberg in *These Ghostly Archives*, with her letters and papers scattered throughout the United Kingdom and the United States. And while copyright belonged to the estate, physical copies of letters belonged to the recipient.

This last became a complicated ethical question when, in 1970, Rosenstein began interviewing Ruth Barnard Beuscher, Plath's former psychiatrist, about her relationship with Sylvia Plath. While the nature of Beuscher's relationship with Plath was obvious enough at the beginning of Plath's treatment in McLean Hospital in 1953–54, by 1962 it was more complicated, since Plath was in England and Beuscher Massachusetts. Their relationship was reduced to letters, but Plath seems to have held on to the belief that Ruth was her doctor until the end of her life. Throughout nine of the fourteen letters in Rosenstein's possession, as Plath pours her heart out to Beuscher about the disintegration of her marriage to Ted Hughes, she begs her: *I need help. Let me pay you.* Her letter from Friday, July 20, 1962, begins "[P]lease charge me some money." Her letter of Monday, July 30, 1962, opens, "I do hope you will agree to a few paid letter sessions." On September 4, 1962, Plath asks again for a response to her request for "paid letter sessions."

Beuscher did eventually write back—two letters from the time are held at Smith College, one dated September 17, 1962, the next the twenty-sixth of the same month. She tells her the "paid business" is "not silly, but irrelevant." *Are you asking me for psychiatric help or something more?* Beuscher asks Plath, before advising her to divorce Hughes, get a good nanny, and, in a line Hughes hated and used verbatim in his poem "Howls and Whispers," "Keep him out of your bed." In America, Beuscher tells her, sleeping with one's husband after the husband has been unfaithful is seen as legally condoning the affair. Both letters end with Beuscher expressing her frank love for Sylvia, with the first closing, "I have often thought, if I 'cure' no one else in my whole career, you are enough. I love you."

Beuscher's letters have a distinct tonal difference from Plath's. They offer practical advice, but little psychiatric counsel, which is what Plath explicitly seeks in her letters to the woman she saw as her doctor. Writing on October 21, she says, "My relation to Ted was . . . gravely regressed. . . . I was calling on him to be a father & hating myself for it." Plath uses the language of psychiatry, of analysis, which she learned, partly, from her sessions with Beuscher. We know this definitively, now, because Rosenstein's archive includes Beuscher reading her session notes from Plath's appointments (from 1954 and 1959) directly into Rosenstein's tape recorder.

As the recipient of the letters, Ruth Beuscher owned them outright—but did her status as Plath's psychiatrist preclude her from sharing them with a biographer? Olwyn Hughes thought so. She had been in touch with Dr. Horder, who had shown her a letter Dr. Beuscher had written to him, letting him know that she had been speaking at length with a young scholar named Harriet Rosenstein. The Rosenstein papers include a September 15, 1970, letter from Olwyn to Ruth Beuscher, asking her to stop discussing Sylvia with Harriet Rosenstein. That letter contains a telling handwritten annotation. Where Olwyn has typed "I know that [Rosenstein's] work is in connection with her studies at Brandeis but I know too that her real wish and intention is to write an autobiography," she has inked out "auto." In the margin, she has handwritten in black ink, "Interesting slip—I think this is about right in Harriet's case!" Soon enough, Beuscher would develop a close relationship with Rosenstein, one the biographer Carl Rollyson characterized in *The Last Days of Sylvia Plath* as "[Beuscher] continuing a relationship with Plath that at times had seemed simply too painful to bear."

Already, by 1970, Rosenstein was understood by some of those closest to Plath's life and work as a stand-in for the writer herself, someone so connected to Plath, it unnerved them. When Rosenstein met Wilbury Crockett, Sylvia's influential high school English teacher, she went back repeatedly for visits. They sat by the fire, talking and drinking sherry—just like Sylvia, who in her journals described doing exactly this. When Rosenstein wrote that her dissertation contained "personal information," did she exclusively mean personal information connected to Sylvia Plath? Or had it become her story as well? And if it had become her story, was this the reason, or one of the reasons, she decided against the completion or publication of her book?

There is no mention of Harriet Rosenstein in any of the Plath biographies from the 1980s and '90s. Rosenstein appears to have published nothing beyond her article in *Ms.* and a handful of reviews. The only available material from her dissertation is her prospectus, a draft of which is included in her archive. The prospectus contains compelling arguments about Plath's life and work and material from Ted Hughes on his late wife's poetry that has appeared nowhere else in print. Hughes's thoughts can only have come from Rosenstein's 1969 visit to Court Green, but the prospectus offers no further information about this trip, and it is missing its notes, in what must have been an act of deliberate removal—Rosenstein was granted her PhD, and a prospectus without sources would never have been approved. Even in archival material—outside of her own—about Plath, Rosenstein is a shadowy figure, appearing rarely in Hughes's papers.

So, what happened to her? And what happened to her book? A December 10, 1991, letter from Olwyn Hughes to Janet Malcolm contains a possible clue to Rosenstein's mysterious disappearance:

> Apparently Harriet had a big breakdown about [1976], and when I again wrote her . . . that we could go ahead with . . . her biog.[*sic*] . . . I got only a baffled little note from her. . . . Peter Davison reported seeing her, much changed. . . . She is of course the girl who could have done a first class book on Plath.

The same archive contains a handwritten note by Janet Malcolm, on *New Yorker* stationery, that reads, "Harriet Rosenstein 'in insane asylum.'"

Jillian Becker's 2002 memoir about Sylvia Plath also contains a brief, strange reference to Rosenstein:

> In 1973 a woman from Boston found me and asked me to tell her what I remembered about Sylvia's last days . . . [for] *Ms.* . . . [W]hen I heard how wrong [what she knew] was, I couldn't resist the temptation to put her right. . . . [F]or a time . . . we corresponded. I sent her a copy of [Sylvia's] autopsy. When I went to New York to see my publishers about a book . . . , I took a bus to . . . the would-be biographer and I talked about Sylvia again. On my return to London I wrote to her once more, but received no answer. . . . [M]onths . . . passed without a line from her or a copy of *Ms.* with her expected piece in it. . . . I . . . was told that she'd had a "breakdown," was in a psychiatric hospital, had given up her intention to write about Sylvia, and earnestly entreated others who were planning to write about her to do the same "or they too would go crazy."

Becker's timeline here is off. Her letters to and from Harriet Rosenstein and Rosenstein's interview with her are part of the Rosenstein Papers (no tapes of this interview exist). All of these documents postdate Rosenstein's *Ms.* magazine article, which ran in 1972 and which, in one letter, Becker praises and asks for permission to quote from in her own work on Plath. But Becker did send Rosenstein a copy of Plath's coroner's report, which was delivered to Becker by Mr. Goodchild, a coroner, with whom she discussed, "over tea and biscuits, murder, suicide, road-accidents, and the old days of hanging in our local Pentonville prison." Becker notes that the coroner's report states on the second page that Plath died with "recent bruises on right forehead and the scalp in right occipital region" and wonders to Rosenstein if Plath had banged her head as she was dying, attempting to get up. Heather Clark also posits this in *Red Comet*, but Goodchild insisted this was impossible, stating that Plath would have been paralyzed by the gas within thirty seconds, unable to move at all.

Rosenstein seized on the bruises, suggesting Plath had deliberately banged her head as a ritualistic act, an effort to mimic the events of her 1953 suicide attempt, during which she scraped her face on the concrete and was left with a scar. Becker's take dispensed with mystical symmetries: she wondered if Hughes had been there that night and hit Plath, since Becker hadn't noticed any bruises on Plath's forehead the weekend prior to Plath's death, which Plath had spent at Becker's home. Hughes wasn't with Plath the last night of her life, but the estranged couple had been together Friday afternoon, February 8. Since Plath wore a heavy bang in the last months of her life, any bruises on her right forehead could conceivably have been obscured. She also wrote a poem called "Contusion" on February 4, 1963, a week before her death, full of genuinely terrifying images of bruised flesh and the end of one's life, which ends with the line, "The mirrors are sheeted."

Writing to Plath biographer Linda Wagner-Martin on April 1, 1987, Plath's friend Clarissa Roche struggled to recall what Plath had told her of her marriage during Roche's November 1962 visit to Court Green: " 'Contusion,' she writes "might be Ted's blow. . . . The tales I've forgotten have much to do with brutality."

There is no way to know if there was a final episode of violence between Hughes and Plath in the last days of her life. But it is telling that Jillian Becker, who knew Plath well, thought the possibility distinct enough to put it in writing to a biographer whose work she took seriously, under contract with a major publisher. It points to the ways that in the first fifteen years after Plath's death, her friends and family attempted to speak on her behalf to researchers. When that information failed to enter the public record, whether because of neglect, theft, loss, intimidation, excision, or suppression, the idea that Plath had once been a victim of intimate partner violence was treated like a foggy, distant memory or a rumor.

When Plath's letters to Ruth Beuscher reemerged in 2017, much of the accompanying discourse leaned toward *Why now?*, the classic trope to silence survivors of sexual assault and domestic violence: Why wait? Why now? What is she up to? Harriet Rosenstein's archive stands as a stark reminder of a period when Plath as a victim of IPV was a recent reality, not a distant rumor. But the archive is the present and the past—a lame tautology, but a tautology nonetheless. Rosenstein's papers, so long unseen by any eyes but hers, return us to a time when a version of Plath's story was emerging. Fifty years later, that story is still coming out.

IN HER 2017 *HUFFINGTON POST* piece "Good Girls: How Powerful Men Get Away with Sexual Predation," Kate Manne writes of the ways women's silence in the wake of sexual assault allows male perpetrators to move along as though they have not committed sexual violence—or to be exonerated from it entirely. Manne's essay ultimately functions as a moral imperative to report sexual violence, but also points out that absolute silence rarely accompanies an assault. Writing about the "mandatory reporting" clause of Title IX—the part of the law requiring faculty and staff at American educational institutions to make an official record any time a student discloses a campus sexual assault to them—she responds to the philosopher Martha Nussbuam, who questions the wisdom of the mandate in her lecture "Sexual Violence: Accountability in a Culture of Celebrity."

Nussbaum fears that laws like mandatory reporting discourage victims from disclosing their assaults to trusted confidantes out of a terror of setting legal wheels in motion, with the law inevitably on the side of powerful men: "Law cannot fix this problem," Nussbaum writes. Given the aspersions typically cast upon a victim's character when they do speak up, this is a valid fear. In the long march toward his conviction, Bill Cosby filed multiple defamation suits against his accusers. Among them, notably, was supermodel Beverly Johnson, who wrote about her alleged assault by Cosby for *Vanity Fair* in 2014. In his suit, Cosby alleged that Johnson only wrote about the incident to resuscitate a dying career and that she "played" her allegation "to the hilt"—language of gross sexual innuendo, something Manne would surely attribute to the way violent men, faced with these scenarios, cleverly turn themselves into the victims of attacks they perpetrated.

In her lifetime, Plath faced a version of this. Jonathan Bate reports that just prior to her death, Ted Hughes brought a note to Plath's Fitzroy Road flat that threatened legal action if she didn't "stop spreading lies." Plath killed herself five days after this encounter.

Unlike Nussbaum, Manne argues that mandatory reporters should make an official record of a rape and that rape victims almost always tell at least one person what happened to them, consequences be damned: "People spill; they spill over," she writes at the top of a bulleted list of reasons in support of mandatory reporting. Without these official reports, especially at or near the time of the event, the possibility of action, in the form of consequences for the perpetrator—not to mention the likelihood that the victim stands a chance of being believed—practically disappears.

Manne's *Huffington Post* article debuted a month before the world learned about Sylvia Plath's fourteen letters to Ruth Beuscher, just as the #MeToo movement was gaining traction. Like the victims Manne describes, Plath's claim in her letter of September 22, 1962, that Ted Hughes had "beat [her] up physically," an event she said caused her to miscarry the couple's second child, was read by many as both opportunistic and too little, too late. This was a common refrain in the case of Cosby's victims, with the press often ignoring the reality that many of those women had come forward, either to friends, family, or the police, years earlier. Plath's second volume of *Letters* includes a foreword by her only survivor, Frieda Hughes, in which she describes the agony of reading her mother's narration of the deterioration of her parents' marriage. When it came time for Frieda Hughes to address Plath's allegation that Hughes had beaten her, Frieda wrote, "This assault had not warranted a mention in [an earlier letter to Beuscher]. . . . But . . . what woman would want to paint her exiting husband in anything other than the darkest colours?" In other words, why hadn't her mother written about it in earlier letters to her therapist? *Why now?*

THIS RHETORICAL QUESTION IS all too frequently aimed at survivors who come forward after the fact. In the same way that Beverly Johnson (and later, fellow supermodel Janice Dickinson) was seen as motivated to lie about Cosby raping her by a need to reinvigorate her failing career, Frieda Hughes attributes her own mother's claims of domestic battery at the hands of her father as alternately false or greatly exaggerated. "What, I asked myself, would qualify as a physical beating? A push? A shove? A swipe?" she writes. And when we lie, we need a reason to lie—hence Frieda Hughes's reasoning that her mother, angry at her husband's infidelity, would need to "paint him" in the worst possible light and so lie about him beating her so badly that she lost their child.

Similar reactions accompanied the publication of Plath's second volume of letters, with some reviewers calling Plath a liar outright and others claiming her writing to be the manipulative attention seeking of a woman we have long seen as an unreliable narrator. Given that doubt is cast on Plath's word at the front of her own book, and by her own daughter, this is unsurprising. In his review of Plath's second volume of letters for the *New Statesmen*, Craig Raine quotes Plath, writing to Beuscher, that Hughes "beat [her] up physically." Raine "[detects] in that otiose 'physically' the anxious pedantry of the perjurer."

As we saw in the previous chapter, Kate Manne, reading Kristie Dotson, extends Dotson's definition of testimonial smothering to the ways police officers, meeting women victims of domestic violence, are unable to hear, or understand, how they testify to their experience. This frequently leads to no police intervention on behalf of the victims. Plath, it seems, never contacted the police about any of her experiences with Hughes. But there are many ways to police someone's language—or behavior. Might I suggest that Plath, even in death, is policed by a good old boys club that amounts, in word and deed, to the poetry cops?

This policing is another example of what Miranda Fricker calls "collective systematic cognitive failings" about the experiences of victims of "long-term domestic violence." Fricker writes of how "a given misinterpretation stems from a collective failure to understand the nature of some type of social experience," which leads to "hermeneutical injustice." This is evident in Jonathan Bate's reading of the violence in the Plath-Hughes marriage. To be wholly fair, Bate's biography of Hughes debuted prior to the Plath's letters to Ruth Beuscher. But Bate did have access to McCullough's description of Hughes giving Plath a black eye in 1961, which he quotes in *The Unauthorised Life*.

Reading Susan Fromberg Schaeffer's *Poison*, which includes the story of the beating and resultant miscarriage, Bate casts aspersions on Schaeffer's decision to include the story, which he disbelieves: the "tender" writing Plath did about Hughes after her miscarriage "give[s] the lie to the claim," he writes. He is apparently unaware of what experts in IPV call the "honeymoon" period in the cycle of abuse, or the period after physical violence when the abuser showers the victim with affection. Bate decries Schaeffer's inclusion of this story in her novel because "the accusation feeds the myth of Ted himself as the monster. That is the pernicious aspect of the book. At times, *Poison* is itself a kind of poison." This is another way that we "exonerate men," as Kate Manne writes. Abusers are monsters; Ted Hughes is not a monster; therefore, Ted Hughes was not abusive.

Manne's most potent example of this is the so-called Stanford rape case, in which Brock Turner was convicted of raping Chanel Miller (then the anonymous "Emily Doe") but received a sentence so light that the ensuing public outrage caused the judge in question to be removed from the bench. One way that Turner's lawyers achieved this light sentence was to solicit character witnesses who spoke and wrote to the judge on his behalf. One young woman wrote that Turner's sexual assault of Miller bore no resemblance to "real" rape, between two strangers: "That is a rapist. . . . I know . . . that Brock is not one of those people." "[In] all my life with my father, I'd never seen this side of him," Frieda Hughes writes in her foreword: "in my mind . . . my father was not the wife-beater that some would wish to imagine he was."

Manne quotes Chanel Miller's victim impact statement, which describes how, in light of the fact that she had no memory of the rape (which took place while she was unconscious), Turner's version of events—which included the claim that an unconscious Miller had orgasmed during the assault—were taken during the trial as the factual narrative. "I was warned," Miller wrote, "he is going to get to write the script. . . . His attorney constantly reminded the jury, the only one we can believe is Brock, because she doesn't remember." In the wake of Sylvia Plath's suicide, Ted Hughes famously "[got] to write the script" of his life with Sylvia Plath. Anything he remembered, we remembered. What he forgot was thought to be lost. If anyone might have rewritten that script, it was Harriet Rosenstein, who said as much in her email to the poet, Plath scholar, and *New Yorker* writer Dan Chiasson in 2018. Chiasson had written that Hughes assaulted Plath in his *New Yorker* review of Plath's second volume of letters. Rosenstein thanked him, telling him he had written much of what she would have, "had I been able to." Why wasn't she able to? What prevented her?

When I wrote to ask her about her work she responded, in August of 2021, that "[c]ertain constraints" kept her from discussing her work on Plath and wished me well in the writing of this book, which she said she would like to read. That same summer, I taught an online course about her archive for the university where I teach. On September 18, Rosenstein emailed me asking about my course on her archive—the course description included the ways we would "unravel the mystery" of Rosenstein's archive. This didn't sit well with her, and she told me as much, writing that she hoped my work was "derive[d] from solid source material," something she said was important to her. She requested "the full text of your course," and reiterated her good wishes and interest in this book.

I wrote back immediately, assuring her that the course was about the contents of the archive, offering specific examples of materials we discussed. I offered to send her the slides. The next day, she wrote and thanked me for my "generous-spirited reply." She also told me that as she read what I wrote to her, she wanted to talk back to me, but this was "an impulse" she had learned to quell long ago. She left off with a kind of warning—maybe, someday, I would learn the same lesson (and, presumably, pipe down). Nonetheless—"Your book should be fascinating."

In January 2022, I tried once more to speak to her. To my surprise and delight, she agreed, telling me, "Your determination reminds me of my own repeated knocking on certain Plath doors. Now I'm knocking on yours." She reminded me she had never spoken to any other "Plath researchers," and requested a number of documents to review, including my book proposal. I wrote back to Harriet Rosenstein, sending all of documents and information she had requested.

The next day, she turned me down.

Plath's "blue, [f]loating" saints inside the church at North Tawton, Devon, a stone's throw from Court Green, where Harriet Rosenstein stayed with Ted Hughes and his children during her research for her unfinished book on Plath.

The House of the Ruler

—⋘◆⋙—

> The word *archive*, Jacques Derrida tells us, comes from the ancient Greek . . . *arkheion*, "the house of the ruler." When I first learned about this etymology, I was taken with the use of *house* (a lover of haunted house stories, I'm a sucker for architecture metaphors), but it is the power, the authority, that is the most telling element. What is placed in or left out of the archive is a political act, dictated by the archivist and the political context in which she lives.
>
> —Carmen Maria Machado, from *In the Dream House*

JUDITH KROLL, ONE OF THE EARLIEST SYLVIA PLATH SCHOLars, wrote that, studying Plath in the late 1960s, she found the elements of a detective story. As a doctoral student at Yale, Kroll undertook what was probably the first-ever dissertation on Plath's poetry. In 1976, she published *Chapters in a Mythology: The Poetry of Sylvia Plath*. It was reissued in 2007 with a new foreword.

Plath's work was so new to the literary world in the 1960s that

Kroll was tasked not only with writing her dissertation but with proving that her subject was dissertation-worthy in the first place. She writes that she

> felt somehow protective about [Plath's] poetry and her literary reputation. The ways in which critics . . . spoke of her dismissively and trivialized her achievement, disturbed me. Her genius and the . . . power of her imagery, these critics claimed, might be seen as symptoms. . . . A moralistic stance about how she had attended to her life . . . crept into commentary on her work, as if her suicide testified to a weak character, as if she should have been buried at a crossroads.

In the 1960s and '70s, there were no archives holding Plath's manuscripts. Her poetry was not yet collected in a single volume. Kroll worked from *The Colossus, Ariel*, and the many journals and magazines where Plath had been published over the years. In 1971, she ordered a limited-edition Plath volume called *Crystal Gazer and Other Poems* from a London publisher calling itself The Rainbow Press and was puzzled by what she read. The versions of the poems differed, in some cases dramatically, from the ones she had been working from in magazines. Kroll wrote to the editor of the Rainbow Press and was surprised to get a response from Olwyn Hughes, confirming the errors as exactly that and asking Kroll to let her know if she found others. By then, Kroll had finished her coursework at Yale and was teaching at Vassar College. Olwyn wondered if Vassar had any desire to purchase Plath's manuscripts for their special collections, and Kroll's department head expressed interest. "Those are the circumstances," Kroll writes, "under which I first came to meet Olwyn Hughes, four years after I began working on Plath. In March 1972, during my spring break, I traveled to London to see the papers."

It was the same year Robin Morgan made her famous claim that Ted Hughes had murdered Sylvia Plath, aided and abetted by "critical necrophiles" Al Alvarez, George Steiner, and Robert Lowell, who had "[patronized Sylvia Plath's] madness, [diluted] her rage, [and buried] her politics"—murder by selective editing and censorship. Morgan would go on to claim that her poem was based on archival documents—letters from Sylvia Plath—which "Plath scholars" had shown her. Judith Kroll, by contrast, was interested in how Plath's literary influences might be made clear by the careful study of her manuscripts. Both writers were invested in wresting Plath's reputation from an establishment they viewed as dangerous or demeaning to her, but only Kroll was championed by that same establishment. Positioned as yet another Plath avatar (she, too, graduated from Smith College and worked closely with the same literature faculty as Sylvia), she was seen as someone who could, with the backing of the Ivy League and Seven Sisters, exalt Plath to her proper place in the literary canon: "You have convinced me that she is a major American poet," Kroll's dissertation adviser, New Critic Cleanth Brooks, told her when she received her PhD.

Morgan, by contrast, was seen as an upstart, her work described by Harriet Rosenstein in a 1972 letter to Olwyn Hughes as "crazy and outrageous," a "hysterical misinterpretation and misidentification" of Sylvia Plath's life and poetry. Rosenstein claimed that she had advised the editors at *Ms.* magazine, which had recently published her long essay on Plath, against printing "Arraignment." As a result, she told Olwyn, Morgan had accused Rosenstein of participating in a "conspiracy of silence." If Judith Kroll was the clever detective, then Robin Morgan was the bungling cop, policing the right of Ted Hughes and his "critical necrophiles" to do what they would with Plath's work.

The state and location of Plath's papers in the 1960s and '70s created factious rivalries, inspiring rumors, legends, and the persistent, sometimes correct, belief that something was always going missing. The years immediately preceding Judith Kroll's first visit to England saw Sylvia Plath's papers from the last years of her life passed back and forth between Ted and Olwyn Hughes or stored at Barclays

Bank. Olwyn Hughes was living in London; Ted Hughes between Court Green, London, and his parents' home in West Yorkshire, Heptonstall, where he had purchased an eighteenth-century manor house known as Lumb Bank. In spring 1971, when Lumb Bank was briefly unoccupied and Hughes was traveling through Scotland with his second wife, Carol, and his children, someone set fire to its foyer after deliberately placing a pile of Hughes's and Plath's manuscripts there; everything in the pile was lost. That summer, while Hughes was in Iran working on a theatrical project with the director Peter Brook, someone broke into Court Green and stole some of Sylvia's manuscripts. Emma Tennant, in *Burnt Diaries*, describes a 1976 encounter with Olwyn Hughes at her London flat "on the fringes of Camden Town" that housed "the invaluable relics of a genius." Tennant sensed "chaos" in "the crumpled pieces of paper, long-forgotten letters and bills." She left, nonetheless, with the original manuscript of a then-unpublished Plath story, no questions asked.

Plath's papers inhabited a series of makeshift archives: houses haunted by her corpus, not bricked into the walls, but hidden in plain sight. Tennant writes that the windows to Olwyn's flat had no curtains. Judith Kroll describes Olwyn handing her Plath's manuscripts sight unseen to take them back to her hotel room and work. Arriving back in London in June 1974 at the request of the Hugheses to begin editing a collected version of Plath's poetry, Kroll struggled to work at Olwyn's flat, where Olwyn's boyfriend, Richard, a violent alcoholic she eventually married, now lived. Richard threatened Olwyn and banished Kroll from the house. Kroll returned to smashed glass and bloodstains in the foyer and learned that Richard had chased Olwyn around the house, scattering Plath's manuscripts in the process. Olwyn also told her that Richard had thrown Plath's manuscripts out the window and into the garden. The domestic chaos, then, which had inspired so much of Plath's late writing, now surrounded its remains.

That same summer—1974—Kroll traveled to Court Green with Ted, Carol, and Olwyn Hughes. There she saw, briefly, Plath's original journals, the outline for her missing novel *Doubletake*, and several letters Ruth Beuscher wrote to her former patient in the fall of 1962, urging her to divorce Ted Hughes (these, Kroll writes, were "whisked away"). Eventually, Kroll spoke at length with Ted Hughes about her dissertation; he thought it "rather a brilliant book." He was also sure, however, that Kroll had been "talking with" someone about it, unconvinced she could have come to her own, informed conclusions about Plath's literary influences.

Ted and Olwyn questioned Kroll's reading of Plath's October 1962 poem "Medusa," which Kroll had discerned to be about Aurelia Plath, since "the medusa jellyfish has a subgenus 'also called aurelia.'" The Hugheses agreed with Kroll's "etymological detective work." But they expressed terror that her reading of "Medusa" make it into the world. "I felt a little as if I were being interrogated," Kroll wrote. Ted Hughes called Kroll's work on "Medusa" an "exegesis," following his by-then established pattern of speaking and writing of Plath's work in religious terms; he and Olwyn told Judith Kroll that her reading of the poem would kill Aurelia. "Do you want to be a murderer?" Olwyn asked her.

JUDITH KROLL'S TREATMENT OF "MEDUSA" in *Chapters in a Mythology* is careful, deliberate scholarship, placing it as the twin of "Daddy" and pointing to the ways Plath's late poetry is a high-wire act, with Europe a bloody, patriarchal hell and America the motherly sea. Plath walks the wire between them like a circus queen. In "Medusa," the speaker can access her maternal bloodline through the "old barnacled umbilicus, Atlantic cable" of the telephone line; she can, importantly, talk. In "Daddy," the "black telephone's off at the root." When the speaker tries to talk in her father's foreign tongue, she stutters—"Ich, ich, ich, ich"—the high wire, the telephone wire, of connection has become "a barb wire snare" that strangles language in her mouth. Kroll moves her interpretation inward to Plath's biography (her mother was raised Catholic, hence the image of her in "Medusa" as a "ghastly Vatican"), then spins it out to Greek mythology, Frazer's

The Golden Bough, and the poetry of Dylan Thomas. To reduce it, then, to one small image, and conflate that image with murder, was to ignore years of her scholarship—but that seems, in the case of Ted and Olwyn Hughes, to be part of the pattern, and the point.

Kroll's brief description of her time with Ted and Olwyn Hughes had dual aims. She wanted to reintroduce her book to a new generation of readers. But she also wanted to reclaim it. When it debuted with Harper & Row in 1976, it landed a high-profile review by the critic Karl Miller in the *New York Review of Books*, in which Miller dropped a not so subtle hint that in writing about Sylvia Plath, Kroll had been helped along by Ted Hughes: "Many of her findings have been checked with Ted Hughes, and it is evident that the two of them are keen to draw Plath's verse as far as possible beyond the reach of exploitative biographers." Kroll responded to this review in a letter to the editor, dated May 12, 1977, in which she claimed that Miller accused her of "[conspiring]" with the Hugheses to complete her work. In her foreword, Kroll writes:

> In the preface to *Chapters in a Mythology* that I would write a year after leaving Court Green, I explained the extent and timing of my interaction with Ted Hughes. I stated . . . the phrase "Ted Hughes confirmed" would indicate Ted's confirmation of my conclusions long after I had made them. . . . At the time, this manner of indicating that I'd had no contact with or help from Ted Hughes prior to completing and handing in my dissertation seemed clear and unambiguous to me, to my editor, and to others who read *Chapters in a Mythology* before publication. Although I explained all this in the original preface, some reviewers misunderstood what, in that context, "confirmed" meant, and assumed that anything "confirmed" by Ted Hughes originated with him.

By 1976, it was clear that while Judith Kroll might be the clever girl detective, she could learn nothing without entering the ruler's house.

Gaining entry, however, was a risk. Miller's response to her work evinced the way power and propriety continued to operate in the literary world, which could not conceive of a Sylvia Plath without Ted Hughes, or a Judith Kroll without Ted Hughes's aid. In 2015, writing about Judith Kroll's book for *Ted Hughes: The Unauthorised Life*, Jonathan Bate describes Kroll's 1974 visit to Court Green. He notes Ted Hughes's keen admiration for Kroll's dissertation, "which he thought full of amazing intuitions." But, Bate writes,

> they started work on Sylvia's manuscript drafts . . . it became clear that Kroll's strong suit was . . . not the minutiae of textual bibliography and the investigation of manuscript drafts. Ted completed his work on the collected poems alone.

This last was true—Hughes was listed as sole editor of Sylvia Plath's *Collected Poems*, which was published in 1981. As to the other reasons he might have lacked a coeditor—the threats and violence—nothing is said here.

PLATH'S *COLLECTED POEMS* WAS FILLED with errors, some of which Kroll notes in her 2007 foreword; the poem "Elm," for instance, in the *Collected Poems*, includes the line "Snaky acids kiss" rather than "Snaky acids hiss," which was Plath's final draft. Kroll also writes that she tried to impress upon Olwyn Hughes that using Plath's last recorded edits in the manuscript was standard editing practice on a definitive text. But Olwyn was unconvinced, sure they should stick to edits made by magazines like *The New Yorker*. In a letter Kroll wrote to her husband on June 1, 1974, she describes Olwyn's editorial process as "I like this line better their way, let's keep it like that." Kroll published her foreword eight years prior to the publication of Jonathan Bate's biography, but in his book, Hughes is once more credited as Plath's impresario, while Kroll, an Ivy League scholar who went on to a long career at the University of Texas, is incapable of making line edits.

Judith Kroll's foreword is accurately pitched between the

Hugheses' determination to read the uncanny into her commonsense approach and her own hard literary detective work. But she, too, makes dubious claims. Writing of her dissertation in 2007, Kroll tells the reader that, given the option, she would keep her dissertation the same. After all, she was, she claims, the first writer to mention Assia Wevill in print. In her attempt to prove she cracked the case first, Kroll, like so many of her contemporaries, dismisses the work of her colleague Robin Morgan, who, in "Arraignment," published four years prior to Kroll's dissertation, writes not only of Assia's existence, but also her murder-suicide. But Robin Morgan was long ago banished to the attic, held up as the singular concrete example of the so-called hordes of angry feminists attacking Ted Hughes, who, Janet Badia has rightly pointed out, do not actually exist. For Emma Tennant, as for Sylvia Plath, Hughes embodied the dangerous but ultimately irresistible sex appeal of Heathcliff and Edward Rochester; but Robin Morgan was the thief of the marriage veil, setting fire to the ruler's house.

JUDITH KROLL MANAGED TO ENTER the many houses where Plath's manuscripts were held prior to their official sale to two university libraries. But the literary establishment was locked, evidenced in Karl Miller's review of *Chapters in a Mythology*. Miller knew Hughes and Plath personally; Plath wrote in an April 21, 1960, letter to her mother about having lunch with him in Soho. In the ultimate act of literary insidership, one of the three books Miller reviewed was *Letters Home*, which included that letter and others to and about him, since he was a prominent London critic during Plath's lifetime, the editor at the *New Statesmen*, who reviewed Hughes's work and published Plath's in her lifetime.

That Miller already lived in the house Kroll was trying to gain entrance to is on full display in his review, which jabs at the long-standing rumor of Ted and Olwyn Hughes's incestuous relationship. Early in her marriage, Sylvia Plath seems to have limited her belief to the possibility that Olwyn was in love with Ted, but later, she referenced an incestuous relationship in letters to both her mother and Ruth Beuscher. Clarissa Roche told Janet Malcolm that Plath believed this. (She is on record saying it in her taped interview with Malcolm.) Malcolm wrote off Plath's suggestions as "outrageous" in *The Silent Woman*. Karl Miller wrote around them: he describes Plath's 1962 review of the biography *Lord Byron's Wife* for the *New Statesmen*, for which he was then reviews editor: "a book which she said in a letter she was lucky to receive and had wanted to get her hands on, though it may have been sent (by me) in ignorance of quite why this might have been so." A portrait Plath saw of Byron's sister looked exactly like Olwyn, Plath wrote to her mother around the same time.

Miller's review speaks to anyone with enough knowledge of literary history to know that Byron had an affair with his half-sister, a charge his wife, Annabella, leveled publicly in divorce proceedings in 1816, causing Byron to flee the country. By February 1963, during the last weekend of her life, Plath would beg Hughes to leave the country. Jonathan Bate said that more scandal had attached itself to Ted Hughes's name than to any writer since Lord Byron, but stopped short of suggesting incest between Ted and Olwyn Hughes, writing that Olwyn hated any woman who interfered in her relationship with her brother; she therefore doubted Ted's paternity of Shura Wevill.

At least one newspaper profile of Olwyn, from May 1992, claimed that she told various friends that she and Ted "were indeed lovers." A 1961 letter from Ted to Olwyn, after a disastrous Christmas in Yorkshire during which Olwyn and Plath fought and Ted struck Olwyn, describes how all of the Hughes siblings hated each other's boyfriends and wives simply because they existed: "I don't find reasons to dislike your boyfriends, I just detest them flat. . . . I detest the idea of your boy-friends etc. I dismiss them as unimportant, first as you've always dismissed my girl-friends." Much like the claims of intimate partner violence against Hughes, the claim of incest has been dismissed as "outrageous" or else gone unaddressed in the name of protecting the reputation of, as John Banville wrote, "a fine poet and complicated man." Or as the mock historian Philomena Cunk said of Lord Byron's *Don Juan*, "Must have been a good book if you can overlook the fact he slept with his sister."

THE QUESTION OF WHO RULES the house is at the heart of Carmen Maria Machado's memoir of queer intimate partner violence, *In the Dream House*, which begins with a discussion of Machado's disdain for prologues: "If what the author has to say is so important, why relegate it to the paratext?" She never answers her own question, unless writing two prologues for a book that begins with its stance against them is a kind of answer, a way to warn her reader that before they enter the story, which is its own archive, its own haunted house, there are things they need to know. Machado's question of what should be relegated to paratext haunts my writing on Sylvia Plath, whose life has historically been relegated to the paratext of her famous death. All Plath biographies end with her death, but many also start there. In attempting to wrestle Plath's life and afterlife away from those who, in my view, had blown it up to monstrous proportions and then shrunk it down to nothing in their funhouse mirrors, I occasionally felt trapped in my own mirrored hall: reflecting me, reflecting back Plath's death in the kitchen at 23 Fitzroy Road ad infinitum: a woman writing a dead woman, writing, a woman, writing a dead woman, writing . . .

I began *In the Dream House* during the last month of a surprise pregnancy, at the age of forty, during the third of four "nonstress tests" where, for the very first time, a cheerful nurse asked me the question, "Are you safe at home?" Despite having survived a prior violent relationship with my older son's father, I had, by then, for so long been safe at home that the question confused me. It should not have: it was October of 2020, and in the year that passed, almost every household had suffered some factor that made the conditions for intimate partner violence worse. According to one source, domestic violence had increased anywhere from 25 to 33 percent globally. People had less money, were out of work with nowhere to go, and were drinking more. As ever, these problems were, and are, truer for pregnant people. Disappearing one's self is more difficult when you are carrying another human being inside your body: "And I have no face / I have wanted to efface myself," Sylvia Plath writes in her great poem "Tulips."

In *The Art of Cruelty*, Maggie Nelson reads these, and other lines by Plath, as addressing the horror of having your face ripped off, a recurring Plathian theme. This is certainly true, but the word *efface* also, of course, refers to the thinning of the cervix as you near labor. Plath wrote "Tulips" soon after she miscarried her second pregnancy, a loss she later attributed to being beaten by Ted Hughes, with whose birthday she said the unborn child shared a due date. She wrote "Tulips" in response to the experience of having an appendectomy three weeks after her miscarriage, in March 1961. According to *Bitter Fame*, Plath walked to the hospital for her appendectomy and got lost, eventually being driven there by a couple of whom she had asked directions, telling them, "I'd rather have a baby; at least you've got something to show for it," before breaking down.

The spring of 1961 also saw the composition of a little-discussed poem called "Widow," in which Plath's speaker moves between the subject positions of a black widow spider, and a widow recalling the enraged murder of her husband: "That is the fear she has—the fear / His soul may beat and be beating at her dull sense." The repetitive use of the words "beat/beating" in concert with the repetition of "the fear . . . the fear" suggests to the reader that this speaker is recalling violence in response to violence. The speaker also, notably, *loves* the man she killed, pointing to a paradox: the impossible, but actual, concurrence of love and violence: he is someone she would want to kill again, just to be close to him once more. This returns us to Miranda Fricker's use of a survivor of "long-term domestic violence" who attacks her husband as the most potent example of "hermeneutic injustice," or a group whose experience is so little attended to that we simply fail to hear it, much less understand it. Given that it took fifty-six years for Plath's reports of IPV in the winter of 1961 to come to broad public knowledge, it's hardly a surprise that "Widow" has been overlooked.

"Widow" is also an important precursor to "The Detective," a quick parting of the drapes to offer us a view inside the ruler's house, where nothing is as it seems, where an impossible language, which is "dead," a "shadow," and "an echo," "exposes" a secret passageway that leads to more emptiness. In "The Detective," the speaker's mouth "disappears" as a punishment for its greed, something Maggie Nelson reads as another version of being effaced—but it is also, as previously discussed, punitive. The mouth was greedy for love, food, and speech and so had to be punished. In "Widow," language dies before it can even attempt to name experience, and the speaker transmutes into a sheet of newspaper laid onto the fire. The language is another presentiment of Plath's legacy, body turned to corpus, corpus turned to ash. The widow recalls a time when she tried to warm herself not with fire but with her husband's letters, which were once so vibrant to her, they could warm her as if the paper they were written on was live skin.

We are reminded of Plath's delight in Hughes's letters during their brief separation at the beginning of their marriage, in October 1956, when Hughes remained in Yorkshire with his family and Plath returned to Cambridge University for the fall term of the second year of her Fulbright. In her own letters to Hughes, Plath describes being "perpetually freezing cold" without him, wondering "when will the Word, these words I cram my eye with, assuage this hunger for your sweet incredibly dear flesh." In the same letter, she decries Saint Paul's letter recommending celibacy, since she now has "a private holy spirit in small letters, an earth-faith which flickers." No longer able to warm herself with her husband's letters, the widowed speaker becomes paper to burn, becomes "that great, vacant estate!" as though in anticipation of her home: Court Green, which by the 1970s was ruled by her widower husband, who housed, and then destroyed, her estate.

WHAT STORIES ARE MISSING, OR struck, from the archive? By the time Carmen Maria Machado's memoir found me in what felt like an act of Plathian bibliomancy, I was living in my own dream house—a four-bedroom condominium in my hometown with my husband and our two children, his daughter from a previous relationship and my son from the same. The paratext that led me to safely read about intimate partner violence at a doctor's appointment, rather than live through it, is one undercurrent of this story. Between 2010 and 2012, I lived with a violent drug addict, with whom I had a son. There is scant official record of what happened to us in those years, an open gap in the paper trail. I told almost no one what happened. Those I did speak to heard whispers, sentences that trailed off. This both is and is not what the writer Saidiya Hartman calls "the violence of the archive"— "stories," Machado writes, "sometimes . . . destroyed, and sometimes . . . never uttered in the first place." Machado writes into the particular silence of queer intimate partner violence "even newer, even more shadowed" than that which exists between straight couples. Although "the abused woman has certainly been around as long as human beings have been capable of psychological manipulation and interpersonal violence . . . she . . . did not exist until about fifty years ago."

What a body endures and what institutions will recognize, name, and codify into law are two separate things. A book, like a court of law, looks for *proof*: a split lip, contusions. By the time the law becomes involved in many domestic disputes, the only available proof is the woman's dead body, a silent house:

> A 12-city study . . . conducted of [homicide-suicide] cases found that intimate partner violence had previously occurred in 70 percent of them. Interestingly, only 25 percent of prior domestic violence appeared in the arrest records. . . . Researchers uncovered much of the prior domestic violence through interviews with family and friends of the homicide victims.

We are reminded of Hughes's repeated phrase upon Plath's death: *It was either her or me.* We are reminded that events do not necessarily enter the record. It can take years, if it happens at all. Machado dates the abused woman's entrance into the official record at "about fifty years ago," or sometime around 1970, at least seven years before any of Sylvia Plath's manuscripts, letters, papers, or photographs entered an official archive. In 1970, Plath was already understood as the polar opposite of a survivor of her own life, much less a survivor of intimate partner violence. But this was as much a historical problem as a political one, or a question of who to believe.

By the 1970s, Plath was already so closely associated with both suicide and feminist political aims that she occupies a whole page in Susan Brownmiller's 1975 book on rape. Brownmiller writes that Plath's violent relationship was one cause of her suicide, offering Plath as a high-profile example of the masochism women in heteronormative relationships were required to possess to endure them. This masochism had "gotten out of hand" for Plath by the time she killed herself. In trying to write a history of rape, Brownmiller had to first build the case that it was even a crime. Feminists advocating for the prosecution of domestic violence faced a similar struggle. The earliest attempts in the United States to criminalize intimate partner violence in the 1960s

> were designed to do everything possible to avoid formal legal processing of men who beat their wives or partners. . . . [Police] were trained to do anything except arrest violent husbands. For many years, police culture portrayed domestic violence as the most potentially dangerous situation for police officers, with elevated risks of serious injury or death; subsequent data proved this false.

How do you survive something that doesn't legally exist? How do you talk about it?

When the nurse asked me if I was safe at home, even though

the answer by then was *yes*, the horrors of my old life reared up at me. By telling her my (dream) home was safe, did I perform an irrevocable silence against the story of my first, terrifying pregnancy? Women's bodies, queer bodies, Black and brown bodies have been, still are, individual repositories of time spent in the ruler's house, struck from the official record; but like the archives they stand in for, these bodies are not created equal. Hartman's violence of the archive refers not to the individual stories of white women, but to the collective and systematic excision of stories of enslaved people—young women, in particular—from the archive. As recently as February 2023, National Public Radio reported a story about the so-called need for forensic nurses in hospitals to use "blue or purple light" to better detect bruises on "victims with darker skin," without which, the article hints, the claims of these same victims would not be believed. One wonders less at the ways this sheds metaphorical light on the systemic disbelief of women of color than that a major American journalistic outlet was celebrating this as a win for Black women, given that the presence of blue or purple light is hardly a new discovery.

Bodies are houses of bad memory. My own is still the house where I cowered behind locked bathroom doors, in dark closets, where I wept in the shower, apologizing out loud to my still-unborn son. Like Sylvia Plath's, my body is an archive with hidden rooms, a straw thatch, a *wall of old corpses*, and a ruler, long gone. And yet here I sit, writing this book, using my body to help tell the story of hers. I need no special light to do so.

BEFORE THE NURSE EVEN RETURNED to peel the fetal monitors from my body, I told her: *I am safe, now. But there was a time when I wasn't*. What if someone had asked me then, *Are you safe at home*? Could I have answered honestly? This last question—what we do with escape routes when we are not yet ready to run—haunts my study of Sylvia Plath, who is always just about to break free of her famous death, just about to get out of the collective memory that we have built around her. *In the Dream House* understands how we get stuck in our stories, how they build houses around us with hidden staircases and trapdoors. One chapter, "*Dream House as* Choose Your Own Adventure," admonishes the reader page by page to move forward or backward in the book: "Are you a monster? You might be a monster. END. Go to page 177."

As a bookish kid, I wanted to love *Choose Your Own Adventure* books. The glamorous titles called out to me—*The Mona Lisa Is Missing*—take me to Paris to find her. But it was impossible to get lost in their narratives, which was why I read in the first place. The books in the series circled back on themselves too quickly and ended in what felt like no time at all. The problem wasn't necessarily that they were short: Sylvia Plath's life was barely thirty years long; and incredibly, to me, I lived with my abusive ex for less than two years. The problem was how quickly they wrapped up loose ends. You either found the Mona Lisa and went back home or fell down a mineshaft and died. What I want, I know now, is a story of any length that can't, or won't, resolve. The escape hatch beckons, but the heroine won't budge. Still, we return, laden with hope. *You wake at 4 a.m. The babies sleep. It is still dark. The milkman's bottles have yet to rattle. The pain is real. It exhausts you. You sit down at your desk to write. You live another day. Go to page 31.*

BUT SHE DIDN'T SURVIVE.

When Sylvia Plath killed herself with sleeping pills and domestic cooking gas in the kitchen of her flat at 23 Fitzroy Road in London's Primrose Hill district, she is alleged to have left behind a letter to her mother that she wrote hours before her death. This sheds light on one of her last acts: around midnight, she visited her downstairs neighbor, Trevor Thomas, and asked him for stamps. Plath may have expressed a desire for someone else to be custodian of her writing or her children in that letter to her mother, but we can't know, as Hughes refused to allow Aurelia to see it. According to Gail Crowther's *Three-Martini Afternoons at the Ritz: The Rebellion of Sylvia Plath and Anne Sexton*, when Mrs. Plath pressed the issue, he threatened to keep her grandchildren from her for the rest of her life. The letter has never resurfaced. "Days [before her death], Aurelia had sent $4,000 to her daughter as a gift," Crowther reports. "She noted that she never received this money back either."

I read this private censor as the start of Hughes's wresting control of his estranged wife's legacy from anyone else who had loved her in life. Over the course of thirty-five years, Hughes admitted anecdotally and in print to either actively burning or losing Plath's journals, poems, letters, and her third novel-in-progress. Diane Middlebrook describes the poetry of Hughes and Plath as a conversation that began when Sylvia Plath quoted Ted Hughes's own poem to him upon their first meeting at a Cambridge party in 1956—"I did it, I"—and continued until Hughes's death.

The morning after the couple met—February 26, 1956—Plath wrote a long, now-famous journal entry about how, upon shouting "I did it, I," at him, she bit him on the face, how he pulled her earrings from her ears, her red headband from her head, "bark[ing]" "Ha, I shall keep." She followed it up with "Pursuit," a terrifying poem that opens, "There is a panther stalks me down: / One day I'll have my death of him." But by late spring, making love to Hughes in the open air of Cambridge meadows, she wrote "Ode for Ted," a poem celebrating Hughes's fecund sexuality, able to produce not just children but fruits, greens, and grains; animals, too, attend to him: "For his least look, scant acres yield: / . . . heaves forth stalk, leaf, fruit-nubbed emerald." In the last stanza, the speaker calls herself "adam's woman," a nod to Plath's perception of Cambridge, verdant in the spring of 1956, as the couple's personal Eden. Six months later, during her brief separation from Hughes, she would write:

> Oh Teddy, how I repent for scoffing in my green and unchastened youth at the legend of Eve's being plucked from Adam's left rib; because the damn story's true; I ache and ache to

return to my proper place, which is curled up right there, sheltered and cherished.

But if the poets were talking in poetry, that conversation also included semaphores of annihilation: bonfires, theft, loss, and death. Hughes wrote no poetry about burning Plath's work (or, if he did, we don't have it), but Plath did write about burning his. In August 1962, she built a bonfire made of Hughes's papers, hair, dandruff, and fingernail clippings in her backyard and set it on fire. "Now," she told it, "speak." Plath claimed the fire threw off a piece of paper with Assia's name on it. She immortalized this experience in her poem "Burning the Letters," written the same month. "And here is an end to the writing," she wrote in the poem's second stanza, a line traditionally read as her relief at watching Hughes's letters to his lover disappear before her eyes. But if she was writing about the end of Hughes's writing, she was also writing about the end of her own—not literally, as she was entering one of the great creative periods in the history of English literature, often compared to Keats's *annus mirabilis*. By the fall of 1962, Plath was no longer Adam's woman.

Like Eliza Doolittle in George Bernard Shaw's *Pygmalion*, Plath had "got a little of [her] own back." Eliza, a Cockney flower girl, is part of a wager by the linguist Henry Higgins, who bets he can teach her to speak proper English and pass her off as a member of the aristocracy at the forthcoming Ascot Ball. His bet pays off, and Eliza is a hit. But their relationship is revealed as the fraud it has always been when Henry refuses to give Eliza credit for her accomplishments, characterizing her instead as his Frankensteinian creation: "I tell you I have created this thing out of the squashed cabbage leaves of Covent Garden," the garbage-littered inverse of Hughes and Plath's Cambridge Eden, with its emerald greenery. When Eliza, reverting to her Cockney accent of origin, tells him she has recovered a sense of herself, Higgins tells her, "You have wounded me to the heart." In the musical version of the play, *My Fair Lady*, Eliza closes the scene by singing to him about his insignificance to the broader world to which he has introduced her: "Art and music will thrive without you. / Somehow Keats will survive without you." This is a third prescient relational moment to Plath and Hughes; a fourth occurs when Eliza asserts her independence from Higgins. In turn, he strangles her.

Almost as soon as they began seeing one another, Plath, despite being by far the better published writer, practically apprenticed herself to her soon-to-be husband, writing to him that she "[had] no desire, above my typewriter and my cows, to do anything except work for you, slave for you, make myself an always enriching woman for you; and that is that." This was a theme Hughes continued after her death. Plath was a summa cum laude graduate of one of the best English literature programs in the United States, and a Fulbright Scholar, yet he wrote to Anne Stevenson in 1986, "as for her mastery of literature I was mainly astounded—and I mean astounded—by what she had not read."

It is true that one function of intimate partner violence is to break the victim down until they no longer recognize themselves. It is true that this is easier to do when the victim "has just moved somewhere new," a practice called "dislocation," as Carmen Maria Machado wrote in *In the Dream House*: "She is made vulnerable by her circumstance, her isolation. Her only ally is her abuser, which is to say she has no ally at all." This is often helped along by the frenetic sense of brand-new love, like the green new Eden Plath believed she and Hughes were going to inhabit, just after she had moved across an ocean. "In dreams," Machado writes of the house she inhabited with her violent ex-girlfriend, "it sits behind a green door, for reasons you have never understood. The door was not green."

In her book *Revising Life*, Susan Van Dyne traces the ways that Plath's *Ariel* poems seek to destroy the dual images she had built of Ted Hughes as both ideal husband and the ideal poet/teacher whose creative and commercial success Plath chased after throughout their marriage. For Van Dyne, "Burning the Letters" is not simply Sylvia Plath deciding that she will have creative primacy in their relationship. It is a declaration of war: "'Burning the Letters' demonstrates that all of Plath's revenge plots from the fall of 1962 have twin objects for her rage: Hughes's sexual betrayal and his poetic primacy." In it, Plath literally destroys Hughes's image and his image-making (that is, his poems, some of which she burned) and kills the project that began with "Pursuit" in 1956—writing poetry that celebrated her husband's creative and sexual powers. "The more he writes poems, the more he writes poems," Sylvia wrote to her mother when she first fell in love with Hughes. Now she was saying the same thing about herself.

"Ode for Ted" makes use of one of Hughes's so-called totem animals, the red fox, which, the poem claims, is "stalked" by the Adamlike hero of the verse. Hughes, of course, also wrote one of his most celebrated poems about a fox. "The Thought-Fox" was published in *The New Yorker* and included in *The Hawk in the Rain*, Hughes's book that Plath organized, typed, and submitted for publication in the first year of their marriage. As Van Dyne points out, "The Thought-Fox" takes place in a dark, snowy landscape, while "Burning the Letters" takes place in a summery backyard—but drafts of "Burning the Letters," held at Smith College, include the lines "It never snows in the country. That is the trouble. / There is never a gallon of white on the doorstep," lines that Van Dyne believes "strongly [suggest] Plath, stalled in her own composition, got her fresh start by re-reading "The Thought-Fox."

"Burning the Letters" makes dramatically different use of the fox—Plath ends her poem about lighting Hughes's letters and poems on fire by comparing the flames to a pack of dogs tearing a fox: "This is what it is like— / A red burst and a cry." In a letter to Anne Stevenson about Plath's destruction of his papers and his friends' angry responses to that destruction, Hughes stole Plath's metaphor to describe her own behavior. Janet Malcolm includes a long excerpt from this letter in *The Silent Woman*, writing that the letter "works its way toward a stunning culmination: . . . 'It was like trying to protect a fox from my own hounds while the fox bit me. With a real fox in that situation, you would never have any doubt why it was biting you.'" With a real fox in that situation, of course, you would never pick it up—the fox's singular function is to be killed by the hounds, which the owner has set upon the fox.

Poems like "Burning the Letters" underscore the high stakes of the game both poets were playing with language, sex, and love, one that left a scorched earth of manuscripts in its wake, a stubborn silence we try to fill. This is one version of archival silence, stories destroyed or cast out of the official record: feathery piles in the ash can, bodies on the ocean floor. In "Venus in Two Acts," Saidiya Hartman's essay about the archives of the Atlantic slave trade, Hartman says that she writes "at the limit of the unspeakable and the unknown" to "[describe] as fully as possible the conditions that determine the appearance of Venus and that dictate her silence." Venus, a captive girl on the slave ship *Recovery*, was murdered by its captain, John Kimber. Her name appeared only once during Kimber's trial, when the ship's surgeon confirmed her presence on the *Recovery*. Yet on the basis of this handful of words, Hartman calls into question the methods and meaning of history, its representations, and its repositories. Hartman writes against the gaps in the archive and "wrestles with the impossibility of discovering anything about [Venus] that hasn't already been stated."

This is a version of the problem new writers on Plath are said to face: *No more Plath, please*. The idea that we know everything we can ever know about Sylvia works with the silence of her burnt and missing pages, producing a tense gap that begs us to speak on her behalf, a need Hartman urges us to resist, suggesting instead that we write "at the limit of the unspeakable and the unknown."

But what was unspeakable for Sylvia Plath? Her tendency to obsessively record the events of her life, often in multiple forms, has left us with a remarkable historical record of those events, sometimes retold in the fact-laden style of a journalist, sometimes transformed into poetry or fiction. Compared with Hartman's gobsmacking truth that "There is not one extant autobiographical narrative of a female captive who survived the Middle Passage," what we know of Plath's life seems enormous, the stuff of luck and legend, a bounty we should fall over ourselves in gratitude for and leave as it is.

If the archive, as Hartman, quoting Foucault, writes, "returns the dead to us 'in the very form in which they were driven out of the world,'" then it would seem that Sylvia Plath left the world writing, a practice she took up seriously at the age of eight, when she published her first poem in the *Boston Traveler*. But since much of the writing Plath did right up to her death has vanished, we are left with Hartman's archival violence: we lack the physical letters, which may have contained her last wishes for her children, her body, and her body of work. Absent these, her body landed in a lonely, vandalized grave, and the archive seems hacked at, moth-eaten, torched, and reconstructed, a version of what Hartman, describing the barracoon, calls "an episteme." It returns a Sylvia Plath that never looks quite right to us, from whom we nevertheless must learn. Faced with this off-kilter Plath, we revisit the sites of her life and death, double- and triple-checking for what has gone missing.

The image of a censored Plath led to an understanding of her as Janet Malcolm's "silent woman" and has, in this way, conflated her with the subaltern, the colonial subject who lives outside of the hierarchy of state-sponsored power. Hartman's work deals directly with the impossibility of subaltern speech, a problem posed by Gayatri Spivak in her pivotal essay. Where Plathian discourse tells us that there is nothing left to say about Plath because we already know everything, Hartman's question of subaltern discourse exists as its direct opposition—there is nothing left to say of Venus because Venus couldn't speak in the first place. Her appearance in the archive is an aberration that, in its very aberrance, points out the everyday commonplace of deadly violence in the Atlantic slave trade. Instead of putting words in her mouth, Hartman wants to "*tell a story* . . . predicted upon impossibility: redressing the violence that produced numbers, ciphers, and fragments of discourse, which is as close as we come to a biography of the captive and the enslaved."

"Venus in Two Acts" is undertaken as part of a larger project of freedom that "[enables] a place for the living" where we imagine a different future than the present we inhabit, which is structured upon the power lines of race, sex, class, and gender that took root in the world that saw Venus as refuse.

A version of these power lines allowed for Hughes's censor of Plath—but I in no way want to offer the false equivalence of Venus with Sylvia Plath. Plath's place in the hierarchies of race, class, and gender allowed her to enter her written word into the historical record before she turned ten and allowed for her continued contributions to that record even after her death. Where Venus appears once, Plath's almost every known written word is preserved by university libraries dedicated to their perpetuity. To understand her as a "silent woman" is an irony that perpetuates these same oppressive lines.

And yet silences exist and call out to us to fill them. Sylvia Plath's endorsement, at the height of her fame in the 1970s, by the second-wave feminist movement has suffered a similar fate as Sylvia herself—the silencing and reduction of a group of complex, vocal women into a single voice who was painted to look like a foolish liar. There is no more potent example of this than Robin Morgan and her poem "Arraignment." Published as part of her 1972 collection *Monster*, "Arraignment" almost didn't make it into the book. In an article Morgan published in the now defunct *Feminist Art Journal*, Morgan detailed how, when she already had the galleys for *Monster*, her editor called her in for a meeting with Random House lawyers to ask her to withdraw the poem from the collection, under concern that its inclusion would trigger a libel suit from Ted Hughes. The poem in its original form begins, "I accuse / Ted Hughes," and goes on to charge Hughes with the "murder" of his wife, among other things.

In the article, Morgan defends her original draft and discusses the trauma of revising it (she writes that the meetings with lawyers became so nasty that she took Dramamine ahead of time to stop the nausea she would feel in them). The newer, published version reads, "*How can* / I accuse / Ted Hughes," a clever rhetorical turn that, via line breaks, accomplishes some of the work of the original (with "I accuse" on its own line) and points to the impossibility of feminist critique under a patriarchy. Morgan's published opening lines roll a cheeky eye at a critique she already knows is coming ("How *could* you?"), while also working out the problem on the page: How can I do this impossible thing—say what must be said, what no one else will say? Since Morgan has now been forbidden to publish her original draft by her (powerful) publisher, the question is also literal.

The second version, with its rhetorical question, was published in *Monster*. Rather than gain fame, the poem gained infamy. As a twenty-year-old woman schooled in contemporary American poetry, with its insistence that I "show, not tell" what my poems were "about," I found Morgan's poem to be an interesting historical relic, but a bad example of verse. When, preparing to write this book at the age of forty, I revisited it, I was stunned to discover how "Arraignment" anticipated much of my own argument about the ways Plath's life and death were covered up and miscast.

Held up as the chief example of the "simplified feminist ideology" that led women to truck up dark Yorkshire hills and chisel the "Hughes" off of Sylvia Plath's tombstone, her poem was criticized as being full of not just rhetorical excesses, but lies—chiefly, the lie that Ted Hughes had been violent with Sylvia Plath, which Elaine Feinstein publicly criticized in the 2015 BBC documentary *Ted Hughes: Stronger Than Death*. The irony, of course, is that a writer as revered as Feinstein would state publicly that Morgan was writing literally when she said that Hughes murdered Plath (a large portion of the poem goes on to be about the killing of her other corpus, her textual body, via selective editing, plagiarism, and censorship) or that she and her fellow feminists planned to murder him. Morgan, in her article for *Feminist Art Journal*, told Random House's lawyers that she was writing in a long literary tradition of poetic excesses against one's enemies (she cites Dante, Marvell, and Swift, among others, as her predecessors). The problem, it seemed, was not that someone was writing a satirical poem about murder. The problem was that the person writing the satirical poem about murder was a woman, writing about a man.

Or that was one of the problems. Morgan goes on, in her article, to discuss some of the others, chiefly that she was perceived as actually accusing Hughes of intimate partner violence and rape against Sylvia Plath, which the Random House lawyers deemed a libel risk. Morgan wrote that it was not—or anyway, it was not in 1972—libel to say a husband raped his wife, because in 1972, the act was still legal (it wouldn't be declared illegal in the United Kingdom and the United States until 1993 and 1994, respectively). As for intimate partner violence, Morgan declares the following:

> One of the interesting highlights into my research on Plath's death was the uncovering of some twenty-odd last letters of hers, in which she talks of Hughes' torturing her . . . appearing periodically (although they were separated) to rape her and beat her up and terrorize the children. . . . In one letter she asks rhetorically, "Why must the killing of me be so elaborate?"—a purely Plath line.

Feminist Art Journal went out of print in 1977. It's no wonder, then, that Plath's letters to Ruth Beuscher were described in the press as going "unseen" by anyone but Harriet Rosenstein for half a century, lending them an air of grim secrecy and giving credence to the idea that Plath's claims were false (that is, Why now?). As Kate Manne reminds us, "People spill; they spill over." Most of us are wobbly vessels rather than locked boxes. Someone, whether Harriet Rosenstein or Ruth Beuscher, spilled—they showed Robin Morgan the Beuscher letters, because the line "Why must the killing of me be so elaborate?" comes directly from a letter Sylvia Plath wrote to her therapist on October 21, 1962. The phrase appears in no other letter or poem she wrote. Morgan's estimation of the letters ("about 20") is out of line with the actual number—fourteen—but some of the letters are so long, the total word count of the fourteen runs to almost eighteen thousand, so it's easy to see why, without them in front of her, Morgan might have guessed twenty. It's also possible she saw other letters that have since disappeared or been destroyed.

The silencing of Sylvia Plath, then, was compounded. Harriet Rosenstein may have sat on those letters and their "explosive" claims until she tried to sell them for almost one million dollars. But Robin Morgan talked. She wrote about their contents in the original version of "Arraignment," and when Random House reneged on their agreement to publish it, she went elsewhere (she comments in her *Feminist Art Journal* article about their commitment to feminist ideals). Absent a wide audience, the testimonies of Plath, and one of the only people to ever see Plath's claims of intimate partner violence in print, were functionally erased. The letters wouldn't surface for another forty years.

This is one reason that Sylvia Plath's work entered the house of the ruler and she emerged as a figure of imperious silence rather than the woman who gained fluency in every written discourse she took up. When we try, as Hartman does, to write into the silences of Plath's vast archive, the burnt and missing texts somehow become as vast as the archive itself, the flames hissing at us that, had we the novel, the journals, the letters, we would be replete with the knowledge that Plath herself had: like the dead woman in "Edge," we, too, might be perfected. But this is a trapdoor we fall through, one that tells us that Plathian discourse is too much, in need of an end to the story, a house closed up forever, a novel in flames. Write into it to learn once more: the ideal marriage is a fantasy in a dream house, built on sand. When Sylvia set it on fire, it gave up her rival's name. There is no resolution in the ruler's house. This story has no end.

In the Boneyard

※

> DOCTOR: Her death was doubtful,
>   And, but that great command o'ersways the order,
>   She should in ground unsanctified been lodged
>   Till the last trumpet . . .
> LAERTES: Must there no more be done?
> DOCTOR: No more be done.
>
> —From *Hamlet*, Act V, Scene I

ABOUT A QUARTER MILE FROM SYLVIA PLATH'S GRAVE IN HEP-tonstall, West Yorkshire, there is a wooded path lined with sycamore and oak trees. The path is steep and slippery and harder to get down than climb up. To find it, you cross over grassy hills and go through two tiny gates like something from a doll's house. Stone stairs lead up to the first small gate; the other one opens to the same, carved into the hillside, sloping down toward a moss-covered stone wall, which you follow to the wooded path lined with sycamore and oak trees.

At the top of the path is Lumb Bank, the eighteenth-century

manor home that Ted Hughes bought in the early 1970s, shortly after Assia Wevill killed herself and their daughter, Shura, in March of 1969. In the week before she ended her life, Wevill was in West Yorkshire with Hughes, looking for a home where they could live together. Lumb Bank wasn't in the running at the time, but they saw several other homes, none of which seemed suitable. Wevill was in despair; according to her journals of March 20, 1969, she asked Hughes why he couldn't commit to a life with her, to marriage and their family. In the years since Plath's suicide, Assia and Shura had often lived with Hughes, with Assia caring for Frieda and Nicholas. But it always ended badly. " 'It's Sylvia—it's because of her,' " Wevill records him telling her: "Ted drunk—stroking my shoulder." The next day, Wevill went to Haworth, the village up the road where the Brontës lived and wrote and died, and bought Seconal sleeping pills from the druggist. Two days later, she killed herself and her daughter in the kitchen of her London flat.

Ted Hughes took Assia Wevill to Lumb Bank with the intention of purchasing it in 1963. In an unpublished note about this, held by the British Library, he describes the visit as a happy one. Wevill's journals from the time tell a different story: "My insides raging. Anger and a silly flapping spite." Then, two days later: "I feel undocile. Endless idiotic conversations." The sale fell through, and the couple continued to bounce between London, Devonshire, and, for a time, the west coast of Ireland. Hughes's note indicates that Assia loved Lumb Bank and wanted to live there, but it is almost impossible to imagine her living in Heptonstall, which even today feels shuttered and insular, trapped in time. The stone is very old and the hills are very steep. Everywhere you look there is forbidding beauty. It rains and rains, and your boots slip on the cobblestones, so you move from the cobblestones to the sidewalks, which, in October, are slippery with fallen leaves. You are relieved to move to the crisscrossed walking paths of the surrounding woods, except that leaves blanket the uneven ground there, rocky with unseen stones, which gives way to mud and mulch. You never quite know what you're stepping on.

You feel the locals are onto you, and you imagine, as you can't help but do, the way they must have looked askance at a young Sylvia Plath, who visited for the first time in the late summer and early fall of 1956, after spending her honeymoon summer abroad in France and Spain with her new husband. Ted Hughes is a son of Heptonstall—at the top of a hill, with a view down to the village, sits his parents' home, The Beacon, where the couple stayed during their visits. There is a picture of Plath from this time, perched on a stone wall with her typewriter, wearing her signature headband and a chic sweater. Even at young people's Cambridge, where Plath was then studying English literature on a two-year Fulbright fellowship, her brightly colored clothes marked her as a flashy American; she must have seemed like a movie star against the gray stones of Heptonstall.

In 1963, Assia Wevill was thirty-six, famous in London for her beauty. Like Hughes, she was dark, with almost black hair that made her light-colored eyes jump from her face. Photographs of Wevill astonish those unfamiliar, or just learning, this terrible story. Some audibly gasp. "They look <u>exactly alike</u>," Plath wrote of Ted Hughes and Assia Wevill on October 21, 1962.

But I am more interested in the similarities between Sylvia and Assia, how, in Heptonstall, both must have felt like huge exotic birds forced into a gray stone cage as villagers watched them wander through the town like kept women. How, like a man in a fairy story, Ted Hughes tried to take them both from the London life they thrived in, to his gray stone tower. It feels like a tower, this place. You could let down your hair; the rain would lash it to the stones, and there, like lichen, it would stay.

ON THE SURFACE—AND PROBABLY BELOW IT—the details of Sylvia Plath's burial are unremarkable. Ted Hughes held a funeral for her in Heptonstall on February 18, 1963, in St. Thomas the Apostle Church. The church was built in the nineteenth century after a storm destroyed the original, the Church of St. Thomas a' Becket, built between 1256 and 1260. The ruins of the medieval church stand adjacent to the newer one, open to the public and filled with ancient graves, their inscriptions lost to time. Hughes buried Plath in the new graveyard, a stone's throw from the ruins. According to Plath's friend Jillian Becker, who took the train up from London to attend, the snow in Heptonstall was deep and the hole in the ground "a yellow trench in the snow."

Hughes asked for a moment alone after Plath was interred, and the other mourners left him. After, there was a small lunch at a local pub, where, according to Becker, Hughes repeated a series of strange phrases: "Everybody hated her," "She made me professional," and, strangest of all, "It was either her or me." If the goal of a rivalry is to beat, or blot out, your rival, Hughes began the process in the seven years after Plath's death as her grave, far from friends or family in either America or England, remained unmarked. When a stone was finally erected, it was a speckled gray granite inscribed with "In Memory," Plath's maiden and married names, her dates of birth and death, and a single line Hughes claimed was from the Bhagavad Gita: "Even amidst fierce flames, the golden lotus can be planted." The line is not from the Bhagavad Gita but from the sixteenth-century Chinese novel *Monkey*, by Wu Cheng'-en.

But it wasn't the quote that caused trouble for Hughes in the years to come, it was his choice to put "Sylvia Plath Hughes" on her headstone. Hughes wrote in a 1989 letter to the *Guardian* that he was convinced by the mason to use raised lead lettering for Plath's name rather than a carving. It was a choice he regretted, since, beginning in the early 1970s, people began to chisel the name "Hughes" off of the stone with ease (the letters were replaced multiple times). In the late 1980s, Hughes had the stone removed to be repaired or replaced, and for a time, a makeshift wooden cross with Plath's name and dates written across it in green marked the grave. The repaired stone was eventually erected, but in the time since has been repeatedly defaced. At various points, people (or a person) have covered the stone with thick lines of pink chalk. When I visited in October 2018, the "Hughes" had been whited out, possibly with bleach; it was the

A makeshift memorial near Sylvia Plath's grave in Heptonstall, West Yorkshire, when I visited in October 2022.

same when I was there in October 2022. Also there, in October 2022, was a makeshift, primitive memorial just below the grave, a wooden cross laid flat against a halo of wicker. It gave me an eerie feeling, but then, Heptonstall is an eerie place, especially in the October dusk, with the ruins in full view, gray stone against the gray sky, and the bones of your idol beneath your feet.

Plath's grave became a scandal when two young women, college students named Julia Parnaby and Rachel Wingfield, wrote a 1989 letter to the *Guardian* to protest its neglect. They had recently gone to visit it for the first time and found the graveyard unkempt, Plath's stone absent, and scant instructions for its location available—nothing but "a scrap of paper pinned to the notice board in the entrance of the village church [which] gave vague clues to its location." Their letter went on to offer sympathy for Ted Hughes, both for his loss and for the fact that people had chosen to vandalize the grave, but asked, pointedly, what he expected, since he had chosen to include his surname on Plath's stone and to bury her in his home, near his parents' graves. Their letter does not say *rather than near her own family in America or near one of her two English homes*, because it doesn't have to. Being in Heptonstall makes it clear. Sylvia Plath is an exile.

Julia Parnaby and Rachel Wingfield's letter received two near-immediate responses. The first, from a group of artists and writers that included Joseph Brodsky, Al Alvarez, and a number of Hughes's old friends, demanded to know whether Ted Hughes had removed the stone so it could be repaired or replaced, or if he had chosen to leave the grave unmarked. The second was from Hughes himself. Unfortunately for Parnaby and Wingfield (whose surnames Hughes, in his letter, used with repeated, deleterious effect, so that they began to sound like a pair of shifty Dickensian lawyers), they made a single factual error in their original letter to the *Guardian*, writing that Plath had signed divorce papers prior to her death.

In his letter, Hughes seized on this error as a way to mock and invalidate their project, which was to draw attention to the neglect of Plath's grave and improve its condition. Responding to their protest, Hughes gave a succinct history of the grave's vandalization and the stone's removal. In going to talk with the mason about the best course of action—to repair the original stone or make a new one "of a shape that could not easily be shattered, in which the letters would be deeply incised"—he discovered that the mason had gone ahead and repaired the original stone. Hughes encouraged the mason to "give it another go and set it up." The letter ended with a rare joke: "If he has not yet done so, I'm sure I agree with him that there is no hurry."

Hughes's letter was also a protest letter, but it was a curious line of resistance, given Parnaby and Wingfield's concerns—the missing gravestone and the overgrown cemetery hundreds of miles from any person or place Plath loved. Plath thought Yorkshire's Calder Valley extraordinarily beautiful and wrote several poems and one short story set there, but she found its inhabitants mostly narrow

A close-up of Sylvia Plath's grave from my October 2022 visit.

and provincial. Frieda's first Christmas, spent at The Beacon, ended in disaster when Plath and Olwyn had a shouting match over her head. When Hughes offered to bring her and the children there for Christmas 1962, which would be her last, she refused. One could argue that Heptonstall, with its proximity to the Brontës, those other giants of women's literature, is a suitable place for her burial, as though Plath and Emily stalk the moors at night. But, as Julia Parnaby and Rachel Wingfield point out, "It does not take an expert in anthropology to recognise that funerals are not only important for the dead and their relatives, but also as a symbol of what they indicate about a society and its values."

In response, Hughes, like Hamlet, wonders at the disrespect of those who visit his first wife's graveside: "Has this fellow no feeling at this business, who sings at grave-making?" But if he is Hamlet, he is also the gravedigger who, when Hamlet asks, "Whose grave's this, sirrah?" responds, "Mine." Ownership is the chief subject of Hughes's protest, the ownership of, as he wrote in another letter about his life with Sylvia Plath, the facts of his own life. It's true that Hughes and Plath never filed for divorce. It's also true that he buried Sylvia Plath in a graveyard overgrown with weeds and populated by strangers, rather than in "undulating Devon," where she told Jillian Becker she wanted to lie: "Soon after we met she told me, speaking of her death as a far-off event, that she'd like to be buried in the churchyard next to Court Green. Had she never said as much to Hughes?"

Maybe not. In Hughes's letter, Plath's grave becomes another version of her poetic legacy, a flinty mausoleum like Hughes's *Ariel*, a book made of granite that, like her gravestone, was difficult to shatter, the letters carved too deep to knock off.

TWO YEARS BEFORE SHE DIED, Assia Wevill made an unofficial will with instructions for her burial. These included the specification that her body should reside in a country cemetery in England, for which she planned to pay the church £50 (ostensibly because she thought the church would resent a suicide in their grounds), and that her gravestone should read, "Here lies a lover of unreason and an exile." It is possible she was planning filicide even then; the beginning of the document gives instructions for who should receive Wevill's money "in the event of my daughter not surviving," a line that sent a shudder through me. In the same document, she willed some of her jewelry and elegant clothing to Frieda Hughes, to whom she also left her love, love she similarly granted to Frieda's brother, Nicholas, whom she had cared for since he was a year old—"my most tender love." "I kissed Nick's neck over and over again," she wrote in a 1963 journal entry. "It kills me when he gurgles with it."

Hughes and Wevill never married and were living apart at the time of her death, with Hughes in Devon at Court Green, Wevill in a London flat with Shura. Her father, Lonya Gutmann, and her sister, Celia Chaikin, were both living in Canada at the time of her death;

her mother had died of cancer several years earlier. Hughes was tasked with the funeral and burial of his lover and daughter. Despite Jewish law forbidding cremation and Wevill's written instructions for her body, Hughes had both Assia and Shura cremated. He wrote a series of poems about it, some of which made their way into print. Others, unpublished, are preserved in his archives. "Ashes" grimly puns on Wevill's first name. It returns to the imagery of Nazism that Hughes first used in the summer of 1962, when he was leaving Plath. Then he had written that he left Plath because Hitler came to him in a dream and ordered him to do so; here he takes the place of Hitler, whom Wevill and her family fled in the lead-up to the Second World War: "So there were your ashes, plump . . . what Hitler was looking for / And I had found." The poem treats the cremation of Assia and Shura and the neglect of their remains passively, as if Hughes had not made these choices. In the poem, Hughes "[finds]" his lover's ashes on his bedroom bookshelf, as if they had been placed there by someone else.

It was long my understanding that Ted Hughes had scattered or buried Assia and Shura's ashes at an unknown site. The closest to a real location is found in *Ted Hughes: The Unauthorised Life*, where Jonathan Bate writes that Hughes scattered the ashes in a Kentish graveyard. But in the June 2020 issue of the *Ted Hughes Society Journal*, the poet and Hughes scholar Steve Ely claims to have uncovered a precise location. In "The Key of the Sycamore," Ely writes about Hughes's "planning materials" for *Capriccio*, his short book of poetry about Wevill, which includes notes detailing the specifics of the burial of the ashes in an unmarked grave just below Lumb Bank. Ely writes of how, in the notes, Hughes recalls his 1963 visit with Wevill to Lumb Bank, when she thought one day she would be mistress of the house, unable to imagine that instead he would live in it without her and her ashes would be buried nearby. Ely traces references to Wevill's burial on the path below Lumb Bank throughout a series of Hughes texts, including the "Epilogue" poems of his 1977 book *Gaudete*, which Wevill had helped him draft in the 1960s, when Hughes initially planned it as a film script. But it is *Capriccio* and its notes that confirm for the reader where Hughes buried his lover and daughter.

Capriccio was published in collaboration with the sculptor Leonard Baskin. Hughes had befriended him when Baskin was teaching alongside Sylvia Plath at Smith College in the 1957–58 academic year. The two became lifelong friends, and Baskin's woodcut prints were the covers for many of Hughes's later books, most famously 1970's *Crow*, which Hughes dedicated to Assia and Shura the year after their deaths. In "The Key of the Sycamore," Ely attributes this dedication as one way that Hughes attempted to memorialize his lover and child, but he does so in a footnote attached to the sentence, "She simply disappeared and was almost forgotten." This echoes Hughes's poetry about Assia Wevill, with its passive, fated voice that gives itself over to mythology and destiny, justifying not just Wevill's murder-suicide, but also Hughes's decision to cremate Assia and Shura and hide their final resting place from the world. Wevill did not simply disappear. She was nearly erased by someone who claimed to love her as his "true wife" yet could not be bothered to mark her grave.

THE DESECRATION OF SYLVIA PLATH'S grave has been criticized by fans and scholars of both Plath and Hughes, with Plath (and Assia Wevill) scholar Julie Goodspeed-Chadwick writing that the grave "has been the symbolic target of anger on one hand and the site of solidarity with respect to Plath on the other." But what if that anger and solidarity are two sides of the same coin? Anouilh's Antigone, describing her condemned burial of her brother, tells her sister, "You had your chance to come with me in the black night, creeping on your hands and knees. You had your chance to claw up the earth with your nails, as I did; to get yourself caught like a thief, as I did." Antigone has removed her brother's body from the open air to sacred ground, while those who alter Plath's gravestone deface the stone that marks it. But the act is informed by a similar ethical motivation, a desire to restore Plath, in death, to some semblance of what she sought in life: fame, good company, and love. By removing the name of the man who brutalized her and leaving the name she published under, it's possible they think they are performing that restoration, even if that restoration occurs by way of destruction.

The incandescent rage that hallmarks Plath's greatest work is the same anger that allowed me, in the years immediately following the end of a violent relationship, to rebuild my life. Plath taught me that I deserved that anger just as I deserved my life, that, contrary to popular notions of anger, especially in women, as a purely destructive passion, anger was a necessary tool for survival. Once, just before I fled, my ex waved a manila folder in my face, in which, he said, were the papers to take our infant son from me. If I didn't do as he said, he would file them. *Think, Emily, think*, he taunted. *Think, think, think*. The anger I felt; the power of it, spinning like the wheels of a simple machine. I took our son and left the next day, at dawn.

So, I understand and honor the legitimate anger that inspires people to draw on, or chisel words off of, Sylvia Plath's grave. But I went to visit it for the first time in a state of excited anticipation and joy. The thought of doing harm to the grave never occurred to me. It was a gorgeous October day, in 2018, and I carried pink roses in homage to Plath's poem "Fever 103" and also tracing paper to get an etching. Once I found the grave, I watched a fat, furry caterpillar crawl up the granite. I took pictures. I talked to a passerby who asked me to tell him more about Sylvia Plath. I left the roses tied in the old red bandana I had worn for years as a tribute to Sylvia, who is wearing one in my favorite photograph of her, which I have tattooed on the back of my left shoulder. Maybe thirty minutes passed. And then I stood to go, because I wanted to eat something and move onto the nearby Brontë Parsonage.

And then the strangest coincidence of my life happened. I heard a voice say, "I can never remember where grandmum and granddad are buried," and it was the voice of Frieda Hughes, who was visiting Heptonstall that weekend to participate in a festival devoted to her father's poetry. Sylvia's body resides just a few yards from the graves of Frieda's grandparents, Edith and William Hughes, whose shared headstone I had just passed, leaving behind one of the three roses I had intended for Sylvia. I was able, therefore, to tell their granddaughter where they were, which was how we began a halting, unforgettable conversation. Months later, when I wrote about this encounter, another Plath scholar messaged me and said, "Ok, spill it—what was Frieda like?" But the truth was, there was very little to spill. Or so I thought at the time. Frieda was friendly enough, but guarded, and deeply suspicious of me. I can warrant a fair guess that this was because I was an American woman visiting her mother's grave, a person who coded, or read, as "angry feminist." And I am angry. And I am a feminist. That day, however, I felt nothing but gratitude for a world that had brought me to Heptonstall to have a quiet moment with Sylvia Plath's grave in the sunshine. And yet, so conscious was I of the way I read—so very American, with my short hair and my *Jane Eyre* tote bag and my hipster sunglasses—that as I walked closer to Frieda Hughes, I said, aloud, with my hands in the air, palms open, "I don't have a chisel."

In other words, I disarmed myself of her perception of me as someone dangerous to her parents' legacy (and, by extension, to her) before I dared to speak to the woman whose mother taught me that anger is a tool. So, too, is a chisel, is chalk. Using tools is what makes us human, according to anthropologists. But then, Catharine MacKinnon, the landmark feminist thinker, has asked in her work, "Are women human?" We don't have to look far to see this question's abiding connection to Sylvia Plath. And while MacKinnon's work tackles, among other things, grave questions about women as human traffic in the modern-day sex trade, women's anger at the way Ted Hughes treated Sylvia Plath during their marriage and neglected and distorted her legacy after her death is a legitimate extension of MacKinnon's central question. If women were human, we would be allowed the full range of the human experience and the emotions that accompany that experience.

Plath, in expressing the rage she felt at Hughes's betrayal of her, and her larger rage at a system and culture that relegated women's lives to, as she famously said, an "awful tragedy" solely because of the accident of birth, was denigrated as an inhuman monster. Her admirers, along with many feminist scholars, in attempting to defend or legitimize her anger, her work, and her life, have suffered a shadow of this same critique. Absent the tools at the disposal of people whose anger *is* considered "legitimate"—namely, recognition of the realities of what Plath suffered in both life and death—we should not be surprised when this anger smashes patronymic letters off a stone. The people who vandalize Sylvia Plath's grave don't smash the stone to bits or write angry graffiti against Sylvia Plath. They engage in an act of legitimate protest against Ted Hughes—one of the few available to them.

One of Ted Hughes's continued protests about his treatment by Sylvia Plath's fans was their relegation of him to the position of a fictional man in a tragedy, rather than allowing him to experience the full scope of human tragedy. Ironically, the poems Hughes published about Assia Wevill and Sylvia Plath in the last eight years of his life make them victims of the very same fate. Although Steve Ely calls the poem "Snow" "one of Hughes's most tender elegies," we would do well to remember the function of an elegy—to honor and sing the memory of the dead. "Snow," like the majority of the poems in *Capriccio*, turns Assia Wevill from a human being into a literary trope, a "Walk down the cobbled hill into the oven / Of empty fire." Ely's stated belief in "The Key of the Sycamore" is that Wevill only matters because she appears in Hughes's poetry. He extends this line of thinking to Assia's desired epitaph, "Here lies a lover of unreason and an exile," which he calls her "attempt to frame the post-mortem reception of her life, perhaps knowing that she would be posthumously recognised as an important character in the biography of a famous poet, if not for her own achievements." He extends it even to Assia's religion, Judaism, which Ely writes was "in many ways more important to Hughes than it was to her" after arguing that Wevill was not actually Jewish, as the line is matrilineal, and only her father was Jewish. But Wevill was Jewish enough to have fled Hitler's Germany with her family. She was Jewish enough to have specified burial, rather than cremation, of her body—or, as Ely writes, her "disposal," his chosen term for Hughes's burial of Assia and Shura's ashes, as though the woods near Heptonstall were a dumping ground for bodies unwanted, unclaimed.

This forces us to contend with the way Hughes's "disposal" of not just Assia's and Shura's ashes, but also their legacies, has done real harm. In Ely's article, whether he means to or not, he answers MacKinnon's question about whether or not women are human with a resounding *no*. His project shows little care for the fact that he has discovered the burial place of two human beings, one of whom was a four-year-old child. In an article that spans twenty-plus pages, there is no acknowledgment, until the final paragraph, that this might now be an opportunity for Wevill's family, some of whom are still living, to visit her grave. The possibility that Frieda Hughes, Shura's half-sister, might visit is never brought up, since to do so would reckon with the reality that Hughes had an illegitimate child who he functionally abandoned, and other Hughes scholars—notably Terry Gifford, in the same issue of the *Ted Hughes Society Journal* as Ely's article—continue to cast doubt on Shura's paternity.

I thought Ely had one concern: to prove that Assia and Shura Wevill matter only because they exist as obscure characters in Ted Hughes's poetry, which Ely likens to a matryoshka doll: a way to hide his actions in plain sight, an old argument about Hughes's brilliance. Diane Middlebrook made it, as well, in *Her Husband*:

> Withholding from others something important to himself, by hiding it in plain sight—that is a defensive stance so prominent in Hughes's character, as far back as you can track him, that you might as well say it *is* his character. Hughes's life as an artist was ruled by the need to secrete meanings in his writing

that only he would know about. In each important work lies a horde of images imprinted with urgent personal references.

Hughes, then, can hide his sins in a poem layered like a mille-feuille: a girl-child inside a woman inside a myth inside a man's dark mind. But it occurred to me, during my most recent visit to Heptonstall, as I tramped through the woods around Lumb Bank, knowing Assia and Shura were somewhere beneath my feet, hidden in plain sight on a public footpath, that in choosing to publish the burial place of Assia and Shura Wevill in a scholarly journal with a tiny readership, Ely was taking his cues from his subject, a man about whom, in her will, Assia Wevill made no bones: "To Ted Hughes, their father," she wrote, "I leave my no doubt welcome absence and my bitter contempt."

THE PATH THAT LEADS TO Assia and Shura's gravesite is, as Ely says, "frequented by dog walkers, mountain bikers, creative writers, tourists and hikers." When I visited, I had the guidance of two English friends familiar with the area and an American who had relocated to Heptonstall. We had just enough daylight to get there and lay the clay stone I had made earlier in the week with my aunt, a potter, and my eleven-year-old son, the one I took with me when I fled the violent relationship that nearly destroyed my life. I have been, almost, disappeared, which must be why I was compelled to make something permanent to mark the burial of Assia Wevill and her daughter, Shura, who was only four when her mother killed her in a murder-suicide. "And I have no face / I have wanted to efface myself," Plath wrote in "Tulips," lines that live deep in my body, the place that thought, once, *I'll forget—I'll forget all he's done, to me, to our son, to other women, the cheating and the violence, I'll forget, and it will be okay.* I could not forget, which is part of why I took our son early one fall morning and fled. But that longing woman still lives in me. I thought of her as my son helped my aunt and me trim the gravestone we were sculpting for Assia and Shura.

"Doing this with all of you feels powerful," one friend said as we walked over the Heptonstall hills toward Lumb Bank. She had visited the spot in advance to find the right place, or as close as we could get to it. Holding the stone I had lugged in my carry-on from Newark International Airport to Heathrow, then on the Tube, and then the train to Leeds, and then the train to Hebden Bridge, and then up the steep hill to Heptonstall. I walked in circles, looking at the trees and the stones. The sky darkened. I leaned down and nestled the stone at the base of a sycamore, in a hollow made by a gnarled root, which seemed to hug the baked clay. "It will last about three years and slowly dissolve into the earth," my aunt had told me. "In the meantime, we'll make a permanent one, and we'll bring it back."

It was about three years from the time I left my ex before I felt the ground beneath my feet again, rather than the sense that I was walking on water, being waked by a nearby boat. As an American like Sylvia, I was raised on a barrier island, not the English moors, which were, Plath wrote her mother, the only place where she didn't miss the sea. I wanted to feel at home in those woods, but I did not, feeling, instead, the warmth of the women surrounding me as I placed the stone and my friend read the mourner's Kaddish, a prayer described as "a primary weapon in the war against forgetting."

After, we walked up to one of Heptonstall's two pubs in the dark, and my other friend held me back from the group. "You have to banish him," she said, holding my arm gently, staring at me with her intent eyes. "While you're here. We should make a circle around you, and banish him." She meant Ted Hughes, whose presence is nowhere larger than it is in Heptonstall, near Lumb Bank where he was once the lord of the manor, below which he buried his mistress and illegitimate daughter in an unmarked grave and then, according to one source, carved his own initials into an adjacent tree. My friend's brown eyes peered into my own and I saw, in my mind's eye, my son's hands as they pieced together a tiny Star of David, made from clay, to attach to Assia and Shura's stone, while, with my own, I carved Assia's epitaph into the clay: *Here lies a lover of unreason and an exile.* The stylus gripped in my hand, my anger transformed to creative joy as soon as it found another tool.

Ahead of us, in the gloaming, our friends wavered out of view.

ON MY THIRD DAY IN West Yorkshire, I visited the Brontë Parsonage and purchased, in the gift shop, a tiny hanging sign that reads, "Better to be without logic than without feeling," a quote from Charlotte Brontë's novel *The Professor.* The phrase was with me as I trudged over the green hills and down the path away from Lumb Bank, and it is with me now. How do you describe a feeling of surety that something was, something is, something continues to be?

This is the chief problem of writing about Ted Hughes and Sylvia Plath, and now Assia Wevill—you know Hughes made it hard for these women, you know they feared him. You know he made it hard for the women who wanted to write about them. You know somehow he still does, although he is no more, scattered ashes somewhere on Dartmoor. There is a sign in Poets' Corner in Westminster Abbey, the place where a funeral was held for him as poet laureate of England, the place where he was eulogized by King Charles, who once referred to Hughes as his "guru." You know it was hard for Princess Diana, too; you see in her coltish legs and sly smile a trace of Sylvia Plath—Plath, who was trapped, alone, far from home, and trying to escape a crushing love with a sneering, violent poet.

Coltish legs and memories both are and aren't facts; traces have no logic. It is not possible to explain that as my friends and I crossed into a particular part of the woods below Lumb Bank, the temperature dropped suddenly and an icy wind picked up. It is not possible to explain that it felt like a dangerous place, except to say it felt like a dangerous place. It was a dangerous place. It told me to turn back, but I didn't listen. The day before her suicide, Assia Wevill wrote, "The tenderness with which these terrible relationships are evoked, once the players are dead. Their lives are so compost for the sentimental bouquets of 'compilers' of the future." It is a fact that the lesser-used definition of the word quagmire is "a soft, boggy area of land that gives way under foot." I tried to find my footing. My boots sank into mulch.

Lumb Bank is owned now by the Arvon Foundation, a literary nonprofit that offers workshops, retreats, and grants to practicing writers. Ted Hughes leased it to them in 1974. On my last day in England, I went there with a friend to record a panel on Sylvia Plath for the Open University of the United Kingdom. We recorded in the library, with its view of the wooded valley below. It was my first, and surely only, time being inside a home Ted Hughes owned and occupied, and I quashed my discomfort by making jokes. Inside the bathroom, I took a mirror selfie and pulled a face, then rounded the corner to peer into what was once his bedroom. "Assia and Shura's ashes were there, for years, in a plastic bag," my friend told me and I felt nothing but a rising anxiety, like the woman in a horror movie who, as the house hisses *Get out*, fingers the crown molding with loving care.

When, at the end of the panel, I was asked what Sylvia Plath means to me, I choked up as I tried to answer. We, too, have a relationship. "She is a part of every single thing I've been and done. Oh god, no, this is embarrassing," I said, as tears came down my face. My heart hurt, there, in that room, with its view of the wooded valley. It yearned to cross the sea, and be home.

Afterword

The Heart in the Fire

IN THE END, WHAT DOES IT MEAN TO LOVE SYLVIA PLATH?

As Maggie Nelson reminds us in *The Art of Cruelty*, "to be called the Sylvia Plath of anything is *a bad thing*," a signal that you're extremist, suicidally depressed, hysterical, angry, or misandrist, to name just a few of the character traits we associate with my favorite writer. Anyone really familiar with Sylvia Plath's life and work knows this is a reductive stereotype about her. But it is a powerful one. For decades, I was told that writing about Plath from the perspective of an admirer was disastrous. If I loved the work and life of a woman who was so grim, so fated to die, then surely I, too, was grim and, if not fated to die, then unnaturally interested in death and dying. And the truth was, I was curious about death and dying, like most of us. But this was somehow pathologized when it was attached to my interest in Sylvia Plath. Why, for instance, is the exploration of death and suicide seen as a mark of pathology in Plath, or her readers, but Norman Mailer could stab his wife with six witnesses and later be invited to moderate a debate on feminism? The simple answer is, he is a man; but that's not an answer, in the end.

In death, Plath suffered hostilities that were portrayed as the just consequence for her choice to end her life. The resulting discourse centered her suicide in a way that many saw as in need of righting. Over the years, my attempts to correct Plath's easy association with suicide sometimes led me to hyperfocus on the joyful events in her life: childbirth, daffodil planting, traipsing, as a graduate student, through Paris with the Italian man who lent her his typewriter. I did this, I see now, as though I might erase the tragedy of her death. But then I was struck by a passage from Jacqueline Rose's landmark book *The Haunting of Sylvia Plath*, in which she criticizes the feminist position that we might gain a "whole Plath" by recovering work Ted Hughes censored. Rose believes this is predicated on the false notion that an "uncensored" Plath materializes if we read her work "in terms of a positive emergence of selfhood . . . a narrative progression from suffering into self-discovery or flight. Are we not at risk in doing this of putting ourselves, putting feminism, in the place of the idealised and idealizing mother who can bear to see nothing bad in her daughter?" In other words, a restored Plath does not cancel out a Plath who killed herself. For Rose, it made more sense to read Plath "in terms of the unbearable coexistence of opposites," Plath at her most triumphant and at her nadir, a writer who is neither essentialized nor moralized in an essentialist way. For me, it makes sense to love Sylvia Plath in the same way.

Loving Sylvia Plath has long been essentialized as a young woman's game, a phase to pass through and grow out of in order to be taken seriously. The writer Meghan O'Rourke once wrote of a colleague, "a well-read journalist," responding to her declaration of affection for Plath with "You mean you liked her when you were eighteen?" Plath's only published novel, *The Bell Jar*, is often pitched as a young adult novel despite its intense themes of madness, breakdown, suicide, mental hospitals, and sexual assault. But I remain firm in my suspicion that young women are taught they must grow out of their love of Plath because grown women should love men, or, minimally, women who survived their thirties. Plath's suicide is frequently presented as the capricious choice of a spoiled girl seeking revenge, rather than the culmination of a mental health crisis. Her poetic interest in death and dying is conceived as, to quote the poet Marianne Moore, "so grisly." (During her lifetime, Moore also wrote against Plath's application for a Guggenheim, noting that the then-pregnant Plath should not be "subsidized for having a baby, especially in view of the world population explosion.")

Yet bright, joyful images of Sylvia Plath, rather than being welcomed as a balance to this "[grisliness]," are also met with the criticism that Plath is a serious writer who should at all times look serious. This was especially the case in 2017, when the first volume of her published letters debuted in the United Kingdom. The cover image was Plath, aged twenty-one, smiling on a beach, wearing a modest two-piece bathing suit. "It's time to stop sexualizing a serious author to sell books," went the headline in the *Guardian*. The story was picked up by *Jezebel* and *Entertainment Weekly*, which ran with the idea that the "real" Plath was studious, with her "real" brown hair. "Cover of New Sylvia Plath Volume Sells Her as a Blond in a Bikini," went the *Jezebel* headline, as if Plath couldn't possibly have been "a blond in a bikini" or as if either of those descriptors was inherently bad. This inability to understand Plath as many different types of women within her lifetime mirrors her earliest critics' inability to synthesize her popularity with her artistic success: *Pick one Plath*, it says. *You can't have both.*

But we have to have both, because Sylvia Plath was both of those people, and many more, throughout her short life. To write a book about loving her, I had to love the Sylvia Plath in the bikini, twenty-one years old and in love with three different men and all her possible futures. And I had to love—I do love—the Sylvia Plath, *so grisly*, who died by her own hand, in London, at dawn, and is buried in the north of England, far from her American home. I had to love the cemetery where she is buried, and which, as much as any other place, is emblematic of how love transcends time and moves through it, as, too, does Sylvia Plath. At her grave, all the time, are flowers, pens, poems, stones, red bandanas, homemade memorials—proof of the many ways so many people love a Sylvia Plath they never knew, and return to her across generations. There is much to love in that idea alone.

When I began this book, someone I trusted told me, "You have to get everything right. Because everyone is going to come for it." In my attempt to do so, I became closer to Sylvia Plath scholars who had been at this much longer than me. They were unfailingly generous. But their generosity sometimes made me feel ashamed, as though I was not allowed to learn from them. I felt I should have known everything prior to the writing, rather than, as anyone who has written anything knows, learning from the writing itself. I believe this, too, is part of the way we conceive of Sylvia Plath—as a writer we already know everything about, one we must be done with. "'Sylvia'; No More Plath, Please," went a 2003 *New York Times* editorial by a Florida man named Horace Hone in response to a review of the 2003 biopic *Sylvia*. "Do we need this plethora of Plath?" Hone wondered.

I don't actually disagree with Mr. Hone. A plethora is an excess, more and more of the same. We have come to know a Sylvia Plath whose life *is* her famous death, or else its prologue, the apocryphal Chekhovian shotgun over the mantelpiece that had better go off by the end. We need new stories about Sylvia Plath and new stories about we who love her. When the trusted person told me, "You have to get everything right," I jumped right in with the proper response, the one I had been trained to give—"It has to be textual, not rhetorical," I said, and they said, "Yes, exactly." Texts are enormously important to any book that sits, as I hope this one does, at the crossroads of theory, imaginative literature, and biography. But I could not have written it without the embodied experience of loving Sylvia Plath—tramping across graveyards and into the British Library, standing alone on a dark March night outside the London home where Plath killed herself, trying to leave, and feeling, each time I turned to go, that something called me back. This book is as much about that embodiment as it is about the life and afterlife of Sylvia

Plath, because the afterlife of Sylvia Plath, while hugely textual, is also a legacy of survival in the generations of readers who love her.

I wrote this book to celebrate and interrogate the living Plath, the conditions of her life, death, and literary afterlife, and the way she has transformed and informed every stage of my life. When I was a depressed teenager, she took me seriously, and she spurred me to take myself seriously and to demand better for myself—not, as the stereotype about her goes, to give in and die. When, as a young, first-time mother, I fled a violent relationship, it was her incandescent outrage at her husband that helped me rebuild my life and believe, in my worst moments, that I deserved a life at all. When I was a struggling single mother, Plath's transcendental love of her children gave me faith that my son could teach me how to live. And when, years later, in the midst of writing this book, I had a second son at the age of forty with a loving partner, I recited Plath's poem for her own infant son, "Nick and the Candlestick," as his father laid him in my arms for the first time.

Turning Sylvia Plath's writing about suicide, death, and dying into a question of moralism, pathology, or both has kept us from a true valuation of her extraordinary contribution to literature about death—about what it meant to observe it as a living person, its processes and effect on the living, what it meant to desire it, or pursue it, the terror and relief that it produced. Plath wrote of death ironically, whimsically, full of humor and despair, through the endless expanse of her wit, observation, and imagination. And in between the Plath writing of death and suicide and the daily Plath who baked pies and changed nappies, there is a wildness that I continue to seek. "I must be lean & write & make worlds beside this to live in," she wrote in her journal in March 1957. I wrote this book to explore the worlds that Sylvia Plath built, of which I am the smallest part: a bluebird she painted on her daughter's doll cradle, a tulip on her snowy grave, a red heart she tossed onto the fire as she danced, laughing, around the flames: *Now*, she whispered, *speak*.

ACKNOWLEDGMENTS

To Danielle DeTiberus, my first and best reader and my best friend. Thank you for every phone call, email, text message, vacation, big cry, and bigger laughs. I also thank her husband, Ryan, who I have known and loved as long as her. To my husband, Vincent DiGiacinto, for his unconditional love, riotous humor, and willingness to become a de facto expert on Sylvia Plath. To our three beautiful children, Stella, Hank, and Bowie, thank you for being the best reason to keep trying to make the world a better place. Every day I think I couldn't love you all more, but then I do. Thanks to April Isidro for being my co-mother and kindred spirit.

In addition to Beth Vesel, to whom this book is dedicated, I'd like to thank her former assistants, Grey Moran and Calla Deitrick, who read drafts of the proposal and talked me through any challenges I encountered in the process. Thanks to Lauren Champlin, also at the Beth Vesel Agency, for everything she did to help bring this book into the world. To my editor Jill Bialosky, and her former assistant, Drew Weitman, who took a chance on a difficult subject, gave me the necessary space and time to finish, and, with their invaluable edits, turned this into a book worth reading. Thank you so much. If the world knows a different version of Sylvia Plath now, it's because of both of you. To Laura Mucha—I will be eternally grateful that your "academic Rumspringa" coincided with the production of this book. You have been a source of constant support and I am grateful to call you a friend. Thank you, as well, to Gabrielle Nugent and Meredith Dowling, who worked tirelessly and creatively to get the message of this book into the world.

Thank you to everyone at Norton, especially Rivka Genesen and Lauren Abbate, for their help putting this book together, from the art to the permissions. Thanks also, to Don Rifkin for his keen and careful eye. To the two Janets!—Janet Greenblatt and Janet Byrne were absolutely ace copyeditors, who gave this book a style and panache it otherwise lacked, and talked me out of my much-too-long paragraphs. Thank you both.

To Corinne Segal, my former editor at *Literary Hub*, where the roots of this book lie—thank you for your guidance, brilliance, and friendship.

Thank you to my loving parents, John and Scottie Van Duyne, for filling our home with books and teaching me to fight for what I love. Thanks to my sisters, Julie and Gretchen, for being my lifelong best friends and for our group text, which keeps me laughing and sane. Thanks to Susan and Catherine Van Duyne, who have been my aunts, big sisters, and best friends all in one, and who have propped me up with unconditional love my whole life. Thanks to my Uncle Tom and Aunt Bette, who, when I was a small child, taught me to love art, beauty, jazz, and cats. Thanks to my mother's family, the Metzgers, who are always there to offer love, humor, and well-timed sarcasm when I need it most—thanks especially to my cousin David Metzger, for his lifelong love and support, and for driving Hank and me to the airport when we had to run, all those years ago. You're my brother, and I love you.

To Gail Crowther, who, tramping through England, Ireland, Greece, and America with me, taught me how to listen to the dead. Your friendship means the world to me, and this book wouldn't exist without your input and edits. To Julie Goodspeed-Chadwick, for her friendship and belief in this book, and for her groundbreaking work on Assia Wevill, which continues to expand and enhance Plath Studies—thank you. To Janet Badia, of whose work I thought, at many points, Why should I try when Janet's book is already in the world? Thank you for inspiring me to keep working.

To Linda Wagner-Martin, for your intrepid work on Sylvia Plath, your generosity of spirit, and your box of treasures—I can never thank you enough. Thanks to Susan and Jennifer Plath for their generous permission to mention Assia's letters to their grandmother. Thank you to Kathleen Aguero and Laure-Anne Bosselaar for teaching me how to write poetry. Laure-Anne—you told me to listen to Hank, that he would teach me how to live. And he did. Thank you.

I have often wondered how Sylvia Plath might have fared with consistent, loving childcare. For this reason, and many others, I send love and gratitude to Chery Lemmerman. Without her love, empathy, and constancy in those first terrible months after I left a violent relationship with my young baby, I couldn't have survived or built a life. Thanks also to the staff over the years at her Montessori school, most especially her mother, Darlene, Katie Sutor-Costello, and Abby Chort, who care for our son as though he is their own.

Thanks to the Fulbright and Mid-Atlantic Arts Foundations and Emory University, which generously supported my work on Sylvia Plath with research and creative fellowships. Thank you to Stockton University's Research & Professional Development Committee, which generously supported my work on Plath.

Thanks to the librarians at the British Library, the Cambridge University Library, Smith College's Neilson Library, Yale's Beinecke Rare Book & Manuscript Library, and Emory University's Rose Manuscript, Archives, and Rare Book Library, but most especially Karen V. Kukil, whose groundbreaking work on Sylvia Plath changed the world's understanding of, and access to, my favorite writer. Special thanks also to Kathy Shoemaker, Gabrielle Dudley, and Carrie Hintz, of Emory's Rose Rare Book and Manuscript Room, for providing scans and photocopies from afar. Thanks to Courtney Chartier, now at Columbia University, for her incredible generosity and kindness during my time at Emory. Thanks to Nick Twemlow for sharing new materials at the Rose I would never have known were there. Thanks to Frieda Midgley for the tour of Newnham College's grounds and archive, and for introducing Gail and me to Jean Gooder. Thanks to Penny Ramon at the Lilly Library of Indiana University for her help securing permissions for photographs.

Thank you to all of my incredible students and colleagues at Stockton University, but especially: Kristin Jacobson, Rodger Jackson, Jacob Camacho, Emily August, Di Strelczyck, Betsy McShea, Betsy Erbaugh, Marcy Isabella, Cindy King, Rob Gregg, Claire Lopatto, Liz Masterson, Shawn Manuola, Lauren Rivera, Kirsten DiPatri, Eddie Horan, Sarah Holt, Moneeba Khan, Aurora Landaman, Cassandra Rosamond, Liz Myers, and Isabella Bruno. Bella—you changed this book for the better with your reading of "Widow."

Thank you to my students and colleagues at Aristotle University of Thessaloniki, but especially Dr. Tatiani Rapatzikou, Dr. Lydia Roupakia, Athina Papadopolou, and Chaido Skylanda. Thanks also to Maria Mytilinaki-Kennedy for her generosity and friendship.

Thank you to Dora Psoma for your friendship and for the $1 text messages—despite your not being a fan of Sylvia Plath, I am your biggest fan.

Thanks to Stephanie Cawley for their friendship and for introducing me to Linda Gregg. Thanks to Sara Franklin for loving Judith Jones as much as I love Sylvia Plath. Thanks to Amy Reading for reading an early draft of this book and convincing me it was worth publishing. Thank you to Kelly McAllister for much-needed support at a crucial time. Thanks to Ali Velshi, Lily Corvo, and Hannah Holland for letting me talk about Sylvia Plath for their excellent "Banned Book Club."

The Sylvia Plath community is filled with writers, scholars, and fans who have given me much support over the years and become friends. I want to especially thank Suzanne Demko for the laughs, the champagne, and the side commentary. Thanks to Paul Alexander for allowing me to interview him about his important work on Sylvia Plath, and for responding quickly to emails and text messages about the same. Thanks also to Diane Demko, Jessica Ferri, Giulia Listo, Carl Rollyson, Ash Caton, A. E. Stallings, Nic Presley, Emma Bolden, Sarah Corbett, Eilish Mulholland, Maeve O'Brien, Nels Highberg, Sarah Viren, Muffy Bolding, Greg Mulhern, Kathleen Ossip, Peter Fydler, Peter K. Steinberg, Anne Theriault, Sandra Beasley, and Ash Trebisacci for friendship and collegiality and for handily sharing letters, laughs, documents, and links whenever I needed them. Thanks to Martin Baker for his spirited correspondence about his dear friend Assia Wevill, and for allowing me to publish his photographs of Assia and Shura in this book. Thank you to Mark Wormald for generously sending me scans of his book *The Catch: Fishing For Ted Hughes*, which is not yet available in the United States, and for discussing our shared interest in the ways our lives intersect with our heroes.

Gratitude for the friendship of Jamie Bittar, Ming Tran, Diane Shapiro, Natalie Pryor, Justin Pryor, Meredith Granieri, Andrea Madden, Christine Salvatore, Maxine Patroni, Emari DiGiorgio, Nancy Reddy, Richard Russell, Heather McGovern, Deb Gussman, Meghan Privitello, Benjamin Paloff, Meghan Thomas, Strummer Hoffston, Ciara Barrick, Patricia Durante, Bill Thomas, Patrick Davis, Patricia Barasch, Gina Innocente, Michelle Salvato, and Julia Zabihach and her two beautiful girls, Zorianna and Daria.

Finally, in memoriam: Alicia Smith, Jennifer Cakert, Dawn Henson Farley, Susan Ingargiola, Lauren Campbell, and Joel Frankel—who called me "Sylvia" in high school, and helped me survive, then, whether he knew it or not.

NOTES

Introduction: Gaslight

1   **"If you are dead":** Sylvia Plath, *The Unabridged Journals of Sylvia Plath*, ed. Karen V. Kukil (New York: Anchor Books, 2000), 478.
1   **Sylvia Plath's psychiatric records:** See the 2016–17 emails between Harriet Rosenstein and Frieda Hughes. Harriet Rosenstein research files on Sylvia Plath, Box 2, Folder 4. Stuart A. Rose Manuscript, Archives, and Rare Book Library, Emory University.
2   **"Unseen Plath Letters Claim Domestic Abuse":** Danuta Kean, "Unseen Sylvia Plath Letters Claim Domestic Abuse by Ted Hughes," *Guardian*, April 11, 2017.
2   **similar ones in major newspapers:** For a relatively comprehensive list of these, see Peter K. Steinberg, "The Harriet Rosenstein Sylvia Plath archive, Update," *Sylvia Plath Info* (blog), April 12, 2017.
2   **"Shock" can be caused:** *Merriam-Webster Dictionary*, "shock."
2   **she died without a will:** For a thorough account of the legalities of this, and the consequences it had on the publication of Plath's work, see the final chapter of Carl Rollyson, *The Last Days of Sylvia Plath* (Jackson: The University Press of Mississippi, 2020).
3   **"felt the full collection":** Ted Hughes, "Publishing Sylvia Plath," reprinted in *Winter Pollen: Occasional Prose*, ed. William Scammel (New York: Picador, 1994), 166.
3   **"more personally aggressive":** Ted Hughes, "Collecting Sylvia Plath," reprinted in *Winter Pollen: Occasional Prose*, ed. William Scammel (New York: Picador, 1994), 172.
3   **Beginning in 1971:** Plath's uncollected poems from the *Ariel* period were initially published in the volumes *Winter Trees* and *Crossing the Water* (London: Faber & Faber, 1971) and later in her *Collected Poems* (Faber & Faber, 1981). In 2004, her original order for the collection was published as *Ariel: The Restored Edition* (Faber & Faber).
3   **allegations about Hughes's violence:** Paul Alexander, *Rough Magic* (Cambridge, MA: Da Capo Press, 2003), 194.
3   **brutal fights and sexual encounters:** Plath, *The Unabridged Journals of Sylvia Plath*.

3   **only possible to be shocked:** Emily Van Duyne, "Why Are We So Unwilling to Take Sylvia Plath at Her Word?" *Literary Hub*, July 11, 2017.

3   **victim impact statement:** Chanel Miller, "Here's the Powerful Letter the Stanford Victim Read to Her Attacker," Buzzfeed, June 3, 2016.

3   **first Women's March:** "The Women's March, 2017," *National Museum of American History: Behring Center*. The list of women accusing Trump is long, but here are two powerful examples: E. Jean Carroll, "Hideous Men: Donald Trump Assaulted Me in a Bergdorf Goodman Dressing Room 23 Years Ago. But He's Not Alone on the List of Awful Men in My Life," *New York*, The Cut: First Person, June 21, 2019; Kate Manne's preface to *Down Girl: The Logic of Misogyny* (Oxford: Oxford University Press, 2017), 5–10. Manne's preface treats not only Ivana Trump's accusations, in her divorce suit, of both sexual assault and intimate partner violence, but also similar accusations against Andrew Puzder by his ex-wife Lisa Fierstein; Trump had nominated Puzder to be his secretary of labor (the nomination was eventually withdrawn).

3   **#MeToo movement:** Jodi Kantor and Megan Twohey, "Harvey Weinstein Paid Off Sexual Harassment Accusers for Decades," *New York Times*, October 5, 2017.

4   **biopic *Sylvia*:** *Sylvia*, directed by Christine Jeffs (New Zealand: Focus Features, 2003). Set in 1961, the film includes a scene in which Hughes repeatedly hits Plath in the face after she accuses him of having an affair with a BBC producer.

4   **"gaslit so often":** Chanel Miller, "A Conversation with Chanel Miller." Online lecture in honor of Asian American & Pacific Islander Heritage Celebration, Stockton University, April 30, 2021.

4   **The word *gaslighting*:** See *Merriam-Webster Dictionary*, "gaslighting."

4   **Gaslight:** John Van Druten, Walter Reisch, and John L. Balderston, *Gaslight*, directed by George Cukor (Culver City, CA: Metro-Goldwyn-Mayer, 1944). Digital, 2023.

4   **Gaslighting became a hot topic:** Stephanie Sarkis, "Donald Trump Is a Classic Gaslighter in an Abusive Relationship with America," *USA Today*, October 3, 2018; Amanda Carpenter, *Gaslighting America: Why We Love It When Trump Lies to Us* (New York: HarperCollins, 2018).

5   **"anything that is not a hard fact":** Miller, "A Conversation with Chanel Miller."

5   **Hughes admitted to destroying:** Hughes's foreword to the 1982 edition of *The Journals of Sylvia Plath*, ed. Frances McCullough (New York: Anchor Books, reprinted 1998); Ted Hughes, "Sylvia Plath and Her Journals," in *Winter Pollen: Occasional Prose*, 177–92.

5   **As Janet Badia wrote:** *Sylvia Plath and the Mythology of Women Readers* (Amherst: University of Massachusetts Press, 2011), 28.

6   **New Criticism held that a poem:** The Poetry Foundation, Glossary of Poetic Terms, "New Criticism."

6   **"the personal is political":** Carol Hanisch, "The Personal Is Political," 1969.

6   **embraced by second-wave feminists:** Honor Moore, "After Ariel," *Boston Review*, March 1, 2009.

6   **confessional school of poetry:** The Poetry Foundation, Glossary of Poetic Terms, "Confessional Poetry."

6   **cited as influences:** In her October 1962 interview with Peter Orr for the British Council, Plath named Lowell's *Life Studies* and Sexton's work, specifically about mental illness and motherhood, as influencing her *Ariel* poetry, which she was then in the process of composing. That summer, Sexton had sent Plath a copy of her 1962 book *All My Pretty Ones*, and Plath wrote her back a warm letter of admiration and thanks for the book, which she said "absolutely stunned and delighted" her. The August 21, 1962, letter is published in Vol. 2 of Plath's *Letters* (p. 812). Listen to Plath's interview with Orr here: https://www.youtube.com/watch?v=ePbVT4nNc9I

6   **women speaking about the domestic:** Kyla Bishop, "A Reflection on the History of Sexual Assault Laws in the United States," *Arkansas Journal of Social Change and Public Service*, April 15, 2018.

7   **anthology *Sisterhood Is Powerful*:** Sylvia Plath, "The Jailer," in *Sisterhood Is Powerful*, ed. Robin Morgan (New York: Vintage Books, 1970), 510–11. For a history of second-wave literature about Plath, see Lauren Ryan, "Arraignment," *The Feminist Poetry Movement*. Williams College, December 11, 2021.

7   **"Arraignment":** Robin Morgan, "Arraignment," in *Monster* (New York: Vintage Books, 1972), 76–78.

7   **changes in the American legal system:** Robin Morgan, "Conspiracy of Silence Against a Feminist Poem," *Feminist Art Journal* (Fall 1972).

7   **"We began to read differently":** Moore, "After Ariel."

7   **backlash against both feminism and Plath's fame:** Lyndall Gordon, "Red Comet by Heather Clark Review: Rescuing Sylvia Plath from the Cult of Her Fans," *Telegraph*, October 10, 2020.

7   **Rose scoffed at the biographical readings:** Janet Malcolm, *The Silent Woman: Sylvia Plath and Ted Hughes* (New York: Knopf, 1994), 18.

7   **Janet Badia cites the scholar:** Badia, *Sylvia Plath and the Mythology of Women Readers*, 13.

7   **"Because she was dead":** Liz Jones, "Haunted by the Ballad of Ted and Sylvia, Poetry's Most Toxic Love Story: Frieda Hughes Reveals Why Her Parents' Secrets Still Cast a Shadow on Her Own Career," *Daily Mail*, June 10, 2017.

8   **mythologized as a woman born to die:** See Jacqueline Rose, *The Haunting of Sylvia Plath* (Cambridge MA: Harvard University Press, 1992); Badia, *Sylvia Plath and the Mythology of Women Readers*; and Carl Rollyson, *The Last Days of Sylvia Plath*.

8   **Roland Barthes's definition of myth:** Badia, *Sylvia Plath and the Mythology of Women Readers*, 22.

8   **"kingmaker":** Carl Rollyson, *American Isis* (New York: St. Martin's Press, 2013), 176.

9   **"priestess" of their "cult":** Al Alvarez, "Prologue: Sylvia Plath," in *The Savage God: A Study of Suicide* (New York: W. W. Norton, 1990), 46.

9   **"The tragedy of Plath's death":** Jonathan Bate, "Review: *The Letters of Sylvia Plath*, edited by Peter K. Steinberg and Karen V. Kukil" in *The Times*, September 8, 2018.

9   **in London in 1960:** Alvarez, "Prologue: Sylvia Plath."

9   **"A Poet's Epitaph":** Al Alvarez, "A Poet's Epitaph," *Observer*, February 17, 1963.

Notes

9 **Time magazine ran an unsigned review:** "Books: The Blood Jet Is Poetry," unsigned review, *Time*, June 10, 1966.

9 **Newsweek called Plath:** See "Russian Roulette," unsigned review, reprinted in Linda Wagner-Martin, ed., *Sylvia Plath: The Critical Heritage* (London: Routledge, 1988), 88–90.

10 **"Dying Is an Art":** George Steiner, "Dying Is an Art," in *The Art of Sylvia Plath*, ed. Charles Newman (Bloomington: Indiana University Press, 1970), 211–18.

10 **"At the moment of writing":** See Peter Davison, "Inhabited by a Cry: The Last Poetry of Sylvia Plath," *Atlantic*, August 1966.

10 **In his foreword:** Robert Lowell's foreword to *Ariel* (New York: Harper & Row, 1966), vii–ix.

10 **"was a murderous art":** Alvarez, "Sylvia Plath," in *The Art of Sylvia Plath*, ed. Charles Newman (Bloomington: Indiana University Press, 1970), 68.

10 **Keats's poetry about death:** Alvarez, "Sylvia Plath."

10 **deadly strain of tuberculosis:** *Letters of John Keats*, ed. Robert Gittings (Oxford: Oxford University Press, 1992), xvii–xviii.

10 **borrowing language from his last letter:** Gittings, *Letters of John Keats*, 388–89.

11 **last recorded letter:** See Plath's February 4, 1963, letter to Ruth Beuscher in *The Letters of Sylvia Plath, Vol. 2: 1956–1963*, ed. Peter K. Steinberg and Karen V. Kukil (New York: HarperCollins, 2018), 967–69.

11 **Robert Lowell made the case:** Robert Lowell's foreword to *Ariel*, viii.

11 **"Are these final poems":** Steiner, "Dying Is an Art," in *The Art of Sylvia Plath*, 218.

11 **"The intensity of Plath's poems":** Denis Donoghue, "You Could Say She Had a Calling for Death," *New York Times*, November 22, 1981.

11 **"destroyed her marriage":** Al Alvarez, *Where Did It All Go Right?* (London: Bloomsbury, 2002), 229.

12 **"the work of a poet":** Denis Donoghue, "You Could Say She Had a Calling for Death," *New York Times*, November 22, 1981.

12 **new definition of misogyny:** See Kate Manne's introduction to *Down Girl: The Logic of Misogyny*, "Eating Her Words," 1–54.

12 **interchangeable with sexism:** Manne, introduction to *Down Girl: The Logic of Misogyny*, 1–54.

13 **Misogyny is moralistic:** Manne, introduction to *Down Girl: The Logic of Misogyny*, 1–54.

13 **"a literary dragon":** "Books: The Blood Jet Is Poetry."

13 **"blood and brain":** "Russian Roulette," in *Sylvia Plath: The Critical Heritage*, 88–90.

13 **"speak quietly but do not mumble":** Quoted in Lidija Haas, "The World of Adrienne Rich," *Dissent*, Fall 2016.

13 **read as plagiarized:** See Sylvia Plath's April 5, 1961, letter to Judith Jones in *The Letters of Sylvia Plath, Vol. 2*, 601.

14 **"a subtle larceny":** Steiner, "Dying Is an Art," 211–18.

14 **"history's bad gendered bargains":** Preface to Manne, *Down Girl: The Logic of Misogyny*, xix.

14 **"[M]isogyny . . . directed at female public figures"**: Preface to Manne, *Down Girl: The Logic of Misogyny*, xiv.
15 **the most famous poet in England**: For a lengthy treatment of this, see Jonathan Bate, "Famous Poet," in *Ted Hughes: The Unauthorised Life* (London: William Collins, 2015).
15 **"Whatever it was I missed"**: See Richard Howard, "Sylvia Plath: 'And I Have No Face, I Have Wanted To Efface Myself . . . ,'" in *The Art of Sylvia Plath*, 79.
15 **"insufficiently caring and attentive"**: Preface to Manne, *Down Girl: The Logic of Misogyny*, xiv.
15 **"a shirt of nettles" . . . "in an Auschwitz all her own"**: "Books: The Blood Jet Is Poetry."
16 **"*is* morally in the wrong"**: Preface to Manne, *Down Girl: The Logic of Misogyny*, xiv.
16 **"entirely interior, mental"**: Stephen Spender, "Warnings from the Grave," reprinted in *Sylvia Plath: The Critical Heritage*, 69–73.
16 **"That she was creating"**: See Dido Merwin's interview in the transcript for *Sylvia Plath: Voices and Visions*, 21. https://test-learnermedia.pantheonsite.io/wp-content/uploads/2019/02/sylvia-plath.pdf
17 **willful silence of Hughes's friends**: Janet Malcolm, *The Silent Woman: Sylvia Plath & Ted Hughes* (New York: Knopf, 1994), 103.
17 **a 2006 biography**: Yehuda Koren and Eilat Negev, *Lover of Unreason: Assia Wevill, Sylvia Plath's Rival and Ted Hughes's Doomed Love* (Cambridge, MA: Da Capo Press, 2006).
17 **"the baying pack"**: Badia, "We Did Not Wish to Give the Impression," chap. 3 in *Sylvia Plath and the Mythology of Women Readers*, 98.
17 **both Plath and Hughes**: Badia, "We Did Not Wish to Give the Impression."
17 **"repeated . . . dead ends"**: Badia, "We Did Not Wish to Give the Impression," 98.
17 **twenty years or more after**: Another example of this can be found in Erica Jong's December 12, 2004, article "An Art Like Everything Else," from the *New York Times*, in which she claims that she was "picketed by an angry posse because [she] refused to mouth the feminist orthodoxy of the time, that Hughes had murdered Plath" at a Plath-centered event at the 92nd Street Y, which she said took place in 1971. Actually, it took place in 1973; Jong was part of a panel on Plath that included Robert Baggs and Elizabeth Hardwick, who wrote about it in a February 2, 1973, letter to Robert Lowell, in which she said that at the event, "rows of radical lesbians" were angry about Lowell's introduction to *Ariel*; Hardwick responded by asking them, "Why are y'all against that—uh? I think it's kinda good, you know." Hardwick, *The Dolphin Letters, 1970–1979*, ed. Saskia Hamilton (New York: Farrar, Straus and Giroux), 307.
17 **"credibility as a witness"**: Badia, "We Did Not Wish to Give the Impression," 99.
18 **"The history of feminist attacks"**: Badia, "We Did Not Wish to Give the Impression," 96.
18 **"neither original nor radical"**: Dale Spender, quoted in *Feminist Theory: A Reader*, 4th ed., ed. Wendy K. Kolmar and Frances Bartkowski (New York: McGraw-Hill, 2013), 9.

18 **criticized as flimsy:** Elizabeth Frank, "A Long Romance with Death," *New York Times*, October 6, 1991; see also Paul Alexander, "The Psychiatrist Who Tried to Save Sylvia Plath," *Literary Hub*, 2018.
18 **libelous:** In his archive at Emory University, there is a thick file of unpublished libel threats from Ted Hughes's lawyer to Penguin, which originally published *Rough Magic*. Carl Rollyson quotes from the exchange in *American Isis*, 258.
18 **"Poetry Is Not a Luxury":** Audre Lorde, *The Selected Works of Audre Lorde*, ed. Roxane Gay (New York: W. W. Norton, 2020), 3.
19 **"Here are stories":** Plath, *Unabridged Journals*, 476.
19 **"In that collection":** See Linda Wagner-Martin's email to author of January 10, 2023.
20 **as essential as bread or water:** See Sylvia Plath's interview with Peter Orr of the British Council, recorded for the BBC, October 30, 1962.
20 **Stanford professor Sandra M. Gilbert:** Sandra M. Gilbert, "'A Fine, White Flying Myth': Confessions of a Plath Addict," in *Massachusetts Review* 19, no. 3 (Fall 1978): 585–603.
20 **"personal material":** Gilbert, "'A Fine, White Flying Myth,'" 588.
20 **twenty-eighth birthday:** See the Introduction to *The Letters of Sylvia Plath*, Vol. 2, xxxix.
20 **wrote in her diary:** See Plath's entry of January 27, 1959, in *The Unabridged Journals of Sylvia Plath*.
21 **on a par with Virginia Woolf:** See Headline Reading: Heather Clark & Ruth Fainlight, Hosted by Helen Meller. The Waterfront Hall, Town Hall, Hebden Bridge, West Yorkshire, United Kingdom, October 22, 2022. https://plathfest.co.uk/headline-reading-heather-clark-ruth-fainlight/

Love, My Season: A Brief History of Sylvia Plath

23 **"How can Lady Lazarus":** Elizabeth Winder, *Pain, Parties, Work: Sylvia Plath in New York, Summer 1953* (New York: HarperCollins, 2013), 179.
23 **At Robinson Memorial Hospital:** Heather Clark, "Do Not Mourn," chap. 2 in *Red Comet: The Short Life and Blazing Art of Sylvia Plath* (New York: Knopf, 2020).
23 **bachelor of arts in classical languages:** Linda Wagner-Martin, "Childhood: 1932–40," chap. 1 in *Sylvia Plath: A Biography* (New York: St. Martin's Griffin, 1987), 17–18.
23 **master of arts in German:** Wagner-Martin, "Childhood: 1932–40," 11.
24 **were Austrian immigrants:** Clark, "The Beekeeper's Daughter," chap. 1 in *Red Comet*, 22.
24 **"our name Schober":** See Aurelia Plath's introduction to *Letters Home by Sylvia Plath: Correspondence 1950–1963*, ed. Aurelia Schober Plath (New York: Harper & Row, 1975), 4.
24 **"interest in minority groups":** A. Plath, *Letters Home*, 4.
24 **Aurelia met Otto:** A. Plath, *Letters Home*, 9–10.
25 **Her father "told his colleagues":** A. Plath, *Letters Home by Sylvia Plath*, 12.
25 **"somewhat chilling":** Wagner-Martin, "Childhood: 1932–40," 19.
25 **"the man who gets what he wants":** A. Plath, *Letters Home*, 12.

25 **transitioning into a marriage:** A. Plath, *Letters Home*, 13.
25 **"if not idyllic, [then] close":** Wagner-Martin, "Childhood: 1932–40," 15.
25 **STOP sign as "pots":** Wagner-Martin, "Childhood: 1932–40," p. 22.
25 **Otto had begun to suffer:** Wagner-Martin, "Childhood: 1932–40," 25.
25 **"The moon is a lock":** See the transcript for the documentary *Voices & Visions: Sylvia Plath*, produced by the New York Center for Visual History: 1988, p. 5. https://test-learnermedia.pantheonsite.io/wp-content/uploads/2019/02/sylvia-plath.pdf
26 **"Ocean 1212-W":** Sylvia Plath, *Johnny Panic and the Bible of Dreams: Short Stories, Prose, and Diary Excerpts, ea.* Ted Hughes (London: Faber & Faber, 1979), 117–24.
26 **The actual timeline was slower:** Wagner-Martin, "Childhood: 1932–40," 28.
26 **"She loved his praise":** See the transcript for the documentary *Voices & Visions: Sylvia Plath*, p. 4.
26 **"cut down a uniform":** See the transcript for the documentary *Voices & Visions: Sylvia Plath*, p. 4.
26 **"I'll never speak to God again":** See the transcript for the documentary *Voices & Visions: Sylvia Plath*, p. 4.
26 **"Years":** Sylvia Plath, *The Collected Poems*, ed. Ted Hughes (New York: Harper & Row, 1981), 255–56.
26 **"Lyonnesse":** Plath, *The Collected Poems*, 233–34.
27 **left her grief unresolved:** Plath writes movingly in her journal of going to her father's gravestone for the first time as an adult in an entry from March 9, 1959. See her *Unabridged Journals*, ed. Karen V. Kukil (New York: Anchor Books, 2000).
27 **"I laid my face":** Sylvia Plath, *The Bell Jar* (New York: Harper & Row, 1971), 189.
27 **For a brief time:** See Wagner-Martin, "Childhood: 1932–40," and "Adolescence: 1940–47," chaps. 1 and 2 in *Sylvia Plath: A Biography*, 29–33.
27 **suburb of Wellesley:** A. Plath, *Letters Home*, 29.
27 **in her journals and letters:** Plath dealt with this "problem" of her stifling relationship with her mother in therapy with Ruth Beuscher, in both 1953–54 and 1958–59. She wrote about it in a poignant journal entry dated December 12, 1958—see her *Unabridged Journals*.
27 **"Off, off, eely tentacle!":** See "Medusa" in Plath, *The Collected Poems*, 224–26.
28 **The Tempest:** Clark, "The Shadow, 1940–45," chap. 3 in *Red Comet*, 71.
28 **Plath's thirteenth Christmas:** Clark, "The Shadow, 1940–45," 78.
28 **Years later, studying at Cambridge:** See Plath's February 2, 1956, letter to her mother in *The Letters of Sylvia Plath, Vol. 1: 1940–1956*, ed. Peter Steinberg and Karen V. Kukil (New York: HarperCollins, 2017), 1094–96.
28 **the Wellesley Award:** Clark, "My Thoughts to Shining Fame Aspire," chap. 4 in *Red Comet*, 91.
28 **Cleanth Brooks and Robert Penn Warren:** Brooks was the dissertation adviser for Judith Kroll's *Chapters in a Mythology: The Poetry of Sylvia Plath*, the first-ever book-length study of Plath; Penn Warren reviewed *Ariel* with a rave when it debuted in the United States in 1966. His review was used as jacket copy.

28   **Wellesley High School:** Clark, "The Voice Within: Wellesley, 1947–1948," chap. 5 in *Red Comet*.
28   **"inject[ing] a sour note":** A. Plath, *Letters Home*, 38.
29   **a signed copy of her first book:** Clark, "The Voice Within: Wellesley, 1947–1948," in *Red Comet*, 107.
29   **twice won the *Atlantic*:** Clark, "Summer Will Not Come Again, 1948–1950," in *Red Comet*, 134.
29   **"Bitter Strawberries":** Plath, *The Collected Poems*, 299–300.
29   **yearbook graduation photo:** Clark, "Summer Will Not Come Again, 1948–1950," 136.
29   ***Seventeen* accepted her story:** Clark, "Summer Will Not Come Again, 1948–1950," 122.
29   **inspired a fan letter:** Many of Plath's letters to Cohen were lost, but you can read the ones that are available in *The Letters of Sylvia Plath, Vol. 1: 1940–1956*.
30   **second letter to Cohen:** See Plath's August 11, 1950, letter to Cohen in *The Letters of Sylvia Plath, Vol. 1: 1940–1956*, 165–76.
30   **"Out in the strawberry field":** Plath's August 11, 1950, letter to Cohen in *The Letters of Sylvia Plath, Vol. 1: 1940–1956*, 165–76.
30   **poetic masterpiece, "Ariel":** Plath, *The Collected Poems*, 239–240.
30   **scholarship to Wellesley:** Clark, "Summer Will Not Come Again, 1948–1950," 135.
31   **"Middle-class Americans":** Anne Stevenson, "A Smith Girl," chap. 2 in *Bitter Fame: A Life of Sylvia Plath* (London: Penguin, 1999), 19.
31   **"four or five football players":** See p. 3 of Rosenstein's 1971 interview notes with William Sterling (Box 4, Folder 14), and p. 8 of her interview notes with Crockett, conducted the same year (Box 1, Folder 19), in Harriet Rosenstein research files on Sylvia Plath, Stuart A. Rose Manuscript, Archives, and Rare Book Library, Emory University.
31   **a vivid description of sexual assault:** See Plath's journal entry marked #45 from the winter of 1951, her first year at Smith College, in her *Unabridged Journals*.
32   **Plath recording snide comments:** See Plath's journal entry marked #41 from fall 1950, in her *Unabridged Journals*.
32   **a comedic centerpiece:** Plath, *The Bell Jar*, 66.
32   **Dick was at Yale:** See Clark, "The White Queen," chap. 7 in *Red Comet*, for a long description of the beginnings of Plath's romantic relationship with Dick Norton.
32   **Buddy Willard "offers":** Plath, *The Bell Jar*, 75.
32   **Norton quickly began to exhibit:** See Clark, "The Ninth Kingdom," chap. 9 in *Red Comet*, to learn more about the disintegration of Plath's romantic relationship with Dick Norton.
32   **"Sunday at the Mintons":** Plath, *Johnny Panic and the Bible of Dreams*, 148–59.
33   **In Plath's reply to Strauss:** See Plath's July 8, 1952, letter to Strauss in *The Letters of Sylvia Plath, Vol. 1: 1940–1956*, 463.
33   **November 3, 1952, journal entry:** See the entry marked #154 in Plath's *Unabridged Journals*.

33   **From 1939 to 1980:** "When Joan Didion Met Jean Stafford," April 22, 2021, at the Library of America.
34   **"Jose the Cruel Peruvian":** See Plath's diary entry for July 14, 1953, in her *Unabridged Journals*.
34   **"Both men were predators":** Winder, *Pain, Parties*, 176–79.
34   **writing to Wilbury Crockett:** See p. 5 of Harriet Rosenstein's interview notes with Crockett in Box 1, Folder 19, of Harriet Rosenstein research files on Sylvia Plath, Stuart A. Rose Manuscript, Archives, and Rare Book Library, Emory University.
34   **ECT was often used:** Clark, "The Hanging Man," chap. 11 in *Red Comet*.
35   **what "terrible thing" she has done:** Plath, *The Bell Jar*, 161.
35   **over two hundred articles:** These were collected by Plath scholar Peter K. Steinberg and can be read at Smith College's Neilson Library.
35   **At McLean, Plath struggled:** Plath's medical records from McLean are (ethically questionably) available to read in Box 3, Folder 10, of the Rosenstein papers. They detail her treatment and include notes from her attending physicians' time with her and their interviews with Aurelia Plath.
35   **her last at Smith:** Wagner-Martin, "Smith, A Culmination: 1954–55," chap. 7 in *Sylvia Plath: A Biography*, 118–19.
36   **Tragedy, Practical Composition & Criticism:** Clark, "Channel Crossing," chap. 15 in *Red Comet*.
36   **Amateur Dramatic Club:** See Plath's October 9, 1955, letters to her mother in *The Letters of Sylvia Plath, Vol. 1: 1940–1956*, 974–79.
36   **wrote for *Varsity*:** For both the quote and an image of the photograph in *Varsity*, see Diane Middlebrook, "Meeting (1956)," chap. 1 in *Her Husband: Ted Hughes & Sylvia Plath, A Marriage* (New York: Penguin, 2003), 13–14.
36   **young man named Richard Sassoon:** See Clark, "The Lady or the Tiger," chap. 13 in *Red Comet*, which describes Plath's time in the United States with Sassoon.
36   **"traveling by motor scooter to Vence":** Stevenson, "Pursuit, 1955–1956," chap. 4 in *Bitter Fame*, 67–69.
36   **not to contact him:** Stevenson, "Pursuit, 1955–1956," chap. 4 in *Bitter Fame*, 71.
36   **Born August 17, 1930:** Hughes's early life is described at length in Jonathan Bate, "Capturing Animals," chap. 2 in *Ted Hughes: The Unauthorised Life* (London: William Collins, 2015).
37   **"an exhibition" at Pembroke College:** Bate, "Goddess," chap. 4 in *Ted Hughes: The Unauthorised Life*, 81.
37   **stop writing literary criticism:** Bate, "Burnt Fox," chap. 5 in *Ted Hughes: The Unauthorised Life*, 98–99.
37   **"he'd bash my head in":** See Plath's letter marked "Dec. 15–16" to Marcia Brown in *The Letters of Sylvia Plath, Vol. 2: 1956–1963*, ed. Peter K. Steinberg and Karen V. Kukil (New York: HarperCollins, 2018), 35.
37   **dating a nurse:** Bate, "Burnt Fox," 106.
37   **"Hughes was already":** Danuta Kean, "Unseen Sylvia Plath Letters Claim Domestic Abuse by Ted Hughes," *Guardian*, April 11, 2017.
37   **Plath did go:** Middlebrook, "Meeting (1956)," chap. 1 in *Her Husband*.

38   **morning journal entry:** See the February 25, 1956, entry in Plath's *Unabridged Journals*.
38   **"too clever, too sophisticated":** Clark, "Channel Crossing," chap. 15 in *Red Comet*.
38   **"Is this the better":** See the entry for February 26, 1956, in Appendix VII of Sylvia Plath's *Unabridged Journals*.
38   **a celebrity on campus:** Clark, "Mad Passionate Abandon," chap. 16 in *Red Comet*.
38   **Susan Alliston, the poet:** Clark, "Yeats' House," chap. 33 in *Red Comet*.
38   **"simply went on up":** See "St. Botolph's" in Ted Hughes, *Collected Poems*, ed. Paul Keegan (New York: Farrar, Straus and Giroux, 2003), 1051–52.
38   **an ugly girl:** See the entry for February 26, 1956, in Appendix VII of Plath, *Unabridged Journals*.
39   **"sleepless holocaust":** See the entry for March 26, 1956, in Appendix VII of Plath, *Unabridged Journals*.
39   **"Ridiculous to call it love":** Bate, "18 Rugby Street," chap. 8 in *Ted Hughes: The Unauthorised Life*, 138.
39   **"I think he is":** See Plath's July 14, 1956, letter to her mother in *The Letters of Sylvia Plath, Vol. 1: 1940–1956*, 1217–21.
39   **publishing six new poems:** See Plath's October 1, 1956, letter to Ted Hughes in *The Letters of Sylvia Plath, Vol. 1: 1940–1956*, 1255–59.
39   **onetime college boyfriend, Peter Davison:** See Plath's September 30, 1956, letter to Peter Davison in *The Letters of Sylvia Plath, Vol. 1: 1940–1956*, 1251–55.
40   **A journal entry from January 1958:** See Plath's January 7, 1958, entry in her *Unabridged Journals*.
40   **Clarissa Roche, Plath's good friend:** Roche's taped (now digitized) interviews with Malcolm are held by Yale's Beinecke Rare Book & Manuscript Library.
41   **Plath took on additional grading:** Plath writes throughout her journals from 1957–58 of grading exams for other members of the department.
41   **engaged in a violent fight:** See Plath's June 11, 1958, entry in her *Unabridged Journals*.
41   **1958–59 in Boston:** See Stevenson, "Electra on Azalea Path," chap. 7 in *Bitter Fame*, for a thorough discussion of the Hugheses time with the literary elite in Boston.
42   **"The Barfly Ought to Sing":** See the Fall 1966 issue of *Triquarterly* magazine, which is devoted to Plath. This essay was also reprinted in Charles Newman, *The Art of Sylvia Plath* (Bloomington: Indiana University Press, 1970).
42   **Arriving in London in January:** Stevenson, "Ariel in the Tree, 1959–1960," chap. 9 in *Bitter Fame*.
43   **"Frieda is my answer":** See Plath's September 30, 1960, letter to Lynne Lawner in *The Letters of Sylvia Plath, Vol. 2: 1956–1963*, 520.
43   **Plath was pregnant again:** Plath described this event in her September 22, 1962, letter to Ruth Beuscher; Jonathan Bate also details it in "Famous Poet," chap. 11 in *Ted Hughes: The Unauthorised Life*, 215–16.
43   **Her copious notes from the hospital:** These can be read in Plath's *Unabridged Journals*.
43   **the famous "Tulips":** Plath, *The Collected Poems*, 158–62.

43 **"Love set you going"**: Plath, *The Collected Poems*, 156–57.
44 **"my first son"**: See Plath's diary entry of January 17, 1962, included as part of her notes on her Devon neighbors, in her *Unabridged Journals*.
45 **"Elm," a poem**: Plath, *The Collected Poems*, 163–64.
45 **Assia Wevill telephoned**: See Plath's July 11, 1962, letter to Ruth Beuscher for a description of this in *The Letters of Sylvia Plath, Vol. 2: 1956–1963*, 790–95.
45 **Plath and Hughes attempted to reconcile**: Bate, "The Grass Blade," chap. 12 in *Ted Hughes: The Unauthorised Life*, 238–40.
46 **"How can I ever get free?"**: See Plath's October 9, 1962, letter to Ruth Beuscher in *The Letters of Sylvia Plath, Vol. 2: 1956–1963*, 851–53.
46 **she wrote to Beuscher**: See Plath's October 21, 1962, letter to Ruth Beuscher in *The Letters of Sylvia Plath, Vol. 2: 1956–1963*, 876–80.
47 **legendary "seducer" she had met**: See Plath's February 26, 1956, entry in her *Unabridged Journals*.
47 **"creating two other poets"**: See Hughes's letter marked "late summer 1962" to Olwyn in *Letters of Ted Hughes*, ed. Christopher Reid (London: Faber & Faber, 2007), 203–6.
47 **"a secret life"**: See Hughes's letter marked "late summer 1962" to Vicky Watling in *Letters of Ted Hughes*, 206–7.
47 **"he wants to be an 'international catalyst'"**: See Plath's October 21, 1962, letter to Ruth Beuscher in *The Letters of Sylvia Plath, Vol. 2: 1956–1963*, 876–80.
47 **Hughes sounds unhinged**: These letters were sold by Frieda Hughes to Emory University in spring 2021 and are available in Subseries 1.1, Box 4, Folder 8, of the Ted Hughes papers, Stuart A. Rose Manuscript, Archives, and Rare Book Library, Emory University.
48 **"in a gentlemanly considerate way"**: Bate, "That Sunday Night," chap. 13 in *Ted Hughes: The Unauthorised Life*, 242.
48 **"he picks up Finns"**: See Plath's October 21, 1962, letter to Ruth Beuscher in *The Letters of Sylvia Plath, Vol. 2: 1956–1963*, 876–80.
48 **"I was ecstatic"**: See Sylvia Plath's October 21, 1962, letter to Ruth Beuscher in *The Letters of Sylvia Plath, Vol. 2: 1956–1963*, 876–80.
49 **her grandmother was "possibly Jewish"**: See Rosenstein's interview notes in Box 3, Folder 3, of Harriet Rosenstein research files on Sylvia Plath, Stuart A. Rose Manuscript, Archives, and Rare Book Library, Emory University.
49 **her friend Anne Sexton**: Plath's letter of August 21, 1962, thanking Sexton for the book, is in *The Letters of Sylvia Plath, Vol. 2: 1956–1963*, 812.
50 **Sexton's clever syntax**: Anne Sexton, "Letter Written on a Ferry While Crossing Long Island Sound," Poetry Foundation; Plath, "Fever 103" in *The Collected Poems*, 231–32.
50 **"Whatever her father did to her"**: Leon Wieseltier, "In a Universe of Ghosts," *New York Review of Books*, November 25, 1975.
50 **The FBI investigated Otto Plath**: Cynthia Haven, "New FBI Files: Was Sylvia Plath's Daddy 'Pro-Nazi?'" Stanford University Book Haven (blog), August 20, 2012.
50 **Hitler came to him**: See Hughes's letter marked "late summer 1962" to Olwyn in *Letters of Ted Hughes*, 203–6.

50　**"pure ego-Fascist"**: See Plath's July 30, 1962, letter to her mother in *The Letters of Sylvia Plath, Vol. 2: 1956–1963*, 802–7.
50　**who wrote *Tarka the Otter***: Bate, "Tarka, Rain Horse, Pike," chap. 3 in *Ted Hughes: The Unauthorised Life*.
51　**"the smell of polish"**: See Plath's *Collected Poems*, 208–9.
51　**"that antique billhook"**: See Plath's *Collected Poems*, 209–10.
51　**"The Jailer," the most potent**: See Plath's *Collected Poems*, 226–27.
52　**"the slippage between victims and sweethearts"**: Saidiya Hartman, "Venus in Two Acts." *Small Axe* 12, no. 2 (2008): 1–14.
52　**described a wife as a slave**: See, for example, Betsy Warrior, "Housework: Slavery or Labor of Love," in *Radical Feminism*, ed. Anne Koedt, Ellen Levine, and Anita Rapone (New York: Times Books, 1973), 208–12.
52　**"Like a Belsen label"**: See Plath's October 9, 1962, letter to Ruth Beuscher in *The Letters of Sylvia Plath, Vol. 2: 1956–1963*, 851–53.
53　**"Letter in November"**: See Plath's *Collected Poems*, 204–5.
53　**a sign on Fitzroy Road**: See Plath's November 7, 1962, letter to her mother in *The Letters of Sylvia Plath, Vol. 2: 1956–1963*, 897–99.
53　**She signed a five-year lease**: Clark, "Castles in Air, October–November 1962," in *Red Comet*, 823.
53　**a series of challenges**: The difficulties at the end of Plath's life are well documented. Details from these two paragraphs are taken from Middlebrook, "Parting (1962–1963)," chap. 7 in *Her Husband*, 182–211.
54　**"Once one has seen God"**: See Plath's *Collected Poems*, 268–69.
54　**the famous "Edge"**: See Plath's *Collected Poems*, 272–73.
54　**"What appals [sic] me"**: See Plath's February 4, 1963, letter to Ruth Beuscher in *The Letters of Sylvia Plath, Vol. 2: 1956–1963*, 967–69.
55　**he planned to "auction" it**: Clark, "Your Wife Is Dead," epilogue in *Red Comet*, 899. Hughes is reported to have said this to his friend, the poet David Ross, and to Hughes's lover, Susan Alliston, when they visited Fitzroy Road together in the days after Plath's death.
55　**£150,000 a year**: Ted Hughes gave this number to both Luke Myers and Ben Sonnenberg. See Middlebrook, "Curing Himself (1967–1998)," chap. 9 in *Her Husband*, 257.
55　**With the help of his sister**: See Olwyn's correspondence with David Machin and Elizabeth Anderson of William Heinemann, Ltd., Plath's British publishers, as well as all business correspondence related to the initial publication of *Ariel* in the United Kingdom and the United States, held in Box 1, Folder 23, in Olwyn Hughes's papers at Emory University's Stuart A. Rose Manuscript, Archives, and Rare Book Library.
55　**"was not really prepared"**: See letter of November 9, 1964, from Judith Jones to Ted Hughes, Box 1, Folder 24, in Olwyn Hughes's papers at Emory University's Stuart A. Rose Manuscript, Archives, and Rare Book Library.
55　**"Can Harper's have *Ariel*?"**: Undated airmail letter, probably early 1965, from Donald Hall to Ted Hughes, Box 1, Folder 25, in Olwyn Hughes's papers at Emory University's Stuart A. Rose Manuscript, Archives, and Rare Book Library.

55 **Knopf "seemed nonplussed":** Ted Hughes, "Publishing Sylvia Plath," reprinted in *Winter Pollen: Occasional Prose*, ed. William Scammel (New York: Picador, 1995), 166.
56 **"It is her":** Ted Hughes, "Sylvia Plath: *Ariel*," in *Winter Pollen*, 162.
56 **"chapters in a mythology":** Ted Hughes, "Notes on the Chronological Order of Sylvia Plath's Poems," in *The Art of Sylvia Plath, Tri-Quarterly* no. 7 (Fall 1966): 88.
56 **but not his last:** Hughes took up this line of argument again in his introduction to Plath's *Collected Poems*, 13–17, which he edited.
57 **"teenagers at college":** See Hughes's May 19, 1966, letter to Aurelia Plath in *Letters of Ted Hughes*, 258.
57 **more than a month to write:** See Ted Hughes's March 15, 1963, letter to Aurelia Plath in *Letters of Ted Hughes*, 214–15.
57 **"You won't be":** See the scholar Catharine Rankovic's translations of Aurelia Plath's shorthand annotations on her letters. Rankovic published her findings as the essay "Medusa's Metadata: Aurelia Plath's Gregg Shorthand Annotations," in *The Bloomsbury Handbook to Sylvia Plath*, ed. Anita Helle, Amanda Golden, and Maeve O'Brien (London: Bloomsbury, 2022).
57 **"Sylvia's marriage hit":** This quote is taken from extensive notes Hughes sent to Aurelia Plath in January 1975, when she was coediting *Letters Home*. Copies are held at Emory University in the Stuart A. Rose Manuscript, Archives, and Rare Book Library, Subseries 1.2, Box 16, Folder 3.
57 **"in those days":** Ted Hughes's foreword to *The Journals of Sylvia Plath*, ed. Frances McCullough (New York: Anchor Books, 1982), xiii.
58 **poem "Amnesiac":** See Plath's *Collected Poems*, 232.
58 **"Thanks to her habit":** See Kathleen Ossip's poem "No Use" in her book *The Do-Over* (Louisville: Sarabande, 2015), 65–66.

Loving Assia Wevill

59 **began translating the work:** See Yehuda Koren and Eilat Negev, *Lover of Unreason: Assia Wevill, Sylvia Plath's Rival and Ted Hughes's Doomed Love*, (Cambridge, MA: Da Capo Press, 2006), 166–67, for a description of Wevill's relationship with Amichai and her translation process. Wevill's translations were initially published in 1968 by Faber & Faber in England and Harper & Row in the United States. They were recently published in Assia Wevill, *The Collected Writings of Assia Wevill*, ed. Julie Goodspeed-Chadwick and Peter K. Steinberg (Baton Rouge: Louisiana State University Press, 2021), 226–61.
59 **Wevill had met Amichai:** Jonathan Bate, "The Iron Man," chap. 15 in *Ted Hughes: The Unauthorised Life* (London: William Collins, 2015).
59 **She and Hughes presented the translations:** See the transcript for the BBC recording in *The Collected Writings of Assia Wevill*, 268–80. The original is held by Emory University's Stuart A. Rose Manuscript, Archives, and Rare Book Library.
60 **Amichai's family left Wurzburg:** See "Yehuda Amichai," the Poetry Foundation.
60 **moving to Tel Aviv in 1934:** Koren and Negev, "A New Life," chap. 2 in *Lover of Unreason*, 10–17.

60 **"Nazi ideology described":** Koren and Negev, "Childhood," chap. 1 in *Lover of Unreason*, 5–6.
60 **he brought his family to Palestine:** Koren and Negev, "Childhood," chap. 1 in *Lover of Unreason*, 5–6.
60 **their Palestinian home:** Koren and Negev, "Childhood," chap. 1 in *Lover of Unreason*, 5–6.
61 **began to publish his poetry:** See "Yehuda Amichai," the Poetry Foundation.
61 **They sent her to the Tabeetha School:** Koren and Negev, "A Tabeetha Girl," chap. 3 in *Lover of Unreason*, 18–24.
61 **rave reviews:** P. J. Kavanagh, "An Awkward Shyness," *Guardian*, July 12, 1968.
61 **"Draft Constitution":** See Ted Hughes's 1968 letter to Assia Wevill, marked "Draft Constitution." Held by Emory University's Stuart A. Rose Manuscript, Archives, and Rare Book Library, MSS 1058, Box 1.
61 **his poem "Dreamers":** See "Dreamers" in Ted Hughes, *Collected Poems*, ed. Paul Keegan (New York: Farrar, Straus and Giroux, 2003), 1145–46.
62 **from her young family:** Koren and Negev, "A New Life," chap. 2 in *Lover of Unreason*, 10–17.
62 **traveled back to Germany:** Koren and Negev, "A New Life," chap. 2 in *Lover of Unreason*, 10–17.
62 **marriages between Christians and Jews:** Koren and Negev, "A New Life," chap. 2 in *Lover of Unreason*, 10–17.
62 **relationship with her sister:** Koren and Negev, "A New Life," chap. 2 in *Lover of Unreason*, 10–17.
62 **She was born Assia Esther Gutmann:** Koren and Negev, "Childhood," chap. 1 in *Lover of Unreason*.
63 **reentered the workforce:** For a thorough analysis of Wevill's contributions to the golden age of advertising, see Julie Goodspeed-Chadwick, "Assia Wevill as Author, Artist, and Translator," chap. 4 in *Reclaiming Assia Wevill: Sylvia Plath, Ted Hughes, and the Literary Imagination* (Baton Rouge: Louisiana State University Press, 2019), 104–49.
63 **second-wave feminism:** Robin Morgan, "Arraignment," in *Monster* (New York: Vintage Books, 1972), 76–78; see also Yehuda Koren and Eilat Negev, "On The Trail of Assia," foreword to *The Collected Writings of Assia Wevill*, ix–xiv.
63 **major influence on the lives:** See Goodspeed-Chadwick, "Sylvia Plath's Representations of Assia Wevill" (chap. 2, 26–53) and "Ted Hughes's Representations of Assia Wevill" (chap. 3, 54–103), in *Reclaiming Assia Wevill*.
63 **Hughes began a campaign:** Goodspeed-Chadwick treats this problem throughout *Reclaiming Assia Wevill*. See also Janet Malcolm, *The Silent Woman: Sylvia Plath and Ted Hughes* (New York: Knopf, 1994), 102–103. Hughes asked Anne Stevenson not to name Assia Wevill in a letter dated "Sept.–Oct. 1986," which includes his extensive notes on her drafts of her Plath biography, *Bitter Fame: A Life of Sylvia Plath* (1989). Copies of this correspondence are held by Emory University's Stuart A. Rose Manuscript, Archives, and Rare Book Library, Box 147, MSS 644, Folder 6.
63 **"Publicly, Hughes continued":** Koren and Negev, "On the Trail of Assia," xi.

63 "'People are so dumb'": Koren and Negev, "On the Trail of Assia," xi.
63 "his most tasteless lines": Bate, *Ted Hughes: The Unauthorised Life*, 231.
63 "[managed] to hit the nadir of taste": Katha Pollitt, "Peering into the Bell Jar," *New York Times*, March 1, 1998.
64 Her father's brother had been murdered: Koren and Negev, "A Second Husband," chap. 6 in *Lover of Unreason*, 55.
64 "I still believe": See Wevill's September 14, 1954, letter to Celia Chaikin in *The Collected Writings of Assia Wevill*, 60–62.
65 In Hughes's poem "Shibboleth": Hughes, "Shibboleth," in *Collected Poems*, 794–95.
65 In the opening poem "Cappricios": Hughes, "Capriccios," in *Collected Poems*, 783.
67 while the poem "Snow": Hughes, "Snow," in *Collected Poems*, 789–90.
67 almost no one read them: Steve Ely, "A Prologue to *Capriccio*," *Ted Hughes Society Journal* 8, no. 2 (2020): 12–30.
67 long, intimate letters: See Wevill's letters to Yehuda and Hana Amichai, dated July 18, 1967; August 19, 1967; October 31, 1967; November 17, 1967; November 21, 1967; January 11, 1968; March 6, 1968; May 8, 1968; May 29, 1968; June 18, 1968; June 25, 1968; August 8, 1968; and circa December 1968, in *The Collected Writings of Assia Wevill*.
68 his famous poem "A Pity": See Wevill's translation of Amichai's poem in *The Collected Writings of Assia Wevill*, 233–34.
68 "The prospect before me": See Assia Wevill's January 1969 letter to her father in *The Collected Writings of Assia Wevill*, 155.
69 taking her family out of Tel Aviv: Koren and Negev, "First Marriage," chap. 5 in *Lover of Unreason*, 36–48.
69 Assia tried to kill herself: Koren and Negev, "First Marriage," chap. 5 in *Lover of Unreason*, 41.
69 "Reliable studies": Itzhak Levav and Anat Brunstein Klomek, "A Review of Epidemiologic Studies on Suicide before, during, and after the Holocaust," *Psychiatry Research* 261 (2018): 35–39.
69 moved the couple to Canada: Koren and Negev, "First Marriage," chap. 5 in *Lover of Unreason*, 43.
70 reduced to initials: Koren and Negev, "First Marriage," chap. 5 in *Lover of Unreason*, 45.
70 became her second husband: Koren and Negev, "A Second Husband," chap. 6 in *Lover of Unreason*, 49–59.
70 dressing in exotic colors: Koren and Negev, "A Second Husband," chap. 6 in *Lover of Unreason*, 49–59.
70 dressed in the bright reds and blues: Heather Clark, "Mad Passionate Abandon," chap. 16 in *Red Comet: The Short Life and Blazing Art of Sylvia Plath* (New York: Knopf, 2020).
71 David Wevill was seven years younger: Koren and Negev, "Falling in Love," chap. 7 in *Lover of Unreason*, 60.
71 propriety dictated the marriage: Koren and Negev, "A Second Husband, 1956," chap. 6 in *Lover of Unreason*, 51.

71 **Anne Stevenson, one of Sylvia Plath's biographers:** Koren and Negev, "Falling in Love," chap. 7 in *Lover of Unreason*, 65–66.
71 **a successful copywriter:** Koren and Negev, "Falling in Love," chap. 7 in *Lover of Unreason*, 65–67.
72 **submitted their petition for divorce:** Koren and Negev, "Falling in Love," chap. 7 in *Lover of Unreason*, 72.
72 **the newlyweds sailed back to England:** Koren and Negev, "Third Marriage," chap. 8 in *Lover of Unreason*, 75.
73 **A document in the *Capriccio* materials:** Steve Ely, "The Key of the Sycamore," in *Ted Hughes Society Journal* 8, no. 2, 45.
73 **"took over our flat":** See Ted Hughes's winter 1961 letter to Al Alvarez in Hughes, *Letters of Ted Hughes*, ed. Christopher Reid (London: Faber & Faber, 2007), 190.
73 **"A seed of attraction":** Ely, "The Key of the Sycamore," 45.
74 **"[Hughes] promised to work":** Diane Middlebrook, "Separating (1962–)," chap. 6 in *Her Husband: Ted Hughes & Sylvia Plath, A Marriage* (New York: Penguin, 2003), 177.
74 **back with her from Burma:** Koren and Negev, "A Fateful Meeting," chap. 9 in *Lover of Unreason*, 82.
74 **"the wooden tinted cobra":** British Library, Add Ms, 88918/1/17, f. 163.
75 **still a happy couple:** Koren and Negev, "A Fateful Meeting," chap. 9 in *Lover of Unreason*, 85.
75 **learning of their affair:** Koren and Negev, "An Illicit Affair," chap. 10 in *Lover of Unreason*, 98–99.
75 **Middlebrook was the first to report:** Middlebrook, "Separating (1962–)," chap. 6 in *Her Husband*, 177, 166.
76 **"in war paint":** Middlebrook, "Separating (1962–)," chap. 6 in *Her Husband*, 166.
76 **Gehenna Press broadside:** Clark, "Error," chap. 28 in *Red Comet*.
76 **Called "The Wishing Box":** Sylvia Plath, "The Wishing Box," in *Johnny Panic and the Bible of Dreams* (London: Faber & Faber, 1979), 48–55.
77 **"humorous terrible little story":** See Sylvia Plath's October 9, 1956, letter to Ted Hughes in *The Letters of Sylvia Plath, Vol. 1: 1940–1956*, ed. Peter K. Steinberg and Karen V. Kukil (New York: HarperCollins, 2017), 1291–94.
77 **"That month, Assia Lipsey":** Mark Wormald, "'I Fished in Still Water,'" chap. 4 in *The Catch: Fishing for Ted Hughes* (London: Bloomsbury Circus, 2022), 43.
78 **"the claim of fatal attraction":** Koren and Negev, "A Fateful Meeting," chap. 9 in *Lover of Unreason*, 88.
78 **Wevill says he has no memory:** Koren and Negev, "A Fateful Meeting," chap. 9 in *Lover of Unreason*, 88–89.
78 **"to buy into the image":** Bate, *Ted Hughes: The Unauthorised Life*, 231.
78 **"'Dreamers' is the one poem":** Goodspeed-Chadwick, *Reclaiming Assia Wevill*, 97–98.
78 **an Ogre representing Plath's death:** "Fairy Tale," in Hughes, *Collected Poems*, 1146–48.
78 **a single blade of grass:** Koren and Negev, "An Illicit Affair," chap. 10 in *Lover of Unreason*, 95–96.

79 **"Babylonian"**: Middlebrook, "Separating (1962–)," chap. 6 in *Her Husband*, 164, 177.
79 **"staggering"**: Bate, *Ted Hughes: The Unauthorised Life*, 229.
79 **"killed" her first two husbands**: Clark, "Error," chap. 28 in *Red Comet*.
79 **"feral beauty, feral eyes"**: Koren and Negev, "Torn Between Two Lovers," chap. 11 in *Lover of Unreason*, 136.
79 **"The Pit and the Stones"**: "The Pit and the Stones," in Hughes, *Collected Poems*, 793–94.
79 **Hughes married Carol Orchard**: Bate, *Ted Hughes: The Unauthorised Life*, 365.
80 **"so violent and animal"**: Koren and Negev, "An Illicit Affair," chap. 10 in *Lover of Unreason*, 98.
80 **"smelled like a butcher"**: Koren and Negev, "An Illicit Affair," chap. 10 in *Lover of Unreason*, 98.
80 **pregnant with Ted Hughes's child**: Koren and Negev, "Leaving Plath," chap. 11 in *Lover of Unreason*, 114.
80 **nothing to do with her**: Koren and Negev, "The Shadow of Suicide," chap. 12 in *Lover of Unreason*, 115.
80 **representations of Wevill**: Goodspeed-Chadwick, *Reclaiming Assia Wevill*, 20.
80 **"the ghost house"**: See Assia Wevill's March 20, 1963, letter to Jannice Porter in *The Collected Writings of Assia Wevill*, 105.
81 **Plath's study**: See Wevill's August 10, 1963, journal entry in *The Collected Writings of Assia Wevill*, 177.
81 **Sigmund told her no**: Koren and Negev, "Domesticity," chap. 13 in *Lover of Unreason*, 131.
81 **"added her own stamp of ownership"**: Koren and Negev, "Torn between Two Lovers," chap. 14 in *Lover of Unreason*, 132
81 **back to the Highbury flat**: See Wevill's May 20 and May 23, 1963, journal entries in *The Collected Writings of Assia Wevill*, 166–67.
81 **"feelings of immense alienation"**: See Wevill's May 20 and May 23, 1963, journal entries in *The Collected Writings of Assia Wevill*, 168.
82 **"All this has been a summer job"**: See Wevill's May 20 and May 23, 1963, journal entries in *The Collected Writings of Assia Wevill*, 168.
82 **Hughes was running cold**: Koren and Negev, "The Shadow of Suicide," chap. 12 in *Lover of Unreason*, 120.
82 **his source of inspiration**: Ely, "A Prologue to *Capriccio*," 19.
83 **if she couldn't sleep with him**: See Wevill's letter to Ted Hughes marked "late March 1968," in *The Collected Writings of Assia Wevill*, 138.
83 **"Assia valued that which she believed**: Goodspeed-Chadwick, *Reclaiming Assia Wevill*, 81.
84 **one year before her suicide**: See Wevill's letter to Ted Hughes marked "late March 1968," in *The Collected Writings of Assia Wevill*, 138.
84 **"Unfortunately for her"**: Goodspeed-Chadwick, *Reclaiming Assia Wevill*, 81.
84 **entirely her mother's**: Koren and Negev, "Birth," chap. 15 in *Lover of Unreason*, 147.
84 **In "Possession"**: Hughes, "Possession," in *Collected Poems*, 791.
84 **"The Error"**: Hughes, "The Error," in *Collected Poems*, 795–96.

85   **intense and productive creativity:** Koren and Negev, "Birth," chap. 15 in *Lover of Unreason*, 148–53.
85   **short film *Lost Island*:** The *Lost Island* film is available on YouTube. https://www.youtube.com/watch?v=F1Zs7ag9VaM
86   **James Bond films:** Koren and Negev, "Birth," chap. 15 in *Lover of Unreason*, 150–151.
86   **"the Lilith of abortions":** Hughes, "Dreamers," in *Collected Poems*, 1145–46.
87   **Wevill's letters to Hughes:** There are ten letters to Assia published in *Letters of Ted Hughes*.
87   **"F. Wall, Esq.":** Bate, *Ted Hughes: The Unauthorised Life*, 284.
87   **"Well, when we started":** Koren and Negev, "On The Trail of Assia," foreword to *The Collected Writings of Assia Wevill*, ix.
87   **"devoid of Assia's presence":** Koren and Negev, "Torn between Two Lovers," chap. 14 in *Lover of Unreason*, 134.
88   **could do nothing about it:** Koren and Negev, "Agony," chap. 21 in *Lover of Unreason*, 206–18.
88   **Lois Ames, who was appointed:** Ames and Anne Sexton visited Court Green in 1967; Hughes wrote to Anne Sexton about this visit, and Assia wrote one paragraph to Sexton at the close of the letter, dated August 9, 1967. This letter is in *The Collected Writings of Assia Wevill*, 121.
88   **to do so were stymied:** Wagner-Martin wrote of her difficulty with the Plath estate in her preface to *Sylvia Plath: A Biography* (New York: St. Martin's Griffin, 1987), 11–14.
88   **"He always says, *please*":** Malcolm, *The Silent Woman*, 102–103.
88   **controversial poem "Arraignment":** Morgan, "Arraignment," in *Monster*, 76–78.
89   **Koren and Negev doubt:** In an email to me dated January 22, 2023, Koren and Negev wrote: "We are certain that when Assia did what she did, she never thought of Jewish mothers killing their children in the Holocaust or Pogrom sense, as Morgan indicated."
89   **Shura "danced and danced":** Koren and Negev, "Agony," chap. 21 in *Lover of Unreason*, 213.
89   **a "remarkable woman," a "near-genius":** See Wevill's letter to Anne Sexton of August 9, 1967, in *The Collected Writings of Assia Wevill*, 121.
89   **"'very much [those] of a daughter'":** Koren and Negev, "Love Me Back or Let Me Go," chap. 18 in *Lover of Unreason*, 182.
89   **These letters have recently resurfaced:** Warren Plath's daughter, Jenny, confirmed the existence of these letters to me in an email dated March 14, 2023, and graciously permitted me to mention them in this chapter.
89   **Assia Wevill did begin a journal:** The surviving excerpts of Assia's journal are held at Emory University's Stuart A. Rose Manuscript, Archives, and Rare Book Library, and were published in their entirety in *The Collected Writings of Assia Wevill*.
90   **"He's busy espalliering [*sic*] Sylvia":** See Wevill's journal entry of May 20, 1963, in *The Collected Writings of Assia Wevill*, 167.
90   **"planning materials":** British Library, Add Ms, 88918/1/17, f. 163.

90 **"had a delicate, sultry face":** Al Alvarez, *Where Did It All Go Right?* (London: Bloomsbury, 1999), 234–35.
90 **had once been in love:** Jonathan Bate describes Alvarez's affair with Assia in *Ted Hughes: The Unauthorised Life*, 384–386.
91 **Terry Gifford wrote that he doubted:** Terry Gifford, "Review: *Reclaiming Assia Wevill: Sylvia Plath, Ted Hughes, and the Literary Imagination*," *Ted Hughes Society Journal*, 8, no 2 (2020): 65–67.
91 **"A, B, and C":** Bate, *Ted Hughes: The Unauthorised Life*, 331.
91 **"He was a real hunter":** Koren and Negev, "Aftermath," chap. 22 in *Lover of Unreason*, 21.

Nota Bene: The Dead Girls

92 **an October 26, 1984, letter:** See American novelist Susan Fromberg Schaeffer's letter of October 26, 1984, to Ted Hughes, in Box 7, Series 1.1, of Ted Hughes papers, Stuart A. Rose Manuscript, Archives, and Rare Book Library, Emory University.
92 **a prolific American novelist:** For an intimate look at Schaeffer's relationship with both Ted and Olwyn Hughes, you can read their letters to her, which are held by Boston University's Howard Gotlieb Archival Research Center. Schaeffer's letters to Hughes, also delightful, are at Emory University's Stuart A. Rose Manuscript, Archives, and Rare Book Library.
92 **"vampirish warlock appeal":** Erica Jong, "An Art Like Everything Else," *New York Times*, January 12, 2004.
92 **Plath's letters to Ruth Beuscher:** See Sylvia Plath's September 22, 1962, letter to Ruth Beuscher in *The Letters of Sylvia Plath, Vol. 2: 1956–1963*, ed. Peter K. Steinberg and Karen V. Kukil (New York: HarperCollins, 2018), 827–30.
93 **"I don't know if you're aware of it":** Susan Fromberg Schaeffer's October 26, 1984, letter to Ted Hughes, Subseries 1.1, Box 7, Folder 4. Ted Hughes papers, Stuart A. Rose Manuscript, Archives, and Rare Book Library, Emory University.
93 **"as blandly unpretentious":** Janet Malcolm's *The Silent Woman: Sylvia Plath and Ted Hughes* (New York: Knopf, 1994) is rife with criticism of Linda Wagner-Martin's *Sylvia Plath: A Biography* (New York: St. Martin's Griffin, 1987). See, in particular, pp. 24–29.
93 **unaware of its existence:** Personal email to the author from Linda Wagner-Martin, May 18, 2021.
93 **"The rumor was at first":** Sandra M. Gilbert, "'A Fine, White Flying Myth': Confessions of a Plath Addict," *Massachusetts Review* 19, no. 3 (1978): 587–88.
94 **"Why did she die?":** Erica Jong, "An Art Like Everything Else," *New York Times*, January 12, 2004.
94 **"A Biographical Note":** Lois Ames, "Sylvia Plath: A Biographical Note, with Eight Previously Unpublished Drawings by Sylvia Plath," appendix to the first American edition of *The Bell Jar* (New York: Harper & Row, 1971), 279–96.
94 **"all relationships were puppetlike":** Lois Ames, "Sylvia Plath: A Biographical Note," 295–96.
94 **interviews about her:** Al Alvarez, Interview, March 22, 2013, in *Granta*.

94 **"the total purification":** Al Alvarez, "Sylvia Plath," in *The Art of Sylvia Plath*, ed. Charles Newman (Bloomington: Indiana University Press, 1970), 64.
94 **"went down into the cellarage":** Al Alvarez, *Where Did It All Go Right?* (London: Bloomsbury, 1999), 230.
95 **"bright, clean, competent":** See the Prologue, "Sylvia Plath,"in Al Alvarez, *The Savage God: A Study of Suicide* (New York: W. W. Norton, 1990), 22.
95 **Plath took center stage:** Prologue, "Sylvia Plath," in Al Alvarez, *The Savage God: A Study of Suicide*, 27. For a further discussion of the artistic rivalry between Plath and Hughes, see Heather Clark, "But Not the End," chap. 30 in *Red Comet: The Short Life and Blazing Art of Sylvia Plath* (New York: Knopf, 2020).
95 **a series of angry letters:** The letters between Alvarez and Hughes are in the British Library and have never been published in their entirety. Copies of some of the letters are in Ted Hughes's papers at Emory University's Stuart A. Rose Manuscript, Archives, and Rare Book Library, in papers relating to the publication of *The Silent Woman*. Janet Malcolm quotes extensively from Hughes's end of the correspondence in *The Silent Woman*. Alvarez's letters do not appear in her book.
95 **"a sensation-watching":** These quotations are taken directly from copies of the correspondence between Alvarez and Hughes in Ted Hughes's papers related to *The Silent Woman*, at Emory University's Stuart A. Rose Manuscript, Archives, and Rare Book Library, Subseries 3.5, Box 147, File Folder 6.
96 **"Ted and Olwyn knew":** Jonathan Bate, "The Savage God," in *Ted Hughes: The Unauthorised Life* (London: William Collins, 2015), 382.
96 **wrote to ask Alvarez:** See Olwyn Hughes's June 9, 1988, unpublished letter to Al Alvarez, held as part of Alvarez's papers relating to Sylvia Plath in the British Library.
96 **"guardian angel":** These quotations are taken directly from copies of the correspondence between Alvarez and Hughes in Ted Hughes's papers related to *The Silent Woman*, at Emory University's Stuart A. Rose Manuscript, Archives, and Rare Book Library, Subseries 3.5, Box 147, Folder 6.
97 **Sigrid Grosvenor speaking:** Chap. 1 in Susan Fromberg Schaeffer, *Poison* (New York: W. W. Norton, 2006), 9.
97 **Peter tells Sophie and Andrew:** Chap. 1 in Fromberg Schaeffer, *Poison*, 10.
97 **long-standing rumors:** See Harriet Rosenstein's recorded interview with Elizabeth Sigmund, now digitized in the Rosenstein archive at Emory University. In the interview I conducted with Plath biographer Paul Alexander in February 2020, he also told me that Carol Hughes had a history of suicidal threats.
97 **closely mirrors what happened:** For more details of the similarities between Ted Hughes's will and *Poison*, see Jonathan Bate, "Epilogue: The Legacy," in *Ted Hughes: The Unauthorised Life*. More can also be read in Andrew Alderson, "'Dying Wish' of Ted Hughes Splits Family," *Telegraph*, October 27, 2002.
98 **"If you keep carrying on like this":** See Fromberg Schaeffer, *Poison*, 14.
98 **"a monster of the imagination":** Bate, *Ted Hughes: The Unauthorised Life*, 669.
98 **lengthy interview with Elizabeth Sigmund:** Available in Harriet Rosenstein research files on Sylvia Plath, Stuart A. Rose Manuscript, Archives, and Rare Book Library, Emory University.

98   **the first to do so:** See Ted Hughes's undated, unpublished letter to Olwyn Hughes, part of the holdings Frieda Hughes sold to the library in spring 2021. Ted Hughes papers, Stuart A. Rose Manuscript, Archives, and Rare Book Library, Emory University.
98   **Plath's suicide was accidental:** Alvarez, "Prologue: Sylvia Plath," in *The Savage God*, 54–55.
99   **"The end came when she felt":** Alvarez, "Prologue: Sylvia Plath," in *The Savage God*, 55–56.
99   **an unstoppable "blood-jet":** Plath, *The Collected Poems*, 220–21.
99   **"I wonder if you know":** See Olwyn Hughes's June 22, 1988, unpublished letter to Al Alvarez. Held as part of Alvarez's papers relating to Sylvia Plath in the British Library.
100 ***New York Times* bestseller list:** Jill Rodriguez, "Deconstructing Plath's 'The Bell Jar,'" Roger Williams University, March 5, 2013.
100 **"It was a mistake, then":** Alvarez, "Prologue: Sylvia Plath," in *The Savage God*, 55.
100 **Alvarez accused Sylvia Plath's fans:** Alvarez, "Prologue: Sylvia Plath," in *The Savage God*, 55.
100 **Dido had made the initial introductions:** Dido Merwin, "Vessel of Wrath: A Memoir of Sylvia Plath," one of three appendices in Anne Stevenson, *Bitter Fame: A Life of Sylvia Plath* (London: Penguin, 1989).
100 **"inevitable, sooner or later":** Dido Merwin, "Vessel of Wrath," in Stevenson, *Bitter Fame*, 347, 340.
100 **Doctor Horder, whose notes to biographers:** The 1987 handwritten letter from Doctor Horder to Linda Wagner-Martin, which she gifted to me in May 2021, contains some of the same information that he sent to Anne Stevenson and Harriet Rosenstein. It also includes unique information, including that Sylvia Plath took an overdose of sleeping pills prior to gassing herself and that he believed she was in a state of psychosis.
101 **two essays on Plath:** George Steiner's essay appeared in the 1969 issue of the *Cambridge Review*; Alvarez's, a review of the UK edition of *Ariel*, was published in the *Observer* in March 1965.
102 **researchers Klara Toro and Stefan Pollak:** See Klára Törő and Stefan Pollak, "Complex Suicide versus Complicated Suicide," *Forensic Science International* 184, nos. 1–3 (2009): 6–9.
102 **a July 3, 1970, interview:** Although many of Rosenstein's interview notes correspond with recordings (now digitized at Emory University), this one does not. There are nine pages of notes. It can be found in Box 3, Folder 3, of the Harriet Rosenstein research files on Sylvia Plath, Stuart A. Rose Manuscript, Archives, and Rare Book Library, Emory University.
102 **Ted Hughes didn't tell:** Clark, "Epilogue: Your Wife Is Dead," in *Red Comet*, 900.
102 **one of the few that did run:** Ashley Fetters, "There Are Almost No Obituaries for Sylvia Plath," *Atlantic*, February 11, 2013.
102 **Aurelia confided to Harriet Rosenstein:** See Harriet Rosenstein's interview notes from her July 3, 1970, interview with Aurelia Plath in Box 3, Folder 3,

of the Harriet Rosenstein research files on Sylvia Plath at the Stuart A. Rose Manuscript, Archives, and Rare Book Library, Emory University.

102 **"SPEAKING OF DADDIES"**: Harriet Rosenstein's interview notes from her July 3, 1970, interview with Aurelia Plath, 7.

103 ***Atlantic* article by Ashley Fetters**: Fetters, "There Are Almost No Obituaries for Sylvia Plath," *Atlantic*, February 11, 2013.

103 **gourmet food like caviar**: In chap. 3 of *The Bell Jar*, Esther Greenwood visits a women's magazine test kitchen and is fed caviar, avocado, and crab salad, which ends up giving her ptomaine poisoning. Greenwood describes how her grandfather, the head waiter at a local country club, would sneak her lush, exotic foods like caviar and avocado, inspiring her extravagant taste.

103 **Ted Hughes's rush to publish**: Four poems were published in "A Poet's Epitaph," in the *Observer*, six days after her death; by August of 1963, *The New Yorker* reprinted every poem by Plath that they had on hand, per Howard Moss's request and Hughes's agreement, in an exchange from March 1963, held in the New York Public Library.

103 **"far more intimately concerned"**: Alvarez, "Sylvia Plath," in *The Art of Sylvia Plath*, 64.

104 **people still interpret the poem this way**: Sina Queyras, "How Sylvia Plath Calls Out for Connection across Time," *Literary Hub*, April 11, 2022.

104 **"['Lady Lazarus'] anticipates"**: See Mark Ford, "Lady Lazarus" by Sylvia Plath: A close reading, British Library, May 25, 2016.

104 **Nell, dies by her own**: Shirley Jackson, *The Haunting of Hill House* (New York: Penguin, 2006), 182.

104 **A lonely young woman trapped**: Jackson, *The Haunting of Hill House*, chap. 1.

104 **Nell is mysteriously compelled to climb**: Jackson, *The Haunting of Hill House*, chap. 9.

105 **Elizabeth Hardwick, whose long**: Elizabeth Hardwick, "On Sylvia Plath," *New York Review of Books*, August 12, 1971.

105 **"dispel the posthumous miasma"**: Quoted in Janet Malcolm, *The Silent Woman: Sylvia Plath and Ted Hughes* (New York: Knopf, 1994), 24.

105 **Janet Malcolm, who extended**: Malcolm, *The Silent Woman*, 96.

105 **they don't believe them**: See *The Haunting of Hill House*. Episode 5, "The Bent-Neck Lady." Aired October 12, 2018, on Netflix.

106 **Nell, like the character**: *The Haunting of Hill House*. Episode 5, "The Bent-Neck Lady."

106 **"inevitable, even justified"**: Al Alvarez, "Poetry in Extremis," reprinted in Linda Wagner-Martin, ed., *Sylvia Plath: The Critical Heritage* (London: Routledge, 1988), 55–57.

107 **"A Picture of Otto"**: Ted Hughes, *Collected Poems*, ed. Paul Keegan (New York: Farrar, Straus and Giroux, 2003), 1167.

107 **"Little poltergeist girl"**: Heather Clark quotes this poem at length in *Red Comet: The Short Life and Blazing Art of Sylvia Plath* (New York: Knopf, 2020), 853.

107 **"seems never to tire"**: Terry Castle, "The Unbearable," *New York Review of Books*, July 13, 2013.

108 **"the surprise, the shimmering":** See Robert Lowell's foreword to the first American edition of Sylvia Plath's *Ariel* (New York: Harper & Row, 1966), viii.
108 **"It has frequently been asked":** Malcolm, *The Silent Woman*, 58.
108 **unique form of censorship:** For a sampling of this trend in criticism on Plath, see the many reviews of her first epistolary collection, *Letters Home* (Harper & Row, 1976), in which writers as erudite as the novelist Anne Tyler claim that we should only ever read Plath's last poems; anything else is worthless. A generous sample of these reviews can be found in Wagner-Martin, *Sylvia Plath: The Critical Heritage*.
108 **"I am content to live in silence":** For a thorough analysis of this and other Linda Gregg poems, see Gabriel Fine, "'I Am Supposed to Look': Linda Gregg's Prolific Vision," *Los Angeles Review of Books*, March 29, 2019.

The Haunting of Ted Hughes

110 **last poem of his lifetime:** You can read "The Offers" in Ted Hughes, *Collected Poems*, ed. Paul Keegan (New York: Farrar, Straus and Giroux, 2003), 1180–83. You can read more about its significance and its publication in Jonathan Bate, "Sylvia Plath's Death Was the Central Fact of Ted Hughes's Life," *Times*, September 28, 2015.
110 **Howls & Whispers:** While *Howls & Whispers* is now printed in its entirety in Hughes's *Collected Poems*, it was initially printed in a limited edition of 110 copies by the Gehenna Press, run by Hughes's longtime friend, the sculptor Leonard Baskin. You can read more about its original print run (and about all of Hughes's book publications) at the webpage for the Ted Hughes Society.
110 **revised and reworked:** Jonathan Bate describes the drafts of this poem in great detail in his epilogue to *Ted Hughes: The Unauthorised Life* (London: William Collins, 2015), 682–86.
110 **Plath seems yellow and aged:** Hughes, *Collected Poems*, 1178–80.
111 **"Purdah," which Plath wrote:** Sylvia Plath, *The Collected Poems*, ed. Ted Hughes (New York: Harper & Row, 1981), 243–44. Interestingly, Hughes had nothing to say about this poem in his extensive biographical and editorial notes for Plath's *Collected Poems*.
111 **Hughes translated:** See Hughes's translation of *The Oresteia* (London: Faber & Faber, 1999).
111 **In "The Applicant":** Plath, *The Collected Poems*, 221–22.
112 **"Whereas Clytemnestra kills unfaithful":** See Bate's epilogue to *Ted Hughes: The Unauthorised Life*, 684.
112 **Diane Middlebrook similarly reads:** See the introduction, "Becoming Her Husband," in Diane Middlebrook, *Her Husband: Sylvia Plath & Ted Hughes, A Marriage* (New York: Penguin, 2003), xv–xx.
112 **discussing it on National Public Radio's:** "Sylvia Plath's Husband, Ted Hughes, Lived a Life of Poetry and Tragedy," on *Weekend Edition Saturday*, with Scott Simon, October 10, 2015.
112 **Like Diane Middlebrook:** See the introduction to *Her Husband*, xx.
113 **Hughes's translation of Euripides's *Alcestis*:** Bate, "The Return of Alcestis," in *Ted Hughes: The Unauthorised Life*.

Notes

113 **"*Alcestis* moment":** Bate, the epilogue to *Ted Hughes: The Unauthorised Life*, 684.
113 **"perhaps because they were too painful":** Bate, "The Return of Alcestis," in *Ted Hughes: The Unauthorised Life*, 646.
113 **in the poem "The Shot":** Hughes, *Collected Poems*, 1052–53.
113 **In the poem "Trophies":** Hughes, *Collected Poems*, 1054.
113 **"the solar system married us":** Hughes, *Collected Poems*, 1051–52.
114 **the poem "Flounders":** Hughes, *Collected Poems*, 1084–85.
114 **"the wind shifted":** Middlebrook, "Prospering," in *Her Husband*, 116; the scene of Hughes and Plath nearly lost at sea is also memorably re-created in Christine Jeffs's 2003 film *Sylvia*.
114 **Middlebrook reads the poem as a fight:** Middlebrook, "Prospering," in *Her Husband*, 116. The major English poet and novelist Robert Graves (1895–1985) was especially important to Ted Hughes's later work on his marriage to Sylvia Plath; Middlebrook posits that his is the driving influence behind *Birthday Letters*, which she says was in many ways the embodiment of Graves's book *The White Goddess* (New York: Farrar, Straus and Giroux, 1997), a book that claimed that all true poetry was in service of the White Goddess, a true and ancient female muse who, according to the British Library's website, "governs birth, life and death in the three aspects of maiden, mother and crone."
114 **"A Pink Wool Knitted Dress":** Hughes, *Collected Poems*, 1064–65.
115 **In "Your Paris," Hughes contrasts:** Hughes, *Collected Poems*, 1065–67.
115 **"You Hated Spain," the first:** Hughes, *Collected Poems*, 1068.
115 **In "Moonwalk," Hughes tells:** Hughes, *Collected Poems*, 1069–70.
115 **earlier poem "Shibboleth," in *Capriccio*:** Hughes, *Collected Poems*, 794.
115 **In "Drawing," Plath's practice:** Hughes, *Collected Poems*, 1071.
116 **"Fever," in which Hughes:** Hughes, *Collected Poems*, 1072–73.
116 **she is "crying wolf,":** Hughes, *Collected Poems*, 1073.
116 **In Hughes's poem "The Hands":** Hughes, *Collected Poems*, 1161–62.
116 ***Two of a Kind*:** Ted Hughes and Sylvia Plath, "Two of a Kind: Poets in Partnership." Interview by Owen Leeming for the BBC, January 18, 1961. Audio, 23:56.
117 **practitioners of psychology:** See "Power and Control," The National Domestic Violence Hotline.
117 **Frieda wrote in her brief foreword:** Sylvia Plath, *The Letters of Sylvia Plath, Vol. 1: 1940–1945*, ed. Peter K. Steinberg and Karen V. Kukil (New York: HarperCollins, 2017), xii.
117 **published two books:** *The Colossus* debuted in England with William Heinemann in 1960 and in the United States with Knopf in 1962; *The Bell Jar* was published by Heinemann under the pseudonym Victoria Lucas on January 14, 1963.
118 **"We were working toward it":** Frieda Hughes, foreword to Sylvia Plath, *Ariel: The Restored Edition* (New York: HarperCollins, 2004), xiii.
118 **"The Laburnum":** Hughes, *Collected Poems*, 1176–77.
118 **Molly Bloom:** See the last pages of James Joyce's *Ulysses*, in which Leonard Bloom's wife Molly gives her famously affirmative soliloquy.
118 **"I *told* her":** Jillian Becker, *Giving Up: The Last Days of Sylvia Plath* (New York: St. Martin's Press, 2003), 46.

118 **Becker knew that was impossible:** Becker, *Giving Up*, 46.
118 **the chilblains that had "demoralized" her:** See Plath's letter to Helga Huws of March 29, 1962, in which she describes the intense challenges of living with two children in a house without central heat (including "CHILBLAINS"). *The Letters of Sylvia Plath, Vol. 2: 1956–1963*, ed. Peter K. Steinberg and Karen V. Kukil (New York: HarperCollins, 2018), 804.
119 **Plath was writing to Ruth Beuscher:** See Plath's letters to Ruth Beuscher of July 11, 1962, in *The Letters of Sylvia Plath, Vol. 2: 1956–1963*, 842.
119 **"He wanted to have a homebase":** See p. 3 of Harriet Rosenstein's July 3, 1970, interview notes from her interview with Aurelia Plath, Box 3, File Folder 3, part of the Harriet Rosenstein research files on Sylvia Plath, Stuart A. Rose Manuscript, Archives, and Rare Book Library, Emory University.
119 **"I can't be [a] sweet homebase":** See Sylvia Plath's letter to Ruth Beuscher of July 11, 1962, in *The Letters of Sylvia Plath, Vol. 2: 1956–1963*, 845.
119 **Ted Hughes married Carol Orchard:** See Jonathan Bate's "The Savage God," in *Ted Hughes: The Unauthorised Life*, for a thorough treatment of this period of Hughes's life.
119 **"a deeply affecting portrait":** Michiko Kakutani's review of *Birthday Letters*, "A Portrait of Plath in Poetry for Its Own Sake," *New York Times*, February 13, 1998.
119 **"[Hughes] loved [Plath]":** Bate, epilogue to *Ted Hughes: The Unauthorised Life*, 687.
120 **"took enormous courage":** Bate, epilogue to *Ted Hughes: The Unauthorised Life*, 682–83.
120 ***Publishers Weekly* said:** See the magazine's online entry for *Birthday Letters* from February 1998.
120 **"sickeningly anti-Semitic":** Becker, chap. 5 in *Giving Up*, 59–60.
120 **propagandistic images of Jews:** Hughes, *Collected Poems*, 1145–46; "Exhibition: Rothschilds in Caricature. 10: Musee des Horreurs," Rothschild Archive.
120 **monstrous in "The Ventriloquist":** Hughes, *Collected Poems*, 1159–60.
121 **"Cut," an illness:** Plath, *The Collected Poems*, 235–36.
121 **Plath's poem "Medusa":** Plath, *The Collected Poems*, 224–25.
121 **In "The Error":** Hughes, *Collected Poems*, 1121–22.
122 **in her poem "Wintering":** Plath, *The Collected Poems*, 217–18.
122 **Writing of Davies:** See Plath's letter to her mother, dated January 24–27, 1962, in *The Letters of Sylvia Plath, Vol. 2: 1956–1963*, 768.
122 **"I was your nurse":** Hughes, *Collected Poems*, 1148.
122 **moralizing reread of "The Jailer":** Plath, *The Collected Poems*, 226–27.
123 **inhabited five different homes:** I arrived at this number by including the five homes the Hugheses established in the towns where they lived and worked: 55 Eltisley Avenue in Cambridge, their Elm Street apartment in Northampton, 9 Willow Street in Boston, 3 Chalcot Square in London, and Court Green. I recognize that they spent long vacations in Spain and Cape Cod, but chose these five as established places of residence.
124 **host literary salons:** See the chapter "Yeats's House" in Heather Clark's *Red Comet: The Short Life and Blazing Art of Sylvia Plath* (New York: Knopf, 2020)

for a lengthy description of the ways Plath was especially interested in building a literary community of women writers like Stevie Smith, Emily Hahn, and Doris Lessing in her Fitzroy Road flat.

124 **he moved himself:** See Bate's chapter "That Sunday Night," in *Ted Hughes: The Unauthorised Life*, for a detailed treatment of Hughes's actions in the last months before Sylvia Plath's suicide and the months immediately after.

124 **Hughes's Cambridge girlfriend:** See Bate's chapter "A Complex Index of Everything to Follow," in *Ted Hughes: The Unauthorised Life*, for a detailed treatment of Hughes's relationship with his longtime girlfriend Shirley, who he dated just prior to meeting Sylvia Plath.

124 **"murder his pale freckled":** See Plath's journal entry of March 2, 1958, when the couple was living in Northampton, Massachusetts: *The Unabridged Journals of Sylvia Plath*, ed. Karen V. Kukil (New York: Anchor Books, 2000).

124 **"I'd rather have my Ted":** Middlebrook, "Romance," in *Her Husband*, 30.

124 **called "The Rival":** Plath, *The Collected Poems*, 166–67.

125 **"seemed effaced":** Al Alvarez, "Prologue: Sylvia Plath," in *The Savage God: A Study of Suicide* (New York: W. W. Norton, 1971), 22.

125 **"Sylvia had changed":** Alvarez, "Prologue: Sylvia Plath," in *The Savage God*, 28.

125 **"a strong, close" one:** Alvarez, "Prologue: Sylvia Plath," in *The Savage God*, 28.

125 **"Not even temporary insanity":** See Ted Hughes's letters to Al Alvarez. Although their original correspondence is held by the British Library, these quotes are taken from copies of the originals held in Hughes's archive at Emory, in his papers related to Janet Malcolm's 1994 book *The Silent Woman*.

125 **"fame and its legendary temptations":** Clark, "But Not The End," chap. 30 in *Red Comet*, 753.

125 **"It was either her or me":** Heather Clark reports on p. 899 of her epilogue in *Red Comet* ("Your Wife Is Dead") that Hughes said this odd phrase to Suzette Macedo on February 11, the day Plath died. On p. 44 of *Giving Up: The Last Days of Sylvia Plath*, Jillian Becker says that Hughes repeated it to her and her husband, Gerry, multiple times at Plath's funeral luncheon.

126 **Gayatri Spivak, writing about women:** See Spivak's 1983 essay "Displacement and the Discourse of Women," reprinted in *A Critical and Cultural Theory Reader*, ed. Anthony Easthope and Kate McGowan (Buckingham: Open University Press, 1992), 171.

126 **"Well, what about my system?":** See Sylvia Plath's July 11, 1962, letter to Ruth Beuscher in *The Letters of Sylvia Plath, Vol. 2: 1956–1963*, 846.

127 **associated herself with Electra:** Plath wrote often in her journals about her so-called Electra complex, and in her description of "Daddy" for a BBC recording of the poem, said that the poem was spoken by "a girl with an Electra complex."

127 **"Electra on Azalea Path":** Plath, *The Collected Poems*, 116–17.

How Reliable a Witness?

128 **generations of proof:** One of the most intriguing and comprehensive examples of how this problem extends across time is examined in Kate Manne's "Eating Her Words," her lengthy introduction to *Down Girl: The Logic of Misogyny*

(Oxford: Oxford University Press, 2017). I will return to this introduction repeatedly in this chapter.

128 **wielded threats as a weapon:** Hughes sued Trevor Thomas, Sylvia Plath's neighbor at the time of her death, for libel after Thomas wrote a memoir about Plath's last days (the memoir was privately published). Janet Malcolm recounts this lawsuit in *The Silent Woman: Sylvia Plath and Ted Hughes* (New York: Knopf, 1994). Heather Clark also discusses Thomas at length in "Yeats' House," chap. 33 in *Red Comet: The Short Life and Blazing Art of Sylvia Plath* (New York: Knopf, 2020).

128 **Rough Magic:** There is a thick file of letters back and forth between Ted and Carol Hughes, their lawyer Katy Baldock, and lawyers for Penguin, USA, who published *Rough Magic*, in the Ted Hughes archive at Emory, in Series 3, Subseries 3.5, Box 147, Folder 1.

128 **"We would like you to send":** Ted Hughes archive at Emory, Series 3, Subseries 3.5, Box 147, Folder 1. See the Hugheses' unpublished letter to Baldock of November 5, 1992.

129 **Hughes also threatened Anne Stevenson:** See Hughes's November 4, 1989, letter to Anne Stevenson, a copy of which is held by Emory University in Hughes's archive in Series 3, Subseries 3.5, Box 147, Folder 9, literature related to Janet Malcolm's *The Silent Woman*. Although Malcolm published excerpts from this letter in her book, she left everything concerning Hughes's lawsuits, threatened and actual, out of her book.

129 **"an old friend of mine (female)":** See Hughes's November 4, 1989, letter to Anne Stevenson, a copy of which is held by Emory University in Hughes's archive in Series 3, Subseries 3.5, Box 147, Folder 9, literature related to Janet Malcolm's *The Silent Woman*.

129 **one alleged conversation:** Paul Alexander, "Abroad," in *Rough Magic* (Cambridge, MA: Da Capo Press, 1999), 194.

129 **including "The Jailer," "The Rabbit Catcher":** Sylvia Plath, *The Collected Poems*, ed. Ted Hughes (New York: HarperCollins, 1981), 226–27, 193–94, 222–24.

129 **One of Plath's 1962 letters:** See Sylvia Plath's September 22, 1962, letter to Ruth Beuscher in *The Letters of Sylvia Plath, Vol. 2: 1956–1963*, ed. Peter K. Steinberg and Karen V. Kukil (New York: HarperCollins, 2018), 882.

130 **Miranda Fricker's 2010 article:** Miranda Fricker, "Epistemic Oppression and Epistemic Privilege," *Canadian Journal of Philosophy* 29 (1999): 191–210.

130 **result in "collective systematic cognitive failings":** Fricker, "Epistemic Oppression and Epistemic Privilege," 18.

130 **lived under "long-term domestic violence":** Fricker, "Epistemic Oppression and Epistemic Privilege," 18.

130 **"have turned this story into":** Jacqueline Rose, *The Haunting of Sylvia Plath* (Cambridge, MA: Harvard University Press, 1992), 68.

131 **"it is hard to determine":** Sarah Churchwell, "Ted Hughes and the Corpus of Sylvia Plath," *Criticism* 40, no 1 (Winter 1998): 101.

131 **1962 poem "The Detective":** Plath, *Collected Poems*, 208–209.

131 **"a hundred times [I] sniff":** See Plath's February 22, 1958, journal entry in *The Unabridged Journals of Sylvia Plath*, ed. Karen V. Kukil (New York: Anchor Books, 2000).

264 | Notes

131 **"[F]or at least the last 3 years"**: See Sylvia Plath's October 9, 1962, letter to Ruth Beuscher in *The Letters of Sylvia Plath, Vol. 2: 1956–1963*, 903.

131 **"sherry . . . or roast beef"**: See Sylvia Plath's October 9, 1962, letter to Ruth Beuscher in *The Letters of Sylvia Plath, Vol. 2: 1956–1963*, 903.

131 **"I feel this . . . desire to torture"**: See Sylvia Plath's October 9, 1962, letter to Ruth Beuscher in *The Letters of Sylvia Plath, Vol. 2: 1956–1963*, 903.

132 **"The Courage of Shutting-Up"**: Plath, *Collected Poems*, 209–210.

132 **Poe's short story "The Black Cat"**: See Edgar Allan Poe's "The Black Cat," first published in *The Saturday Evening Post* in August 1843 (reprinted September 2, 2011).

133 **"just like [Plath], but permanent"**: See Ted Hughes's brief essay "Sylvia Plath: Ariel," which originally accompanied the 1965 Faber & Faber edition of the book as the choice for the *Poetry Book Society Bulletin* in February 1965. I quote here from the essay's inclusion in Ted Hughes, *Winter Pollen: Occasional Prose*, ed. William Scammell (New York: Picador, 1994), 162.

133 **"a kind of hermeneutical affirmative action"**: Fricker, "Epistemic Oppression and Epistemic Privilege," 21.

133 **"The Body of the Writing"**: Rose, *The Haunting of Sylvia Plath*, 29–64.

133 **picking her nose:** See Plath's January 25, 1953, journal entry in her *Unabridged Journals* (New York: Anchor Books, 2000), 165.

134 **"and then he kissed me"**: See Plath's February 26, 1956, journal entry in her *Unabridged Journals*, 212.

134 **his girlfriend Shirley:** In March 2022, while visiting Cambridge, I was lucky enough to hear the story of Plath's and Hughes's meeting from an eyewitness, Jean Gooder, professor emerita at Newnham, who was Plath's classmate there in her course on tragedy. She was also a close friend of Shirley. I asked her if Shirley had a happy life, and she told me that unfortunately, she did not, and traced much of her unhappiness to the night of Plath's first meeting with Hughes. It was another reminder of the ways this story reverberates throughout time.

134 **abridged edition of Plath's *Journals*:** Sylvia Plath, *The Journals of Sylvia Plath*, ed. Frances McCullough (New York: Anchor Books, 1998), 112.

134 **another lover, Richard Sassoon:** Plath, *The Journals of Sylvia Plath*, 114–44.

135 **"Arrived in Paris":** See Plath's journal entry for March 26, 1956, in *Unabridged Journals*.

135 ***Venus in the Seventh* and *Falcon Yard*:** Copies of this are held in the Ted Hughes papers at the Stuart A. Rose Manuscript, Archives, and Rare Book Library at Emory University, Subseries 3.2: Sylvia Plath, Box 140, Folder 11.

135 **"Love bites":** Jonathan Bate, "18 Rugby Street," chap. 8 in *Ted Hughes: The Unauthorised Life* (London: William Collins, 2015), 136.

135 **"Color floods to the spot":** "Contusion," in Plath, *Collected Poems*, 271.

135 **what she calls "epistemic oppression":** Fricker, "Epistemic Oppression and Epistemic Privilege," 18.

136 **"If someone or some group":** Fricker, "Epistemic Oppression and Epistemic Privilege," 19.

137 **experiences IPV and suicidality:** See the Agenda Alliance's report *Underexamined and Underreported: Suicidality and Intimate Partner Violence:*

Connecting Two Major Public Health Domains, "Executive Summary" and "Findings," February 2023.

137 **"the life after death:** Anne Stevenson, *Bitter Fame: A Life of Sylvia Plath* (London: Penguin, 1999), xii.

138 **Paul Alexander's *Rough Magic*:** Alexander's chapter "Abroad," in *Rough Magic*, 194.

138 **"Things improved after they moved":** Stevenson, *Bitter Fame*, 93.

139 **"all could happen":** Stevenson, *Bitter Fame*, 93.

139 **"Suddenly, Sylvia found herself":** Stevenson, *Bitter Fame*, 93.

139 **"You Hated Spain":** Ted Hughes, *Collected Poems*, ed. Paul Keegan (New York: Farrar, Straus and Giroux, 2003) 1068.

139 **dislike of the bullfights:** See Plath's July 14, 1956, letter to her mother in *The Letters of Sylvia Plath, Vol. 1: 1940–1956*, ed. Peter K. Steinberg and Karen V. Kukil (New York: HarperCollins, 2017), 1217–21.

140 **ran as a serial in *The New Yorker*:** The story originally ran in the magazine in August 1993: Janet Malcolm, "The Silent Woman," *New Yorker*, August 23, 1993. Malcolm also quotes Alexander's description at length in *The Silent Woman*, 167.

140 **her introduction, "Eating Her Words":** See the introduction to Kate Manne's *Down Girl*, 1–3.

140 **"a simple assault":** Anne Saker, "48 States Have Toughened Laws on Strangulation, A Factor in Domestic violence. But Not In Ohio." *Training Institute on Strangulation Prevention*, December 14, 2021.

140 **Strangulation is deliberate:** Manne, *Down Girl*, 2.

140 **"You can train her not to say 'strangle'":** Manne, *Down Girl*, 4.

141 **routinely exist in testimonial smothering:** Kristie Dotson, "Tracking Epistemic Violence, Tracking Practices of Silencing," *Hypatia* 26, no. 2 (Spring 2011): 244.

141 **two high-profile examples:** See Manne, *Down Girl*, 7–18, for extensive descriptions of Fierstein's and Piccard's experiences of strangulation, IPV, and being forced to "eat their words."

142 **"Vocal Changes":** Manne, *Down Girl*, 7.

142 **Jonathan Bate includes it:** Bate, "Marriage Is My Medium," chap. 9 in *Ted Hughes: The Unauthorised Life*, 152.

143 **"[t]he friend . . . is not an entirely":** Bate, "Marriage Is My Medium," chap. 9 in *Ted Hughes: The Unauthorised Life*, 703, note 16.

143 **"[One] afternoon while she and Ted":** Alexander, *Rough Magic*, 194.

144 **"a ten- to fifteen-second":** Manne, *Down Girl*, 16.

144 **"chief aim":** Malcolm, *The Silent Woman*, 167.

144 **"horrible story":** Malcolm, *The Silent Woman*, 167.

145 **"like standing in a room":** Becker, *Giving Up*, 57.

145 **Malcolm intersperses descriptions:** Malcolm, *The Silent Woman*, 147–70.

145 **I suspect so:** See C. Roche (3); Alvarez (5) (2), undated. Janet Malcom papers. Yale Collection of American Literature, Beinecke Rare Book and Manuscript Library.

146 **Tennant's memoir *Burnt Diaries*:** Emma Tennant, *Burnt Diaries* (Edinburgh: Canongate Books, 1999).

146 **"Ted leans down"**: Tennant, Burnt Diaries, 195–96.
147 **"whether she should have revealed"**: See John Banville's review of *Burnt Diaries*: "Every Love Affair Delivers a Hostage to Fortune," *Irish Times*, October 30, 1999.
147 **"Tennant indulges in fantasies"**: See Lesley McDowell's review of *Burnt Diaries*: "An Accident Just Waiting to Happen," *Herald*, September 29, 1999.
147 **Hughes claimed to have burned**: See Hughes's foreword to the 1982 edition of *The Journals of Sylvia Plath* (New York: Anchor Books), xiii.
147 **now-famous poem "The Rabbit Catcher"**: Plath, *The Collected Poems*, 193–94.
148 **Jonathan Bate wondered**: Bate, "The Grass Blade," chap. 12 in *Ted Hughes: The Unauthorised Life*, 231.
148 **two D. H. Lawrence poems**: D. H. Lawrence, "Rabbit Snared in the Night," in *Look! We Have Come Through*, Project Gutenberg; and D. H. Lawrence, "Cruelty and Love," The Poetry Foundation.
148 **Plath read Lawrence extensively**: For a few passages in Plath's *Unabridged Journals* about her interest in, and love of, the work of D. H. Lawrence, see her entries of February 23, 1958; March 2, 1958; and September 15, 1958; Plath's notes from her time at the obscenity trial at the Old Bailey can be found in Appendix 10 of her *Unabridged Journals*.
148 **Diane Middlebrook writes in *Her Husband***: For Middlebrook's lengthy take on this topic, see her section "The Rabbit Catcher" in chap. 6, "Separating (1962–)," in *Her Husband: Ted Hughes & Sylvia Plath, A Marriage* (New York: Penguin, 2003), 170.
148 **his prose inspired her to write**: See Plath's journal entry of February 23, 1958, *Unabridged Journals*, 337–38.
148 **"[was] killed by" this mess**: See Plath's July 11, 1962, letter to Ruth Beuscher, *The Letters of Sylvia Plath, Vol. 2: 1956–1963*, 845.
148 **Ted Hughes bought Sylvia Plath**: See the prologue to Heather Clark's 2020 biography *Red Comet*.
149 **his poem of the same name**: See "The Rabbit Catcher" in Ted Hughes, *Collected Poems*, ed. Paul Keegan (New York: Farrar, Straus and Giroux, 2003), 1136–38.
150 ***Difficulties of a Bridegroom*, which he**: For an extensive discussion of the effect this broadcast had on Sylvia Plath, see Clark, "Yeats' House," chap. 33 in *Red Comet*.
150 **The play has never been published**: This information comes from transcriptions made from the typescript in Hughes's papers in the British Library, with gratitude to Peter Fydler, who typed it for me when I was unable to get to England.
150 **Daniel Huws speculated**: Clark, "Yeats' House," chap. 33 in *Red Comet*.
150 **"shamanic animal"**: Clark, "Yeats' House," chap. 33 in *Red Comet*.
150 **"Sylvia invited Ted"**: Clark, "Yeats' House," chap. 33 in *Red Comet*.
150 **Plath drafted "Kindness"**: Plath, *The Collected Poems*, 269–70. Handwritten drafts and Plath's typescripts of "Kindness" are held by Smith College's Mortimer Rare Book Room.
151 **Frieda's tears**: See Plath's January 22, 1963, letter to Olive Higgins Prouty, in *The Letters of Sylvia Plath, Vol. 2: 1956–1963*, 1013.

Notes | 267

152 **Hughes began drafting:** Middlebrook, "Separating (1962–)," chap. 6 in *Her Husband*, 169–70. Hughes also describes drafting the play in two letters, one from May 24, 1962, to the Merwins, and one to his sister, Olwyn, marked June 1962 in *Letters of Ted Hughes*, ed. Christopher Reid (London: Faber & Faber, 2007), 198–201.

152 **As Lenny and Doreen dance:** Sylvia Plath, chap. 2 in *The Bell Jar* (New York: Harper & Row, 1971), 18.

153 **Leonard: Hero:** Clark, "Life Studies," chap. 21 in *Red Comet*.

154 **"[lure] us into this labyrinth":** Middlebrook, "Coda" to *Her Husband*, 287.

154 **women's interpretations of social experiences:** Fricker, "Epistemic Oppression and Epistemic Privilege,' 18.

154 **her friends had a debate:** Manne, *Down Girl*, 4 (note 4).

154 **"self-masking":** Manne, preface to *Down Girl*, xix.

154 **"is golden for the men":** Manne, introduction to *Down Girl*, 18.

154 **Let us shriek:** See "Elm" in Plath, *Collected Poems*, 192–93.

Harriet the Spy

155 **"The Descent of Ariel":** Copies of Hinchliffe's thesis are held at the University of Maryland in Frances McCullough's papers, in Special Collections, and in Al Alvarez's papers at the British Library. I worked with scans from the Frances McCullough papers, Special Collections, University of Maryland Libraries. Writings of others, bulk: 1972–1984, Box 4, Folder 4.

155 **Lois Ames, a writer:** From everything I can gather, Ames has only ever granted one interview about this subject, with a man named Doug Holder, for his Somerville, MA, public access television show *Poet to Poet: Writer to Writer*. Holder published a transcript of it on the website authorsden.com ("Interview with Lois Ames: Confidante to Anne Sexton and Sylvia Plath"). Ames spoke about her contract and about working with the Hughes family.

156 **"prim and rather fussy":** Elizabeth Hinchliffe, *The Descent of Ariel: The Death of Sylvia Plath, Part One: London, 1962*, 14.

156 **"had never even heard of a plunger":** Hinchliffe, *The Descent of Ariel*, 18, 16.

157 **doesn't want to overdose:** There are two copies of Hinchcliffe's play, *The Descent of Ariel*, held by the British Library. The play is not held in connection to either Plath or Hughes, but as part of a collection of the scripts of every play ever performed in the United Kingdom since 1824, *The Modern Playscripts Collection*. It was known as *The Lord Chamberlain's Collection* until 1968.

157 **Olwyn Hughes used Ames's name:** See, for examples, Olwyn's letters of September 15, 1970, to Ruth Beuscher; October 13, 1970, to Harriet Rosenstein; November 19, 1971, to then president of Brandeis University, all available in Box 2, Folder 5, of the Harriet Rosenstein research files on Sylvia Plath, 1910-2018, at the Stuart A. Rose Manuscript, Archives, and Rare Book Library, Emory University.

157 **"A full biography could not":** See Ted Hughes's spring 1966 letter to Aurelia Plath in Series 1.1, Correspondence, Subseries 1.5, Box 55, Folder 2, Ted Hughes papers, Stuart A. Rose Manuscript, Archives, and Rare Book Library, Emory University.

268 | Notes

157 **a joint letter:** Wevill's portion of the letter (written August 9, 1967) is included in *The Collected Writings of Assia Wevill*, ed. Julie Goodspeed-Chadwick and Peter K. Steinberg (Baton Rouge: Louisiana State University Press, 2021), 121. Hughes's portion of the letter is in *Letters of Ted Hughes*, ed. Christopher Reid (London: Faber & Faber, 2007), 275–76.

158 **daughter of Elizabeth Ames:** Doug Holder, "Interview with Lois Ames: Confidante to Anne Sexton and Sylvia Plath," AuthorsDen.

158 **taught together at McLean:** Doug Holder, "Interview with Lois Ames."

158 **"biographical sketch":** Ames's sketch is not typically included in newer editions of *The Bell Jar*, but it can be found in the first American edition, published in 1971 (New York: Harper & Row), 279–96.

158 **"completely given up on":** See McCullough's letter to Ted Hughes of October 11, 1973, in Subseries 1.2, Business Correspondence, Box 15, Folder 2, Ted Hughes papers, Stuart A. Rose Manuscript, Archives, and Rare Book Library, Emory University.

158 **"I was the first one":** Lois Ames, interview by Doug Holder: "Lois Ames: Confidante to Anne Sexton and Sylvia Plath," AuthorsDen, accessed January 1, 2024.

158 **Olwyn Hughes had met Rosenstein:** Olwyn tells Ruth Beuscher, in her letter of September 15, 1970, that Rosenstein "rang me" when she was in London.

159 **"After all the solid work":** See Olwyn's August 8, 1978, letter to Rosenstein, in Box 2, Folder 5, of the Harriet Rosenstein research files on Sylvia Plath, 1910–2018, at the Stuart A. Rose Manuscript, Archives, and Rare Book Library, Emory University.

159 **with one exception:** See Olwyn's August 8, 1978, letter to Rosenstein. In the same letter, Olwyn tells Rosenstein that she is relieved to have received her letter of July 27, in Box 2, Folder 5, of the Harriet Rosenstein research files on Sylvia Plath, 1910–2018, at the Stuart A. Rose Manuscript, Archives, and Rare Book Library, Emory University

159 **declared the legal owner:** For a relatively detailed account of the proceedings between Smith College and Rosenstein, see Carl Rollyson, chap. 2 in *The Last Days of Sylvia Plath* (Jackson: University of Mississippi Press, 2020), 7–11. See also Peter K. Steinberg's blog post of September 12, 2018, "Sylvia Plath Collections: Letters to Ruth Beuscher," on *Sylvia Plath Info*.

159 **article on Plath in *Ms.* magazine:** Harriet Rosenstein's article, "Reconsidering Sylvia Plath," appeared in the September 1972 issue of *Ms.* magazine, 44–57.

159 **a contract with Knopf:** Rosenstein's contract with Knopf and her check stubs from her book advance are in Box 1, Folder 1, of the Harriet Rosenstein research files on Sylvia Plath, 1910–2018, at the Stuart A. Rose Manuscript, Archives, and Rare Book Library, Emory University.

159 **long interviews with Plath's friends:** Rollyson's *The Last Days of Sylvia Plath*, 5, reveals that there are "fifty-three cassette tapes and two reel-to-reel recordings" in Rosenstein's archive.

160 **"I never met a Smith girl":** Harriet Rosenstein interview with Ruth Barnhouse (Beuscher), undated (side B) [original: audio cassette], Box: AV1. Harriet Rosenstein research files on Sylvia Plath, Manuscript Collection No. 1489, Stuart A. Rose Manuscript, Archives, and Rare Book Library, Emory University.

160 **"a very ambitious rather heady":** See Merwin's June 29, 1988, letter to Ted

Hughes in Series 1.1, Box 4, Folder 1, of the Ted Hughes papers, Stuart A. Rose Manuscript, Archives, and Rare Book Library, Emory University.

160 **"I'm angry . . . he wasn't nice to me":** Elizabeth Sigmund, interview recording, parts 5 and 6, undated [original: audio cassette], Box: AV1. Harriet Rosenstein research files on Sylvia Plath, Manuscript Collection No. 1489, Stuart A. Rose Manuscript, Archives, and Rare Book Library, Emory University.

160 **"trunks full of Sylvia":** Elizabeth Sigmund, interview recording, parts 3 and 4.

160 **on Plath's "Ariel":** See Plath's *Collected Poems*, 194–95.

161 **"the shock of recognition":** See Plath's January 25, 1953, entry in her *Unabridged Journals*.

161 **Smith College, then Newnham:** See *The Descent of Ariel*; Hinchcliffe's CV is included as the last two pages of her thesis.

161 **inflict agony on Ted Hughes:** The most recent example of this idea can be found in Steve Ely, "The Key of the Sycamore," *Ted Hughes Society Journal* 8, no. 2 (Summer 2020): 42–64. Hughes scholar Steve Ely posits that Assia Wevill only killed Shura Wevill to hurt Ted Hughes more intensely than Plath intended with her own suicide. Jillian Becker also said as much on p. 40 of her brief memoir *Giving Up: The Last Days of Sylvia Plath* (New York: St. Martin's Press, 2002).

162 **her heroine Lady Lazarus:** Plath, *Collected Poems*, 244–46.

162 ***Three Women*, Plath's 1962 radio play:** Plath, *Collected Poems*, 176–87.

162 **as Esther Greenwood says:** Sylvia Plath, *The Bell Jar* (New York: Harper & Row, 1971), 143.

162 **"accused by . . . the white mute faces":** Plath, *Collected Poems*, 176–87.

163 **"I see her in my sleep":** Plath, *Collected Poems*, 182.

163 **read about Harriet Rosenstein:** For a thorough description of Rosenstein's appearance in Frances McCullough's papers, see Carl Rollyson, "In the Temple of Isis: Among the Hierophants (1963–)," chap. 8 in *American Isis* (New York: St. Martin's Press, 2013).

163 **Janet Malcolm mentions Rosenstein:** Janet Malcolm, *The Silent Woman: Sylvia Plath and Ted Hughes* (New York: Knopf, 1994), 35.

163 **belied Malcolm's real interest:** See C. Roche (3); Alvarez (5) (2), undated. Janet Malcom papers, Yale Collection of American Literature, Beinecke Rare Book and Manuscript Library.

163 **"a prime position":** Rollyson, *American Isis*, 246.

164 **"Unseen Sylvia Plath Letters":** Danuta Kean, "Unseen Sylvia Plath Letters Claim Domestic Abuse by Ted Hughes," *Guardian*, April 11, 2017, updated April 12, 2017.

164 **October 21, 1962, claim:** Sylvia Plath, *The Letters of Sylvia Plath, Vol. 2: 1956–1963*, ed. Peter K. Steinberg and Karen V. Kukil (New York: HarperCollins, 2018), 876–80.

164 **"The extent of [Plath and Hughes's] estrangement":** Danuta Kean, "Unseen Sylvia Plath Letters Claim Domestic Abuse by Ted Hughes," *Guardian*, April 11, 2017.

164 **remember Frieda Hughes's note:** Frieda Hughes, foreword to *The Letters of Sylvia Plath, Vol. I: 1940–1956*.

165 **by the *Irish Times*:** "Sylvia Plath Letters Reveal Abuse by Ted Hughes," *Irish Times*, April 20, 2017.

165 **Ted Hughes's own accounts:** See Ted Hughes's poem "18 Rugby Street," in *Birthday Letters*, in *Collected Poems*, ed. Paul Keegan (New York: Farrar, Straus

and Giroux, 2003), 1055–58, and Jonathan Bate's account of the night Hughes and Plath first slept together in London, in March 1956. Bate's chapter is also called "18 Rugby Street"; see chap. 8 in *Ted Hughes: The Unauthorised Life* (London: William Collins, 2015), 137.

165 **their book *These Ghostly Archives*:** Gail Crowther and Peter K. Steinberg, *These Ghostly Archives: The Unearthing of Sylvia Plath* (Oxford: Fonthill Media, 2017), 54.

165 **McCullough spent time in Devon:** Jonathan Bate also describes this trip at length, and Ted Hughes's reactions to it in his journals, in "The Arraignment," chap. 21 in *Ted Hughes: The Unauthorised Life*, 428.

165 **"[slap Plath] out":** This 1974 note is held in Box 8, Folder 54, of the Frances McCullough papers, Special Collections, University of Maryland Libraries.

166 **an addendum from Carol Hughes:** The addendum can be accessed here: https://www.theguardian.com/books/2017/apr/11/unseen-sylvia-plath-letters-claim-domestic-abuse-by-ted-hughes.

166 **Frieda Hughes agreed:** F. Hughes, foreword to *The Letters of Sylvia Plath, Vol. 2: 1956–1963*.

167 **never been made available:** See the notes to Rollyson, *The Last Days of Sylvia Plath*, 222.

167 **between Harriet Rosenstein and Frieda Hughes:** See the emails between Frieda Hughes and Harriet Rosenstein in Box 2, Folder 4, of the Harriet Rosenstein research files on Sylvia Plath, Stuart A. Rose Manuscript, Archives, and Rare Book Library, Emory University.

167 **"my mother's taped interview":** See Frieda Hughes's email to Harriet Rosenstein of December 27, 2017, Box 2, Folder 4, of the Harriet Rosenstein research files on Sylvia Plath, Stuart A. Rose Manuscript, Archives, and Rare Book Library, Emory University.

168 **a marble composition notebook:** See Box 1, Folder 6, in the Harriet Rosenstein research files on Sylvia Plath, 1910-2018, at the Stuart A. Rose Manuscript, Archives, and Rare Book Library, Emory University.

169 **1970s version of viral:** See Anne Sexton's May 15, 1974, letter to Rosenstein in Box 4, Folder 8, in the Harriet Rosenstein research files on Sylvia Plath.

169 **dangling financial carrots:** These letters can be found in Rosenstein's general correspondence, Box 4, Folder 2, in the Harriet Rosenstein research files on Sylvia Plath.

170 **"enjoyed our pleasant meeting":** See Olwyn Hughes's letters to Rosenstein in Box 2, Folder 5, in the Harriet Rosenstein research files on Sylvia Plath.

170 **interviewing Ruth Barnard Beuscher:** Rosenstein's archive contains what remains of her taped interviews with Beuscher, and a notebook, Box 1, Folder 6, in the Harriet Rosenstein research files on Sylvia Plath.

170 **Their relationship was reduced to letters:** All of Plath's letters to her former therapist were published in *The Letters of Sylvia Plath, Vol. 2: 1956–1963*: July 20, 1962, p. 796; July 30, 1962, p. 803; September 4, 1962, p. 817.

170 **Beuscher did eventually write back:** These letters are unpublished and can be found in the Sylvia Plath papers, Smith College Archives, CA-MS-00142, Smith College Special Collections, Northampton, Massachusetts.

170 **"Keep him out of your bed"**: Ted Hughes, *Howls & Whispers*, in *Collected Poems*, ed. Paul Keegan (New York: Farrar, Straus and Giroux, 2003), 1178–79.
171 **"My relation to Ted"**: Plath, *The Letters of Sylvia Plath, Vol. 2: 1956–1963*, 876.
171 **September 15, 1970, letter:** See Olwyn Hughes's letter to Ruth Beuscher, Box 2, Folder 5, in the Harriet Rosenstein research files on Sylvia Plath, 1910-2018, at the Stuart A. Rose Manuscript, Archives, and Rare Book Library, Emory University.
171 **"[Beuscher] continuing a relationship"**: Rollyson, *The Last Days of Sylvia Plath*, 13.
172 **Rosenstein met Wilbury Crockett:** Rosenstein's correspondence with Crockett and interview notes from her time with Crockett are in Box 1, Folder 19, in the Harriet Rosenstein Research Files on Sylvia Plath, 1910-2018, at the Stuart A. Rose Manuscript, Archives and Rare Book Library, Emory University.
172 **just like Sylvia:** See Plath's journal entry marked #152 from fall 1952, where she discusses a lengthy visit and discussion with Crockett about her future in *The Unabridged Journals of Sylvia Plath*, ed. Karen V. Kukil (New York: Anchor Books, 2000).
172 **material from her dissertation:** See Box 3, Folder 15, in the Harriet Rosenstein research files on Sylvia Plath.
172 **"Apparently Harriet had a big breakdown"**: See Olwyn Hughes's letter to Janet Malcolm in Janet Malcom papers, Series I: Research materials and writing, 1950-2010, Box 14, Yale Collection of American Literature, Beinecke Rare Book and Manuscript Library
173 **"Harriet Rosenstein 'in insane asylum'"**: See Malcolm's folder marked "Harriet Rosenstein" in Janet Malcom papers, Series I: Research materials and writing, 1950-2010, Box 10, Yale Collection of American Literature, Beinecke Rare Book and Manuscript Library.
173 **"In 1973 a woman from Boston"**: Becker, *Giving Up: The Last Days of Sylvia Plath*, 55.
173 **Becker praises:** See Becker's January 24, 1974, letter to Rosenstein in Box 1, Folder 8 in the Harriet Rosenstein research files on Sylvia Plath.
173 **Plath's coroner's report:** See Becker's June 3, 1974, letter to Rosenstein in Box 1, Folder 8, in the Harriet Rosenstein research files on Sylvia Plath; the copy of Plath's coroner's report is also there.
174 **Heather Clark also posits this:** Heather Clark, "Epilogue: Your Wife Is Dead," in *Red Comet: The Short Life and Blazing Art of Sylvia Plath* (New York: Knopf, 2020).
174 **Rosenstein seized on the bruises:** See Rosenstein's June 11, 1974, letter to Becker in Box 1, Folder 8, in the Harriet Rosenstein research files on Sylvia Plath.
174 **dispensed with mystical symmetries:** See Becker's June 14, 1974, letter to Rosenstein Box 1, Folder 8, in the Harriet Rosenstein research files on Sylvia Plath.
174 **"The mirrors are sheeted"**: Plath, *Collected Poems*, 271.
174 **Clarissa Roche struggled to recall:** This letter is unpublished; Linda Wagner-Martin generously gave me a copy.

175 **"Good Girls: How Powerful Men":** Kate Manne, "Good Girls: How Powerful Men Get Away with Sexual Predation," *Huffington Post*, March 24, 2017, updated March 28, 2017.
175 **"mandatory reporting" clause:** "Intersection of Title IX and the Clery Act," 2014 White House Task Force to Protect Students from Sexual Assault, April 2014.
175 **"Law cannot fix this problem":** "Martha Nussbaum, "Why Some Men Are Above the Law," *Huffington Post*, January 15, 2016.
175 **Bill Cosby filed multiple defamation suits:** Ralph Ellis, "Bill Cosby Sues Supermodel Beverly Johnson for Defamation," CNN, December 22, 2015; Stephanie Marcus, "Bill Cosby Sues Seven of His Accusers for Defamation," *Huffington Post*, December 15, 2015.
175 **supermodel Beverly Johnson:** Beverly Johnson, "Bill Cosby Drugged Me. This Is My Story," *Vanity Fair*, December 11, 2014.
176 **foreword by her only survivor:** F. Hughes, foreword to *The Letters of Sylvia Plath, Vol. 2: 1956–1963*, xv–xxv.
177 **"This assault had not warranted":** F. Hughes, foreword to *The Letters of Sylvia Plath, Vol. 2: 1956–1963*, xxi.
177 **supermodel Janice Dickinson:** "Janice Dickinson Tells Court Bill Cosby Raped Her after Drug Left Her 'Motionless,'" *Guardian*, April 12, 2018.
177 **"What, I asked myself":** F. Hughes, foreword to *The Letters of Sylvia Plath, Vol.2: 1956–1963*, xxi.
177 **Raine quotes Plath, writing to Beuscher:** Craig Raine, "'Ted is [a] liar. Ted beats me up. Ted wishes me dead.': Sylvia Plath Descends into Madness and Misery," *Spectator World*, September 13, 2018.
178 **Fricker calls "collective systematic cognitive failings":** Miranda Fricker, "Epistemic Oppression and Epistemic Privilege," *Canadian Journal of Philosophy* 29 (1999): 207.
178 **the "tender" writing Plath did:** Bate, "Epilogue: The Legacy," in *Ted Hughes: The Unauthorised Life*, 669.
178 **the "honeymoon" period:** See "Supporting Someone Who Keeps Returning to an Abusive Relationship," National Domestic Violence Hotline.
178 **"the accusation feeds the myth":** Bate, "Epilogue: The Legacy," in *Ted Hughes: The Unauthorised Life*, 669.
178 **we "exonerate men":** Kate Manne, "Exonerating Men," chap. 6 in *Down Girl: The Logic of Misogyny* (Oxford: Oxford University Press, 2017), 196–205.
178 **Manne's most potent example:** Manne, "Exonerating Men," in *Down Girl*, 196–205.
179 **no resemblance to "real" rape:** Manne, "Exonerating Men," in *Down Girl*, 198.
179 **"[In] all my life with my father":** F. Hughes, foreword to *The Letters of Sylvia Plath, Vol.2: 1956–1963*, xxi.
179 **Chiasson had written:** See "Sylvia Plath's Last Letters" in *The New Yorker*, October 29, 2018.
179 **"had I been able to":** See Harriet Rosenstein's email to Dan Chiasson in Box 1, Folder 17.

180 **she turned me down:** I sent Dr. Rosenstein a copy of *Loving Sylvia Plath: A Reclamation* when it was published in July 2024. She responded a month later to say that she had enjoyed the book but would have liked to correct certain errors, which she did not identify. I was working on the paperback at that point and reached out several times to Dr. Rosenstein alerting her to the production schedule and asking for her corrections. She responded once to say that a list would be forthcoming; it had not materialized as of the date of this writing in April 2025.

The House of the Ruler

182 **"The word *archive*":** See "*Dream House as* Prologue" in Carmen Maria Machado's *In the Dream House: A Memoir* (Minneapolis: Graywolf Press, 2019), 4.
183 **"felt somehow protective":** Kroll, *Chapters in a Mythology*, xv–xvi.
183 ***Crystal Gazer and Other Poems*:** Kroll, *Chapters in a Mythology*, xx–xxi.
183 **"Those are the circumstances":** Kroll, *Chapters in a Mythology*, xxi.
183 **Robin Morgan made her famous claim:** Robin Morgan, *Monster* (New York: Vintage Books, 1972), 76–78.
184 **"You have convinced me":** Kroll, *Chapters in a Mythology*, xxiii.
184 **"crazy and outrageous":** See Harriet Rosenstein's letter to Olwyn Hughes of November 1972, in the Harriet Rosenstein research files on Sylvia Plath, 1910–2018, the Stuart A. Rose Manuscript, Archives, and Rare Book Library, Emory University.
184 **the editors at *Ms.*:** Harriet Rosenstein's letter to Olwyn Hughes of November 1972.
184 **the clever detective:** Kroll, *Chapters in a Mythology*, xxx.
185 **Court Green, London, and his parents' home:** For a description of this time in Ted Hughes's life, see Jonathan Bate, "The Savage God," chap. 18 in *Ted Hughes: The Unauthorised Life* (London: William Collins, 2015).
185 **someone set fire:** Bate, "The Savage God," in *Ted Hughes: The Unauthorised Life*, 372.
185 **broke into Court Green:** Bate, "The Savage God," in *Ted Hughes: The Unauthorised Life*, 380.
185 **Emma Tennant, in *Burnt Diaries*:** Emma Tennant, "Spring 1976: Sylvia Plath and Her Relics," in *Burnt Diaries* (Edinburgh: Canongate Books, 1999), 45–47.
185 **Tennant writes that the windows:** Tennant, *Burnt Diaries*, 45.
185 **Kroll struggled to work:** Kroll, *Chapters in a Mythology*, xxv–xxvi.
185 **That same summer—1974:** Kroll, *Chapters in a Mythology*, xxvii–xxviii.
186 **"rather a brilliant book":** Kroll, *Chapters in a Mythology*, xxix.
186 **questioned Kroll's reading:** Kroll, *Chapters in a Mythology*, xxx–xxxi.
186 **Kroll's treatment of "Medusa":** Kroll, "Resolutions of the Myth," in *Chapters in a Mythology*, 132–134.
186 **"old barnacled umbilicus":** Sylvia Plath, *The Collected Poems*, ed. Ted Hughes (New York: Harper & Row, 1981), 224–26.
186 **"black telephone's off":** Plath, *The Collected Poems*, 222–24.

274 | Notes

187 **"Many of her findings"**: Karl Miller, "Sylvia Plath's Apotheosis," *New York Review of Books*, June 24, 1976.
187 **letter to the editor:** See Judith Kroll's May 12, 1977, letter to the editor of the *New York Review of Books*, "Not a Conspiracy."
187 **"In the preface to *Chapters*":** Kroll, *Chapters in a Mythology*, xxix–xxx.
188 **Jonathan Bate describes Kroll's:** For a description of the summer of 1974 in Ted Hughes's life, see "The Arraignment," chap. 21 in Bate, *Ted Hughes: The Unauthorised Life*.
188 **"which he thought full of amazing intuitions":** Bate, *Ted Hughes: The Unauthorised Life*, 427.
188 **"they started work on Sylvia's manuscript":** Bate, *Ted Hughes: The Unauthorised Life*, 428.
188 **filled with errors:** Kroll, *Chapters in a Mythology*, xxiv, footnote 12.
188 **"I like this line better":** Kroll, *Chapters in a Mythology*, xxvi.
189 **the first writer to mention Assia:** Kroll, *Chapters in a Mythology*, xxxiv.
189 **Robin Morgan, who, in "Arraignment":** Robin Morgan, "Arraignment," in *Monster*, 76–79.
189 **Janet Badia has rightly pointed out:** For a nuanced discussion of the ways Robin Morgan became a stand-in for the angry, Plath-obsessed feminist, and how many claims of "feminists" protesting Ted Hughes's readings by reciting "Arraignment" seem dubious, at best, see Janet Badia, "We Did Not Wish to Give the Impression," in *Sylvia Plath and the Mythology of Women Readers* (Amherst: University of Massachusetts Press, 2011).
189 **having lunch with him in Soho:** See Plath's letter to her mother in *The Letters of Sylvia Plath, Vol. 2: 1956–1963*, ed. Peter K. Steinberg and Karen V. Kukil (New York: HarperCollins, 2018), 513.
189 **editor at the *New Statesmen*:** Plath makes repeated references to Miller in her letters from 1960 to 1962. See *The Letters of Sylvia Plath, Vol. 2: 1956–1963*.
190 **Clarissa Roche told Janet Malcolm:** There are three tapes from Malcolm's time at Roche's home in Somerset, England, in 1991; Roche tells Malcolm about alleged incest between Ted and Olwyn Hughes, as Plath reported it to her, on the first of the three Janet Malcom papers, Yale Collection of American Literature, Beinecke Rare Book and Manuscript Library.
190 **"outrageous":** Janet Malcolm, *The Silent Woman: Sylvia Plath and Ted Hughes* (New York: Knopf, 1994), 50.
190 **"a book which she said":** Karl Miller, "Sylvia Plath's Apotheosis," *New York Review of Books*, June 24, 1976.
190 **Byron's sister looked:** See Plath's November 29, 1962, letter to her mother in *The Letters of Sylvia Plath, Vol. 2: 1956–1963*, 975.
190 **an affair with his half-sister:** See Stacy Schiff's November 30, 2018, review of *In Byron's Wake: The Turbulent Lives of Lord Byron's Wife and Daughter: Annabella Milbanke and Ada Lovelace* in the *New York Times*.
190 **to leave the country:** Bate, "That Sunday Night," chap. 13 in *Ted Hughes: The Unauthorised Life*, 259.
190 **Olwyn hated any woman:** Bate, "The Custodian," chap. 14 in *Ted Hughes: The Unauthorised Life*, 274.

190 **"were indeed lovers":** The quote is taken from a May 1992 profile of Olwyn Hughes in a local Camden (London) magazine called *Scallywag*, printed from 1991 to 1995. Scans of the profile were sent to me by Dr. Gail Crowther in October 2022.

190 **"I don't find reasons":** See Ted Hughes's letter to Olywn Hughes in the Ted Hughes papers, Subseries 1.1, Box 188, Folder 3, Ted Hughes papers, Stuart A. Rose Manuscript, Archives, and Rare Book Library, Emory University.

191 **Byron's *Don Juan*:** See *Cunk on Britain*. Season 1, episode 3.

191 **"If what the author has to say":** See *"Dream House as* Overture" and *"Dream House as* Prologue" in Machado, *In the Dream House*, 3–5.

191 **25 to 33 percent globally:** Liz Mineo, "'Shadow Pandemic' of Domestic Violence: Law School's Marianna Yang Examines Rise in Factors, Hurdles in Courts for Victims," *Harvard Gazette*, June 29, 2022.

192 **"And I have no face":** Plath, "Tulips" in *The Collected Poems*, 160–62.

192 ***The Art of Cruelty*:** Maggie Nelson, "Face," in *The Art of Cruelty: A Reckoning* (New York: W. W. Norton, 2012), 229–30.

192 **miscarried her second pregnancy:** Plath lost her second pregnancy in February of 1961 while the Hugheses were living at 3 Chalcot Square, London; she later attributed this loss to Ted Hughes's beating her, in a September 22, 1962, letter to Ruth Beuscher. See *The Letters of Sylvia Plath, Vol. 2: 1956–1963*, xlix, 830.

192 **"I'd rather have a baby":** Anne Stevenson, "Warnings," chap. 10 in *Bitter Fame: A Life of Sylvia Plath* (London: Penguin Books, 1998), 208.

192 **poem called "Widow":** Plath, *The Collected Poems*, 164–65. I owe a debt of gratitude to my student Isabella Bruno for her astute reading of this poem in my Fall 2022 freshman seminar, "Sylvia Plath and Silent Women."

193 **something Maggie Nelson reads:** Nelson, *The Art of Cruelty*, 230.

193 **"perpetually freezing cold":** See Plath's October 3, 1956, letter to Ted Hughes in *The Letters of Sylvia Plath, Vol. 1. 1940–1956*, ed. Peter Steinberg and Karen V. Kukil (New York: HarperCollins, 2017), 1275.

193 **"a private holy spirit":** *The Letters of Sylvia Plath, Vol. 1: 1940–1956*, 1274.

194 **"the violence of the archive":** Saidiya Hartman, "Venus in Two Acts," *Small Axe* 12, no. 2 (June 2008): 1–14.

194 **"stories," Machado writes:** Machado, *"Dream House as* Prologue," *In the Dream House*, 4.

194 **queer intimate partner violence:** Machado, *"Dream House as* Prologue," *In the Dream House*, 5

194 **"A 12-city study":** Bernie Auchter, "Men Who Murder Their Families: What the Research Tells Us," *National Institute of Justice Journal*, no. 266 (May 2010): 10–12.

195 **at least seven years:** Aurelia Plath sold a significant amount of her daughter's papers to the Lilly Library at Indiana University in 1977. See "Sylvia Plath: About" for a brief history of the sale on the library's webpage.

195 **Brownmiller writes:** Susan Brownmiller, *Against Our Will: Men, Women, and Rape* (New York: Fawcett Books, 1975).

195 **"gotten out of hand":** Brownmiller, *Against Our Will*, 327.

195 **"were designed to do everything":** Jeffrey Fagan, *The Criminalization of Domestic Violence: Promises and Limits*, a research report published by the

National Institute of Justice for their 1995 conference on criminal justice research and evaluation, 14.

196 **National Public Radio reported:** Carrie Johnson, "New Research Could Help Nurses, Police Detect Bruises on People with Dark Skin," at NPR, February 21, 2023.

197 ***"Dream House* as Choose Your Own Adventure":** Machado *"Dream House as* Choose Your Own Adventure," *In the Dream House*, 162–76.

197 **According to Gail Crowther's:** Gail Crowther, "Suicide," chap. 8 in *Three-Martini Afternoons at the Ritz: The Rebellion of Sylvia Plath & Anne Sexton* (New York: Gallery Books, 2022), 211.

198 **actively burning or losing:** Carl Rollyson covers the loss of Plath's manuscripts in depth in "In the Temple of Isis: Among the Hierophants," chap. 8 in *American Isis* (New York: St. Martin's Press, 2013).

198 **now-famous journal entry:** See Plath's journal entry of February 26, 1956, in *The Unabridged Journals of Sylvia Plath*, ed. Karen V. Kukil (New York: Anchor Books, 2000).

198 **"Pursuit," a terrifying poem:** Plath, *The Collected Poems*, 22–23.

198 **she wrote "Ode for Ted":** Plath, *The Collected Poems*, 29–30.

198 **"Oh Teddy, how":** See Plath's letter to Ted Hughes dated October 7–8, 1956, in *The Letters of Sylvia Plath, Vol. 1: 1940–1956*, 1284.

199 **her poem "Burning the Letters":** Plath, *The Collected Poems*, 204–5.

199 **Like Eliza Doolittle:** See George Bernard Shaw's *Pygmalion*, 1912, Project Gutenberg EBook.

200 **"[had] no desire":** See Plath's October 9, 1956, letter to Ted Hughes in *The Letters of Sylvia Plath, Vol. 1: 1940–1956*, 1293.

200 **"as for her mastery of literature":** See Ted Hughes's 1986 letter to Anne Stevenson in Box 147, MSS 644, Folder 6—correspondence related to *TSW*, Janet Malcolm. Ted Hughes papers, Stuart A. Rose Manuscript, Archives, and Rare Book Library, Emory University.

200 **a practice called "dislocation":** Machado, *"Dream House* as Worldbuilding," *In the Dream House*, 72.

200 ***Revising Life***: Susan Van Dyne, *Revising Life: Sylvia Plath's* Ariel *Poems* (Chapel Hill: University of North Carolina Press, 1993).

201 **"'Burning the Letters' demonstrates":** Van Dyne, *Revising Life*, 41.

201 **"The more he writes poems":** See Plath's April 19, 1956, letter to her mother in *The Letters of Sylvia Plath, Vol. 1: 1940–1956*, 1165.

201 **Now she was saying the same:** See Sylvia Plath's October 21, 1962, letter to Ruth Beuscher in *The Letters of Sylvia Plath, Vol. 2: 1956–1963*, 877.

201 **"The Thought-Fox" was published:** Ted Hughes, *Collected Poems*, ed. Paul Keegan (New York: Farrar, Straus and Giroux, 2003), 21.

201 **"It never snows in the country":** Van Dyne, *Revising Life*, 40.

201 **Janet Malcolm includes a long excerpt:** Malcolm, *The Silent Woman*, 143.

202 **she writes "at the limit of":** Hartman, "Venus in Two Acts," 2.

202 **"There is not one extant":** Hartman, "Venus in Two Acts," 4.

203 **"returns the dead to us":** Hartman, "Venus in Two Acts," 6.

203 **posed by Gayatri Spivak:** Gayatri Spivak, "Can the Subaltern Speak?" *Die Philosophin* 14, no. 27 (2003): 42–58.
203 **"tell a story . . . predicted":** Hartman, "Venus in Two Acts," 3.
204 **now defunct *Feminist Art Journal*:** See Robin Morgan's article "Conspiracy of Silence Against a Feminist Poem" in the first-ever issue of *Feminist Art Journal*, Fall 1972. Morgan's assistant was kind enough to send me scans of the article in the spring of 2019.
204 **begins "I accuse / Ted Hughes":** *Feminist Art Journal* printed the original version alongside Morgan's article about the publishing process.
205 **"simplified feminist ideology":** Stevenson, epilogue to *Bitter Fame*, 304.
206 **"One of the interesting highlights":** Robin Morgan, "Conspiracy of Silence Against a Feminist Poem," *Feminist Art Journal* (Fall 1972), 21.

In the Boneyard

208 **About a quarter mile:** Parts of this chapter appeared as the article "Diary of a Pilgrimage: Marking the Gravesite of Assia and Shura Wevill," *Literary Hub*, November 9, 2022.
208 **Lumb Bank, the eighteenth-century manor:** Jonathan Bate, "Then Autobiographical Things Knocked It All to Bits, as Before," chap. 16 in *Ted Hughes: The Unauthorised Life* (London: William Collins, 2015), 344.
209 **Wevill was in West Yorkshire:** Bate, "Then Autobiographical Things," 334.
209 **why he couldn't commit:** Assia Wevill, "Journals," in *The Collected Writings of Assia Wevill*, ed. Julie Goodspeed-Chadwick and Peter K. Steinberg (Baton Rouge: Louisiana State University Press, 2021), 195.
209 **Wevill went to Haworth:** Wevill, "Journals," in *The Collected Writings of Assia Wevill*, 194.
209 **Two days later, she killed herself:** Bate, chap. 16 in *Ted Hughes: The Unauthorised Life*, 335–36.
209 **an unpublished note:** Steve Ely, "The Key of the Sycamore," *Ted Hughes Society Journal* 8, no. 2 (June 2020): 55.
209 **"My insides raging":** Wevill, "Journals," in *The Collected Writings of Assia Wevill*, 169.
210 **young people's Cambridge:** For the most comprehensive description of Plath's time at Cambridge, see chaps. 15, 16, and 17 in Heather Clark, *Red Comet: The Short Life and Blazing Art of Sylvia Plath* (New York: Knopf, 2020).
210 **"They look exactly alike":** See Sylvia Plath's October 21, 1962, letter to Ruth Beuscher in *The Letters of Sylvia Plath, Vol. 2: 1956–1963*, ed. Peter K. Steinberg and Karen V. Kukil (New York: HarperCollins, 2018), 877.
210 **On the surface:** For the most comprehensive narrative of Plath's funeral, see Jillian Becker, *Giving Up: The Last Days of Sylvia Plath* (New York: St. Martin's Press, 2002).
210 **The church was built:** For a history of the current church and its ruins, see the online article "St. Thomas the Apostle Heptonstall: A Brief History."
211 **"a yellow trench in the snow":** Becker, *Giving Up*, 43.
211 **"Everybody hated her":** Becker, *Giving Up*, 44.

211 **her grave, far from friends:** See Peter K. Steinberg's October 5, 2021, article "Sylvia Plath's Grave," on his blog *Sylvia Plath Info*.
211 **claimed was from the Bhagavad Gita:** See the epilogue to Anne Stevenson, *Bitter Fame: A Life of Sylvia Plath* (London: Penguin Books, 1998), 304.
211 **raised lead lettering:** See Hughes's April 20, 1989, letter in the *Guardian*.
212 **named Julia Parnaby and Rachel Wingfield:** Julia Parnaby and Rachel Wingfield, "In Memory of Sylvia Plath," April 7, 1989, letter in the *Guardian*.
213 **two near-immediate responses:** "Problems Strewn on the Path to Sylvia Plath's Grave," April 11, 1989, letter in the *Guardian*.
213 **from Hughes himself:** See Hughes's April 20, 1989, letter in the *Guardian*.
213 **several poems and one short story:** See Plath's poems "Hardcastle Crags," "Wuthering Heights," and "November Graveyard" and her short story "All The Dead Dears," among others: Sylvia Plath, *The Collected Poems*, ed. Ted Hughes (New York: Harper & Row, 1981).
214 **Frieda's first Christmas:** See Plath's January 4, 1961, letter to Ruth Beuscher in *The Letters of Sylvia Plath, Vol. 2: 1956–1963*, 562–67.
214 **proximity to the Brontës:** The Brontës were born, raised, and died in Haworth, West Yorkshire, about ten miles from Heptonstall.
214 **Hughes, like Hamlet:** See Act V, Scene I, of Shakespeare's *Hamlet*, or "the Gravedigger scene," as it is sometimes called, in which Hamlet happens upon two men digging Ophelia's grave, and the skull of his former court jester, Yorick.
215 **"undulating Devon":** Becker, *Giving Up*, 41.
215 **a flinty mausoleum:** Ted Hughes, "Sylvia Plath: *Ariel*," in *Winter Pollen: Occasional Prose*, ed. William Scammell (New York: Picador, 1995), 162.
215 **Assia Wevill made an unofficial will:** Wevill, "The Will of Assia Esther Wevill," in "Miscellaneous Texts," in *The Collected Writings of Assia Wevill*, 266–67.
215 **"I kissed Nick's neck":** Wevill, "Journals," in *The Collected Writings of Assia Wevill*, 169.
215 **Hughes and Wevill never married:** For a careful description of Hughes's last interactions with Wevill, and Wevill and Shura's funeral, see Bate, "Then Autobiographical Things Knocked It All to Bits, as Before," chap. 16 in *Ted Hughes: The Unauthorised Life*, 324–46.
216 **Jewish law forbidding cremation:** Rabbi Naftali Silberberg, "Why Does Judaism Forbid Cremation?" Chabad.org.
216 **made their way into print:** Ted Hughes, "The Locket," "Folktale," "Snow," "Smell of Burning," and "The Error," in *Capriccio*, in *Collected Poems*, ed. Paul Keegan (New York: Farrar, Straus and Giroux, 2003), 783–99.
216 **"Ashes" grimly puns:** For a detailed discussion of "Ashes," see Ely, "The Key of the Sycamore," 53–54.
216 **Hitler came to him:** See Ted Hughes's letter to Olwyn Hughes, marked "Late summer 1962," in *Letters of Ted Hughes*, ed. Christopher Reid (London: Faber & Faber, 2007), 203–4.
216 **in a Kentish graveyard:** Bate, "Then Autobiographical Things Knocked It All To Bits, as Before," chap. 16 in *Ted Hughes: The Unauthorised Life*, 341.

216 **"The Key of the Sycamore," Ely writes:** Ely, "The Key of the Sycamore," *Ted Hughes Society Journal* 8, no. 2 (June 2020): 42–64.
217 ***Capriccio* was published:** For a long meditation on *Capriccio*'s history, development, and meaning, see Ely, "A Prologue to *Capriccio*," *Ted Hughes Society Journal* 8, no. 2 (June 2020): 12–30.
217 **Baskin was teaching:** Plath wrote and dedicated her poem "The Sculptor" to Baskin, in honor of visiting his studio. Plath, *The Collected Poems*, 91–92.
217 **"She simply disappeared":** Ely, "The Key of the Sycamore," 58.
217 **"true wife":** See Ted Hughes's April 14, 1969, letter to Celia Chaikin, Assia Wevill's sister, in *Letters of Ted Hughes*, ed. Christopher Reid (London: Faber & Faber, 2007), 290–91.
217 **"has been the symbolic target":** Goodspeed-Chadwick wrote about this in a paper she delivered as part of a Zoom symposium called "The Troubling Graves of Sylvia Plath & Assia Wevill," which took place March 6, 2022, and included work by Gail Crowther, Jessica Ferri, and myself.
217 **Anouilh's Antigone:** See Jean Anouilh, *Antigone: A Tragedy*, trans. Lewis Galantière (New York: Random House, 1946).
218 **"Fever 103 degrees":** Plath, *The Collected Poems*, 231–32.
219 **"Are women human?":** Catharine A. MacKinnon, *Are Women Human?: And Other International Dialogues* (Cambridge, MA: Harvard University Press, 2006).
220 **"awful tragedy":** See Plath's July 1951 entry marked #91 in *The Unabridged Journals of Sylvia Plath*, ed. Karen V. Kukil (New York: Anchor Books, 2000).
220 **"one of Hughes's most tender elegies":** Ely, "The Key of the Sycamore," 60.
220 **epitaph, "Here lies a lover of unreason":** Ely, "The Key of the Sycamore," 64.
221 **cast doubt on Shura's paternity:** In his review of Julie Goodspeed-Chadwick's book *Reclaiming Assia Wevill: Sylvia Plath, Ted Hughes, and the Literary Imagination*, which immediately follows Ely's "The Key of the Sycamore," Terry Gifford (*Ted Hughes Society Journal* 8, no. 2, June 2020) writes, "Shura's paternity is assumed to be Hughes, although Assia was still sleeping with David Wevill who only found out about the affair from Plath and was not told by Assia that their marriage was over until 1966." Assia Wevill knew definitively that Shura was Hughes's daughter, as did Hughes; he was named on her birth certificate as her father. For more information about this, see Yehuda Koren and Eilat Negev, *Lover of Unreason: Assia Wevill, Sylvia Plath's Rival and Ted Hughes's Doomed Love* (Cambridge, MA: Da Capo Press, 2006).
221 **"Withholding from others":** Diane Middlebrook, *Her Husband: Ted Hughes & Sylvia Plath, A Marriage* (New York: Penguin, 2003), 55.
222 **"To Ted Hughes, their father":** Wevill, "The Will of Assia Esther Wevill," *The Collected Writings of Assia Wevill*, 256–67.
222 **"frequented by dog walkers":** Ely, "The Key of the Sycamore," 63.
222 **"And I have no face":** Plath, *Collected Poems*, 161–62.
223 **she didn't miss the sea:** See Plath's June 17, 1957, letter to her mother in *The Letters of Sylvia Plath, Vol. II: 1956–1963*, 148.
223 **"a primary weapon":** See the article "Mourner's Kaddish: Central to Jewish Prayer," on Kronish Funeral Services, June 28, 2018.

224 **scattered ashes somewhere on Dartmoor:** For a detailed description of Ted Hughes's public and private funerals, his burial on Dartmoor, his relationship with King Charles III, and his monument in Westminster Abbey's Poets' Corner, see Bate, "The Legacy," in *Ted Hughes: The Unauthorised Life*, 656–87.
224 **his "guru":** Bate, "The Legacy," in *Ted Hughes: The Unauthorised Life*, 658.
224 **"The tenderness with which":** Wevill, "Journals," in *The Collected Writings of Assia Wevill*, 196.
224 **"a soft, boggy area":** See Oxford Languages definition of *quagmire*.
225 **Ted Hughes leased it:** Bate, "Farmer Ted," chap. 19 in *Ted Hughes: The Unauthorised Life*, 397.

Afterword: The Heart in the Fire

226 **"to be called the Sylvia Plath":** Maggie Nelson, *The Art of Cruelty: A Reckoning* (New York: W. W. Norton, 2011), 141.
226 **Mailer could stab his wife:** Mailer stabbed his second wife of six, Adele Morales, in 1960, at their apartment during a late-night party. Morales had two children with Mailer, but died in poverty at the age of ninety. See "Norman Mailer's Ex-Wife Dead at 90, Found Fame as a Stabbing Victim," *Chicago Tribune*, November 23, 2015.
226 **a debate on feminism:** Mailer moderated what has been described as a "raucous" debate on feminism in 1971 in New York City called "A Dialogue on Women's Liberation." A documentary film about this night, called *Town Bloody Hall*, was later produced in 1979, and in 2017, a stage play based on it was produced in England. You can read about all of this in Travis Diehl, "Norman Mailer v Germaine Greer: How the Town Hall Row Still Rages," *Guardian*, March 31, 2017.
227 **"in terms of a positive emergence":** Jacqueline Rose, "The Archive," in *The Haunting of Sylvia Plath* (Cambridge, MA: Harvard University Press, 1992), 87.
227 **Meghan O'Rourke once wrote:** Meghan O'Rourke, "Subject Sylvia," *Poetry*, March 2004.
227 **pitched as a young adult novel:** Vanderbilt University hosts a website with literacy resources for K–12 teachers; *The Bell Jar* is at the top of its list of YA novels: https://my.vanderbilt.edu/yabooklists/topics/the-bell-jar/. The book is also listed on the website "YA Books Central": https://www.yabookscentral.com/the-bell-jar/. These are just two examples of many.
227 **spoiled girl seeking revenge:** See the introduction to this book for a lengthy treatment of this problem.
228 **"so grisly":** Heather Clark, "Life Studies," chap. 21 in *Red Comet: The Short Life and Blazing Art of Sylvia Plath* (New York: Knopf, 2020).
228 **application for a Guggenheim:** Julianne Neely, "Kill Your Heroes: Examining Marianne Moore's Fraught Racial, Misogynistic, and Capitalist Politics," *VIDA*, April 27, 2018. The article includes an image of Moore's letter to the Guggenheim board.
228 **"It's time to stop sexualizing":** Cathleen Allyn Conway, "Sylvia Plath's Bikini Shot: It's Time to Stop Sexualising a Serious Author to Sell Books," *Guardian*, September 28, 2017; Christian Holub, "Sylvia Plath Bikini Book

Cover Slammed as Inappropriate," *Entertainment Weekly*, October 2, 2017; Stassa Edwards, "Cover of New Sylvia Plath Volume Sells Her as a Blonde in a Bikini," *Jezebel*, September 28, 2017. I also wrote about this (pro-bikini) for *Electric Literature*.

229 **"'Sylvia'; No More Plath, Please"**: Horace Hone, "'Sylvia'; No More Plath, Please," *New York Times*, October 26, 2003.

230 **"I must be lean"**: See Plath's journal entry of March 4, 1957, in Sylvia Plath, *The Unabridged Journals of Sylvia Plath*, ed. Karen V. Kukil (New York: Anchor Books, 2000).

230 **a bluebird she painted:** Ted Hughes built a cradle for Frieda's baby dolls for Christmas 1961. Plath decorated it with bluebirds and flowers. The cradle is part of Plath's papers and effects in the Mortimer Library at Smith College, her alma mater, along with her prom dress, books, and a host of other incredible objects.

230 **a tulip on her snowy grave:** See Plath's 1961 poem "Tulips," in *The Collected Poems*, 160. It was first published in *The New Yorker* and then as part of *Ariel* (Faber & Faber, 1965). See also Gail Crowther's introduction to her book *The Haunted Reader and Sylvia Plath* (Oxford: Fonthill Media, 2017), in which Crowther visits Plath's grave in winter and lays red tulips in the snow.

SELECTED BIBLIOGRAPHY

Alexander, Paul. "The Psychiatrist Who Tried to Save Sylvia Plath." *Literary Hub*, October 23, 2018.
———. *Rough Magic*. 2nd ed. Cambridge, MA: Da Capo Press, 2003.
Alvarez, A. "A Poet's Epitaph." *The Observer*, February 17, 1963.
———. *The Savage God: A Study of Suicide*. New York: W. W. Norton, 1990.
———. "Sylvia Plath." In *The Art of Sylvia Plath*, edited by Charles Newman, 56–68. Bloomington: Indiana University Press, 1970.
———. *Where Did It All Go Right?* London: Bloomsbury, 2002.
Badia, Janet. *Sylvia Plath and the Mythology of Women Readers*. Amherst: University of Massachusetts Press, 2011.
Bate, Jonathan. "Review: *The Letters of Sylvia Plath*, edited by Peter K. Steinberg and Karen V. Kukil." *The Times*, September 8, 2018.
———. *Ted Hughes: The Unauthorised Life*. London: William Collins, 2015.
Bishop, Kyla. "A Reflection on the History of Sexual Assault Laws in the United States." *Arkansas Journal of Social Change and Public Service*, April 15, 2018.
"Books: The Blood Jet Is Poetry." *Time*, June 10, 1966.
Brain, Tracy. *The Other Sylvia Plath*. New York: Routledge, 2001.
Brockes, Emma. "Chanel Miller on Why She Refuses to Be Reduced to the 'Brock Turner Sexual Assault Victim." *Guardian*, September 25, 2019.
———. "I Am Grateful to Trump for One Thing: Mainstreaming 'Gaslighting.'" *Guardian*, December 1, 2022.
Brownmiller, Susan. *Against Our Will: Men, Women and Rape*. New York: Fawcett Books, 1975.
Carpenter, Amanda. *Gaslighting America: Why We Love It When Trump Lies to Us*. New York: HarperCollins, 2018.
Carroll, E. Jean. "Hideous Men: Donald Trump Assaulted Me in a Bergdorf Goodman Dressing Room 23 Years Ago. But He's Not Alone on the List of Awful Men in My Life." The Cut: First Person, June 21, 2019.
Castle, Terry. "The Unbearable." *New York Review of Books*, July 11, 2013.
Churchwell, Sarah. "Ted Hughes and the Corpus of Sylvia Plath." *Criticism*, 40, no. 1 (1998): 99–132.
Clark, Heather. "Headline Reading: Heather Clark and Ruth Fainlight." Keynote

lecture, the Sylvia Plath Literary Festival, the Waterfront Hall, Town Hall, Hebden Bridge, October 22, 2022.

———. *Red Comet: The Short Life and Blazing Art of Sylvia Plath*. New York: Knopf, 2020.

"Confessional Poetry." Glossary of Poetic Terms. Poetry Foundation.

Crowther, Gail. *Three Martini Afternoons at the Ritz: The Rebellion of Sylvia Plath & Anne Sexton*. New York: Gallery Books, 2021.

Crowther, Gail, and Peter K. Steinberg. *These Ghostly Archives: The Unearthing of Sylvia Plath*. Oxford: Fonthill Media, 2017.

Cukor, George, dir. *Gaslight*. 1944; Culver City, CA: Amazon Prime Video, 2023. Digital.

Donohue, Denis. "You Could Say She Had a Calling For Death." *New York Times*, November 22, 1981.

Dotson, Kristie. "Tracking Epistemic Violence, Tracking Practices of Silencing." *Hypatia*, 26, no. 2 (2011): 236–257.

Ely, Steve. "The Key of the Sycamore," *Ted Hughes Society Journal* 8, no. 2 (June 2020): 42–64.

———. "A Prologue to *Capriccio*," *Ted Hughes Society Journal* 8, no. 2 (June 2020): 12–30.

Fitzhugh, Louise. *Harriet the Spy*. New York: Yearling, 1964.

Flangan, Mike, dir. *The Haunting of Hill House*. Season 1, episode 5, "The Bent-Neck Lady." Aired October 12, 2018, on Netflix.

Frank, Elizabeth. "A Long Romance with Death." *New York Times*, October 6, 1991.

Fricker, Miranda. "Epistemic Oppression and Epistemic Privilege." *Canadian Journal of Philosophy* 29 (1999): 191–210.

Gilbert, Sandra M. "'A Fine, White Flying Myth': Confessions of a Plath Addict." *Massachusetts Review* 19, no. 3 (Fall 1978): 585–603.

Goodspeed-Chadwick, Julie. *Reclaiming Assia Wevill: Sylvia Plath, Ted Hughes, and the Literary Imagination*. Baton Rouge: Louisiana State University Press, 2019.

Goodspeed-Chadwick, Julie, and Peter K. Steinberg, "Ted Hughes' Trunk at Emory." *Sylvia Plath Info* (blog), February 11, 2018.

Gordon, Lyndall. "Red Comet by Heather Clark Review: Rescuing Sylvia Plath from the Cult of Her Fans." *Telegraph*, October 10, 2020.

Hanisch, Carol. "The Personal Is Political," 1969.

Harriet Rosenstein research files on Sylvia Plath, Stuart A. Rose Manuscript, Archives, and Rare Book Library, Emory University.

Hartman, Saidiya. "Venus in Two Acts." *Small Axe* 12, no. 2 (2008): 1–14.

Haven, Cynthia. "New FBI Files: Was Sylvia Plath's Daddy 'Pro-Nazi?'" Stanford University Book Haven (blog), August 20, 2012.

Hughes, Ted. *Collected Poems*. Edited by Paul Keegan. New York: Farrar, Straus and Giroux, 2003.

———. *Letters of Ted Hughes*. Edited by Christopher Reid. London: Faber & Faber, 2007.

———. "Notes on the Chronological Order of Sylvia Plath's Poems." *The Art of Sylvia Plath, Tri-Quarterly* no. 7 (Fall 1966): 88.

———. *Winter Pollen: Occasional Prose*. Edited by William Scammell. New York: Picador, 1994.

Hughes, Ted, and Sylvia Plath. "Two of a Kind: Poets in Partnership." Interview by Owen Leeming of the BBC. January 18, 1961. Audio, 23:56.
Iati, Marisa. "Her Name Is Chanel Miller, Not 'Unconscious Intoxicated Woman' in Stanford Assault Case." *Washington Post*, September 5, 2019.
Jackson, Shirley. *The Haunting of Hill House*. New York: Penguin Classics, 2006.
Jeffs, Christine, dir. *Sylvia*. 2003; New Zealand: Amazon Prime Video, 2023. Digital.
Jones, Liz. "Haunted by the Ballad of Ted and Sylvia, Poetry's Most Toxic Love Story: Frieda Hughes Reveals Why Her Parents' Secrets Still Cast a Shadow on Her Own Career." *Daily Mail*, June 10, 2017.
Kantor, Jodi, and Megan Twohey. "Harvey Weinstein Paid Off Sexual Harassment Accusers for Decades." *New York Times*, October 5, 2017.
Kaufman, James C. "The Sylvia Plath Effect: Mental Illness in Eminent Creative Writers." *Journal of Creative Behavior* 35, no. 1 (March 2001): 37–50.
Kean, Danuta. "Unseen Sylvia Plath Letters Claim Domestic Abuse by Ted Hughes." *Guardian*, April 11, 2017.
Keats, John. *Letters of John Keats*. Edited by Robert Gittings. Oxford: Oxford University Press, 1992.
Kell, Richard. "The Foil of Despair." *Guardian*, March 12, 1965.
Koren, Yehuda, and Eilat Negev. *Lover of Unreason: Assia Wevill, Sylvia Plath's Rival and Ted Hughes's Doomed Love*. Cambridge, MA: Da Capo Press, 2007.
Kroll, Judith. *Chapters in a Mythology: The Poetry of Sylvia Plath*. Stroud, UK: Sutton Publishing, 2007.
Levav, Itzhak, and Anat Brunstein-Klomek. "A Review of Epidemiologic Studies on Suicide before, during, and after the Holocaust." *Psychiatry Research* 261 (2018): 35–39.
Lorde, Audre. "Poetry Is Not a Luxury." In *The Selected Works of Audre Lorde*. Edited by Roxane Gay, 3–7. New York: W. W. Norton, 2020.
———. "Sexism: An American Disease in Blackface." In *The Selected Works of Audre Lorde*. Edited by Roxane Gay, 45–51. New York: W. W. Norton, 2020.
Lowell, Robert. "Foreword" to *Ariel*. New York: Harper & Row, 1966.
Machado, Carmen Maria. *In The Dream House: A Memoir*. Minneapolis: Graywolf Press, 2019.
Malcolm, Janet. *The Silent Woman: Sylvia Plath and Ted Hughes*. New York: Knopf, 1994.
Manne, Kate. *Down Girl: The Logic of Misogyny*. Oxford: Oxford University Press, 2017.
———. "Good Girls: How Powerful Men Get Away with Sexual Predation." HuffPost, March 28, 2017.
Middlebrook, Diane. *Her Husband: Ted Hughes & Sylvia Plath, A Marriage*. New York: Penguin, 2003.
Miller, Chanel. "A Conversation with Chanel Miller." Online lecture in honor of Asian American & Pacific Islander Heritage Celebration, Stockton University, April 30, 2021.
Moore, Honor. "After *Ariel*: Celebrating the Poetry of the Women's Movement." *Boston Review*, March 1, 2009.
Morgan, Robin. "Conspiracy of Silence Against a Feminist Poem." *Feminist Art Journal* (Fall 1972).

———. *Monster*. New York: Vintage Books, 1972.
Morrison, Toni. *Beloved*. New York: Vintage Books, 2004.
"New Criticism." Glossary of Poetic Terms. Poetry Foundation.
Newman, Charles, ed. *The Art of Sylvia Plath*. Bloomington: Indiana University Press, 1970.
Ossip, Kathleen. *The Do Over: Poems*. Louisville: Sarabande Books, 2015.
Pereira, Malin Walther. "Be(e)ing and 'Truth': Tar Baby's Signifying on Sylvia Plath's Bee Poems." *Twentieth Century Literature* 42, no. 4 (Winter 1996): 526–34.
Plath, Sylvia. *Ariel*. London: Faber & Faber, 1965; New York: Harper & Row, 1966.
———. *Ariel: The Restored Edition*. Foreword by Frieda Hughes. New York: HarperCollins, 2004.
———. *The Bell Jar*. New York: Harper & Row, 1971.
———. *The Collected Poems*. Edited by Ted Hughes. New York: Harper & Row, 1981.
———. "The Jailer." In *Sisterhood is Powerful*, edited by Robin Morgan, 510–11. New York: Vintage Books, 1970.
———. *The Journals of Sylvia Plath*. Edited by Frances McCullough. New York: Anchor Books, 1998.
———. *The Letters of Sylvia Plath, Volume 1: 1940–1956*. Edited by Peter K. Steinberg and Karen V. Kukil. New York: HarperCollins, 2017.
———. *The Letters of Sylvia Plath, Volume 2: 1956–1963*. Edited by Peter K. Steinberg and Karen V. Kukil. New York: HarperCollins, 2018.
———. "Ocean 1212-W." In *Johnny Panic and the Bible of Dreams: Short Stories, Prose, and Diary Excerpts*. Edited by Ted Hughes, 21–27. New York: Harper Perennial, 2008.
———. Sylvia Plath interview with Peter Orr of the British Council. "The Poet Speaks: Interviews with Contemporary Poets." Recorded for the BBC. October 30, 1962. Audio, 14:32.
———. *The Unabridged Journals of Sylvia Plath*. Edited by Karen V. Kukil. New York: Anchor Books, 2000.
Pollitt, Katha. "Peering into the Bell Jar." *New York Times*, March 1, 1998.
Rollyson, Carl. *American Isis: The Life and Art of Sylvia Plath*. New York: St. Martin's Press, 2013.
———. *The Last Days of Sylvia Plath*. Jackson: The University Press of Mississippi, 2020.
Rose, Jacqueline. *The Haunting of Sylvia Plath*. Cambridge, MA: Harvard University Press, 1992.
Ryan, Lauren. "Arraignment." *The Feminist Poetry Movement*. Williams College, December 11, 2021.
Sarkis, Stephanie. "Donald Trump Is a Classic Gaslighter in an Abusive Relationship with America." *USA Today*, October 3, 2018.
Schaeffer, Susan Fromberg. *Poison: A Novel*. New York: W. W. Norton, 2006.
Scholes, Robert. "Esther Came Back Like a Retreaded Tire." *New York Times*, April 11, 1971.
Sexton, Anne. "The Barfly Ought to Sing." In *The Art of Sylvia Plath*. Edited by Charles Newman, 174–181. Bloomington: Indiana University Press, 1970.
———. "Letter Written on a Ferry while Crossing Long Island Sound." Poetry Foundation.

Spender, Dale. Quoted in "Feminism." In *Feminist Theory: A Reader*. Edited by Wendy K. Kolmar and Frances Bartkowski, 9. New York: McGraw-Hill, 2013.
Spender, Stephen. "Warnings from the grave." In *The Art of Sylvia Plath*. Edited by Charles Newman, 199–203. Bloomington: Indiana University Press, 1970.
Steinberg, Peter K. "The Harriet Rosenstein Sylvia Plath Archive, Update." *Sylvia Plath Info* (blog), April 12, 2017.
Steiner, George. "Dying in an Art." In *The Art of Sylvia Plath*. Edited by Charles Newman, 211–220. Bloomington: Indiana University Press, 1970.
Stevenson, Anne. *Bitter Fame: A Life of Sylvia Plath*. London: Penguin, 1989.
"Sylvia Plath Letters Reveal Abuse by Ted Hughes." *Irish Times*, April 20, 2017.
Sylvia Plath: Voices & Visions; 1988. New York: Produced by the New York Center for Visual History. Documentary Film.
Ted Hughes papers, Stuart A. Rose Manuscript, Archives, and Rare Book Library, Emory University.
Temmant, Emma. *Burnt Diaries*. Edinburgh: Canongate Books, 1999.
Törő, Klára, and Stefan Pollak. "Complex Suicide versus Complicated Suicide." *Forensic Science International* 184, nos. 1–3 (2009): 6–9.
Trinidad, David. "Hidden in Plain Sight: On Sylvia Plath's Missing Journals." *Plath Profiles* 3 (2010): 124–57.
Van Duyne, Emily. "Diary of a Pilgrimage: Marking the Gravesite of Assia and Shura Wevill." *Literary Hub*, November 9, 2022.
———. "Sylvia Plath and the Communion of Women Who Know What She Went Through." *Literary Hub*, February 24, 2020.
———. "Why Are We So Unwilling to Take Sylvia Plath at Her Word?" *Literary Hub*, July 11, 2017.
Wagner-Martin, Linda, ed. *Critical Essays on Sylvia Plath*. Boston: G. K. Hall, 1984.
———. *Sylvia Plath: A Biography*. New York: St. Martin's Griffin, 1987.
Wevill, Assia. *The Collected Writings of Assia Wevill*. Edited by Julie Goodspeed-Chadwick and Peter K. Steinberg. Baton Rouge: Louisiana State University Press, 2021.
"When Joan Didion Met Jean Stafford." *Library of America*, April 22, 2021.
Wieseltier, Leon. "In a Universe of Ghosts." *New York Review of Books*, November 25, 1976.
Winder, Elizabeth. *Pain, Parties, Work: Sylvia Plath in New York, Summer 1953*. New York: HarperCollins, 2013.
"The Women's March, 2017." National Museum of American History: Behring Center.

INDEX

Page numbers in *italic* refer to illustrations.
Page numbers beginning with 237 refer to notes.

Agenda Alliance, 137
Alcestis (Euripides), 113
Alexander, Paul, 3, 128, 138, 139–40, 143–44, 242
Alliston, Susan, 38, 54
All My Pretty Ones (Sexton), 49–50, 239
Alternative Values (Hughes), 2
Alvarez, Al
  about, 94
  Hughes family and, 96–97
  as "kingmaker," 8
  "Letter in November" poem, 53
  Morgan's writings and, 183–84
  mythology of Plath and, 8, 9, 10–11, 99–100, 103
  Plath and Hughes rivalry, 125
  as Plath poetry authority, 94
  Plath's tombstone and, 213
  Rosenstein interviews, 160
  on suicide as accidental, 98–99, 101
American Isis (Rollyson), 163
Ames, Lois, 94, 155–56, 157, 161–62, 267
Amichai, Yehuda, 59–61, 67, 68, 91
"Amnesiac" (Plath), 58
"And Summer Will Not Come Again" (Plath), 29
anger, 217–18, 219–20
anti-Semitism, 70, 120. *See also* Holocaust; Nazis

appendectomy, 43
"Applicant, The" (Plath), 111
appropriation, 14
archive as political, 182
archives, 202–3
archives, violence of, 194, 196, 203
"Ariel" (Plath), 28, 30
Ariel (Plath)
  countryside inspiration, 48, *48*
  "daddys" in, 19
  depression and, 56
  dolls in, 121
  Elm tree, 81
  Faber & Faber publishing, 55–56
  homunculi in, 121
  Hughes as ideal and, 200–201
  Hughes on, 56–57, 133
  Hughes's book ads in, 55
  Hughes's edit of, 3, 56, 122, 132
  influences of, 239
  Lowell's introduction, 241
  marriage breakup and, 16–17, 45
  "Morning Song" placement, 43
  as sacrifice, 11–12
  The Savage God and, 100
  second-wave feminism and, 6
  suicide and mythology, 9–12, 16–17
  Time's review of, 15
  R. Warren and, 243
  A. Wevill and, 81

Ariel (Plath) (*continued*)
  writing, 19, 46, 48–49
  See also individual poems
"Arraignment" (Morgan), 7, 88–89, 184, 189, 204–6, 207
"Art Like Everything Else, An" (Jong), 241
Art of Cruelty, The (Nelson), 192, 226
Art of Loving, The (Fromm), 81
"Ashes" (Hughes), 216
Atlantic writing contests, 29
Auden, W. H., 13
Auschwitz, 15–16

Badia, Janet, 5, 7, 8, 17, 189
Bannon, Steve, 142
Barber, Jill, 17, 146
"Barfly Ought to Sing, The" (Sexton), 42
Baskin, Leonard, 217
Bate, Jonathan, 9, 50, 76, 78, 96, 98, 110, 111–13, 119–20, 135, 136, 138, 142–43, 144, 145–46, 165, 176, 216
Becker, Jillian, 54–55, 118, 120, 145, 173, 174, 211, 215, 269
Bell Jar, The (Plath)
  about, 152
  as bestseller, 100
  biographical note in, 94
  dedication of, 122
  Faber & Faber publishing, 55
  grave visits in, 27
  Hughes as author of, 17
  IPV in, 129, 152–53
  Nolan as Beuscher, 35
  Plath's body and, 134
  shock treatments in, 34–35
  social life in, 32
  William Heinemann publishing, 52
  writing, 43–44
  as young adult literature, 227, 280
Beuscher, Ruth Barnhouse, 1, 18, 35, 42, 45, 46, 126, 160, 168, 170, 206–7, 243

Birthday Letters (Hughes), 58, 61, 63, 78, 86–87, 113, 114, 117, 119–20, 121, 127, 139, 165, 260
Bitter Fame (Stevenson), 30–31, 88, 129, 137, 138–39
"Bitter Strawberries" (Plath), 29
"Blackbird, The" (Hughes), 122–23
"Black Cat, The" (Poe), 132–33
Blackface, 51–52
Black women, 196
Brain, Tracy, 7
Brodsky, Joseph, 213
Brontë, Charlotte, 66
Brooks, Cleanth, 28, 243
Brownmiller, Susan, 195
Buddy Willard (character), 32
"Burning the Letters" (Plath), 199, 200–201
Burnt Diaries (Tennant), 146–47, 185
Byron, George Gordon, Lord, 190–91

Cambridge University, 35–40, 70–71
Canada, 68–70
Capriccio (Hughes), 63–64, 66–67, 72–73, 84, 217
"Capriccios" (Hughes), 66
Castle, Terry, 107
Catch, The (Wormald), 76
censorship
  Ariel, 3, 56, 122, 132, 133
  "Arraignment," 204–5
  Bitter Fame, 129
  of IPV, 128–29, 142–43, 204–5
  journals, 57, 142
  overview, 3, 133
  Plath suicide and, 94, 96–97, 176
  Rosenstein's archive, 172
  Rough Magic, 128–29, 242
  The Silent Woman and, 263
  Plath's pre-suicide letter, 197–98
  "whole Plath" and, 227
Change of World, A (Rich), 13
Chapters in a Mythology (Kroll), 182–83, 186–87, 243
Charles, king of England, 224

Chiasson, Dan, 179
"Chlorophyll" (Hughes), 78
choking. *See* strangulation
Choose Your Own Adventure (book series), 197
Churchwell, Sarah, 131, 133
Clark, Heather, 21, 28, 76, 125–26, 142–43, 150, 174
class, 44
Cohen, Eddie, 29–30
Cold War, 29
Collected Plays (Yeats), 53
Collected Poems, The (Plath), 188
Collected Writings of Assia Wevill, The (Wevill), 63, 67, 87. *See also* Goodspeed-Chadwick, Julie
Colossus, The (Plath), 13, 29, 42, 43, 55
Communism, 29
competition, 14
"Complex Suicide versus Complicated Suicide" (Toro and Pollak), 102
Compton, Elizabeth and David, 44
confessionalism, 6
conservatism, 30–31
"Contusion" (Plath), 99, 174
coroner's report, 173–74
Cosby, Bill, 174–75, 177
"Courage of Shutting-Up, The" (Plath), 51
Crain, Nell (character), 105–7. *See also* Vance, Eleanor (Nell)
Crockett, Wilbury, 29, 31, 172
Crow (Hughes), 217
Crowther, Gail, 165, 197–98
"Cruelty and Love" (Lawrence), 148–49
cults, 7, 9, 20. *See also* fanaticism
"Cut" (Plath), 121

"Daddy" (Plath), 13, 48–49, 50, 129, 186
Davies, Winnifred, 91, 122
Davison, Peter, 20–21, 39–40, 165, 169
"Death of Assia G., The" (Hughes), 67
depression
    Ariel poems and, 15, 56, 99
    cold weather and, 36, 45, 53, 119, 193
    ECT and, 34, 35
    "Edge" and, 56
    February 4, 1963, 54
    Hughes's knowledge of, 164
    at Smith College, 33
    writing about death and, 99
    See also suicide
Descent of Ariel, The (play) (Hinchcliffe), 156–57
"Descent of Ariel, The" (thesis) (Hinchcliffe), 155, 156
"Detective, The" (Plath), 51, 131–32, 193
diabetes, 25
"Dialogue of the Damned" (Plath), 29
Difficulties of a Bridegroom (Hughes), 150, 151–52
dislocation, 200
dolls, 121
domestic abuse. *See* intimate partner violence
Domestic Abuse Intervention Project, 117
Doolittle, Eliza (character), 199–200
Dotson, Kristie, 130, 141
Doubletake (Plath, unfinished novel), 52, 80
Down Girl (Manne), 12, 140–42. *See also* "Eating Her Words"; Manne, Kate
"Drawing" (Hughes), 115
"Dreamers" (Hughes), 58, 61–62, 75, 76, 77–78, 85, 120
dreams, 75–78

"Eating Her Words" (Manne), 140–41, 154
"Edge" (Plath), 54, 56, 99
Eleanor Vance (Nell) (character), 104–6
"Electra on Azalea Path" (Plath), 127
electroconvulsive therapy (ECT), 34–35
Eliza Doolittle (character), 199–200
"Elm" (Plath), 45
Elm tree, 81

Ely, Steve, 72–74, 82, 216–17, 220, 222, 269
emotions, 5, 20–21
enslaved people, 196, 202–4
epistemic injustice, 135–38
epistemic oppression, 136–37
"Epistemic Oppression and Epistemic Privilege" (Fricker), 130, 133
"Error, The" (Hughes), 84, 121
Euripides, 113
Evans, Phillip, 156

"Fairy Tale" (Hughes), 78
Falcon Yard/Venus in the Seventh (Plath, unpublished novel), 135, 136
fanaticism, 7, 9, 20, 226
"Fanaticism" (Hughes), 82–83
fans, 7, 20, 56, 100, 217–18, 226, 227–29
fascism, 48–49. *See also* Hitler, Adolf; Nazis
Feinstein, Elaine, 8, 205
feminism
  backlash against, 7, 17, 204–5
  F. Hughes and, 219
  T. Hughes and, 17–18, 189, 205, 241
  idealizing Plath, 227
  racism and, 51–52
  re-creating, 18
Fetters, Ashley, 103
"Fever" (Hughes), 116
"Fever 103" (Plath), 50, 218
Fierstein, Lisa, 141–42, 238
First Love (Turgenev), 85
Fisher, Alfred, 40
Fitzhugh, Louise, 155
Fitzroy Road flat, 53–54, 80, 81, 123–24
"Flounders" (Hughes), 114
Ford, Mark, 104
forgetfulness, 57–58, 63, 67
foxes, 201–2
Fricker, Miranda, 130, 133, 135–37, 154, 178
Fromm, Eric, 81

Fulbright Scholarships, 35–36, 70
"Full Fathom Five" (Plath), 28
Full Severity of Compassion, The (Kronfeld), 91

Gaslight (Cukor, film), 4
gaslighting, 4
Gaudete (Hughes), 216–17
Gibian, George, 40
Gifford, Terry, 90–91, 279
Gilbert, Sandra M., 20, 93–94
Giving Up (Becker), 120, 269
Glascock Poetry Contest, 36
God, 26–27
Goodchild (coroner), 173–74
Gooder, Jean, 264
"Good Girls" (Manne), 175
Goodspeed-Chadwick, Julie, 78, 80, 83, 90–91, 217
grass, 78–79
Graves, Robert, 114, 260
"Great Odes" (Keats), 10
Greenwood, Aurelia (grandmother), 24, 25, 26
Gregg, Linda, 108
Grosvenor, Peter and Sigrid (characters), 97
Guggenheim Fellowship, 228
Gutmann, Assia. *See* Wevill, Assia
Gutmann, Lonya and Elisabeth ("Lisa"), 60, 62, 68, 69–70, 71–72, 215–16

Half-Remembered (Davison), 165
Hall, Donald, 55
Hamlet (Shakespeare), 208, 214–15
"Hands, The" (Hughes), 116
Hardwick, Elizabeth, 42, 105, 241
Harper & Row, 55
Harriet the Spy (Fitzhugh), 155
Hartman, Saidiya, 52, 194, 196, 202–4
Haunting of Hill House, The (Jackson), 104–7, 108
Haunting of Hill House, The (Netflix limited series), 105–7
Haunting of Sylvia Plath, The (Rose), 130–31, 227

Hawk in the Rain, The (Hughes), 37, 40, 41
Hayman, Ronald, 7
"Hearing the Gods" (Gregg), 108
Hebrew, 65
Hedden, Brenda, 91
Henry Higgins (character), 199–200
Heptonstall, England, 208–13, 214, 218–19, 222–25
Her Husband (Middlebrook), 148, 221
hermeneutic injustice, 130, 135–36, 178
Higgins, Henry (character), 199–200
Hill House, 104–7, 108
Hinchcliffe, Elizabeth, 155, 156, 161–62
Hitler, Adolf, 50, 60, 216
Hobsbaum, Philip, 71
Holder, Doug, 267
Holocaust, 15–16, 64, 69, 254
homunculi, 120–21
Horder, John, 43, 56, 99, 100–101, 160, 257
Howls & Whispers (Hughes), 110, 112, 114, 118, 119–20
Hughes, Carol (second wife), 97–98, 119, 128, 166. *See also* Orchard, Carol
Hughes, Frieda Rebecca (daughter)
  birth of, 43
  in "Dreamers," 85
  on fans, 7
  first Christmas, 214
  Hughes's cradle for, 44
  in 1965, 84
  Orchard and, 91
  parents' breakup and, 151
  on parents' marriage, 117, 126–27, 176–77, 179
  Plath letters and, 166
  Plath on, 43
  Rosenstein and, 1–2, 167
  truth about Plath's death, 96–97
  Van Duyne and, 218–19
  Wevill and, 215
Hughes, Nicholas (son), 44, 84, 85, 91, 96, 107, 215

Hughes, Olwyn (sister)
  Alvarez and, 92, 96
  Ames and, 157
  Ariel publishing and, 55
  Beuscher and, 171
  caring for Frieda and Nicholas, 84
  Frieda's first Christmas, 214
  incestuous relations with Ted, 189–91
  Kroll and, 183, 185–89
  Plath's archives and, 184–86, 188
  on Plath's death, 99
  Poison and, 97
  Rosenstein and, 158–59, 169–70, 171, 172
  as talented, 37
Hughes, Ted
  about, 36–37
  as abuser; *see* intimate partner violence
  as adulterer, 48, 54, 91–92, 119, 146–47; *see also* Orchard, Carol; Wevill, Assia
  Alliston and, 38, 54
  Alvarez and, 96–97
  Ames and, 157
  Amichai and, 59
  Amichai credit and, 91
  as anti-Semitic, 120
  on *Ariel*, 56–57, 133
  Ariel publication overview, 3
  as author of *The Bell Jar*, 17
  "Daddy" poem and, 49
  death of, 97, 110
  dream fox, 37
  edit of *Ariel*, 3, 56, 122, 132
  as famous, 14–15
  fascism interest, 50–51
  forgetfulness, 57–58, 63, 67
  Graves and, 260
  Guggenheim Fellowship, 41
  incestuous relations with Olwyn, 189–91
  King Charles and, 224
  Kroll and, 185–89
  lawsuit threats, 7, 128–29, 176, 204, 242, 263

Hughes, Ted (*continued*)
  letters to Aurelia, 57, 102
  love poem to lovers, 91
  manuscripts burned, 185
  mental health issues, 47–48
  mythology of Plath and, 8, 56–57, 58, 77–78
  mythology of A. Wevill, 77–78, 217
  "The Offers" poem, 110–12, 120, 123–25, 127
  Orchard and, 97–98
  paternity of Shura, 91, 221, 279
  Plath's gravesite and burial, 205, 210–15, 220
  poetry as faithfulness, 112–13
  Poison and, 97
  pseudonyms, 47
  Rosenstein interviews, 160
  St. Botolph's Review, 37–38
  Schaeffer and, 92–93
  secret hiding, 154, 221–22
  Shura and, 89
  as teacher, 39, 41
  as terrorized by feminists, 17–18, 205, 241
  Thomas and, 263
  as translator, 111, 113
  Van Duyne and, 223
  as victim, 121
  after A. Wevill, 79
  A. Wevill affair (*see* Wevill and Hughes)
  D. Wevill and, 74
  A. Wevill death and, 17
  See also censorship; Plath and Hughes; Wevill and Hughes; *individual works*
Huws, Daniel, 37–38

ignorance, 141
incest, 189–91
In the Dream House (Machado), 182, 191, 197, 200
intimate partner violence (IPV)
  in *The Bell Jar*, 152–53
  censoring, 128–29, 139, 142–43, 176, 204–5, 242
  coroner's report and, 174
  COVID pandemic and, 191–92
  criminalization of, 195–96
  as discounted, 21–22
  dislocation, 200
  emotions and, 5
  exoneration and, 178–79
  forgotten, 174–75
  Guardian article, 2
  homicide and, 194–95
  honeymoon in Spain, 39, 138–40
  honeymoon period of, 176
  Hughes and Plath meeting, 38, 134, 152, 198
  Hughes as silent about, 128
  C. Hughes on, 166
  as imaginary, 139, 147, 164
  journals vs. published journals, 135
  letter to Brown (1956), 37
  as literal, 136–38, 139–40; *see also* strangulation
  McCullough's documents and, 165–66
  miscarriage and, 192
  misinterpretation and, 130, 135, 178
  Morgan's writings, 88–89, 183–84, 204–6, 241
  official acknowledgement of, 194–95
  overview, 129
  Plath as survivor, 5, 8
  Plath's journals and, 138–39
  Plath's writings as evidence, 133
  as poetic symbol, 136–38
  in *Poison*, 92
  police intervention and, 177–78
  policing of, 177–78
  "Power and Control Wheel," 117
  in *Red Comet*, 21
  rewriting script, 179
  in *Rough Magic*, 128–29, 139–40
  second-wave feminism and, 6–7
  self-silencing and, 140–41
  sex and, 135
  as "shocking," 3, 4, 138, 140
  strangulation, 138–48, 149, 154

before suicide, 174
suicide and, 137, 195
in *Sylvia* (film), 4, 238
timing of reporting, 175–77
Trumps, 238
Van Duyne and, 194, 195–96
Vocal Changes, 142
Wevill and Hughes, 81, 89
in "Widow," 192–93
Israel, 60–61, 68–69

Jackson, Shirley, 104–7, 108
"Jailer, The" (Plath), 7, 51–52, 122–23, 129
Jane Eyre (Brontë), 66
Jewish people, 49, 60, 62, 64–65, 69, 70, 89, 120, 220–21, 254. *See also* Holocaust; Nazis
"Johnny Panic and the Bible of Dreams" (Plath), 41
Johnson, Beverly, 174–75, 177
Jones, Judith, 13, 55–56
Jong, Erica, 94, 241
Journals of Sylvia Plath, The (Plath), 57–58, 134–35. *See also* Plath's journals
J. Walter Thompson, 86

Kakutani, Michiko, 119
Kantor, Jodi, 3–4
Kean, Danuta, 37, 164–65
Keats, John, 10–11
Kennedy, John F. and Jacqueline, 34–35
"Key of the Sycamore, The" (Ely), 72–74, 216–17, 220–21
"Kindness" (Plath), 99, 143, 149–52
Koren, Yehuda, 60, 63, 72, 74–75, 77, 84, 86, 87, 89, 91, 254
Kroll, Judith, 182–84, 185–89, 243
Kronfeld, Chana, 91

"Laburnum, The" (Hughes), 118
Lacan, France, 43–44
"Lady Lazarus" (Plath), 94, 103–4
Lameyer, Gordon, 39
Larschan, Richard, 89

Last Days of Sylvia Plath, The (Rollyson), 167, 171
Lawrence, D. H., 148
Lenny Shepherd (character), 152–54
"Letter in November" (Plath), 53
Letters Home (Plath), 28, 165–66, 189
Letters of Sylvia Plath, The, Vol. 2 (Plath), 9, 166, 176, 177
"Letter Written on a Ferry While Crossing Long Island Sound" (Sexton), 50
libel, 7, 128–29, 144–45, 204, 206, 242, 263
Life Studies (Lowell), 239
Lilith, 84–85, 86–87
Lipsey, Assia. *See* Wevill, Assia
Lipsey, Richard, 70–72
"Locket, The" (Hughes), 64
Lookout Farm, 29, 30
Lorde, Audre, 18–19
Lost Island (Wevill, short film), 85–86
Lotz, Myron, 33
Lover of Unreason (Koren and Negev), 74–75. *See also* Koren, Yehuda; Negev, Eilat
Lowell, Robert, 6, 10, 11, 20, 42, 183–84, 239, 241
Lumb Bank, 208–9, 216, 223–25
Lupercal (Hughes), 41
"Lyonnesse" (Plath), 26–27

Machado, Carmen Maria, 182, 191, 194–95, 200
Mademoiselle (magazine), 32–33
"Mad Girl's Love Song" (Plath), 34
Mailer, Norman, 226, 280
Malcolm, Janet, 93, 105, 108, 138, 140, 144–45, 163, 173, 201–2
Manne, Kate, 12–13, 14–15, 16, 130, 140–42, 144, 154, 175, 176, 178–79
marital rape, 6–7
Matisse Chapel, 36
McCullough, Frances, 165–66, 169
McLean Hospital, 35, 54
McNeely, Maggie, 167

"Medusa" (Plath), 27, 121, 186
mercy killings, 89
Merwin, Dido, 42, 43–44, 100–101
Merwin, W. S., 42, 43–44, 160
#MeToo movement, 3–4
Middlebrook, Diane, 74, 75, 112, 114, 120, 124, 148, 154, 198, 221
Miller, Chanel, 3, 4, 5, 178–79
Miller, Karl, 186–87, 189
miscarriage, 43, 192
misinterpretations, 130, 135, 178
misogyny defined, 12–13, 14, 16, 154
Monster (Morgan), 7, 204–5
"Moonwalk" (Hughes), 115
Moore, Clement, 54
Moore, Honor, 7
Moore, Marianne, 228
morality, 14
Morgan, Robin, 6–7, 88–89, 183–84, 189, 204–6, 207, 241, 254
"Morning Song" (Plath), 43
motherhood in poetry, 6, 11, 43
mouthing disappearance, 131–32, 193
murder. *See* Morgan, Robin; Wevill, Shura
Murphy, Richard, 45
"Mussel Hunter at Rock Harbor" (Plath), 41
Myers, Lucas, 37–38
My Fair Lady (musical), 199–200
"Mystic" (Plath), 54, 99
mythology
  epistemic injustice and, 137–38
  Hughes and, 8, 56–57, 58, 77–78
  Hughes and Plath's marriage, 113–17
  Rosenstein and, 168
  suicide and, 8, 9–12, 16–17, 58, 63–64, 99–100, 103–8, 137–38
  of Wevill, 77–78, 217

Nazis, 49, 50, 60, 62, 63–64. *See also* Holocaust
Negev, Eilat, 60, 63, 72, 74–75, 77, 84, 86, 87, 89, 91, 254
Nell Crain (character), 105–7. *See also* Vance, Eleanor (Nell)

Nelson, Maggie, 226
New Criticism, 6, 94
Newnham College. *See* Cambridge University
"Nick and the Candlestick" (Plath), 230
Norton, Dick, 32–33
"No Use" (Ossip), 58
Nuremberg Race Laws, 62
Nussbuam, Martha, 175

"Ocean 1212-W" (Plath), 26
"Ode for Ted" (Plath), 198, 201
"Offers, The" (Hughes), 110–12, 120, 123–25, 127, 165
Orchard, Carol, 79, 91. *See also* Hughes, Carol
O'Rourke, Meghan, 227
Ossip, Kathleen, 58
Other Sylvia Plath, The (Brian), 7

Pain, Parties, Work (Winder), 23, 34
Palestine, 60–61, 68–69
Paltrow, Gwyneth, 4
Paris, 115
Parnaby, Julia, 212–13, 214
people of color, 196. *See also* racism
Peter Grosvenor (character), 97
Piccard, Mary Louise, 142
"Picture of Otto, A" (Hughes), 107
"Pike" (Hughes), 75–76
pike fish, 75–76
Pill, Ilo, 29–30
"Pink Wool Knitted Dress, A" (Hughes), 114
"Pit and the Stones, The" (Hughes), 79
"Pity, We Were Such a Good Invention, A" (Amichai), 68
Plath, Aurelia Schober (mother)
  birth of Sylvia, 23, 25
  on "Daddy" poem, 49
  Davies and, 122
  marriage of Sylvia and Ted, 39
  marriage to Otto, 24–25
  "Medusa" poem and, 27, 121, 186, 243
  ostracization of, 24

Index | 297

after Otto's death, 27
Rosenstein interviews, 160
Sylvia biographies and, 157
on Sylvia's death, 102–3
Sylvia's depression and, 34
Sylvia's pre-suicide letter, 197–98
Sylvia/Ted breakup and, 45, 119
Ted and, 57, 197–98
theater visits, 28
wedding dress, 114
A. Wevill and, 89
Plath, Otto (father), 23–25, 26–27, 50, 107, 242
Plath, Sylvia
 in 1955, 24
 Alvarez and, 53, 94–95
 appendectomy, 43
 archive of, 183, 184–86, 189, 202–3, 204; *see also* Rosenstein, Harriet
 Aurelia and, 27, 243
 backlash against, 7
 Beuscher and; *see* Beuscher, Ruth Barnhouse
 biographies of, 155–57, 161–63, 191, 202; *see also* Rosenstein, Harriet; *individual biographies*
 birth of, 23
 body of, 133–34
 at Cambridge University, 35–40
 child rearing and writing, 46–47
 Cohen and, 29–30
 coroner's report, 173–74
 death of father, 26–27, 107
 early years, 25–27
 as established, 38
 Frieda's first Christmas, 214
 grandfather and, 24, 25, 102–3
 gravesite, 208, 210–15, *212, 214,* 217, 220, 228–29
 Hinchcliffe and, 161
 horseback riding, 48
 idealizing, 227
 illnesses, 54, 94, 118–19
 jealous men and, 28, 32–33
 Jones and, 55–56
 joyful images of, 227, 228, 230

Lameyer and, 39
Lawrence and, 148–50, 151
legacy of, 136
as liar, 164–65, 177
loneliness, 28
as *Mademoiselle* guest editor, 34
manuscripts burned, 185
manuscripts stolen, 185
men's scholarship on, 20–21
mental health honesty, 164–65
D. Merwin and, 100
miscarriage, 43, 176, 178, 192
motherhood poetry, 43
in New York (1953), 33–34
North Tawton women and, 121–22
Norton and, 32–33
obituaries for, 9–10
panel in 1973, 241
power as unentitled, 14–15
psychiatric hospital, 35, 54
racism, 30, 51–52
rape story response, 31
rumors of death, 93–94, 100–101, 102
Sassoon and, 36, 39
at school, 27–28
scholarship on, 5, 20–21; *see also* biographies of
as secretary, 41
sexual assault, 31–32
sexualizing, 228
at Smith College, 30, 31–33, 40–41
suicide/death as singular subject, 107–8
suicide of, 54–55; *see also* suicide
as survivor, 8; *see also* intimate partner violence
as teacher, 40–41
on Ted and Olwyn as incestuous, 189–90
theater visits, 28
Thomas and, 157, 197
tombstone of, 205, 211–14, *214,* 217, 220
Van Duyne and, 225–26, 228–30
Wagner-Martin, Linda, 93

Plath, Sylvia (*continued*)
  A. Wevill and, 62, 65–66, 75–81, 88, 90, 118, 199
  A. Wevill as suicide cause, 78–79, 80
  A. Wevill gift to, 74
  writing successes, 52–53
  Yeats's Fitzroy Road flat (*see* Fitzroy Road flat)
  See also depression; suicide; *individual books about*
Plath's awards/recognitions
  Atlantic student writing, 29
  The Bell Jar as bestseller, 100
  Fulbright Scholarship, 35–36
  Glascock Poetry Contest, 36
  Mademoiselle contest, 32–33
  as *Mademoiselle* guest editor, 33
  Poetry Book Society, 56
  Wellesley Award, 28
Plath's death. *See* suicide
Plath's fiction/writing, 1, 26, 29, 33, 34
Plath's journals
  as bildungsroman, 105
  destroyed, 57–58, 87
  father's death, 242
  IPV in, 129, 138–39
  vs. *The Journals of Sylvia Plath*, 134–35
  pages torn, 139, 145
  A. Wevill and, 80–81
  See also Journals of Sylvia Plath, The
Plath's letters, 11, 57, 166, 171. *See also* Beuscher, Ruth Barnhouse; Rosenstein, Harriet
Plath's poetry
  Alvarez and, 94
  as artistic, 29
  biographical reading of, 94
  child rearing and, 46
  childhood poetry, 25
  confessionalism, 6
  as conversation with Hughes, 198–99
  death as primary subject matter, 107–8
  after honeymoon, 39
  Hughes on, 56–57
  loneliness and, 28
  marriage as subject matter, 51–52
  ocean, 25–26
  Plath's biography and, 5–6, 7
  Plath's body and, 134
  Plath's suicide and, 99, 101, 103–4, 107–8; *see also* mythology
  published errors of, 183, 188
  racism and, 51–52
  at school, 28–29
  success of, 108; *see also* mythology
  Yaddo and, 42
  See also Ariel; *Colossus, The*; *individual poems*
Plath and Hughes
  Ariel and Hughes as ideal, 200–201
  birth of Frieda, 43
  birth of Nicholas, 44–45
  in Boston, 41–42
  breakup, 45–46, 57, 150
  breakup and *Ariel*, 16–17, 45
  child custody and, 197–98
  child rearing, 46
  Court Green house, 44
  divorce, 213, 215
  domestic duties, 40
  England (1960), 42–43
  faithfulness in poetry, 112–13
  growing distance, 45
  honeymoon, 39, 114, 115, 138–39
  houses overview, 123, 261
  Hughes appropriating Plath, 121
  Hughes as famous, 125
  Hughes as nurse, 122
  Hughes as stabilizing, 15
  Hughes's advertisements, 55
  Hughes's affairs gossip, 54
  Hughes's credit for *The Bell Jar*, 17
  Hughes's later work and, 58
  Hughes's mental health, 47–48
  Hughes's postcard poem, 39
  Hughes's responsibility and, 16–17, 78
  in Ireland, 45
  Lacan (1961), 43–44
  lawsuit threats, 176

letters during separation, 193, 198–99
London (1963), 54
love of, 119–20
meeting, 36, 37–39, 134, 152, 198, 264
miscarriage, 43, 176, 178, 192
Morgan's writings and, 183–84, 204–6, 241
Northampton fight (1958), 41
as one person, 116–17
overview, 2–3
Plath as master, 121
Plath burning Hughes's work, 199, 201
Plath in Hughes's play, 150
Plath in Hughes's poetry, 113–16, 120, 139
Plath on Hughes during honeymoon, 39
Plath promoting Hughes's poetry, 39–40
Plath's dedication to, 200
Plath's ghost and, 110–12, 123–24, 127
Plath's mental health and, 164–65
Plath posthumous publishing choices, 55, 57–58, 90, 117–18; see also *Ariel*
Plath's sacrifice and, 57
Plath's suffering and, 15
Plath's unpublished writing, 55, 57, 80, 87
poetry as conversation, 198–99
power, 14–15
reconciliation, 45, 118–19
relationship as regressive, 46
rivalry of, 125–27, 211
road trip in 1959, 42
royalties from Plath's work, 55
Shirley and, 124, 134, 264
torture, 206
wedding of, 39, 113–14
A. Wevill affair, 75, 118
A. Wevill and, 199
A. Wevill's characterization by Hughes, 62, 65–66

Wevills' visit (1962), 45, 72
See also intimate partner violence
Plath, Warren (brother), 25, 28
Poe, Edgar Allen, 132–33
poetry (general), 6, 18–19, 260
Poetry Book Society, 56
"Poetry Is Not a Luxury" (Lorde), 18–19
"Poet's Epitaph, A" (Plath), 9
"Point Shirley" (Plath), 41
Poison (Schaeffer), 92, 97–98, 178
Pollak, Stefan, 102
"Possession" (Hughes), 84
power, 14–15
"Power and Control Wheel," 117
Prouty, Olive Higgins, 35
"Publishing Sylvia Plath" (Hughes), 55–56
punishment, 11–13
"Purdah" (Plath), 111
"Pursuit" (Plath), 198, 201
Puzder, Andrew, 141–42, 238
Pygmalion (Shaw), 199

"Rabbit Catcher, The" (Plath), 129, 143, 147–49, 151
"Rabbit Snared in the Night" (Lawrence), 148–49, 151
racism, 30, 51–52, 196
Rainbow Press, 183
rape, 31, 79–80, 175–76, 178–79, 195, 206
readers. *See* fans
Reclaiming Assia Wevill (Goodspeed-Chadwick), 78, 83, 90–91
Red Comet (Clark), 21, 76, 174
refugees, 69
religiosity, 56–57. *See also* mythology
Revising Life (Van Dyne), 200
Rich, Adrienne, 13, 42, 160
"Rival, The" (Plath), 124–25
Roche, Clarissa, 145–46, 160, 174, 190
Roethke, Theodore, 13
Rollyson, Carl, 163, 167, 171
Rose, Jacqueline, 7, 130–31, 133–34, 227

Rosenstein, Harriet, *169*
  archive of, 31, 98, 159, 172, 180, 207
  Becker on, 173
  Beuscher and, 168, 170
  Chiasson and, 179
  Crockett and, 172
  currently, 167–68
  as famous, 168–69
  F. Hughes and, 1–2, 167
  O. Hughes and, 158–59, 171, 172
  Hughes family and, 169–70
  on IPV, 179
  Malcolm and, 163
  mental health of, 172–73
  Morgan and, 184
  Ms. article and, 168–69
  overview of work, 156
  A. Plath and, 102–3, 119
  Plath's early life and, 161
  on Plath's suicide, 174
  research for sale, 161, 166, 167
  research overview, 161–62, 163
  taped interviews, 159–60
  Van Duyne and, 179–81
  A. Wevill and, 88
  witchcraft, 168
Rough Magic (Alexander), 3, 128, 138, 139–40, 143–44, 242
royalties, 55

"St. Botoloph's" (Hughes), 113–14
St. Botolph's Review (journal), 37–38
Sassoon, Richard, 36, 39
Savage God, The (Alvarez), 94, 96, 98–100, 125. *See also* Alvarez, Al
Schaeffer, Susan Fromberg, 92–93, 97–98, 178
Schober, Frank (grandfather), 24, 25, 102–3
scholarship, 5, 20–21
Sea Witch, 86
second-wave feminism, 6–7, 204–5, 241
Seduction and Betrayal (Hardwick), 105
Selected Poems (Amichai), 59

self-silencing, 140–41
Seventeen (magazine), 29
sexism defined, 12–13
Sexton, Anne, 6, 42, 49–50, 158, 169, 239
sexual harassment/assault, 4, 31, 34, 175–77, 195. *See also* intimate partner violence
Shakespeare, William, 28, 208, 214–15
shibboleth, 64–65
"Shibboleth" (Hughes), 65, 67, 115
Shirley (ex-girlfriend/rival caricature), 124, 134, 264
shock treatments, 34–35
"Shot, The" (Hughes), 113
Sigmund, Elizabeth, 98, 122, 150, 160
Sigrid Grosvenor (character), 97
silence, 58, 67, 154, 175, 204
silencing, 58, 140–41, 154, 175, 176, 204, 207
Silent Woman, The (Malcolm), 93, 108, 140, 144–45, 163, 190, 201–2
Sisterhood Is Powerful (Morgan), 7
slavery, 51–52
Smith College, 30, 31, 40–41, 160, 166
"Snow" (Hughes), 67, 220
Spain, 39, 115–16, 138–40
Spender, Dale, 18
Spender, Stephen, 20
Spivak, Gayatri, 126
Stanford rape case, 178–79
Starbuck, George, 42
Steele, John, 68
Steele, Pamela A. E. *See* Wevill, Assia
Steinberg, Peter K., 165
Steiner, George, 11, 14, 101, 183–84
Stevenson, Anne, 30–31, 71, 88, 105, 129, 137, 138–39
strangulation, 39, 138–48, 149, 154
Strauss, Harold, 33
suicide
  as accidental, 98–99, 100–101
  Agnes in "The Wishing Box," 77
  Alvarez and Plath obituary, 9
  Alvarez's reading of poetry, 94

Ames confirming, 94
as complex, 101–2
"Edge" and, 56
focusing away from, 227, 228
N. Hughes, 107
C. Hughes and, 97–98
IPV and, 137, 195
letter to Aurelia, 197
D. Merwin's thoughts of, 100
Morgan's writings and, 88–89
mythology and, 8, 9–12, 16–17, 63–64, 99–100, 103–8, 137–38
1963 events, 54–55
as public, 103
as punishment, 11–12
as revenge, 227–28
in *The Savage God*, 94
Sexton and, 42
sleeping pills and suicide, 35, 101, 157, 209, 257
sleeping pills in 1953, 35
Smith College contemplation, 33
suicide and previous attempts (general), 102
telling the children, 96–97
truth about, 94, 96–97, 102–3
Vance/Crain, 105, 106–7
A. Wevill, 58, 63–64, 69, 81, 91
D. Wevill and, 75
A. Wevill and Plath's, 78–79, 80
"Sunday at the Mintons" (Plath), 32–33
Sylvia (Jeffs, film), 4, 238
Sylvia Plath, 1932–1952 (Rosenstein), 167
Sylvia Plath: A Biography (Wagner-Martin). *See* Wagner-Martin, Linda
Sylvia Plath and the Mythology of Women Readers (Badia), 5, 7, 17
Sylvia Plath: Method and Madness (Butscher), 88

Tarka the Otter (Williamson), 50–51
Tarn, Nathaniel, 74, 80
Ted Hughes Society Journal, 90–91
Ted Hughes: Stronger Than Death (Smith, film), 205

Ted Hughes: The Unauthorised Life (Bate), 76, 96, 98, 110, 111–12, 135, 136, 145–46, 188–89, 216
Tempest, The (Shakespeare), 28
Tennant, Emma, 146–47, 185
testimonial smothering, 140–41
These Ghostly Archives (Crowther and Steinberg), 165
Thomas, Trevor, 156, 197, 263
"Thought-Fox, The" (Hughes), 37, 201–2
Three-Martini Afternoons at the Ritz (Crowther), 197–98
Three Women (Plath), 162, 163
Title IX, 175
Toro, Klara, 102
torture, 206
transgenerational haunting, 130–31
trauma, 106–7
"Trophies" (Hughes), 113
Trump, Donald, 3, 4, 238
Trump, Ivana, 238
"Tulips" (Plath), 43, 192
Turgenev, Ivan, 85
Turner, Brock, 178–79
Twohey, Megan, 3–4
"Two of a Kind: Poets in Partnership" (BBC radio interview), 116–17

Unabridged Journals (Plath), 3. *See also* Plath's journals
Understanding Poetry (Brooks and Warren), 28
"Unseen Sylvia Plath Letters Claim Domestic Abuse by Ted Hughes" (Kean), 2, 164–65

Van Duyne, Emily, 4–5, 67–68, 102, 163–64, 179–81, 191, 194, 195–96, 218–19, 222–26, 228–30
Van Dyne, Susan, 200–201
Vance, Eleanor (Nell) (character), 104–6, 108
Vendler, Helen, 138
"Ventriloquist, The" (Hughes), 120–21

Venus in the Seventh/ Falcoln Yard (Plath, unpublished novel), 135, 136
"Venus in Two Acts" (Hartman), 202–4
"Vessel of Wrath" (Merwin), 44
Vocal Changes, 142

Wagner, Janet, 34
Wagner-Martin, Linda, 19, 88, 93
Warren, Robert Penn, 28, 243
Weinstein, Harvey, 4
Weldon, Fay, 89
Wellesley Award, 28
Wevill, Assia, *83*
　about, 44, 59–60, 62–63
　accent of, 65
　affair with Hughes; *see* Wevill and Hughes
　Aurelia and, 89
　burial of, 215–17, 221, 222, 223–24, 225
　in Burma, 72
　at Cambridge University, 70
　in Canada, 69–70
　as copywriter, 71
　creativity and pregnancy, 85–86
　cremated, 216
　as cruel mother, 84–85
　day before suicide, 224–25
　death of, 17, 63–64, 209
　in "Dreamers," 58, 61–62
　Ely's thoughts on, 220–21
　father and, 68
　as femme fatale, 78–79, 80
　filicide of Shura, 63–64, 89, 209, 254, 269
　first mentioned, 189
　Hedden and, 91
　Holocaust/Nazism and, 63–64, 69
　Hughes scholars and, 90–91
　Lipsey and, 70–72, 77
　mythology of Plath and, 77–78, 217
　Plath and, 62, 65–66, 80–81, 88, 90, 118, 199
　Plath gift, 74
　Plath's biographers and, 88, 90
　Plath's burning of Hughes's work and, 199
　as Plath's suicide cause, 78–79, 80
　poetry of, 71
　Shura and, 85
　Steele and, 68–70
　in Tel Aviv/Palestine, 60–61, 68–69
　tombstone of, 222, 223–24
　as translator, 59, 67, 71, 91
　as vain, 82–84, 85
　Van Duyne learning of death, 67–68
　D. Wevill and, 70–72, 88
Wevill and Hughes
　abortion, 82
　affair, 45, 48, 54, 58, 72–75
　Ames and, 157–58
　birth of Shura, 84
　Capriccio, 66–67
　cruelty, 81–82, 89
　expectations by Hughes, 61, 90
　filicide of Shura and, 269
　at Fitzroy Road flat, 80, 81
　grass, 78–79
　Hughes's erasure of Wevill, 63, 67, 87
　Hughes's responsibility and, 78
　letters, 87
　living apart, 215
　Lumb Bank, 208–9, 216
　in 1961, 72–74
　in 1963, 81–82
　in 1969, 89
　Plath and, 75–81, 118
　Plath's writings and, 80–81, 87
　pregnancy, 80
　rape, 79–80
　sexual chemistry, 83–84
　Wevill as femme fatale, 78–79, 80
　Wevill as seductress, 75–76, 77–79, 86
　Wevill journals, 87, 89–90
　Wevill's characterization by Hughes, 61–62, 63–65, 82–83, 84–85, 120, 220
　Wevill's pike dream, 75–76, 77–78
　will and, 88, 222

Wevill, David
    about, 44, 70–72
    after Assia, 79
    on Assia and Shura, 85
    Assia's infidelity and, 74, 75, 77
    on Assia's pike dream, 78
    Hughes's admiration of, 74
    poetry and Plath, 77
    Shura and, 84, 279
Wevill, Shura, 83, 85
    birth of, 84
    burial of, 215–17, 221, 222, 223–24, 225
    death of, 63–64, 89, 209, 254, 269
    in "Dreamers," 58
    in Hughes's poems, 84
    in 1968, 61
    paternity of, 91, 221, 279
    Plath's biographers and, 88
    tombstone of, 222, 223–24
    Wevill and Hughes as family, 84
White Goddess, The (Graves), 260
"Widow" (Plath), 192–93
Wieseltier, Leon, 50
William Heinemann, Ltd., 52, 55
Winder, Elizabeth, 23, 34
Wingfield, Rachel, 212–13, 214
"Wintering" (Plath), 122
"Wishing Box, The" (Plath), 77
"Words" (Plath), 99
Wormald, Mark, 76, 77

Yaddo colony, 42
"Years" (Plath), 26
Yeats, William Butler, 53
"You Hated Spain" (Hughes), 115, 139
"Your Paris" (Hughes), 115, 116